Low-Wage Workers

in the New Economy

EDITED BY **Richard Kazis
and Marc S. Miller**

Low-Wage Workers

in the New Economy

THE URBAN INSTITUTE PRESS
Washington, D.C.

THE URBAN INSTITUTE PRESS
2100 M Street, N.W.
Washington, D.C. 20037

Library of Congress Cataloging in Publication Data

Low-wage workers in the new economy / edited by Richard Kazis and Marc S. Miller.
        p. cm.
Includes bibliographical references and index.
     ISBN 0-87766-705-5 (alk. paper)
   1. Working poor—United States. 2. Wages—United States. 3. Working poor—Government policy—
United States. 4. United States—Economic policy—1993- I. Kazis, Richard, 1952- II. Miller, Marc S.
     HD8072.5 .L68 2001
     331.2'973—dc21

                                                                        2001004515

Printed in the United States of America

THE URBAN INSTITUTE is a nonprofit policy research and educational organization established in Washington, D.C., in 1968. Its staff investigates the social, economic, and governance problems confronting the nation and evaluates the public and private means to alleviate them. The Institute disseminates its research findings through publications, its Web site, the media, seminars, and forums.

Through work that ranges from broad conceptual studies to administrative and technical assistance, Institute researchers contribute to the stock of knowledge available to guide decisionmaking in the public interest.

Contents

Tables

Acknowledgments

This book is the product of the hard work and cooperation of many individuals and organizations. Most of the chapters were written initially for the *Low-Wage Workers in the New Economy* conference held in Washington, D.C., in May 2000 and attended by more than 400 policymakers, practitioners, researchers, and activists. That conference, organized by Jobs for the Future, was sponsored by a remarkable coalition of national organizations—the AFL-CIO, Jobs for the Future, the National Association of Manufacturers, the National Governors Association, the National League of Cities, the National Urban League, the Urban Institute, and the Welfare to Work Partnership—all of whom brought their perspectives, ideas, and constituencies into the mix. Funding for the conference and related activities that focus on policies to help low-income families advance was provided by the Annie E. Casey, Ford, Charles Stewart Mott, David and Lucile Packard, and Rockefeller foundations. We thank all these organizations for their support. Lisa Dickinson, Mindy Martin, and Michael Bedford, all of Jobs for the Future, ensured that the conference ran smoothly. Hilary Pennington, Marlene Seltzer, Sue Goldberger, Jack Mills, Judy Taylor, and Heath Prince helped plan the event.

We wish to thank the many authors contributing to this book. Working with each of them has been a pleasure; we thank them for their enthusiasm for this project and their responsiveness to our many requests and deadlines. Additional thanks are due to Ed Hatcher of The Hatcher Group and Carmon Cunningham of Jobs for the Future for their assistance in disseminating and promoting the policies and practices advanced in this volume.

Finally, we want to thank the many organizations and individuals around the country who are working tirelessly—at the local, state, and national levels; in business, labor, government, academia, education, and training; and inside disadvantaged communities—to improve the opportunities available to low-income families in this country. The examples, models, and strategies highlighted here are the results of their creativity, commitment, and determination to expand opportunity for all Americans.

Richard Kazis
Marc S. Miller
Boston, Massachusetts
August 2001

Opportunity and Advancement for Low-Wage Workers

New Challenges, New Solutions

Richard Kazis

Political and economic developments in the 1990s sparked a dramatic shift in the national debate about work and poverty. A new concern superceded the long-standing focus on how best to reduce individual dependency on government; the question became how to get significant numbers of people off welfare, out of unemployment, and into jobs. In the policy arena, welfare reform moved work onto center stage, replacing an entitlement to cash support. In the economic realm, a decade of tight labor markets made employers more receptive to public policies that would help them find qualified workers.

The speed with which welfare rolls shrank and the employment of former beneficiaries increased surprised many, regardless of their views on the new welfare policies. Since 1994, welfare rolls have dropped by more than 50 percent nationwide and by as much as 90 percent in some states. More than half these women—and almost all those coming off welfare are women—have moved into unsubsidized, paid employment. That is, some 800,000 people have made the transition from welfare to employment as a result of the felicitous combination of a strong economy and changes in public policies.

Yet the very success of work-centered welfare reform in getting people off welfare and into jobs has brought another, more difficult challenge into sharp relief: *For many people, getting into work doesn't mean getting out of poverty.* Recipients who leave welfare typically find jobs that pay between $6 and $8 an hour, well below the income needed to bring a family of three above the federal poverty level. Moreover, there is little evidence of significant wage increases for those who stay employed, even after three years.

This does not mean that welfare reform has failed: About half of former welfare recipients believe that the quality of their lives has improved, even if their economic situation has not. It does underscore that access to employment—even in the nation's most robust economy in over 30 years—is an insufficient solution to poverty.

As the debate over welfare dependency has cooled, the question has become how to help hardworking Americans find their way out of poverty through work. As welfare recipients join the ranks of the employed, it becomes difficult to distinguish them from the millions of other working Americans whose family incomes are inadequate. Today, fewer than 2 million Americans head families that receive welfare benefits, yet over 9 million *working* Americans earn less than the official poverty level—and one out of four of these individuals works full-time, year-round.

Serious challenges face *all* low-skill workers in today's economy. Entry-level workers cannot easily advance out of poverty simply by staying on the job and moving up through seniority. Traditional routes to advancement for low-skill workers, such as career ladders inside large firms and union-negotiated wages, have become less common. More and more often, employers outsource their low-wage jobs and hire externally for mid-level jobs that they once filled from within. The proportion of American workers who belong to unions has been declining for decades, weakening one of the sources of good wages for relatively low-skill workers. And growing technological complexity and changes in work organization have made a person's skill and educational credentials increasingly important to success—and earnings—in the labor market.

Together, these changes in the structure of employment and the labor market make it difficult for less-skilled workers to earn an income that can support a family. Real wages of workers with a high school diploma or less dropped precipitously in the 1980s and remain lower than they were in the mid-1970s. During the 1990s, a decade of exceptional productivity growth and profitability, income inequality also grew markedly. While incomes of better-educated workers rose, earnings for those in the lowest deciles of the employment distribution began to rise only late in the decade. Today, too many Americans, despite working hard, find it difficult to escape jobs that pay too little, provide minimal benefits, and offer limited security and opportunity for advancement.

Low-Wage Workers in the New Economy is about the men and women for whom the American Dream remains out of reach. It is about the challenges they face in pulling themselves and their families out of poverty through work. Most important, it is about strategies for helping working Americans advance—the policies and practices that can make a real difference in the ability of low-wage workers to support their families, choose their futures, and contribute more fully to society and the economy.

AN EMERGING CONSENSUS

Most of the chapters in this book were prepared initially for a national conference, *Low-Wage Workers in the New Economy: Strategies for Opportunity and Advancement*. Organized by Jobs for the Future, the May 2000 conference was sponsored by a remarkably diverse coalition of national business, labor, civil rights, and governmental organizations, including the AFL-CIO, National Association of Manufacturers, National League of Cities, National Governors Association, National Urban League, Urban Institute, and Welfare to Work Partnership. Over 450 policymakers, practitioners, and researchers gathered in Washington, D.C., to:

- Synthesize and expand knowledge on practices and policies to help low-income individuals achieve long-term economic self-sufficiency;
- Expand the network of organizations and individuals working to create more effective workforce and employment policies and programs; and
- Stimulate the demand for national and state policies that can benefit low-wage workers, their employers, and their communities.

In preparation for the conference, Jobs for the Future asked experts on workforce development, welfare, education, and income and tax policy to synthesize existing knowledge or report on original research. Their papers, along with additional chapters written since the conference, present a rich and provocative analysis. They describe the extent and contours of the challenge facing our nation's working poor. They draw lessons from practice and policy about promising approaches to helping low-wage workers advance into the economic mainstream. And they recommend both principles and specific policy interventions for state and federal policymakers.

There are powerful commonalities in the analyses and prescriptions presented here. Most of the authors recommend a multifaceted set of approaches and policies to helping low-wage workers advance. They acknowledge the complicated combination of challenges facing many low-wage workers that stem from limited skills and educational credentials, obstacles to steady work that are a function of being poor, and the characteristics of the jobs they can obtain. Moreover, in response to these issues, most of the authors propose policy priorities that draw from a generally shared combination of options:

- Skill development that can help entry-level workers advance;
- Child care and other supports that can help workers stay on the job longer;
- Income supports that make low-wage work more rewarding; and
- Economic development strategies that promote the creation of higher-quality jobs.

As a group, the authors acknowledge that evidence is thin on the most effective mix of practices and policies to help low-wage workers move up to better opportunities for work and income. As a result, there are sharp differences of opinion among them on the best ways to invest scarce resources and political capital. Some authors put skill development above all else; others emphasize the need to raise wages at the low end of the labor market; still others focus on nonskill supports that can keep people employed so they can develop skills and advance to better jobs.

At the same time, all the authors share a strong belief that a confluence of factors makes new alliances possible for a coherent policy agenda designed to help low-income families enter and stay in the economic mainstream. If progress is to be made, they argue, now is the time. Employers remain hard-pressed to find qualified employees for many jobs. Welfare has receded as an emotional hot button. The past decade's coupling of great wealth creation with unequal distribution of its benefits has added urgency to calls for improving opportunities for low-wage workers to advance.

Moreover, the American public feels strongly that those who work hard and contribute to the best of their ability should earn enough to stay out of poverty. According to a national survey released at the conference, this issue cuts right to the heart of the American sense of fairness. More than 90 percent of Americans believe that those who "work hard and play by the rules" should be able to support their families through their work. And the same survey found signs that the current strong support for welfare reform is contingent upon whether people believe that former recipients can escape poverty through work.

Support for this agenda extends beyond the public. Important allies can also be found in the business community and among state and federal economic policymakers. Around the country, employers say that finding and keeping qualified workers is one of their most pressing problems—even in a cooling economy. The mismatch between the needs of employers and the skills of available workers is so serious that economic policymakers fear it may constrain future productivity growth and economic performance.

Last year, Federal Reserve Chairman Alan Greenspan highlighted the need for greater and more effective investments in worker training in order to avoid labor shortages and bottlenecks that can stifle economic growth. And he went further, noting that simply matching low-skill workers with low-productivity, entry-level opportunities is insufficient. "It is not enough," he said, "to create a job market that has enabled those with few skills to finally be able to grasp the first rung of the ladder of achievement. More generally, we must ensure that our whole population receives an education that will allow full and continuing participation in this dynamic period of American economic history."

We assembled *Low-Wage Workers in the New Economy* because of our strong belief, generally shared by the authors, in the need for a concerted national effort to help bring less-skilled and disadvantaged workers and their families into the mainstream of the U.S. economy and society. It is a logical next step for the policy agenda that began over a decade ago with state-level welfare reform initiatives. Such an effort can be a "win-win" situation for families who have benefited least from a decade of expansion and for an economy, characterized by continued productivity and growth, that is our country's single, best antipoverty policy. It can elicit the support not just of low-wage workers and their advocates but also of employers desperately seeking qualified workers and a society eager to sustain high levels of productivity growth and prosperity.

PRINCIPLES TO GUIDE POLICY INITIATIVES

What would be the core principles of a concerted campaign to help increase economic opportunity for low-skill and low-wage workers? A synthesis of views emerging from the contributors to *Low-Wage Workers in the New Economy* yields six principles to guide federal and state policymakers:

- *Keep work central.* Work should be the primary goal of social policy. All those who can work should be helped to enter the labor market—and succeed in it. Macroeconomic policies that keep unemployment and inflation low are critical to the tight labor markets that make it easier to keep work at the center of social policy.

- *Promote family-supporting work.* It is not enough to help people find *any* job. The quality of early work experiences greatly influences later employment and earnings. Policy should reward efforts to help less-skilled individuals obtain and advance toward high-quality jobs that can support their families (i.e., jobs with good wages, benefits, training, and other opportunities for advancement).

- *Invest in education and work skills.* In the long run, opportunities for education and skill development are critical to the ability of those outside the labor market and those already employed to advance in work and career. Traditional policies that help people secure an initial job must be augmented with policies that make it easier for working Americans to improve their skills and prepare for better jobs. This will require new strategies, such as incentives for employers to provide and support training; education models for those already working that promote lifelong learning and innovative combinations of learning and earning; as well as more effective partnerships among employers, unions, community-based organizations, and educational institutions.

- *Encourage individuals to stay employed and advance.* Employment policy should encourage and fund supports that can help disadvantaged people keep their jobs longer and build their human capital and work experience. Priorities include child care, transportation, employee assistance programs, health coverage, and other ways to help people cope with the challenges of sustained employment. In addition, federal and state governments should use tax and other policies to continue to find ways to reward work for low-wage individuals and families, including the earned income tax credit (EITC), earnings disregards for welfare recipients, and other work-linked income supports.

- *Encourage employers to hire, train, and support low-skill, low-wage workers.* Employers often take financial and productivity risks when they hire less-skilled workers or invest in improving these workers' skills; frequently, they are unable to know in advance who will succeed on the job and who will stay long enough to justify the investment. Policymakers should encourage greater employer investment in their entry-level workforce through subsidies, incentives, and supports that make it less costly and easier for employers to take these risks.

- *Pursue advancement as a goal across education, work force development, welfare, and economic development policies.* New combinations of public- and private-sector education, economic development, and workforce development policies are needed to help low-wage workers become more productive and help employers who hire them improve the quality of available jobs. Workforce and welfare policies should connect to economic development and employer-targeted policies, such as policies that address the employment needs of particular regions, labor markets, and industries/sectors. Such policies should also be better aligned with those that govern access to and financing of postsecondary education. Public policy should continue to encourage local institutions that improve the market for education and training by connecting employers, labor, government, educational institutions, and community-based organizations for the benefit of local employers, workers, and job seekers.

These principles provide a general framework for action. The contributors to *Low-Wage Workers in the New Economy* go much further toward recommending specific policies to advance the agenda of greater opportunity for advancement for low-skill and low-wage workers. Their work should serve as a resource in local, state, and national policy debates. We hope that it can guide the range of interested parties, including business and labor, federal, state, and local officials, education leaders, and community advocates, as they grapple with the next steps toward sustained productivity, economic growth, and the expansion of economic opportunity in our country.

LOW-WAGE WORKERS IN THE NEW ECONOMY

This book is organized into four sections. Part 1 sets the stage with an overview of the low-wage workforce and of the employers who hire them. Part 2 summarizes the evidence on strategies to improve workers' skills, provide them greater supports on the job, supplement their wages, and develop assets that they can use as they seek to escape poverty. Part 3 focuses on the special challenges encountered by certain groups within the low-wage workforce: women, minorities, and immigrants. Finally, Part 4 assesses the potential contributions of three important institutions to expanding opportunity for low-wage workers: community colleges, employers, and unions.

Part 1—Who Are the Low-Wage Workers in the New Economy? Who Employs Them?

Part 1 of *Low-Wage Workers in the New Economy* presents a portrait of the working poor and of the labor market within which they seek employment and earnings. The authors of these three chapters take on a difficult task: characterizing the large group of low-earners in our economy, the jobs they hold, and the employers who hire them—and assessing their prospects for escaping long-term poverty. Who are our nation's low-wage workers? Why are they unable to support their families through their work experience? Is the problem getting worse or better, in general and for specific groups of the working poor? These questions are critical: They hold the key to assessing the nature and the seriousness of the problem *and* to identifying the highest-leverage and most promising interventions and strategies.

Using data from the National Survey of America's Families, Gregory Acs, Daniel McKenzie, and Katherin Ross Phillips generate a detailed portrait of the "working poor," defining them as families whose earnings are less than twice the federal poverty level and in which the adults work an average of half time or more during the year. This definition recognizes the inadequacy of the federal poverty level as a measure of what it takes to support a family in the country.

Using their new definition, the authors estimate that one in six nonelderly Americans lives in a working-poor family. Although one-parent families with children are typically unable to make ends meet through work, almost two-thirds of the working poor live in families with children and at least two adults present. On average, the primary earner in a working-poor family works full-time, year-round.

What makes it hard for low-wage workers to advance out of poverty? These authors answer: The working poor are more likely to have young children, less likely to be married, and tend to have significantly less education. Moreover, compared with the nonpoor who work, they tend to have jobs that pay far less for equivalent work effort, are less stable, offer fewer benefits, and are in occupations with lower status.

What policy priorities derive from this analysis? Acs, McKenzie, and Phillips argue that strategies to increase the hours worked by prime-age, able-bodied adults in working-poor families could help many more working families earn above 200 percent of the poverty level than would the modest increase in the minimum wage to $6.15 an hour that died in Congress at the end of 2000. They emphasize the value of child care, transportation, and other supports that can make it easier for people to work full-time, year-round. At the same time, they recognize the need for continued income supports, such as the EITC, to help working Americans earn enough to sustain a family over time.

Anthony P. Carnevale and Stephen J. Rose ask a similar set of questions: Who are the low-earners and how serious a problem do low wages pose to our economy? Using a different data source, the Panel Study on Income Dynamics, they can look at earnings trends over multiple years. Thus, they can assess the extent to which low-wage workers remain in poverty over time.

Defining low-earners more narrowly (i.e., those who earn $15,000, roughly poverty-level wages for a family of three), Carnevale and Rose discover a mixed picture. On the one hand, the percentage of long-term low-earners has declined significantly from about 30 percent of the workforce to perhaps 10 percent, which is generally consistent with the estimate by Acs, McKenzie, and Phillips that one in six nonelderly Americans lives in a working-poor family. The female workforce has made great progress over the years, as many women have gained access to higher-paying occupations and jobs. However, women, particularly those with children and with limited education, are also the most likely group to earn low wages in any given year and to stay stuck in low-wage employment over time.

Carnevale and Rose distinguish among groups of low-earners, from young workers living in nonpoor families, through adults who are the second wage earner in a family, to prime-age adults who are primary earners in their families. The authors estimate that while almost one-third of all workers earn below-poverty wages, one-third of these (about 10 percent of the workforce) are persistent low-earners who are responsible for the bulk of their families' income. It is this group, skewed heavily toward women, that policy should be most concerned with helping.

Carnevale and Rose emphasize the importance of lack of education, combined with being a single-parent head of household, in keeping working people in poverty. They argue that policy should promote ways to make education and training more available and more affordable to low-wage workers, including policies for connecting low-wage workers to jobs that provide valuable training. They also advocate for concerted union efforts to organize low-wage jobs and occupations.

Paul Osterman describes and analyzes the labor market within which low-skill and low-wage workers seek employment and opportunity. He discusses the boundaries and size of the low-wage/low-skill labor market and identifies what is distinctive about it.

While cautioning that definitions of the size of this labor market—that is, the number of available jobs—are imprecise, whether based on educational requirements or on hourly wages, Osterman concurs with other estimates that between one-fourth and one-third of all jobs pay low wages or are low-skill, and that about 1 in 10 workers is a low-wage employee living in a low-income family. Osterman warns that distinctions must be made between low-wage jobs that are way stations for young workers and those that offer little career mobility, for they play very different roles in generating and sustaining poverty. At the same time, he emphasizes that the scope of the low-wage labor market is quite significant and is not shrinking. Osterman notes the growing importance of soft skills in this labor market, as well as the continuing role of race in shaping employer hiring and recruitment decisions.

Consistent with his focus on the employers of low-wage workers, Osterman concentrates on policies that can change the nature of low-wage jobs and the behavior of low-wage employers. These include: a coordinated approach to minimum wage laws, hours laws, and health and safety standards that could improve job quality in low-wage jobs; union organizing targeted to low-wage sectors; the promotion of labor market intermediaries that negotiate with training institutions, employers, and government on behalf of low-wage workers; and incentives to employers to provide more training to lower-skill employees. In general, he argues, policy options and investments should be assessed on the basis of their ability to have an impact on large numbers of low-wage workers.

Part 2–Program and Policy Priorities: Strategies to Help Low-Wage Workers Advance

Part 2 summarizes the rich literature about and direct experience with programs and policies that help low-wage workers succeed in the labor market and advance out of poverty. These authors look at experiences from welfare-to-work experiments, workforce and economic development initiatives at the state and local levels, tax incentives, and other practices and policies. They highlight four approaches: (1) skill development for incumbent workers with low skills, particularly education and training approaches that can be pursued while working; (2) investments in child care, transportation, employee assistance programs, and other supports that can help people stay on the job longer, build an employment record, gain training, and move up to better jobs; (3) income supports tied to work and other financial incentives that make work more rewarding to those who cannot make ends meet on their wages alone; and (4) asset development to help low-wage workers accumulate savings they can invest in education, training, and other aids to economic security.

Historically, U.S. workforce policy has focused on helping people get their first job, under the assumption that through seniority and consistent employment, low-skilled individuals would climb toward wage levels high enough to support themselves and their families. There is widening recognition that this approach must be revised for today's changed economy, in which advancement to better-paying jobs is more difficult. Experience upon which to set policy is thin, however. The authors of these chapters offer differing assessments of the mix of policies and programs that would best help less-skilled workers and their families secure middle-class jobs and incomes. For this reason, these authors make a particular effort to identify practices that appear effective or promising and to propose a combination of strategies that policymakers should pursue in concert.

One way to help low-wage workers succeed is to help them stay in early job experiences longer. To advance in the labor market, a person must stay employed long enough to gain experience and relevant training, perhaps build some savings, and make the personal contacts that help make it possible to move to another job. Yet for welfare recipients and other low-wage workers, turnover is frequently quite high and work can be a revolving door of short-term, unsatisfactory job experiences.

Anu Rangarajan draws on the four-city, federally funded Post-Employment Services Demonstration for lessons on organizing job retention services for those with weak attachment to the labor market. She highlights a number of themes echoed elsewhere in this volume, including the importance to job retention of the quality of the job placement (in terms of wages, working conditions, etc.); the need for flexible, individually responsive supports both in preemployment job preparation and once someone has found work; the value of financial incentives and wage supplements that can make work more attractive; and the power of mentoring and job coaching for less-skilled individuals.

Julie Strawn and Karin Martinson build upon these lessons on retention and go further to assess strategies for helping low-wage workers advance in earnings and careers. Like Rangarajan, Strawn and Martinson distill lessons from experience with welfare reform and from rigorous evaluations of welfare-to-work employment programs. They argue that the welfare-to-work research, while complex, can be summarized in a few broad axioms:

- Steady work alone is not a path to higher wages.
- Where someone starts in the labor market—her initial wages and occupation—matters for her future success.
- Postsecondary education or training is a key factor in who advances over time.

Strawn and Martinson conclude that it is possible to help low-income people move into better jobs—with higher pay or with better benefits than they would have secured on their own—even within a relatively short time frame. They present examples of promising practice in three areas: connecting low-wage workers to better jobs, upgrading skills while unemployed, and upgrading skills while working.

Still, success stories are the exception rather than the rule. According to Strawn and Martinson, replicating innovative programs will require significant changes in the way that services are delivered, changes that will require innovations in both policy and practice. To improve access to better jobs, they recommend strategies that promote better information on available jobs, engagement of employers who can offer higher-quality jobs, and performance goals for publicly funded placement agencies that reward job quality. To upgrade skills for the unemployed, Strawn and Martinson make suggestions for improving the quality of job training and work-related basic education and for making training more accessible to those without a high school diploma or GED.

Finally, to encourage skill upgrading for those already working, Strawn and Martinson emphasize the importance of partnerships with employers to provide training at or near the work site; more flexible hours for job advancement services (i.e., nights and weekends); and financial aid and supports that can help low-skill workers afford to upgrade their skills and earn educational credentials. Strawn and Martinson emphasize the importance of involving employers in the design and delivery of services, making occupational training accessible to those with low skills and to those who are working, and making it easier and more affordable for working people to earn postsecondary credits and credentials.

Charles Michalopoulos focuses on one particular strategy advocated by Rangarajan and by Strawn and Martinson: financial incentives that make work more attractive to former welfare recipients. He reviews evidence from 13 programs, all begun since the early 1990s, on how preemployment services and financial work incentives can promote sustained employment and earnings growth. Each program tested the impact of either preemployment supports or financial incentives on single-parent welfare recipients' employment. Taken as a group, the studies suggest several lessons:

- Programs with financial work incentives can promote sustained employment.
- Programs that emphasize going to work immediately can promote sustained employment, but not all programs are equally effective.
- Programs that emphasize skill building through adult basic education can promote sustained employment, but the effects tend to be small.
- Sustained full-time work may be the key to increasing hourly wages.
- Preemployment services focused on getting people to work can result in earnings gains over time, but growth in earnings may be linked to sustained employment.

In recent years, interest has been growing in strategies for helping low-income individuals and families become more self-sufficient by accumulating assets. Many of these new models, such as Individual Development Accounts (IDAs) and Lifelong Learning Accounts, promote and reward individual savings that people can use to buy education and training services. Colleen Dailey and Ray Boshara survey a number of fledgling individual asset-building approaches, summarize lessons from community-level demonstration projects, and offer policy recommendations for creating a large-scale asset-building system for low-income workers.

Dailey and Boshara pay particular attention to the potential for and the many obstacles to making IDAs an employer-provided benefit. They note employer concerns about tax treatment of such accounts, rules that would make it hard to provide benefits to some workers and not others, and potential administrative burdens. They urge that policymakers not isolate asset-building strategies from workforce development initiatives, because these accounts can be a vehicle for combining private, public, and individuals' funds to increase workers' education and training options.

According to Dailey and Boshara, policymakers should incorporate three principles into their efforts. Asset initiatives should build upon existing efforts to help low-wage workers, such as the vouchers under the Workforce Investment Act, and should not undercut important policies, such as the EITC. They should be structured to encourage and reward employer commitment and investment. And they should be available to all low-wage workers, including temporary and self-employed workers, the unemployed, and those employed in traditional arrangements.

The responsibility for designing an effective mix of policies and practices that can help low-wage workers secure employment and support their families is primarily up to states. Federal workforce and welfare laws give states significant flexibility. States can decide to enact their own EITC or to target their economic development resources in ways that reward employers who help low-wage workers gain access to quality jobs.

Of course, the commitment of states to support and fund retention and advancement strategies for their low-wage workers varies greatly. Carol Clymer and her co-authors, Brandon Roberts and Julie Strawn, describe policy innovations in states that are particularly committed to helping low-wage workers advance out of poverty. While the authors acknowledge that state efforts targeted to low-wage workers are modest and new, they point to important innovations in several states—including California, Minnesota, Oregon, Texas, and Washington—that are trying to move toward flexible and balanced policies to help low-wage workers and their families improve their employment, skills, and income.

Clymer, Roberts, and Strawn identify three areas in which state innovation can be particularly valuable:

- Integration of skill development initiatives for low-skill working adults provided through state welfare and workforce systems;
- Policies that reward work by augmenting low wages; and
- Efforts to remove barriers to employment for the working poor, including child care, transportation assistance, and housing and health care assistance.

States that want to make this agenda a high priority can use their budgetary and regulatory authority to:

- Redirect resources to initiatives whose goals are retention and advancement;
- Establish performance measures that reward advancement, not just initial job placement;
- Consolidate service delivery in ways that promote greater efficiency and effectiveness;
- Engage business in ways that take employer needs and interests seriously; and
- Redefine eligibility for benefits or services to include the working poor, not just the unemployed or the welfare population.

Part 3—Different Strokes: Overcoming Barriers Facing Particular Groups

Part 3 looks more closely at the people who make up the low-wage workforce, differentiating among the experience of particular gender, race, and ethnic groups. These authors highlight particular challenges facing women and minorities in the low-wage labor market and suggest policies and practices to help these groups advance.

Harry J. Holzer is concerned that, on average, minorities in the United States earn less than whites and unemployment among them is higher. He assesses the relative impact of several different explanations for these labor market outcomes, which combine to make escaping poverty through work more difficult. Holzer concludes that while the lower educational attainment of African-American and Hispanic workers clearly contributes to their labor market difficulties, it does not fully account for them. Even when they have comparable levels of education to whites, African Americans and other minorities earn less and are less likely to be working. Other factors must be considered, including residential segregation, subtle racial discrimination in hiring and advancement, and, for young minority men, the high rate of criminal activity and incarceration.

Based on this analysis, Holzer proposes policy directions that can help overcome the multiple barriers that less-educated minorities face in the labor market. He advocates for more attention to early education, basic skill development, and work experience for minority youth, because relatively low skills remain the most serious obstacle to their labor market success.

Holzer stresses the importance of improving physical access to jobs and to safer, more integrated neighborhoods. He also emphasizes the importance of comprehensive educational, employment, and training services for disadvantaged, out-of-school youth, especially ex-offenders and others needing a combination of job training, job mobility, job placement and assistance training, and perhaps work experience. Like Osterman, Holzer notes the value of labor market intermediaries in helping connect less-skilled individuals with employers and reducing the effects of persistent discrimination.

Holzer acknowledges that much remains to be learned about effective approaches to helping less-educated individuals succeed. He advocates for continued experimentation and evaluation in four areas: approaches to improving school quality and student performance; school-to-work transition models; work experience programs that can generate credentials of value to private-sector employers; and communitywide education and employment initiatives in low-income neighborhoods.

While Holzer addresses the problems of less-educated Latinos and African Americans, Sonia M. Pérez and Cecilia Muñoz argue that Latinos face particular labor market challenges that make it difficult for them to advance out of low-wage work. Low education levels keep Latino workers in lower-paying jobs and occupations. The changing structure of employment—particularly the decline of manufacturing, the expansion of the low-wage, limited-benefit service sector, and the collapse of career ladders within firms—limits the ability of less-educated Latinos to start at the bottom and advance out of poverty.

Moreover, Latino immigrants face a particularly serious set of barriers. Pérez and Muñoz argue that immigration laws and immigrant provisions in welfare and other laws undermine the workplace rights of immigrants, both legal and undocumented. They make it easier to discriminate against Latinos on the job and make it more difficult for Latino immigrants to gain access to safety net services that offer important income supplements to individuals and families trying to survive on low wages.

Pérez and Muñoz argue that the confluence of record levels of immigration and strong economic growth creates an extraordinary opportunity to address the challenges facing low-wage workers, including immigrant workers. They suggest a policy agenda designed to ensure that immigrant workers and their counterparts in the low-wage workforce benefit as much from their labor as the larger society does from their presence in the workforce. The authors' recommendations fall into four broad areas:

- Investment in human capital;
- Improvements in job quality, including health benefits, training, and mobility tied to work;
- Support for Latino community-based organizations that can serve as intermediaries, can reach immigrants, and are trusted in the community; and
- Stronger protections for immigrants' workplace rights and civil rights through changes in immigration laws and enforcement of equal employment opportunity protections.

Vicky Lovell and Heidi Hartmann examine the particular barriers facing women in the low-wage labor market, with findings that are consistent with those of Carnevale and Rose: The preponderance of persistent low-wage workers are women. Yet Lovell and Hartmann note that women experience the labor market very differently than men do. They work in different occupations, for a different number of hours per week, and take more time out of the workforce to care for their families. The result of this sex-based divergence is that women earn less than men during their working lives and their income is lower when they retire.

Lovell and Hartmann suggest that this is not inevitable. Effective public policy can mitigate the disadvantage of being a member of the sex designated by society as the natural caregiver. However, rather than target policies that would only help low-wage women workers, Lovell and Hartmann argue that public policy strategies that address women's employment security will inevitably and directly benefit low-wage families, particularly those headed by women. They identify four sets of policies that can reduce barriers to women's economic security and be of particular value to women mired in low-wage jobs:

- Policies that would make it easier for workers with caregiving responsibilities to increase their work hours;
- Policies that would increase women's wages through skill development and through changes in wage-setting mechanisms;
- Income supplement policies, such as the EITC and paid family leave; and
- Changes in labor and equal employment opportunity laws that would help strengthen women's bargaining power in the labor market.

In the labor market, race and ethnicity interact with factors that vary geographically, including the characteristics of available jobs in a region. John Foster-Bey and Beata Bednarz of the Urban Institute explore how the mix of industry sectors in four metropolitan areas affects the availability of full-time and living wage jobs for low-skilled individuals in those areas. Their analysis focuses on the interaction between industry characteristics and living wage employment for African-American adult males, a group that has been particularly hard hit by economic change in the past two decades.

Foster-Bey and Bednarz undertook their analysis of these complex interactions to determine whether disaggregated research could help improve the targeting of policies designed to help low-wage workers advance. Their research answers two questions:

Can the effectiveness of targeted industry strategies for low-income individuals be improved by examining the opportunities for living wage employment for less-educated workers? Foster-Bey and Bednarz suggest that employment opportunities for less-educated men could be improved by targeting the economic sectors and occupations that provide the greatest opportunities for living wage employment. They show that it is possible to identify those sectors by analyzing the level of living wage employment opportunities available to less-educated adult workers in different sectors.

Can the effectiveness of targeted industry strategies for less-educated workers be improved if racial differences in living wage employment could be identified and explained by racial differences in the industry and occupational employment mix? Opportunities for employment appear to be strongly related to race and ethnicity. Foster-Bey and Bednarz conclude that an effective workforce development strategy would have to ask what can be done to improve the access of African-American males to employment opportunities in those sectors of the regional economy that offer the greatest opportunities for living wage employment. While the lower probability of employment may not be entirely the result of racial or ethnic discrimination, directly addressing the barriers to employment for less-educated African-American males is critical to any successful targeted industry strategy.

Part 4—Institutions That Can Improve Low-Wage Workers Prospects: Community Colleges, Employers, and Labor Unions

In the final section, the focus shifts to three important institutions that can influence the educational and economic progress of less-skilled and low-wage individuals: community colleges, employers, and labor unions. What practices are effective and promising? And how can new policies strengthen the contributions of these institutions to improving opportunities for low-skill workers to succeed in the labor market?

W. Norton Grubb argues that the comprehensive community college is the best-situated, best-prepared educational institution for helping low-skilled workers. At the same time, he recognizes the serious challenges facing community colleges that want to embrace that mission.

Based on field work, Grubb first identifies five characteristics of work-related education and training programs that are effective for low-skilled workers:

- They understand the local labor market and target jobs with relatively high earnings, strong employment growth, and opportunities for advancement.
- They contain an appropriate mix of academic education, occupational skills, and work-based learning, integrated to the extent possible.
- They provide a variety of supportive services appropriate for the diverse needs of different low-skill and low-wage workers and job seekers.
- They provide students with pathways or "ladders" to further education opportunities.
- They collect information about program results and use that data to improve program quality.

In Grubb's view, community colleges are better equipped to provide these services than most second-chance training programs. However, if the colleges are to succeed for adults who have traditionally not excelled at school and who must balance learning opportunities with earning and family needs, they must:

- Improve the quality of teaching;
- Enhance remedial or developmental educational offerings;
- Provide more effective and available guidance and counseling to students, many of whom have never succeeded in school and know few people who have completed postsecondary degrees;
- Provide easier access to financial support for adult working students with low incomes, to child care, and to other support services that can help students balance learning and family; and
- Cultivate better connections to employers who will hire those who complete the programs.

To promote and sustain such changes, Grubb concludes with recommendations for policymakers. At the federal level, he advocates for financial aid policies that help low-wage workers and for supporting a more active community college role in conducting research on and disseminating best practices. Grubb recommends that states help their colleges take steps to spread good ideas more quickly and efficiently, such as setting up instructional centers focused on improved teaching quality. Further, he challenges states to combine accountability measures with technical assistance and other supports that can help weaker institutions understand and pursue high-leverage reforms of institutional practice.

Edwin Meléndez and Carlos Suárez also see great promise in the community college as an institution that can serve low-wage workers, be attuned to the changing dynamics of the local labor market, and provide flexible, affordable lifelong learning options. These authors focus specifically on the ability of community colleges to serve Hispanics.

Meléndez and Suárez report on demonstration projects at four community colleges that have tried to prepare economically disadvantaged Hispanics for better jobs. Meléndez and Suárez conclude that effective programs for Hispanic students tend to combine four interrelated program-design elements:

- They offer comprehensive case management, proactive mentoring, and tutoring that together address each participant's unique needs and goals.
- They use curricular and instructional approaches that are student focused and put into practice the belief that "good teaching matters."
- They address language, culture, and learning-style barriers to the success of Hispanic college students.
- They have strong ties with local industry and employers.

Looking at employers who choose to provide an unusually high level of workplace education to their less-skilled employees, Amanda Ahlstrand and her colleagues use data from the American Society for Training and Development to try to identify the characteristics and practices that contribute to a firm's role in promoting educational and economic progress. The authors note, for example, that mid-sized firms and health care and family-owned businesses tend to provide more training to lower-wage employees. Also, firms that train more of their low-wage workers tend to be businesses that train a higher percentage of their total workforce. Perhaps most important, the researchers discovered wide variation in employer practices, raising the important question of what can move more firms to provide more training to their low-wage employees.

These authors draw several policy implications from their research-in-progress. First, they have found no evidence that a fear of losing newly trained workers leads employers to forego a potential costly training process for entry-level workers. On the contrary, employers believe that training promotes retention of employees.

Employers *are* concerned about the costs that arise when workers are off the job for training and education, a concern that the authors suggest should influence training program design and delivery. For example, the patterns of employer behavior in their study leads the authors to promote strategies to spread training costs among employers, such as the development of electronic learning technologies. Also, firms might encourage senior managers to quantify the costs and the benefits of training in order to demonstrate the return on such investments. Finally, the authors emphasize that public policies to stimulate on-the-job training for low-wage workers must address the needs of both employers and employees. Publicly funded programs, such as those provided through community colleges, can stimulate more training of low-wage workers—but only if they meet the needs of participating employers.

The third institution discussed in this section is organized labor. Brian J. Turner notes that unions occupy a central place on the issue of low-wage work—at the intersection of jobs, skills, and income. In the past decade, according to Turner, unions have undertaken a range of innovative strategies to aid low-wage workers, from engaging in collective bargaining and public advocacy to expanding their training and job placement programs.

Turner places union-sponsored education and training initiatives in the context of the labor movement's two core goals: raising labor standards through collective bargaining and union advocacy for pro-worker policies, services, and practices. He notes an increased commitment within the labor movement to organizing new members—including low-wage workers in a variety of industries—and to promote policies, such as a higher minimum wage and living wage ordinances, that raise wages for lower-paid workers.

According to Turner, organized labor has made strides in promoting training for low-wage workers through:

- Recruiting minorities and low-wage workers into unions and union jobs, with the provision of education and training to support initial placement and later career advancement;
- Raising standards, in the absence of union contracts, through training or through public campaigns to promote better wages and working conditions and more opportunities for training on-the-job; and
- Education and training services (e.g., ESL, GED) for community and union family members and job referral services for union and nonunion workers in organized units or with unorganized employers.

These strategies are part of organized labor's commitment to building community-union partnerships that address the needs not just of existing union members but also of potential future members. To encourage expansion of union efforts to help low-wage workers secure better skills, wages, and opportunities for advancement, Turner advocates a policy agenda that would expand public funding for regional skills alliance, recognize unions as effective providers of employment-and-training programming funded under Temporary Assistance for Needy Families (TANF), change immigration laws to protect workplace rights, and remove National Labor Relations Board and court-erected barriers to the right to unionize.

PART 1

Who Are the Low-Wage Workers in the New Economy? Who Employs Them?

Playing by the Rules,
but Losing the Game

Americans in Low-Income Working Families

Gregory Acs, Katherin Ross Phillips, and Daniel McKenzie

"It's time to honor and reward people who work hard and play by the rules. . . . No one who works full time and has children should be poor any more."

—Bill Clinton and Al Gore, *Putting People First,* 1992

Since the mid-1990s, as millions of people have moved off the welfare rolls and into low-paying jobs, policymakers and policy analysts have become increasingly concerned about the challenges facing low-income working families. The annual earnings of a full-time, full-year worker making $6 an hour—well above the federal minimum wage ($5.15 an hour)—are too low to lift a family of three above the federal poverty level. Even families with slightly higher earnings and who take advantage of programs like Food Stamps and the Earned Income Tax Credit (EITC) still must pay work-related expenses and struggle to make ends meet.

Discussions of low-income working families have been hampered by the lack of a common understanding of the term. Some analysts only consider those who work full-time and full-year to be working (e.g., Schiller 1994), while others have far less stringent requirements (e.g., Wertheimer 1999). And while the federal government defines an official poverty level, many analysts are concerned with understanding the struggles of low-income families trying to stay out of poverty. How the terms "low-income" and "work" are defined affects the size and composition of the group, as well as possible policy interventions to address its needs.

Using data from the National Survey of America's Families (NSAF), we examine how alternative hours and income thresholds alter the size of the low-income working population.[1] We settle on a broad definition that counts a family as low-income if its income falls below twice the federal poverty level and as working if the average annual hours worked by all adult family members is at least 1,000 hours (approximately one person working half-time). We proceed to examine the demographic characteristics of low-income working families, then compare those with the demographics of low-income families that do not meet our work threshold and to those of higher-income families that do work. We also analyze the job characteristics of low-income working families, again comparing them with both their higher-income and low-income, non-working counterparts as appropriate.

Policies aimed at lifting the incomes of low-income working families can involve increasing their wage rates or enabling or encouraging them to work more hours. While we cannot rigorously evaluate any particular policy option, some basic simulation exercises provide a sense of how many people in low-income working families would become higher-income if the minimum wage were to increase or if all able-bodied, prime-age adults (25- to 54-year-olds) were to work full-time, year-round.

One in six nonelderly Americans live in families we deem to be working low-income in 1996. Further, more than half of all nonelderly persons living in families with incomes below twice the poverty level are in working families. Almost two-thirds of the working low-income live in families with children and at least two adults present. And, on average, the primary earner in a low-income working family works full-time, year-round.

From the simulations, we find that increasing the minimum wage to $6.15 an hour would reduce the size of the low-income working population only slightly. If all prime-age, able-bodied adults in low-income working families were to work full-time, year-round, incomes would rise above twice the poverty level for about one-fifth of the individuals in low-income working families. Simulating an increase in work hours would also affect low-income nonworking families: One in six people living in low-income nonworking families would see their incomes rise above 200 percent of the poverty level; over one-third would become working low-income.

PREVIOUS RESEARCH

Previous research contains a wide range of estimates on the size of the working low-income population. These estimates depend upon who is counted as a worker and how low-income is defined. While much of the research has focused on individuals who are poor by the official U.S. Census Bureau definition, some researchers have looked more broadly at families with incomes above the federal poverty level but below various low-income thresholds.

Three papers by U.S. Bureau of Labor Statistics (BLS) researchers focus on the working poor and adopt a common definition: A worker is poor if his/her family's income falls below the federal poverty level; an adult is a worker if he or she worked or looked for work in at least 27 weeks over the past calendar year. Examining data for 1987, 1990, and 1994, these researchers estimate that the poverty rate among working adults ranges from 5.5 to 5.9 percent (Klein and Rones 1989; Gardner and Herz 1992; Hale 1997).

Altering the standard for working profoundly affects these results. For example, Schiller (1994) only counts adults working full-time and full-year as workers. Using this strict standard, he finds that the poverty rate among workers is only 2.5 percent, less than half the level the BLS researchers report. Kim (1998) uses a much less stringent standard to define workers: any adult that worked at all in the previous calendar year. She finds that 10 percent of workers are poor, almost twice the rate reported by the BLS researchers.

Many researchers argue that the poverty threshold is too low—that many people with incomes slightly above the poverty level are struggling.[2] Consequently, several researchers use more generous income limits. Schwarz and Volgy (1992) consider full-time, full-year workers just as Schiller (1994) does, but they set their poverty threshold at 155 percent of the federal poverty level. Schwarz and Volgy find that 7.4 percent of all workers are low-income, compared with 2.5 percent under Schiller's definition. Kim (1998) shows that the share of workers she counts as working poor rises from 10 percent when she uses the official poverty level to 18 percent when she uses 150 percent of the poverty level as her income threshold for the working poor.

Few researchers report the share of all adults who are working low-income, much less the share of all persons living in low-income families in which the adults work. After all, if an adult is low-income, so are his/her spouse and children. Kim (1998) finds that 7 to 12 percent of all adults are working low-income, depending on whether she uses 100 or 150 percent of the poverty level as her income threshold. Recall that for Kim, anyone who worked at all is counted as a worker. Again, this is much higher than the share we compute using data reported by Schiller (1994): 1.2 percent of all adults work full-time, full-year and live in families with incomes below the poverty level.

Other researchers focus on the share of the poor that is working or living in working families. Klein and Rones (1989), using the BLS definitions, find that one-third of all poor adults work. Wertheimer (1999) reports that 35 percent of all poor children live in families in which either a single parent works 20 hours a week or two parents combine to work at least 35 hours a week.

Two recent papers show that if the poor work more and take advantage of government transfer programs, they are likely to move above the federal poverty level but still have very low incomes. Ellwood (1999) calculates that in 1997, a single mother with two children working full-time, full-year at the minimum wage would have a net income about 13 percent above the poverty level. Ellwood's calculations include the value of the EITC (over $3,600), as well as $1,000 in child support, while subtracting $2,000 for child care costs. Similarly, Sawhill (1999) finds that the poverty rate for all persons in families would fall from 12.2 to 3.6 percent if all family heads worked full-time, full-year. Her measure of family income nets out work-related expenses but adds in the value of the EITC.

It may not be reasonable to expect single mothers with young children to work 40 hours a week. And if the income threshold is something higher than the official poverty level, as several researchers set it (e.g., Kim 1998 and Schwarz and Volgy 1992), then many of these families would still be working low-income.

DEFINING AND COUNTING LOW-INCOME WORKING FAMILIES

Any rigorous discussion of people living in low-income working families must begin by answering two basic questions: (1) Who is low-income? and (2) Who is working?

While the official federal poverty level is considered to reflect the income a family requires to meet its basic needs (adequate food, clothing, and shelter), the poverty thresholds are sufficiently low enough that they exclude families struggling to make ends meet. For example, many people would find it hard to provide for themselves and a child on an annual salary of $17,000 a year—yet this is over 50 percent more than the official poverty threshold for a single parent with one child ($11,235 in 1998). Furthermore, the official poverty threshold does not account for costs associated with working, such as transportation, child care, and other work-related expenses. In recent work, Pearce and Brooks (1999) calculate that a single mother with one child living in Washington, D.C., needs to make almost $34,000 a year—three times the official poverty level—to pay for housing, child care, and other basic needs.

Defining the term *work* is also subjective. An individual who works for a few weeks during a year clearly works in the strictest sense, but this does not demonstrate a strong attachment to the labor force. Alternatively, only counting individuals who work 40 hours a week and 52 weeks a year as working may be too stringent. After all, a single parent holding down a steady, part-time job is demonstrating a strong attachment to the world of work.

Comparing Alternative Definitions of Low-Income Working Families

Table 2.1 examines how the share of all nonelderly persons living in low-income working families varies under six different definitions of working low-income. We define low-income using both the official poverty level and twice the poverty level. We apply three different criteria in determining if a family is working:

TABLE 2.1 Nonelderly Persons in Low-Income Working Families, by Family Work Status, 1996: Alternative Definitions

	Persons in Families with Incomes Less than the Federal Poverty Level (%)	Persons in Families with Incomes Less than Twice the Federal Poverty Level (%)
All persons	14.0	32.2
Total hours worked = at least 1,000	6.4	22.2
Total hours worked = at least 2,000	3.6	16.3
Average hours worked per adult = at least 1,000	4.2	16.7

Source: Urban Institute tabulations from the 1997 National Survey of America's Families.

- The adults in the family worked a total of at least 1,000 hours a year (at least one half-time equivalent worker).
- The adults in the family worked a total of at least 2,000 hours a year (at least one full-time equivalent worker).
- The average hours worked by all adults in the family is at least 1,000 a year.[3]

This third criteria is the most flexible, setting different work standards for one- and two-parent families. To be deemed working, one-parent families must have one half-time equivalent worker, while two-parent families must have at least one full-time equivalent worker (2,000 hours divided by two adults).

> *Of our six possible definitions of the low-income working population, the last—the share of persons living in families with incomes below twice the poverty level and whose average hours worked per adult is at least 1,000—is the most appealing.*

The average-hours approach allows the hours-worked requirement to vary by the number of adults in a family, recognizing that two-parent families have more potential workers than one-parent families. And while the federal poverty level is the official standard for deprivation, many families living just above the poverty level struggle to make ends meet, and are also eligible for some government assistance (food stamps, earned income tax credits, and Medicaid, for example). By the time a family's income exceeds twice the poverty level, it is likely to be free from such government assistance. Consequently, we use 200 percent of the poverty level as our threshold for low income and find that 16.7 percent of all nonelderly persons live in low-income working families.

Work Effort among the Low-Income Population

> *The majority of people living in low-income families live in families that work.*

Depending on the definition, the share of nonelderly persons living in low-income working families ranges from 3.6 to 32.2 percent. Table 2.2 shows that almost one-third of all nonelderly persons are low-income by our definition (below 200 percent of the poverty level). Using that definition, among low-income persons, 52.0 percent live in families in which adults work at least 1,000 hours a year, on average. Even when we examine persons with incomes below the federal poverty level, we find that about 30 percent live in working families.

Table 2.2 also shows how the share of persons in low-income working families varies across states in our sample. Nationally, one out of six nonelderly persons lives in a low-income working family. Across the 13 focal states, the share ranges from a low of 9.1 percent in Massachusetts to a high of 22.7 percent in Mississippi. The share of low-income persons who live in working families ranges from 40.7 percent in New York to 65.3 percent in Wisconsin.

> *There is little correlation between the relative size of a state's low-income population and the share of the low-income population in working families.*

TABLE 2.2 Nonelderly Persons Living in Low-Income Working Families in Relation to Total Population and Low-Income Population, by State, 1996

	Low-Income Working Population (%)	Low-Income Population (%)	Low-Income Working Population As a Percentage of Low-Income Population (%)
U.S. total	16.7	32.2	52.0
Alabama	19.3	38.8	49.7
California	18.0	38.6	46.6
Colorado	15.9	27.4	57.8
Florida	20.1	36.8	54.6
Massachusetts	9.1	22.0	41.5
Michigan	13.3	25.5	52.2
Minnesota	13.5	22.6	59.6
Mississippi	22.7	45.8	49.5
New Jersey	10.0	21.7	46.1
New York	13.3	32.8	40.7
Texas	21.5	39.6	54.4
Washington	14.7	28.4	51.9
Wisconsin	14.3	21.9	65.3
Balance of nation	16.9	31.0	54.6

Source: Urban Institute tabulations from the 1997 National Survey of America's Families.

Note: Families with annual incomes less than 200 percent of the federal poverty level are considered low-income. Families are labeled working if their average annual hours worked per adult is at least 1,000 hours.

For example, in both Texas and Wisconsin, the share of the low-income population in working families exceeds the national average, but Wisconsin's low-income rate (21.9 percent) is among the lowest in our 13 NSAF focal states and Texas's is among the highest (39.6 percent).

Incomes of Low-Income Working Families

The average low-income working family's income is 39 percent above the federal poverty level (table 2.3).

For a single parent with one child, this implies an average income of $15,600; for a two-parent family with two children, it implies an average income of $23,000.[4] Low-income working families in California have the lowest average incomes (124 percent of the poverty level); those in Minnesota have the highest (149 percent of the poverty level).

Focusing on working families with incomes below the official poverty level, we find that their incomes, on average, reach only 76 percent of the poverty threshold. For a one-parent, one-child family, this implies an average income of $8,400; for a two-parent, two-child family, it implies an average annual income of $12,400. The differences in average incomes for working families below the poverty level across states are small, ranging from 73 percent of the poverty level in New York to 81 percent in New Jersey.

TABLE 2.3 Income Relative to the Poverty Level for Nonelderly Persons Living in Low-Income Working Families, by State, 1996

	All Nonelderly Persons Living in Low-Income Working Families	Nonelderly Persons Living in Working Families with Incomes below the Federal Poverty Level
U.S. total	1.39	0.76
Alabama	1.34	0.74
California	1.24	0.79
Colorado	1.40	0.75
Florida	1.36	0.79
Massachusetts	1.45	0.75
Michigan	1.44	0.77
Minnesota	1.49	0.75
Mississippi	1.32	0.75
New Jersey	1.41	0.81
New York	1.39	0.73
Texas	1.32	0.75
Washington	1.41	0.75
Wisconsin	1.45	0.76
Balance of nation	1.44	0.75

Source: Urban Institute tabulations from the 1997 National Survey of America's Families.

Note: Families with annual incomes less than 200 percent of the federal poverty level are considered low-income. Families are labeled working if their average annual hours worked per adult is at least 1,000 hours.

WHO ARE THE MEMBERS OF LOW-INCOME WORKING FAMILIES?

Family Composition

In terms of the types of families in which they live, the working low-income are neither a subset of the low-income population, nor are they just like working families with higher incomes.

They are both similar to and different from both groups. Overall, the biggest difference between low-income working families and other families is the presence of children: More than 80 percent of the working low-income population live in families with children as compared with less than two-thirds of other families.

Nearly two-thirds of the working low-income live in families with children in which two or more adults are present (table 2.4). One out of six people living in low-income working families lives in one-adult families, and 17.9 percent live in families without children. Interestingly, nonworking, low-income individuals—persons in families with incomes below 200 percent of the poverty level and whose average annual hours worked per adult fall below 1,000—are not much more likely to live in one-adult families with children than their working counterparts.

The big differences between the working and nonworking low-income populations are the proportions in families without children (17.9 versus 35.1 percent, respectively)

TABLE 2.4 Family Types, 1996

	Low-Income Working Population (%)	Low-Income Nonworking Population (%)	Higher-Income Working Population (%)
One adult with children	16.8	19.8	3.8
Two or more adults with children	65.3	45.1	57.9
Childless families	17.9	35.1	38.3

Source: Urban Institute tabulations from the 1997 National Survey of America's Families.
Note: Families with annual incomes less than 200 percent of the federal poverty level are considered low-income. Families are labeled working if their average annual hours worked per adult is at least 1,000 hours.

and the proportions in families with children and two or more adults (65.3 versus 45.1 percent, respectively). However, the share of persons in families with two or more adults and children is only slightly higher among the working low-income population than among the nonworking low-income population (65.3 versus 57.9 percent).

Demographic Characteristics of the Low-Income Working Population

In many respects, the low-income working population exists on a continuum between the nonworking low-income and higher-income populations.

Table 2.5 compares the low-income working population with the low-income non-working population and with persons living in working families with incomes over 200 percent of the poverty level. The share of the low-income working population living in female-headed families is 37.0 percent, far lower than the 57.0 percent of persons in low-income nonworking families but greater than the 26.6 percent in higher-income families. Other areas in which the working low-income population inhabits the middle ground include marital status, educational attainment, race, health status, and car ownership.

In terms of the number and age of their children, the low-income working population more closely resembles its nonworking counterpart. Among families with children, just under 60 percent of persons in low-income working and nonworking families have children ages 6 and younger, and more than 40 percent in both groups have three or more children. In contrast, 43.6 percent of persons in higher-income working families have young children, and only 22.9 percent have three or more children.

Demographic Factors Contributing to Economic Differences between Working Low-Income and Higher-Income Families

Differences in the demographic characteristics of the working low-income and higher-income populations may contribute to the lower economic status of the working low-income population through effects on job choices and earnings potential.

First, because low-income working families have more children than higher-income working families, they need more income to meet their families' needs. And because they have younger children, they may have more constrained job prospects.

TABLE 2.5 Nonelderly Persons Living in Families with Given Characteristics, by Family Work and Income Status, 1996

	Low-Income Working Families	Low-Income Nonworking Families	Higher-Income Working Families
Any children in the family	82.1%	64.9%	61.7%
Number of children in family (for families with children)			
One	20.2%	25.2%	35.5%
Two	36.5%	31.6%	41.6%
Three or more	43.3%	43.2%	22.9%
Age of youngest child (for families with children)			
Less than 3 years	33.8%	35.0%	25.1%
Between 3 and 6 years	24.3%	22.8%	18.5%
Number of children per worker (for families with children)	1.6	1.5	0.7
Number of adults in family	1.9	2.1	2.1
Family has more than two adults	9.6%	26.7%	19.0%
Age of family head (average)	35.5	37.7	40.6
Age of family head			
Younger than 25	11.3%	18.1%	3.6%
25 to 54	84.5%	68.4%	87.4%
55 and older	4.2%	13.4%	9.0%
Female family head	37.0%	57.0%	26.6%
Marital status			
Married (including cohabitors)	68.9%	45.2%	83.0%
Widowed/divorced/separated	17.3%	25.6%	8.9%
Never married	13.9%	29.2%	8.1%
Education of family head			
Less than high school	22.4%	35.2%	4.3%
HS grad or GED	45.7%	39.3%	35.0%
Some college	21.5%	17.9%	24.7%
College graduate	10.4%	7.6%	36.0%
Race of family head			
Black	18.0%	26.5%	9.4%
Hispanic	11.6%	10.7%	3.9%
White, non-Hispanic	66.0%	56.2%	82.5%
Nonwhite, non-Hispanic	4.5%	6.6%	4.2%
Family head has a work-limiting health condition	11.6%	27.6%	7.1%
Lives in metropolitan area	73.3%	76.9%	82.4%
Owns a car	84.1%	66.7%	96.4%

Source: Urban Institute tabulations from the 1997 National Survey of America's Families.

Note: Families with annual incomes less than 200 percent of the federal poverty level are considered low-income. Families are labeled working if their average annual hours worked per adult is at least 1,000 hours. In working families, the highest-earning adult in the social family is the family head. In families where no adult works, the adult with the highest education is deemed the family head.

Second, the primary earners in low-income working families have far less education than their counterparts in higher-income families: More than one-third of the higher-income population live in families headed by a college graduate compared with just 1 in 10 of the low-income working population. And, of course, more-educated workers command higher wage rates. Third, the head of a low-income working family is, on average, younger than the head of a higher-income working family. Only 3.6 percent of the higher-income population live in families headed by someone under age 25, compared with 11.3 percent of the low-income working population. Younger workers generally have less labor market experience and earn lower wages than prime-age workers (25- to 54-year-olds). Interestingly, similar proportions of the working higher-income and the working low-income populations live in families headed by prime-age individuals (25- to 54-year-olds): 87.4 and 84.5 percent, respectively.

In addition, when compared with primary earners in higher-income families, the primary earners in low-income working families are less likely to be married, implying that they are less likely to have a potential secondary worker in the family. And heads of low-income working families are more likely to be members of a minority group and to have a work-limiting health condition. Each of these factors is associated with either lower income or reduced earnings potential.

EMPLOYMENT CHARACTERISTICS OF LOW-INCOME WORKING FAMILIES

Hours Worked and Wages Earned

The primary earners in low-income working families are working, on average, full-time, full-year but for lower wages than their higher-income counterparts. Further, higher-income families are far more likely to have secondary workers than working low-income families.

Table 2.6 describes the jobs that the primary earners in low-income working families hold, and it compares those jobs with jobs held by primary earners in higher-income families. Not surprisingly, the median hourly wage of the primary earner in low-income working families ($7.55) is less than half the median of primary earners in families with incomes above 200 percent of the federal poverty level ($16.67). Focusing on one-adult families with children, we find that the median hourly wage of the primary earner in low-income working families is $6.73, compared with $14.42 for the primary earner in higher-income families.

While the wages of primary earners in low-income families are far lower than those of their higher-income counterparts, their work effort is not. Primary earners in both working low-income and higher-income families work full-time, year-round on average. In low-income working families, the median number of annual hours worked by the primary earner is 2,080, just below the 2,184 hours for primary earners in higher-income working families. And the primary earner in both low-income and higher-income working families usually works 52 weeks a year. Work effort among one-adult families with children is almost identical for both working low-income and higher-income families. In addition, there is little difference in the median number of hours

TABLE 2.6 Nonelderly Persons Living in Working Families with Given Job Characteristics, 1996

	All Families		One-Adult Families with Children	
	Low-Income	Higher-Income	Low-Income	Higher-Income
Wage rate of primary earner (median)	$7.55	$16.67	$6.73	$14.42
Number of workers per adult	0.8	0.9	1.0	1.0
Annual hours of work (median) for:				
Primary earner	2,080	2,184	2,058	2,080
Total for family	2,600	3,873	2,080	2,080
Per adult in family	1,508	1,820	2,080	2,080
Annual weeks of work (median) for:				
Primary earner	52	52	52	52
Total for family	52	98	52	52
Primary earner has more than one job	8.0%	11.5%	8.3%	13.7%
Primary earner mainly works between 6 a.m. and 6 p.m.	74.7%	83.0%	75.6%	86.3%
Family receives health insurance through employer	54.3%	88.6%	54.3%	85.6%
Time at current employer (primary earner):				
Less than 1 year	30.8%	13.7%	34.5%	14.7%
1 year or more	69.2%	86.3%	65.5%	85.3%

Source: Urban Institute tabulations from the 1997 National Survey of America's Families.
Note: Families with annual incomes less than 200 percent of the federal poverty level are considered low-income. Families are labeled working if their average annual hours worked per adult is at least 1,000 hours.

worked by the primary earner, with those in low-income families averaging 2,058 hours while those in higher-income families average 2,080 hours.

Even though the primary earners in low-income working families work about as much as those in higher-income families, higher-income families are far more likely to have additional earners working more hours.

For example, the median total number of hours worked by low-income working families is 2,600, substantially less than the 3,873 worked by higher-income families. In addition, the average hours worked per adult is appreciably lower in low-income working families (1,508 per year) compared with higher-income families (1,820 per year).

Quality of Employment

While primary earners in low-income working families work as much as those in higher-income families, the jobs that they hold are less stable and provide fewer benefits.

Primary earners in working low-income families are less likely to hold jobs that provide daytime work hours, are much less likely to have been at their employer for more than one year, and their families are substantially less likely to receive health insurance through an employer.

The primary earner in 74.7 percent of low-income working families works between 6 a.m. and 6 p.m., compared with 83.0 percent of higher-income families. Only 54.3 percent of persons living in low-income working families receive health insurance through an employer, while 88.6 percent of their higher-income counterparts do. Finally, while the primary earner in 86.3 percent of higher-income families has been at his or her job for more than one year, only 69.2 percent of primary earners in low-income working families have been at their jobs for more than one year.

> *Our data on job characteristics indicate that primary earners in low-income working families spend as much time working as those who are better off, but for less money, fewer benefits, and with less predictable hours.*

SIMULATION RESULTS: THE EFFECTS OF INCREASES IN THE MINIMUM WAGE AND HOURS WORKED ON THE SIZE OF THE LOW-INCOME WORKING POPULATION

A substantial number of people live in families in which the adults are committed to working, yet their incomes remain low. Indeed, as noted, one out of six nonelderly persons lives in a working family with income below 200 percent of the poverty level, and one-quarter of the low-income working population falls below the official poverty level. Our profile of the low-income working population indicates that they earn less per hour and have less education than the higher-income working population. They also have more and younger children than the higher-income working population. Primary workers in low-income working families tend to work full-time, full-year. However, the total hours worked by all adults tends to be much lower among the working low-income than the higher-income population because secondary workers work fewer hours in low-income working families.

These differences between the low-income and higher-income working populations suggest that policies aimed at raising the wages or work effort of adults in working low-income families could potentially move some people over the 200 percent of poverty level threshold, into the working higher-income population. There are several approaches policymakers can take to increase the hourly earnings of low-income working families. For example, they can directly raise the wages of the lowest-paid workers by increasing the minimum wage, or they can attempt to raise wages indirectly by helping low-income people obtain more education and training.

Policymakers can also take two general approaches to raising the work effort of low-income working families. One involves reducing obstacles to work—for example, by increasing the supply of subsidized, quality child care and providing transportation assistance. A second approach involves increasing the rewards for work—for example, through the EITC. Attempts to raise the work effort of low-income working families are also likely to encourage nonworking families to work. Of course, policymakers can simply provide more direct assistance to low-income working families through more generous Temporary Assistance for Needy Families (TANF) policies and in-kind transfers, such as food stamps and public health insurance.

We cannot rigorously evaluate all the options, but very basic simulations can provide important insights into how certain policies could affect the size of the low-income working population, and even the size of the low-income nonworking population. With simulations, we examine two scenarios:

- The impact of raising the minimum wage on the size of the low-income working population; and
- The effects of increased work effort among prime-age, able-bodied adults on the size of the low-income working population.[5]

Note that we are not examining a specific policy to increase work effort; rather, we focus on the ultimate impact of a substantial rise in work hours on family incomes. Our primary concern is to estimate the potential impact of a large increase in work effort on the size of the low-income working population; then one can consider specific policy options to increase work effort.

Increases in wages and work effort both will raise some families' incomes, and this has implications for their receipt of means-tested cash assistance and their tax bills. Our simulations do not explicitly model changes in eligibility and receipt of means-tested benefits; however, they do use two extreme assumptions: (1) that families retain all the benefits they had been receiving; and (2) that families stop receiving AFDC/TANF, general assistance, and emergency assistance.[6] The likely outcome (in the absence of an explicit policy change regarding these programs) will fall between the two extremes.

In addition, we make no attempt to calculate a family's work-related expenses, tax liability, or the payment it may receive through the EITC, which can substantially increase the income of a low-income working family. However, by reporting the share of persons still living in low-income working families after an increase in the minimum wage or in hours worked, we demonstrate the number of people who could potentially benefit from the EITC, even if we cannot assess its monetary value.

Of course, increased work effort among nonworkers will affect the size of the low-income nonworking population as well. In addition to presenting what portion of the low-income working population becomes higher-income through increases in the minimum wage and hours worked, we examine what share of the low-income nonworking population is transformed into the working low-income and even into working higher-income populations. We also examine how many persons living below the official poverty level are raised above it by our simulated changes.

Raising the Minimum Wage

Through minimum wage legislation, governments can mandate the lowest wage paid to a majority of the workforce. In 1996, the federal minimum wage was $4.25 an hour; it increased to $4.75 in 1997 and to $5.15 in 1998.[7] Congress is considering an increase in the minimum wage to $6.15 over the next two years. In table 2.7, we estimate the short-run effect of increasing the 1996 federal minimum wage to $6.15 on the share of the nonelderly population living in low-income working families.

To simulate raising the minimum wage to $6.15 per hour, we increase the wages of every worker earning between $4.25 and $6.14 to $6.15.[8] We assume that raising the minimum wage will neither draw workers into the labor market nor encourage workers to increase their hours of work. Similarly, we assume that employers will not lay off workers or cut their hours in response to higher labor costs.[9] Over all, one-third of all workers in low-income working families and 41.3 percent of workers in families with

TABLE 2.7 Effects of Changes in the Minimum Wage, 1996

A. Percentage of Persons Living in Working Families with Incomes below 200 Percent of the Poverty Level

	1996 Minimum Wage (%)	Simulated Minimum Wage = $6.15 (%)
Simulations assuming continued receipt of means-tested cash assistance		
Overall	16.7	16.2
One adult with children	34.3	34.3
Two or more adults with children	20.1	19.6
Childless families	8.0	7.3
Simulations without means-tested cash assistance		
Overall	16.7	16.2
One adult with children	34.3	34.3
Two or more adults with children	20.1	19.6
Childless families	8.0	7.3

B. Percentage of Persons Living in Working Families with Incomes below 100 Percent of the Poverty Level

	1996 Minimum Wage (%)	Simulated Minimum Wage = $6.15 (%)
Simulations assuming continued receipt of means-tested cash assistance		
Overall	4.2	3.5
One adult with children	12.8	10.9
Two or more adults with children	4.4	3.8
Childless families	1.8	1.5
Simulations without means-tested cash assistance		
Overall	4.2	3.7
One adult with children	12.8	11.7
Two or more adults with children	4.4	3.9
Childless families	1.8	1.5

Source: Urban Institute tabulations from the 1997 National Survey of America's Families.

Note: Families are considered working if their average annual hours worked per adult are at least 1,000; at the time of the survey, the federal minimum wage was $4.25; simulations without means-tested cash assistance assume families will no longer receive income from either AFDC/TANF, general assistance, or emergency assistance.

incomes below the official poverty level earn less than $6.15 an hour. Only workers with wages below $6.15 will see their family incomes rise as a result of this simulation.

Minimum Wage Increases and the Low-Income Working Population

Increasing the minimum wage to $6.15 an hour will not have a large effect on the share of persons living in low-income working families.

Such an increase would reduce the share of persons living in low-income working families from 16.7 to 16.2 percent regardless of whether they continued to receive means-tested cash assistance. When we examine one-adult families with children, we find that raising the minimum wage has no effect on the proportion of families deemed working and low-income: It remains stable at 34.3 percent. Among two-adult families with children, increasing the minimum wage reduces the share living in families with incomes below 200 percent of the poverty level from 20.1 to 19.6 percent.

Interestingly, our findings are roughly the same whether or not we assume that workers continue to receive means-tested cash assistance. This suggests that the vast majority of the low-income working population that would move up and into the ranks of the higher-income population does not receive such assistance.

Minimum Wage Increases and Families below the Federal Poverty level

Increasing the minimum wage would also have small impacts on individuals in working families with income below the federal poverty level.

A minimum wage of $6.15 would reduce the percentage of individuals in working families living below the poverty level from 4.2 percent to 3.5 percent, a 16.6 percent decline. If we assume that families would have stopped participating in cash assistance programs, the rate would only fall to 3.7 percent, an 11.9 percent decline. For one-adult families with children, increasing the minimum wage would reduce the share in working families with incomes below the poverty level from 12.8 to 10.9 percent if benefits are retained and to 11.7 if benefits are lost. For two-adult families with children, the share falls from 4.4 to 3.8 percent with means-tested cash assistance and to 3.9 percent without.

Summary of Raising the Minimum Wage Simulations

These simulation results suggest that raising the minimum wage to $6.15 would not lift many low-income working families into the higher-income category.

Indeed, the primary earners in low-income working families earn far more than $6.15 an hour already. Raising the minimum wage high enough to dramatically reduce the size of the low-income working population may not be possible without reducing the number of available low-wage jobs. In addition, this wage would likely have to be substantially higher than any increases being contemplated by Congress. Nevertheless, a higher minimum wage will increase the incomes of some low-income working families, and while it may not lift them above any given income threshold, these families will have more income to meet their needs.

Increasing Hours Worked

Increasing work effort is another way to increase income. Not all adults can work and not all part-time workers can work more hours. However, our simulations gauge the potential impact of dramatic increases in work effort, giving an upper boundary of sorts on the impact of policies to increase work effort.[10] The simulations assume that all prime-age, able-bodied adults work at least 2,000 hours a year. For adults who are not working, we simulate earnings equal to the minimum wage ($4.25) times 2,000 hours of work (a total of $8,500 in annual earnings). For people who are currently working fewer than 2,000 hours a year, we increase their hours to 2,000 and compute their earnings by multiplying their wage rates by 2,000.[11] People working more than 2,000 hours are not affected by this simulated increase. Note that over half of all persons in low-income working families live with an able-bodied adult working less than 2,000 hours a year.

Increasing the Hours of Work among Low-Income Working Families

If all prime-age, able-bodied adults worked at least 2,000 hours a year and all families continued to receive means-tested cash assistance, 3.3 percent of the population would move from the low-income working population into the higher-income working population (table 2.8).

In other words, about 20 percent of the people in low-income working families would become higher-income. Even taking away the welfare benefits of families when their incomes increase, we obtain roughly the same impact.

Not surprisingly, *people in one-adult low-income working families with children are not profoundly affected by an increase in hours worked* because all these adults are already working at least 1,000 hours a year, with most working more than 2,000 hours. Only 5.1 percent of the low-income working population in one-adult families would become higher-income even if they retained all their means-tested cash assistance. In contrast, about one-quarter of the low-income working population in families with two or more adults and children see their incomes rise above 200 percent of the poverty level. By definition, these families have more potential workers than their one-adult counterparts.

Increasing the Hours of Working Families with Incomes below the Federal Poverty Level

Focusing on families with incomes below the federal poverty level, we find that increasing hours lifts one-third of the people in these working families above the poverty level. Among one-adult working families with children and incomes below the poverty level, 12.5 percent are lifted out of poverty through increasing work effort; among two-adult families with children, nearly half will move above the federal poverty level. However, this change affects only 2.2 percent of all individuals in two-adult families.

Whether or not families continue to receive means-tested transfers only affects the share of one-adult working families with children moved above the poverty level. No

TABLE 2.8 Effects of Increasing Work Effort in the Low-Income Working Population to at Least 2,000 Hours per Year, 1996

A. Percentage of Persons Living in Working Families with Incomes below 200 Percent of the Poverty Level

	Low-Income Working Population		Percent That Moves above 200% of Poverty
	Baseline (%)	Family Income Increases to More than 200% of Poverty (percentage points)	
Simulations assuming continued receipt of means-tested cash assistance			
Overall	16.7	−3.3	19.6
One adult with children	34.3	−1.8	5.1
Two or more adults with children	20.1	−4.8	23.7
Childless families	8.0	−1.4	17.8
Simulations without means-tested cash assistance			
Overall	16.7	−3.2	19.3
One adult with children	34.3	−1.8	5.1
Two or more adults with children	20.1	−4.7	23.3
Childless families	8.0	−1.4	17.8

B. Percentage of Persons Living in Working Families with Incomes below 100 Percent of the Poverty Level

	Working Families with Incomes below 100% of Poverty		Percent That Moves above 100% of Poverty
	Baseline (%)	Family Income Increases to More than 100% of Poverty (percentage points)	
Simulations assuming continued receipt of means-tested cash assistance			
Overall	4.2	−1.4	34.8
One adult with children	12.8	−1.6	12.5
Two or more adults with children	4.4	−2.2	48.7
Childless families	1.8	−0.4	20.0
Simulations without means-tested cash assistance			
Overall	4.2	−1.4	33.1
One adult with children	12.8	−1.2	9.3
Two or more adults with children	4.4	−2.1	47.2
Childless families	1.8	−0.4	20.0

Source: Urban Institute tabulations from the 1997 National Survey of America's Families.

Note: Families are considered working if their average annual hours worked per adult are at least 1,000; simulations without means-tested cash assistance assume families will no longer receive income from either AFDC/TANF, general assistance, or emergency assistance.

other family type is substantially affected when we assume receipt of means-tested transfers would cease. As one would expect, this suggests that means-tested cash assistance is a more important source of support for poor single adults with children than for other types of families.

Increasing the Hours Work among Nonworking Families

Increasing the hours worked by prime-age, able-bodied adults will also increase the hours worked among the *nonworking* low-income families (table 2.9). Many of the nonworking low-income population will move into the ranks of the working low-income population while others will be lifted above 200 percent of the poverty level.

More than one-third of the nonworking low-income population will become working low-income and one-sixth will see incomes rise above 200 percent of poverty as a result of increases in their hours worked (see table 2.9). About half the nonworking low-income population will remain nonworking and low-income, indicating that the adults in these families are very young, very old, or disabled. Again, the results are similar whether or not we assume families continue to receive means-tested cash assistance.

More than half the people in nonworking, low-income, one-adult families with children will become working low-income through increased work effort; another 5.1 percent will become higher-income; 42.9 percent will remain in nonworking families. Among nonworking, low-income families with children and two or more adults, increasing work effort will lift one in five above 200 percent of poverty and about half into the ranks of the working low-income population. Fewer than one-third of persons in such families will remain nonworking and low-income.

Increasing the Hours of Nonworking Families with Incomes below the Federal Poverty Level

Overall, 9.8 percent of the nonelderly population lives in families in which the adults work an average of less than 1,000 hours a year and the family's income falls below the federal poverty level. If all prime-age, able-bodied adults worked 2,000 hours a year, we find that more than one-third would be lifted above the federal poverty level if they retained all their means-tested cash assistance. Without this assistance, only 28.7 percent of people in such families would be lifted above the poverty level. One in five would remain in poverty but would be considered a working family if they retained benefits; this share rises to one in four if benefits are lost. Less than half (45.0 percent) of families would still be considered nonworking and still have incomes below the federal poverty level.

People living in families with two or more adults and children whose incomes are below the poverty level are more likely to be lifted above the poverty level through increased work effort than individuals in one-adult poor families with children. More than one-third of people in one-adult nonworking poor families with children would now be working but remain poor even if they continued to receive benefits. Without benefits, the share rises to 46.5 percent as families that had been lifted above the poverty level fall back below it.

TABLE 2.9 Effects of Increasing Work Effort in the Low-Income Nonworking Population to at Least 2,000 Hours per Year, 1996

A. Percentage of Persons Living in Nonworking Families with Incomes below 200 Percent of the Poverty Level

	Baseline (%)	Low-Income Nonworking at Baseline		
		Remain Nonworking Low-Income (%)	Become Working Low-Income (%)	Become Higher-Income (%)
Simulations assuming continued receipt of means-tested cash assistance				
Overall	15.4	45.6	37.7	16.9
One adult with children	37.3	42.9	52.0	5.1
Two or more adults with children	12.8	31.4	48.2	20.4
Childless families	14.5	65.3	16.1	18.5
Simulations without means-tested cash assistance				
Overall	15.4	45.6	38.2	16.2
One adult with children	37.3	42.9	52.2	4.9
Two or more adults with children	12.8	31.5	49.0	19.4
Childless families	14.5	65.3	16.3	18.4

B. Percentage of Persons Living in Nonworking Families with Incomes below 100 Percent of the Poverty Level

	Baseline (%)	Nonworking/Family Income below 100% of Poverty		
		Remain Nonworking, Income Less than 100% of Poverty (%)	Become Working, Income Less than 100% of Poverty (%)	Income Rises above 100% of Poverty (%)
Simulations assuming continued receipt of means-tested cash assistance				
Overall	9.8	45.0	20.1	34.7
One adult with children	33.6	42.6	36.4	21.1
Two or more adults with children	7.6	31.1	19.8	49.2
Childless families	7.8	67.2	5.5	27.3
Simulations without means-tested cash assistance				
Overall	9.8	45.0	26.1	28.7
One adult with children	33.6	42.6	46.5	10.9
Two or more adults with children	7.6	30.9	27.1	41.4
Childless families	7.8	67.2	5.5	27.3

Source: Urban Institute tabulations from the 1997 National Survey of America's Families.
Note: Families are considered working if their average annual hours worked per adult are at least 1,000; simulations without means-tested cash assistance assume families will no longer receive income from either AFDC/TANF, general assistance, or emergency assistance.

Summary of Increasing Hours-Worked Simulations

Our simulation results suggest that increases in the work effort of all prime-age, able-bodied adults can lift some families out of the working low-income population—about one in five will see its income rise above 200 percent of the poverty level. Further, about one in three working families with incomes below 100 percent of poverty will move over that threshold.

In addition, more than half the nonworking low-income population will start working, many will join the ranks of the working low-income population, and some will actually have incomes in excess of 200 percent of the poverty level.

Many families will see their incomes rise as a result of increased work effort, even if they do not rise enough to cross one of our low-income thresholds. However, to the extent that policymakers are particularly concerned about families that work hard and play by the rules, it is important to note that increases in work effort will actually move more people into the ranks of the working low-income population (from formerly nonworking families) than it will lift out. Thus, while most families will be far better off because of increased earned income, on net, about one out of every five people would live in a family we consider to be working low-income. In addition, about half the persons living in nonworking low-income families—about 5 percent of the total population—are unlikely to be able to increase their hours worked because the adults in the families are either over 54, under 25, or disabled.

Finally, keep in mind that these simulations require all prime-age, able-bodied adults to work 2,000 hours a year—a sizeable work effort. As such, the findings suggest an upper bound. Furthermore, for one-adult families with young children, it may be particularly difficult for the adult to work full-time, year round. It may also be unrealistic to assume that a secondary earner would be able to increase work effort, especially in families with young children.[12] In addition, it is not clear whether the economy could generate enough jobs to sustain this level of work effort.

SUMMARY AND IMPLICATIONS

We find that one in six nonelderly Americans lives in a family with income below twice the federal poverty level and in which all adults work, on average, at least 1,000 hours a year: These individuals comprise the low-income working population. Almost two-thirds of the low-income working population lives in families with children and at least two adults present. And, on average, the primary earner in a low-income working family works full-time, year round. However, due to differences in the work effort and presence of secondary workers, total family hours worked are lower for working low-income families than for higher-income families. In addition, primary earners in higher-income families have much higher average hourly wage rates than primary earners in low-income working families: $16.67 versus $7.55 an hour.

Raising the minimum wage will lift the incomes of some of the low-income working population, but most will remain low-income. Alternatively, if all prime-age, able-bodied adults worked at least 2,000 hours a year, about one-fifth of persons living in low-income working families would rise above twice the poverty level. Nonworking low-income families would also increase their work effort, and more than one-third of persons living in nonworking low-income families would join the ranks of the working low-income, while one-sixth would move above 200 percent of the poverty level.

Although there is legitimate disagreement about how to define the terms "working" and "low income," our analysis makes clear that many people live in families in which the adults work at least half-time but the family's income remains low. Even if policies aimed at promoting work—such as child care and transportation assistance—induce a large increase in work effort, a substantial number of people would still live in low-income families. As such, programs that supplement earnings, like the EITC, are vital to the well-being of families that are working and playing by the rules but just making ends meet.

DATA APPENDIX

The analyses rely on data from the 1997 National Survey of America's Families, a nationally representative survey of the noninstitutionalized, civilian population under age 65. The NSAF is part of the Urban Institute's multiyear *Assessing the New Federalism* research project designed to analyze the growing responsibility of state governments for the provision of social assistance.

The 1997 NSAF was fielded between February and November 1997 and has large enough samples from 13 states to permit state-level analyses.[13] Income and employment information were collected for the previous year, 1996. The sample includes more than 145,000 people in over 44,000 households, with cross-sectional data about the social and economic well-being of families. One goal of the survey is to gather information about the economic and social well-being of low-income children and their families. As a result, the NSAF oversamples low-income families and is well suited for an analysis of the working low-income population.[14]

The results in this paper are weighted to represent all individuals under age 65. However, many of the indicators are measured at the family level. For example, family income is used to determine whether or not a person is low-income. We use an NASF-developed definition of family that is broader than the legal definition of family used in other surveys, such as the Current Population Survey. A "legal family" includes people within a household who are legally related to each other through blood, marriage, or adoption. The "social family" definition we use includes members of a household who are part of a legal family as well as unmarried partners and all members of the extended family. The social family concept assumes that people with strong relationship ties will share resources within a household.

The NSAF does not designate a head of household. Because many of our indicators rely on identifying someone in the family who is, or potentially could be, the primary earner, we developed two methods to identify a head of household. In families in which at least one adult works, the person with the highest total earnings in 1996 is deemed the head of household and the primary earner. Total earnings include pay from all jobs plus any self-employment income. In families that have no workers, we select the adult with the highest level of education as the family head. We restrict our sample to nonelderly persons in families in which the head of household is between the ages of 18 and 64 and, for families with primary earners, in which the primary earner's main job is not self-employment (to eliminate the possibility of negative earnings from the sample).

While most of the variables in our analyses are straightforward, some require an explanation:

- *Families with children:* One-adult families with children include only families with at least one child under 18 years old and exactly one adult aged 18 years or older. We are careful not to refer to our one-adult families with children as single-parent families. Single parents can live in a family with more than one adult present.
- *Wage:* Because the NSAF does not include a direct question about wage rates, we calculate wage rates from three variables: annual earnings last year; number of hours worked per week last year; and number of weeks worked last year. In this case, "last year" refers to 1996. For each worker, we multiply the number of hours by the number of weeks to derive an estimate of the number of hours worked in 1996. We then divide annual earnings by the estimated total number of hours worked.[15]

At least two potential sources of error are introduced when computing wage rates from earnings and estimated hours. The first source derives from reporting errors associated with earnings data in surveys. Respondents may not know the exact amount of earnings from the previous year, especially when the question is asked later in the following year or is asked about someone other than the respondent. The second source results from the way the "hours" question is asked. The survey asks about the number of hours usually worked during a week in the previous year. Hours calculations, then, will not include either increases or decreases in usual work effort. However, reported earnings should reflect hour variations throughout the year. For example, if a worker worked part-time for a few weeks during the year, we would overestimate the number of hours worked and underestimate the wage rate (assuming the amount of reported earnings is accurate). On the other hand, if a worker worked overtime during a few weeks, we would underestimate the number of hours worked and overestimate the wage rate.

The question pattern in the NSAF survey introduces another potential source of error. For people working for the same employer when the survey is asked as during the previous year, questions about usual hours of work during the previous year are not asked. For these stable workers, the current usual hours of work are used as a proxy for last year's usual hours. As a result, for workers who changed their hours of work over the past year, we incorrectly assume that they worked at the same level last year as they currently do.

NOTES

This chapter was prepared for and partially funded by the Urban Institute's *Assessing the New Federalism* project and Jobs for the Future. We would like to thank Harry Holzer, Pamela Loprest, Marc Miller, Alyssa Wigton, and Sheila Zedlewski for their helpful comments. All errors are the responsibility of the authors. The opinions expressed here are those of the authors and do not necessarily reflect the views of the Urban Institute or its sponsors. The authors can be contacted at: gacs@ui.urban.org, phone: (202) 261-5522.

1. The 1997 NASF is a nationally representative survey of U.S. families. Unlike many such data sets, it contains large samples from 13 states, allowing for state-level analysis. The NSAF also oversamples families with incomes below 200 percent of the poverty level. For a description of the NSAF survey and a discussion of its reliability, see Brick et al. 1999. For more information about the NSAF, see the Appendix.

2. There is considerable debate about how well poverty is measured. Some argue that the official poverty level is too low; others that it is too high. There is also debate over what should count as income. For more information, see Ruggles (1990) and National Research Council (1995).

3. Anyone over age 18 is considered an adult.

4. These dollar values are based on 1998 poverty thresholds.

5. Prime-age, able-bodied adults are persons between ages 25 and 54 who do not report a physical, mental, or health condition that limits the amount of work they can do.

6. We assume that families in which someone receives SSI (Supplemental Security Income) continue to receive SSI. Also, food stamps are not considered income, and they do not affect our simulations. However, food stamps are an important source of support for low-income families.

7. Nine states and the District of Columbia had minimum wages that exceeded the federal minimum in 1996: Alaska ($4.75), Delaware ($4.65), Hawaii ($5.25), Iowa ($4.65), Massachusetts ($4.75), New Jersey ($5.05), Oregon ($4.75), Vermont ($4.75), Washington ($4.90), District of Columbia ($5.25) (Council of State Governments 1999).

8. We only increase the wages of earners who earned at least the minimum wage. Some of the workers in our sample had calculated wage rates less than $4.25. We assume that these individuals are employed in a job that is not covered by minimum wage legislation.

9. Card and Krueger (1995) argue the disemployment effects of raising the minimum wage in this range are likely to be quite small.

10. Our estimates are only an upper-bound "of sorts": We do not measure the additional impact of the EITC on increasing working family incomes.

11. In the hours simulations, we do not include any response of wages to the increased labor supply. In other words, each worker retains her current wage.

12. In addition to the demands of parenting, workers also may face other barriers to increased work effort. See Loprest and Zedlewski (1999) for a description of some of the obstacles to work experienced by former welfare recipients.

13. The 13 states are: Alabama, California, Colorado, Florida, Massachusetts, Michigan, Minnesota, Mississippi, New Jersey, New York, Texas, Washington, and Wisconsin.

14. Detailed information about the survey is available on the Urban Institute's Web site: http://newfederalism.urban.org/nsaf/index.htm. For a description of the NSAF survey and a discussion of its reliability, see Brick et al. (1999).

15. We topcode wages at $150 per hour.

REFERENCES

Brick, Pat, et al. 1999. "Survey Methods and Data Reliability." *Assessing the New Federalism* Methodology Report No. 1. Washington, D.C.: The Urban Institute.

Card, David, and Alan Krueger. 1995. *Myth and Measurement: The New Economics of the Minimum Wage.* Princeton, N.J.: Princeton University Press.

Clinton, Bill, and Al Gore. 1992. *Putting People First: How We Can All Change America.* New York: Times Books.

Council of State Governments American Legislators' Association. 1999. *The Book of the States.* Lexington, Ky.: Council of State Governments.

Ellwood, David. 1999. "Plight of the Working Poor." Children's Roundtable Report No. 2. Washington, D.C.: The Brookings Institution.

Gardner, Jennifer, and Diane Herz. 1992. "Working and Poor in 1990." *Monthly Labor Review* (December): 20–28.

Hale, Thomas. 1997. "At Issue . . . The Working Poor." *Monthly Labor Review* (September): 47–48.

Kim, Marlene. 1998. "Are the Working Poor Lazy?" *Challenge* 41(3): 85–99.

Klein, Bruce, and Philip Rones. 1989. "A Profile of the Working Poor." *Monthly Labor Review* (October): 3–13.

Loprest, Pamela J., and Sheila R. Zedlewski. 1999. "Current and Former Welfare Recipients: How Do They Differ?" *Assessing the New Federalism* Discussion Paper No. 99-17. Washington, D.C.: The Urban Institute.

National Research Council. 1995. *Measuring Poverty: A New Approach.* Constance Citro and Robert Michael, eds. Washington, D.C.: National Academy Press.

Pearce, Diana, and Jennifer Brooks. 1999. "The Self-Sufficiency Standard for the Washington, DC Metropolitan Area." Washington, D.C.: Wider Opportunities for Women.

Ruggles, Patricia. 1990. *Drawing the Line—Alternative Poverty Measures and Their Implications for Public Policy.* Washington, D.C.: The Urban Institute Press.

Sawhill, Isabel. 1999. "From Welfare to Work." *The Brookings Review* 17(4): 27–30.

Schiller, Bradley. 1994. "Who Are the Working Poor?" *The Public Interest* (Spring): 61–71.

Schwarz, John, and Thomas Volgy. 1992. *The Forgotten Americans.* New York: W.W. Norton and Company.

Wertheimer, Richard. 1999. "Working Poor Families with Children: A Statistical Portrait." Child Trends Research Brief. Washington, D.C.: Child Trends.

3

Low-Earners

Who Are They? Do They Have a Way Out?

Anthony P. Carnevale and Stephen J. Rose

Three of the most important indicators of a country's labor market success are:

- Do people who want jobs find one?
- Do all people with jobs make enough to minimally support themselves and their families?
- And are there enough opportunities for workers to move up the career ladder—and up the pay scale?

Over the last five years, the United States has met the first benchmark: Unemployment has fallen to 4 percent. However, there is great concern that we have not met the second and third measures, despite years of economic expansion. Many critics of the great American job machine argue that most of the new positions are "McJobs"—less-skilled service jobs at or near the minimum wage.

Without doubt, there has been a massive shift in employment from manufacturing to services. Yet in previous work, we showed that the share of workers in less-skilled retail and personal services ("counter") jobs stayed remarkably constant from 1959 to the present (Carnevale and Rose 1998).[1] Meanwhile, the service sector was primarily creating office-type jobs in administrative headquarters, finance, insurance, real estate, business consulting, and government. In addition, the education and health care sectors were growing rapidly. In all these "service" activities, workers were highly skilled (often requiring at least some college training) and earned considerably more than the factory workers they were displacing.

Another critique of the McJobs analysis accepts the premise that many jobs are, indeed, less-skilled service. However, this argument goes, that is not necessarily bad: These jobs go primarily to secondary earners—married women with employed husbands and young people, for example—who use low-paying jobs as stepping stones to more lucrative employment.

This argument rests on two assumptions: (1) low-earners are concentrated primarily among the young; and (2) there is a great deal of mobility out of these jobs. The notion that American workers can start in the mailroom and end up in the executive suite is old and well loved; whole generations of Americans grew up hearing Horatio Alger stories. Still, in today's economy, the fact is that not all low-earners are young. And many low-earners never break out of low-paying jobs.

This chapter utilizes a variety of data sources to paint a nuanced picture of the low-earners. The debate about the "working poor" has been heated, especially when Congress is considering, as it often does, increasing the minimal wage. On the one side are those researchers who think that low earnings are a big problem. They cite data showing that over half of poor families have at least one earner and that at least one-third have "poverty-level earnings"—earnings only adequate to guarantee that a family of four will not be poor if this is the only source of their income. The other side emphasizes the view of low-earners as secondary earners, not the breadwinners. They note that only 6 to 7 percent of earners are in poor households; the vast majority of those earning the minimum wage are in families earning at least twice the poverty level.

Both sides agree that the problem of low earnings is most intensely felt by adults who are the primary source of income for their family, especially if there are children present. Further, the concern is deepened if these workers are stuck in dead-end jobs with few prospects for earnings gains in the future. Yet there has been little research on this mobility question.

We put a face on low-wage earners and evaluate their ability to support their families and move up the wage ladder. In addition to looking at single-year snapshots of U.S. labor markets at different points of time (1979 through 1998), we track individual workers over many years as they age and earn more seniority and workplace skills. This latter analysis required a longitudinal panel data set that surveyed the same individuals yearly over the course of their lifetimes.[2] To draw a complete picture of these workers, we look at their age (this affects their likelihood of staying low-earners), their occupation, and their family status (by total household and share of family income accounted for by each worker).

We define "low-earners" as those making less than $15,000 a year.[3] This is not a high level, but is just above the amount needed to keep a household of three out of poverty. Other earnings levels are low-to-moderate ($15,000 to $25,000), moderate-to-high ($25,000 to $50,000), and high ($50,000 and above).[4] In addition, we define low family income as less than $25,000; a major contributor to family income is anyone who is responsible for at least one-third of total earnings.

HOW MANY LOW-EARNERS WERE THERE?

The most common way to answer this question is to tabulate the number of low-earners in a single year (table 3.1). Of all people who worked in 1998, 32 percent had earnings below $15,000. Another 20 percent fell in the low-to-moderate range of $15,000 to $25,000. This left under half of all workers earning above the moderate level.

TABLE 3.1 1998 Annual Earnings, by Gender and Age

		Less than $15,000 (%)	$15,000–$25,000 (%)	$25,000–$50,000 (%)	More than 50,000 (%)
All		32.2	19.9	31.8	16.1
Young (less than 29)	Male	45.2	22.2	26.2	6.3
	Female	57.8	21.4	18.1	2.7
Prime age (30–59)	Male	12.4	15.3	40.6	31.6
	Female	31.6	23.5	33.8	11.1
Older (greater than 60)	Male	40.4	15.0	22.7	21.8
	Female	58.6	18.1	18.7	4.6

Low earnings can result from either of two things: a low hourly wage or fewer working hours. *In fact, it appeared that most low-earners had neither high hourly wage rates nor full-time, full-year employment.*

Working full-time (defined as 1,750 hours annually or 35 hours a week for 50 weeks), a person would have to earn below $8.50 an hour to bring in less less than $15,000. Fewer than 25 percent of low-earners had hourly wages above $8.50.[5] Moreover, only 32 percent worked more than 1,750 hours in 1998. The majority (54 percent) worked fewer than 1,250 hours. The situation for prime-age workers (ages 30 to 59) was slightly different: 48 percent of males and 35 percent of females who earned below $15,000 worked more than 1,750 hours. Many of these workers probably would have preferred to work full-time, making job loss and layoffs the likely reasons behind their low earnings.

The prevalence of low earnings varied greatly among demographic groups. For example, among prime-age males (ages 30 to 59), only 12 percent were low-earners in contrast to 32 percent of prime-age females. For those under 29 years of age, 48 percent of males and 61 percent of females were low-earners. Workers over 60 also had high rates of low earnings (41 percent for men, 60 percent for women). However, their share of the labor force fell to just 6 percent; thus, only 9 percent of low-earners were over 60.

In the second rung of low-to-moderate earning ($15,000–$25,000), prime-age men had the lowest incidence again: Only 15 percent fell in this range. Consequently, 72 percent of this demographic group earned over $25,000. Among prime-age women, 24 percent were low-to-moderate earners, leaving 45 percent earning above $25,000. Of young male and female workers, 22 percent were in the low-to-moderate range; only 33 percent of males and 21 percent of females earned above $25,000.

It is worth noting the incidence of high earning greater than $50,000 annually. *For the economy as a whole, 16 percent fell into this top category, but those holding these positions were overwhelmingly prime-age men.* Nearly one in three prime-age men (32 percent) was a high-earner. Only 11 percent of prime-age women reached this standard. Few young workers under 29 (6 percent of males and 3 percent of females) made it to high-earner status. Among elderly workers 60 and over, 5 percent of females were high-earners, while a significant share (22 percent) of males remaining in the labor force earned more than $50,000.

It should be noted that the share of the workforce earning below $15,000 has declined since 1979. In the earlier year, almost 38 percent of the labor force were low-earners, but the experience of women totally accounts for this higher level. In 1979, 44.5 percent of prime-age women who worked brought home less than $15,000; in 1998, the comparable figure was 31.9 percent. For prime-age working men, the share of low-earners rose from 10.1 percent in 1979 to 12.6 percent in 1998. Thus, this increase occurred during a period in which the economy grew by over 25 percent per worker and while the educational credentials of the workforce were increasing. Consequently, the share of low earning among men at each education level, especially among those without postsecondary education, increased substantially.

EARNINGS BY OCCUPATION

The reason for many of these differences lies in disparities in the earnings distribution by occupation. In tracking wages by occupation, we used a seven-category breakdown.[6] These categories differ slightly from those reported in government sources. These changes are to include similar job titles in the same overall grouping. (The more traditional government categories have several combinations that seem inappropriate.)

These divisions reflect our belief that the U.S. labor market breaks down into three distinct segments. At the top are "elite jobs": managers, professionals, and technical workers. These workers almost always have some college experience—many have graduate degrees—and they are the most highly paid by far. The next group, termed "good jobs," includes supervisors, craft workers, police, firefighters, and clerical workers. The educational requirements for these jobs vary, but increasingly they require one or two years of college. Finally, the last two categories reflect the "less-skilled jobs": factory operators, laborers, salesclerks, and food and personal service workers. Few of these workers attended college, and their pay is considerably below that of the workers in the other categories.[7]

The seven categories are:

- *Managers and business professionals:* Official sources include managers at fast-food outlets in the same category as corporate executives. We include managers at restaurants and retail stores with supervisors. Official sources include stockbrokers, insurance agents, and sales representatives with salesclerks; we include them with business executives and accountants.
- *High-tech workers:* Engineers, chemists, architects, computer programmers, health care technicians, and specially trained machine workers.
- *Health, education, and related professionals:* Teachers, nurses, doctors, clergy, writers, and professional entertainers.
- *Supervisors, craft workers, police officers, and firefighters:* Blue- and white-collar supervisors, plus self-employed persons who do not define their job as professional or managerial. Official sources include police and firefighters with other personal service workers, such as guards, waitresses, and maids; we include them with supervisors and craft and skilled blue-collar workers.

- *Clerical and related workers:* Secretaries, file clerks, and mail carriers.
- *Less-skilled manual workers:* Factory operators, farm and non-farm laborers, truck drivers, and warehouse workers.
- *Less-skilled sales and service workers:* Salesclerks and food and personal service workers.

The first three categories comprise the "elite" jobs, with the best chances for high compensation, advancement, and prestige. Few workers in elite jobs, especially in the first two categories, were paid under $15,000 a year (table 3.2). In the first two categories (business professionals, managers, and high-tech workers), very few jobholders (one in 10) earned below $15,000 a year, while another 12 percent had low-to-moderate earnings. This left almost four out of five of these jobholders in the moderate-to-high and high-earner categories.

The health and education professional category is perhaps the most educated: The highest percentage of these workers had a bachelor's or higher degree. However, these jobs tended to be in the lower-paying public sector; women held two-thirds of them. In particular, women dominate nursing and teaching, and both fields permit workers to exit and return relatively easily as they adjust to family responsibilities. Consequently, they historically had earnings profiles very different from the previous two categories of elite jobs. In 1998, 21 percent of these workers earned below $15,000; another 15 percent were in the $15,000–$25,000 range. Further, the chances for high pay (with the exception of medical doctors) were relatively low (21 percent) for such a highly educated group.

The "good" job categories—clerical workers and supervisors and related craft workers—also were divided strongly by gender. Of prime-age workers in these fields, 81 percent of clericals were female, while 79 percent of supervisors and related workers were male. In terms of education, clerical workers had a slightly higher concentration of workers with college credits than supervisors and related workers: 55 versus 47 percent.

However, the earnings of clerical workers averaged $23,000, while the average annual pay of supervisors and related workers was $33,000. Thirty-five percent of

TABLE 3.2 Earnings by Occupation, 1998

	Less than $15,000 (%)	$15,000– $25,000 (%)	$25,000– $50,000 (%)	More than $50,000 (%)
Managers and business professionals	9.8	12.2	38.5	39.4
High-tech workers	11.2	12.4	39.0	37.5
Health and education professionals	20.9	14.9	43.0	21.2
Supervisors and craft workers	19.6	20.7	40.6	19.1
Clerical workers	34.6	29.9	31.1	4.3
Less-skilled manual workers	40.1	25.5	29.1	5.3
Less-skilled sales and service workers	68.3	18.6	11.3	1.7
All workers	32.2	19.9	31.8	16.1

clerical workers were low-earners, compared with 20 percent of supervisors and related workers. Another 30 percent of clericals and 21 percent of supervisors and related workers were in the low-to-moderate earning range. Thus, there was a huge gap at the top of the earnings scale. Just 4 percent of clerical workers earned above $50,000; 19 percent of supervisors and related workers had earnings at this level.

The two remaining less-skilled categories also had a strong gender connection. Of prime-age workers, 73 percent of less-skilled manual workers were male, while 68 percent of less-skilled salesclerks and service workers were female. Once again, female-dominated jobs were more likely than male-dominated positions to have workers with at least some college coursework: 35 versus 24 percent. However, service and sales workers were much more likely than less-skilled manual workers to be low-earners, 68 to 40 percent. Conversely, fully one-third (34 percent) of manual workers, but only 13 percent of service and sales workers, reached the $25,000 earnings level.

Thus, a snapshot of the low-wage workforce by job category and education showed more variation than one might expect. Some 59 percent of low-earners were in less-skilled positions, while another 26 percent were in good jobs, and even 14 percent were in elite jobs. Sixty percent had at most a high school diploma; 29 percent had some college credits without a four-year degree; and 11 percent had a bachelor's or graduate degree.

These data illustrated that low-educated workers in less-skilled jobs were only part of the low-earning labor force. Those who worked on commission or were self-employed had periodic bad years, when their earnings fell to very low levels. Women and young workers of both genders could be in good, even elite, jobs that weren't full-time, full-year. These included substitute teachers, temporary clerical workers, and even some construction craft workers who had long spells of under- and unemployment. Finally, the "related-professionals" sector of the health and education professionals category comprised some jobs that low-earners dominated: clergy, artists and entertainers, and writers. And indeed, one-half of low-earners in elite jobs were in the health, education, and related-professionals category.

EDUCATIONAL ATTAINMENT, JOB HOLDING, AND EARNINGS

To the degree that pay and jobs are linked, the question becomes: *How do people qualify for better jobs?* Not surprisingly, educational attainment played a greater role than ever in determining who gets the top managerial, professional, and technical jobs. Highly educated workers were more likely to be in higher-paying positions and tended, on average, to earn more in the same job category than less-educated workers. Nonetheless, there were low-earners among workers with all different levels of education, and only a minority of low-earners were high school dropouts.

In terms of earnings distribution among prime-age males who did not have a high school diploma, 31 percent were low-earners; the comparable figure for prime-age females was 61 percent. By contrast, few prime-age workers with bachelor's degrees failed to earn above $15,000: Only 5 percent of males with a degree and 16 percent of females were low-earners. But prime-age workers who have only high school diplomas were nearly three times more likely to be low-earners: 15 percent of males and 39 percent of females.

Thus, among all low-earners, those without a high school diploma accounted for one in four, and another 35 percent had just a high school diploma. This left 40 percent of low-earners having some postsecondary education (11 percent had bachelor's degrees). Many of these highly educated workers were young and had not fully reached their potential. Yet this includes some highly educated prime-age men having isolated "bad years," comprising 4 percent of all low-earners. Meanwhile, highly educated prime-age females were even more likely to earn below $15,000, comprising 12 percent of all low-earners.

We also looked at the connection between jobs and pay because "bad jobs" and "low pay" are not identical, even if they are connected and essential to discussions of low earnings. There are low-earners in virtually every broad occupation, although the incidence is much higher in certain positions. But even in the lowest-paying occupations, not all workers are low-earners. For example, many food-service workers are employed at fast-food outlets, but some work at upscale restaurants and bars where tips may provide a quite adequate income. Further, some clerks in discount stores earn barely more than the minimum wage, while those at a unionized grocery chain in a major metropolitan area can earn considerably more.[8]

Nevertheless, the connection of education to jobs to pay is very strong. For example, very few individuals without a high school diploma were in elite managerial and professional jobs (4 percent for males, 6 percent for females). One-third of prime-age males found good jobs, while 17 percent of female dropouts had such employment. This left 62 percent of males and 77 percent of female high school dropouts stuck in less-skilled jobs (table 3.3).

Among high school graduates with no further education, slightly more held elite jobs (13 percent of males, 18 percent of females), but this was still considerably behind the approximately 40 percent share of employment in these jobs among prime-age workers as a whole. The remaining jobs were split almost equally between good and

TABLE 3.3 Occupation Type by Educational Attainment, Prime-Age Workers, 1998

	Elite (%)	Good (%)	Less Skilled (%)
Males			
All	36.6	34.5	28.9
Did not finish high school	4.6	33.1	62.3
High school graduate	13.1	43.5	43.4
Some college, no four-year degree	32.0	44.0	24.0
Bachelor's or graduate degree	75.5	18.1	6.4
Females			
All	40.1	32.4	27.5
Did not finish high school	6.0	17.0	77.0
High school graduate	18.1	42.7	39.2
Some college, no four-year degree	38.7	41.1	20.1
Bachelor's or graduate degree	77.3	16.5	6.2

less-skilled jobs. For males, 44 percent were in good jobs, and 43 percent in less-skilled ones; the same numbers for females were 43 and 39 percent, respectively.

Workers with some college credits gained more access to the economy's better jobs. Thirty-two percent of males and 39 percent of females at this educational level were in managerial and professional positions. By contrast, only 24 percent of males and 20 percent of females in this group were in less-skilled jobs.

The real winners in accessing elite jobs were those with four-year college or graduate degrees. Fully 75 percent of males and 77 percent of females with these credentials held the economy's top jobs during their prime earning years.

In fact, many, but certainly not all, of the differences between the earnings and job holdings of blacks, Hispanics, and whites can be attributed to education and age. Just under 30 percent of whites, but 38 percent of blacks and 45 percent of Hispanics were low-earners (table 3.4). In the higher categories (above $25,000), however, 52 percent were whites, 38 percent were blacks, and 30 percent Hispanics. The largest earning differences were among prime-age men earning over $50,000 annually; this plateau was reached by 36 percent of whites, but only 16 percent of blacks and 14 percent of Hispanics.

In terms of educational attainment, only 1 in 16 prime-age white workers had failed to earn a high school diploma. By contrast, 1 in 8 blacks and just over 1 in 3 Hispanics had not reached this minimum standard. At the higher end of the educational spectrum, 1 in 3 whites had a bachelor's or graduate degree, versus 1 in 5 blacks and 1 in 7 Hispanics.

Because a four-year degree is important to getting a managerial or professional job, this discrepancy explained much of the difference in elite job holding. Among prime-age whites, 41 percent of males and 44 percent of females held a managerial or professional job. For blacks, these shares fell to 21 and 30 percent, respectively. But only 16 percent of Hispanic males and 22 percent of Hispanic females were in these slots. For those with

TABLE 3.4 Earnings Levels by Race/Ethnicity

	Less than $15,000 (%)	$15,000– $25,000 (%)	$25,000– $50,000 (%)	More than $50,000 (%)
All Workers				
White	29.5	18.4	33.6	18.4
Black	38.4	23.6	29.3	8.8
Hispanic	44.8	25.4	22.8	7.1
Prime-Age Men				
White	9.6	12.5	41.8	36.1
Black	18.9	23.6	41.1	16.4
Hispanic	26.2	26.9	33.1	13.8
Prime-Age Women				
White	29.4	23.1	35.7	11.9
Black	34.0	25.4	31.0	9.6
Hispanic	48.2	23.6	22.9	5.2

bachelor's degrees, the share of elite job holding was reasonably consistent regardless of race or ethnicity.

HOUSEHOLD STATUS OF LOW-EARNERS

Table 3.5 adds more context about the characteristics of low-earners. Of the 46.2 million workers who brought home less than $15,000, less than half were in households with less than $25,000 in total income. Most but not all of these workers were major contributors to total household income. Thus, 15.6 million workers (approximately one in nine workers) were "low" earners in families with "low" family income in which they were responsible for a "high" share of their family's income. Of this "low/low/high" group, more than one in three were in households with children present.

However, most low-earners were in households with incomes above $25,000 in which they were responsible for a small share (less than one-third) of total earnings. This "low/high/low" group consisted mainly of 10 million children (between ages 16 and 24) still living with their parents, and 10 million wives. There were also 2 million men in households where their wives were the main breadwinner and 1 million elderly workers with total incomes above $25,000 who were supplementing their retirement incomes.

Low-earners were indeed a diverse group. Clearly, this group was neither primarily the major earners in low-income households nor entirely "secondary" workers responsible for a small share of a higher-income household. Instead, the division was close to equal, with slightly less than half in low-income households and slightly more than half in households with total incomes above $25,000.

TABLE 3.5 Characteristics of the Working Poor, 1998

	Share of Labor Force (%)	Number in Millions	Share of Low-Earners (%)
Workers with earnings below $15,000	32	46.2	100
Low-earners in families with incomes below $25,000	14	20.2	43
Low-earners/Low family income and high share of family income	11	15.6	34
Low-earners/Low family income/ High share with children present	4	5.1	13
Low-earners/Family income greater than $25,000/Low share			
Children ages 16–24 living at home	7	10.1	22
Wives	7	10.0	21
Husbands	1	2.0	4
Elderly	2	1.0	6

THE MULTIYEAR PERSPECTIVE

There are several ways to effectively use a longer time frame. On the one hand, we evaluate workforce experience on the basis of a person's more permanent position. Many workers have isolated bad years from which they quickly recover, and they tend to rotate into some jobs for just a short period of time. So one set of analyses is based on five years' worth of experiences, determining average earnings over the entire period, and allocating workers into occupations on the basis of consistently being in the same occupation. In fact, one of the first pieces of information gathered from this approach is the share of workers finding consistent niches versus those who move around.

Second, a "spell analysis" determines how many people had at least one year in five in which they were low-earners. Thus, workers with periodic bad years may have relatively high average multiyear earnings but will also experience bouts of low earnings. Because credit is expensive, these bad years may require paying off outstanding debts built up to maintain one's mortgage and other essential household expenses.

Third, we look at mobility: the transition from one earnings level to another to determine whether low-earners stay low-earners. The mobility analysis is based on single-year to single-year transitions and five-year to five-year transitions. The former approach shows that many people have isolated bad years from which they recover. By contrast, the latter approach shows that a smaller share of workers have persistent low earnings and that workers in this group have a much lower probability of escaping this condition in ensuing years.

Finally, we relate individual earnings, household income, and share of earnings generated by that individual. This is a bit more complicated than the calculations done in a single year because people's household relationships (e.g., divorce, marriage, and remarriage) can change over time.

All of these analyses use the Panel Study on Income Dynamics (PSID) to track the multiyear labor force experiences of workers as they progressed through their careers.[9]

Five-Year Average Earnings

Table 3.6 tracks workers aged 26 to 55 in 1988 until they were 30 to 59 in 1992.[10] Only workers continuously in the labor force were counted, and their distribution of earnings differed considerably from the figures in table 3.1. For prime-age men, the share earning less than $15,000 is more than halved (12.4 percent for a single year, 5.4 percent for five years).[11] For women, the difference does not look so large, but this is misleading because of the different years in each approach. While the share of low-earning men in the early 1990s was similar to that of 1998, the share of low-earners among women was higher in the earlier years. Thus, 35 percent of women in 1989 were low-earners in that year versus 28 percent for the combined years 1988 through 1992. The differences between a single year and five years were particularly pronounced among those with more education. Among men with bachelor's or graduate degrees, fewer than 1 in 10 had average earnings over five years below $25,000.

TABLE 3.6 Five-Year Earnings Distribution of Prime-Age Workers, 1988–1992 (in thousands of 1999 inflation-adjusted dollars)

	<$15 (%)	$15–25 (%)	$25–50 (%)	$50–75 (%)	>$75 (%)	
Men						
All	5	15	43	24	12	
No high school diploma or GED	13	34	46	7	0	
High school diploma only	7	20	52	19	2	
Some college/Associate's degree	4	17	46	24	9	
Bachelor's degree only	3	6	36	33	23	
Graduate degree	2	4	20	37	37	
Women						
All	28	25	39	6	2	
No high school diploma or GED	60	27	12	0	0	
High school diploma only	32	33	32	2	0	
Some college/Associate's degree	26	24	41	8	1	
Bachelor's degree only	13	17	55	11	3	
Graduate degree	13	9	54	17	8	
1976–1980						
Men	3	11	52	24	10	100
Women	34	31	31	3	0	100

Particularly striking is the difference in earnings between males and females. Women comprised fully 82 percent of all prime-age workers with continuous labor force attachment over these five years who earned below $15,000. This difference is much larger than the more common approach that shows a narrowing gender gap. Gender-gap comparisons are usually limited to full-time, year-round workers in a single year. Because women tend to take time off from full-time participation in the labor force, their total hours worked over five years is much lower than comparable men: 56 percent of male workers, but only 18 percent of female workers, averaged over 2,100 hours a year over these years. Thus, differences between male and female workers are much greater when a combined five-year period is used along with shorter hours due to gender occupational segregation.

Women's experiences varied considerably depending on whether they had postsecondary training. Few female workers without a high school diploma earned more than $25,000 over these five years. The situation for women with high school diplomas was better but still nearly two-thirds were below the $25,000 level. Women with some college but not a four-year degree did better: Half earned below $25,000 and half above that level. Women with bachelor's degrees did much better (only 30 percent earned below $25,000), yet their earnings distribution mirrors that of men with only a high school diploma. Women workers with graduate degrees have the most dispersed earnings pattern: one-quarter earned above $50,000 and 22 percent earned below $25,000. This experience puts them at slightly worse off than men with some college but no four-year degree.

The last two rows on table 3.6 show the overall earnings distribution of prime-age workers for 1976 through 1980. In comparing male workers, there is a "shrinking middle," with more men earning over $75,000 and more earning less than $25,000 (where the share rises to 20 percent from 14). For women, there are gains across the board. The share of workers earning less than $25,000 falls to 53 percent from 65. At the top of the ladder, fewer than 1 percent averaged more than $75,000 over five years; in the later period, this figure rose to 2 percent; another 6 percent averaged $50,000 to $75,000.

Table 3.7 relates earnings to job holding over five years. Because workers can hold different jobs over this period, it is necessary to accommodate for this multiyear experience. We choose to define persistence in a job as being in that job in at least four out of five years. Presenting the data in simplified form shows persistence in one of our three occupational tiers—elite, good, and less-skilled jobs. The results do not change much if we disaggregate occupational persistence into the seven categories discussed above. For those who were not persistent in an occupation, the group is divided into those employed in all years and those who had some time out of the labor force.

Very few male workers with persistence in either elite or good jobs had average annual earnings less than $15,000 over five years. This contrasts sharply with table 3.2, which presents occupational data for a single year for male and female workers of all ages. In fact, among these male workers, only 8 percent of those with persistence in elite jobs and 21 percent of those with persistence in good jobs earned less than $25,000. But even among men in the lowest tier of less-skilled jobs, only 9 percent averaged under $15,000 and 25 percent between $15,000 and $25,000. Fully two-thirds of this group averaged above $25,000, demonstrating how the vast majority of prime-age men who stayed consistently in the labor force could earn a minimum of $25,000.

The comparable data for women are very different: Only those persistently in elite jobs could expect to earn above $25,000. For women persistently in good jobs, such as

TABLE 3.7 Earnings Distribution by Five-Year Occupation Holding, 1988–1992 (in thousands of 1999 inflation-adjusted dollars)

	<$15 (%)	$15–25 (%)	$25–50 (%)	$50–75 (%)	>$75 (%)
Men					
Persistently in elite jobs	2	6	28	38	26
Persistently in good jobs	5	16	53	22	5
Persistently in less-skilled jobs	16	28	50	7	0
No persistence, all years employed	9	25	41	17	8
Some time out of labor force	44	14	29	11	1
Women					
Persistently in elite jobs	11	13	57	15	5
Persistently in good jobs	28	31	38	3	0
Persistently in less-skilled jobs	62	27	10	1	0
No persistence, all years employed	41	26	29	3	0
Some time out of labor force	82	8	8	1	0

clerical workers, supervisors, and technicians, 28 percent earned below $15,000 and another 31 percent earned between $15,000 and $25,000. Women stuck as salesclerks and personal and food service workers had few options for higher pay: 62 percent averaged below $15,000; only 11 percent earned more than $25,000. Women in the process of interrupting their working careers for family responsibilities seem to have had little opportunity to work limited hours and earn high wages: 82 percent of this group averaged under $15,000 during the years they worked.

All these figures based on five-year averages hide the fact that many more people experience some years with low income.[12] Even among men, it is common to have at least one year with earnings under $15,000: While only 5 percent average under $15,000, nearly one-quarter of those consistently in the labor force (24 percent) had at least one year at this level (table 3.8). This is an important sign of potential family distress because of high interest costs. Families can maintain their living standards during rough patches by running up credit card balances, second mortgages, or postponing paying bills, but this strategy has costs, and it may take several years to pay off these debts.

It is even more common for men to have experienced at least a single year with earnings below $25,000. This situation was faced by 40 percent of prime-age men, and even by 20 percent of men persistently employed in elite jobs. It was rarer for men to earn less than $25,000 year in and year out (the second column labeled "4+"): only one in six met this fate. Very few men, 4 percent, earned less than $15,000 in four or more years out of five.

For women, fully half of those with consistent five-year employment experienced at least a single year with low earnings, and one-quarter were low-earners in at least four of the five years. Even 28 percent of those persistently employed in elite jobs had a year

Table 3.8 Frequency of Experiencing Low Earnings, 1988–1992

	Years Earning Less than $15,000 (%)		Years Earning Less than $25,000 (%)	
	1+	4+	1+	4+
Men				
Persistently in elite jobs	10	1	21	5
Persistently in good jobs	23	3	40	14
Persistently in less-skilled jobs	28	10	61	37
No persistence, all years employed	28	6	57	25
Some time out of labor force	59	–	70	–
All with 5 years' employment	24	4	40	17
Women				
Persistently in elite jobs	28	8	45	19
Persistently in good jobs	47	17	73	51
Persistently in less-skilled jobs	80	50	94	83
No persistence, all years employed	60	31	79	61
Some time out of labor force	93	–	96	–
All with 5 years' employment	51	25	71	50

of low earnings. If the standard is set higher—minimum earnings of $25,000—71 percent of consistently employed women had at least one year in five below this level.

Low Earnings and Mobility

A key question is whether low-earners are stuck at the bottom. One way to approach this question is to follow the fate of people who were low-earners one, five, and ten years after. Because many low-earners have only isolated bad years, these one-year to one-year transitions will capture workers recovering from their bad years. Thus, we also track people over five-year to five-year experiences. To the degree that five years are more representative of a person's continuing situation, these transitions should show less movement.

As table 3.9 shows, almost half the male workers earning below $15,000 in 1987 were earning above that level five years later in 1992, 19 percent had left the labor force, and 32 percent remained low-earners.[13] Educational attainment was an important indicator of ability to escape low earnings. Among male low-earners in 1988, only 25 percent had moved up the earnings scale in 1992; for high school graduates, the comparable figure was 53 percent; for those with some college, 51 percent; for bachelor's degree holders, 62 percent; and for those with graduate degrees, 75 percent.

Tracking workers in the next category, $15,000 to $25,000, there is a wide variety of transitions. A few moved down or left the labor force, only one-quarter stayed in the same category, and 49 percent had higher earnings.

The numbers display where workers ended up in 1992 on the basis of their starting positions in 1987. However, it is also possible to determine the 1987 origins of 1992 male workers who were below the $15,000 level. Somewhat surprisingly, there is a wide variation: Only 30 percent of 1992 low-earners were 1987 low-earners. The origins of the

TABLE 3.9 Yearly Earnings Transitions, 1983–1992 (in thousands of 1998 dollars)

	1992 or 1988–1992 Earnings Distribution (%)				
	<$15	**$15–25**	**$25–50**	**>$50**	**Out of Labor Force**
Men					
1987 earnings of <$15,000	32	16	27	6	19
1987 earnings of $15–25,000	16	26	39	9	9
1982 earnings of <$15,000	24	16	27	10	23
1982 earnings of $15–25,000	16	25	34	15	10
1983–1987 earnings of <$15,000	48	32	11	2	8
Women					
1987 earnings of <$15,000	53	20	9	0	18
1987 earnings of $15–25,000	25	38	26	1	10
1982 earnings of <$15,000	20	15	31	11	24
1982 earnings of $15–25,000	20	27	38	4	11
1983–1987 earnings of <$15,000	71	17	4	0	9

remaining 1992 low-earners were as follows: 23 percent earned $15,000 to $25,000 in 1987, 28 percent were in the $25,000 to $50,000 range, 10 percent had formerly earned more than $50,000, and 9 percent were not in the labor force in the earlier year.

Women low-earners were less likely than their male counterparts to move out of low earnings. Among those who started below $15,000 in 1987, 53 percent were low-earners in 1992 and another 18 percent were no longer working. To the degree they moved up, most made the short step into the next earnings category of $15,000 to $25,000; only 9 percent earned more than $25,000 in the latter year. Educational attainment played a role: Only 16 percent of high school dropouts who were low-earners in 1987 were not low-earners in 1992. This share increased with more education: 28 percent for high school graduates, 36 percent for those with some college, and 44 percent for the four-year college graduates. Paradoxically, few women (26 percent) with graduate degrees and low earnings in 1987 moved up to higher levels in 1992.

Because of the higher probability of remaining low-earners, the origin of 1992 low-earners was very heavily weighted to their 1987 experiences. Of low-earners in the later period, the experience in 1987 was that 57 percent were low-earners, 16 percent earned between $15,000 and $25,000, 7 percent earned more than $25,000, and 19 percent were not in the labor force.

Table 3.9 also tracks earnings experiences 10 years apart. The added separation led to a weaker connection between earnings this far apart. Among male low-earners in 1983, only 24 percent were low-earners in 1993; 37 percent made more than $25,000 in 1993. However, another 23 percent had left the labor force. For female low-earners in 1983, their 1993 earnings distribution was quite similar to that of male earners: 20 percent were low-earners, 24 percent were not in labor force, and 42 percent made more than $25,000.

Finally, we track earnings transitions on the basis of five-year average earnings. *While the share of low-earners is lower using a multiyear perspective, their likelihood of remaining low-earners is higher.* Once they had established themselves as consistent low-earners over five years, it was very difficult for either men or women to move considerably higher. This is evident by looking at the shares of low-earners in the first period who were able to earn more than $25,000 in the latter period. For males when comparing just two years, if the gap were five years, one-third were able to make this move; with a ten-year gap, almost one-half were big "up-movers." However, when comparing five-year averages, only 13 percent were able to make this forward move. For female workers, only 4 percent who had a five-year earnings average below $15,000 followed this with a five-year average above $25,000.

Combining Long-Term Earnings and Family Responsibilities

We now add some greater detail to table 3.5, which showed that 11 percent of the workforce were "low/low/high"—low individual earnings, low family income, and high share of family earnings. Looking at the age and gender composition of this group, slightly less than half of this group can be expected to remain persistently in this situation. In other words, only 5 percent of workers can be considered permanently low/low/high. In any given year, a number of people face this condition temporarily but not permanently. This group consists of younger workers who have yet to find their best labor force match; workers having an isolated bad year; and single people, with and without children, who will shortly marry a spouse whose earnings will bring the household income above $25,000.

Another way to calculate which people face the more permanent conditions of low earnings and low income is to utilize the multiyear data directly. Table 3.10 combines average individual earnings and household income over five years. However, it also presents a new measure to evaluate a person's contribution to family income. In this analysis, a single individual is considered a separate "family"; therefore, that person is responsible for 100 percent of the earnings of that household. Table 3.10 uses these definitions:

- *Breadwinner:* Responsible for at least 75 percent of total household earnings in at least three out of five years and never responsible for less than 33 percent of earnings;
- *Partner:* Responsible for at least 50 percent of total earnings in three years and at least another year of at least 25 percent;
- *Major contributor:* Responsible for at least 33 percent of total earnings in at least three out of five years;
- *Minor contributor:* Responsible for at least 25 percent of total earnings in at least two out of five years; and
- *Caregiver:* Responsible for at least 25 percent of total earnings in at least two out of five years.

Over the five years from 1988 to 1992, only 13 percent of prime-age adults were in households where the average total income was $25,000. Women were more likely than men to face this condition—16 percent of women and 11 percent of men. The labor force status of these adults varied: One-quarter earned between $15,000 and $25,000, which is above the definition of low-earner. Another 15 percent consisted of people with very little attachment to the labor force (e.g., disabled and women consistently out of the labor force due to family responsibility). Thus, only about 8 percent of prime-age adults were persistent low-earners in persistent low-income families.

TABLE 3.10 Contributions to Household Well-Being

	Breadwinner (%)	Partner (%)	Major Contributor (%)	Minor Contributor (%)	Caregiver (%)
Males	51	34	8	3	4
Low-earners	26	22	13	16	22
Low/Low*	37	20	9	13	20
Females	23	13	17	15	31
Low-earners	9	11	8	20	52
Low/Low*	25	22	5	17	31

*Low/Low = average personal earnings of less than $15,000 and average family income less than $25,000.

In terms of earnings alone, about 9 percent of men and 39 percent of prime-age women averaged less than $15,000 during their years in the labor force. But low personal earnings did not always translate into low family income: One-third of low-earning men and three-quarters of low-earning women were in households with total family income greater than $25,000. This means that 6 percent of prime-age males and 10 percent of women fit the low/low definition over five years.

In terms of contribution to family income, table 3.10 shows that men are much more likely than women to be either breadwinners or partners: 85 percent to 36 percent. However, this represents a large increase in income responsibility over time for women; the comparable shares in the late 1970s were 92 percent for men, 21 percent for women.

Low-earners were much less likely to be responsible for a major share of household income. Because 74 percent of female low-earners were in households with average incomes above $25,000, most of this group were caregivers (52 percent) or minor contributors (20 percent). Male low-earners were almost evenly divided among the five categories of family-income contributor. However, among those with low earnings and low family income, responsibility levels were higher for both men and women: Two-thirds of low/low men and 52 percent of low/low women were at least major contributors to five-year family incomes. The resulting estimates for long-term low/low/high are 4 percent of prime-age men and 5 percent of prime-age women.

TIME TRENDS: A SLOW DECLINE IN THE SHARE OF LOW-EARNERS

The share of the workforce with earnings below $15,000 declined modestly from 1979 to 1995—from 38 percent to 36 percent—then proceeded to decline more sharply in the next three years to 32 percent. Offsetting this decline was an almost equal increase in the share of workers with earnings greater than $50,000, from 11 percent in 1979 to 14 percent in 1998. The share of workers in the two middle categories, low-to-moderate and moderate-to-high pay, changed little. Thus, there was a small but consistent shift up the earnings ladder, with high-earners the biggest gainers, rising to 17 percent of the labor force in 1998.

At first glance, the size of this shift seems too small, given the economy's growth of nearly one-third (measured by either GDP per capita or personal income per capita). Why didn't the share of low-earners, as defined by a fixed, inflation-adjusted level, fall even more?

The answer is complex. In fact, over these years, the labor market changed dramatically in terms of age, educational attainment, gender, race/ethnicity, and job characteristics. Most of these changes shifted the composition of the workforce to workers *less* likely to be low-earners. These factors should have caused the share of low-earners to decline.

We roughly estimated the size of each factor's effect by simulating what the share of low-earners would have been in 1998 had the demographic characteristics of 1979 applied:

- *Age:* In 1979, baby boomers were beginning their careers, and 43 percent of workers with some labor force experience were 29 years old or younger; by 1999, the share of younger workers was 28 percent. This shift could be responsible for a 3-percentage-point decline in the share of low-earners.

- *Educational attainment:* Among prime-age workers in 1979, 41 percent of men and 33 percent of women had some postsecondary education; by 1998, the shares rose to 59 and 58 percent, respectively. Paralleling these increases were big declines in the share of workers without a high school diploma and the share of females with just a high school diploma. Given the strong correlation between education and earnings, this upgrading of the labor force could yield a 5-percentage-point decline in the share of low-earners.
- *Gender:* There was little change over these years: The female share of workers who worked at any time during the course of a year grew from 45 percent in 1979 to 47 percent in 1998. Given that women earn less than men, this shift could be responsible for a half-point increase in the share of low-earners.
- *Race/ethnicity:* In 1979, non-Hispanic whites comprised 83 percent of the labor force; by 1998, the figure was 74 percent. The share of working African Americans rose slightly, from 10 to 11.5 percent; the share of Hispanics doubled from 5 to 10 percent. Since white workers were much less likely to be low-earners than black or Hispanic workers, this demographic shift could be responsible for a 3-percentage-point increase in the share of low-earners.
- *Job distribution:* Between 1979 and 1998, professional/managerial/technical jobs rose from 24.6 percent of the total to 33.1 percent. This rise was offset by a modest decline in the share of good jobs—from 34 to 32 percent—and a larger decline in less-skilled jobs (from 41 to 35 percent). The gains in professional/managerial/technical jobs were widespread but concentrated among managers and business professions (10.7 to 15.4 percent). This shift had broad implications. As high-paying slots replaced lower ones, it could be responsible for a 5-percentage-point drop in the share of low-earners.

All of these factors interact—especially education and job holding—so it is not correct to simply add up their separate contributions. Moreover, the earnings distribution of demographic groups has changed in some ways. For example, relatively fewer blacks were low-earners in 1998 than in 1979. This improvement (which did not apply to Hispanics) would have decreased the share of low-earners by almost a percentage point.

In contrast to these mostly positive factors, which should have led to a decrease in the share of the low-earners, the incidence of low earnings increased among men. In 1979, 42 percent of male workers under the age of 29 were low-earners; the comparable figure in 1996 was 50 percent, before declining to 45 percent in 1998. For prime-age men, the low-earning share started at 8 percent in 1979, rose to 12 percent in 1995, then fell to 10 percent in 1998.

This change in the fate of men was closely correlated to educational attainment. Only 19 percent of men without a high school diploma were low-earners in 1979, a figure that rose to 32 percent in 1998. For men with a high school diploma but no postsecondary education, the rise in low-earners was from 8 to 15 percent. Even men with some college were affected: Their low-earner share rose to 10 percent from 8 percent. These shifts might be responsible for a 3-percentage-point increase.

The clearest case of the changing economy and the rising importance of education concerned prime-age men in factory-type jobs and with no higher education. In 1979, even among those without a high school diploma, 21 percent were low-earners, and 26 percent were in the low-to-moderate category; this meant that 53 percent earned more than $25,000. For men with a high school diploma in these jobs in this year, only 9 percent were low-earners and 18 percent in the low-to-moderate group. Thus, 73 percent earned more than $25,000, with 17 percent earning greater than $50,000.

By 1995, the share of low-earners among prime-age men in these jobs rose sharply to 38 percent for those without a high school diploma and 21 percent for those with one. In this year, only 31 percent of those without a diploma and 53 percent of those with one were above $25,000 in earnings. In both cases, there was a 20-percentage-point drop from 1979 in the share earning at least a moderate salary. Thus, the earnings potential in the major employment option for men without higher education worsened dramatically. Conditions improved a bit in the hot economy from 1995 to 1998, but they still were much worse than 1979.

For women, the trends were positive, except for women without a high school diploma, where the share of low-earners increased to 65 percent in 1998 from 61 percent in 1979. By contrast, the share of low-earners declined over these years, from 45 to 39 percent for women with a high school diploma, from 39 to 29 percent for those with postsecondary education without a four-year degree, and from 28 to 16 percent for those with four-year or graduate degrees. For this last group of best-educated women, new horizons opened: The share earning over $50,000 grew from 8 percent in 1979 to 26 percent in 1998.

CONCLUSION

With a 4 percent unemployment rate, the economy offers jobs for those who want them, but can people support their families with those jobs? And can they move into better-paying jobs from low-paying ones?

The conclusions are mixed. On the one hand, the percentage of low-earners in the workforce has declined from about 38 percent in 1979 to perhaps 32 percent in 1998, which is very good news indeed. This finding shows the importance of a strong economy that is running on all cylinders.

For women workers, there was more good news. Women have started to move more confidently up the earnings ladder. In 1979, 44 percent of women were low-earners, 29 percent low-to-moderate, 24 percent moderate-to-high, and 3 percent high-earners. In 1998, the comparable figures were 33, 25, 35, and 7 percent, respectively.

That is only part of the story, though. Much of the growth in earnings between 1979 and 1988 was concentrated at the top of the scale: The number of workers making over $50,000 went from 13 percent of all workers to 18 percent. And, overall, shouldn't earnings have risen more, given that the economy's inflation-adjusted output rose 30 percent per person between 1979 and 1998?

Then there is the matter of those workers—11 percent—stuck in low-earning jobs. Many are prime-age women, and about 28 percent of those women are single parents. Contrary to the views of some, these data show that not all low-earning women are members of stable families where a spouse is bringing in a larger income. Of prime-age men with these earnings (13 percent), 9 percent are persistent low-earners.

For the most part, the advantage these persistent low-earners lack most is education. Workers with even some postsecondary education fare far better than those without, gaining access to jobs that train for advancement. Unfortunately, workers with no postsecondary education are unlikely to land jobs that offer training, creating a cruel "catch-22" situation.

This country must do better at making education accessible and affordable to less-skilled workers. Moreover, government programs must do a better job of helping low-wage workers locate jobs that offer training. Outside of government, labor unions should consider organizing efforts targeting these lowest of low-wage jobs and occupations.

While the timing of these recommendations—help for low-wage workers when the economy is running full barrel—may seem off to some people, this, in fact, is the *best* time. The continuing labor shortage means that the economy would benefit from having more workers gainfully employed. The nation will continue to need a highly educated workforce in the years ahead; addressing access to education and other problems now may help keep the economy from getting derailed later.

- *Children (primarily between the ages of 16 and 24) in families with working parents and reasonably high family incomes:* These young people work for a variety of personal reasons but account for only a small share of family income. Some young workers do not plan to continue their education; it is important that they have opportunities to develop useful skills and good workplace habits.
- *Adults, sometimes called secondary earners, who are supplementing their retirement incomes (primarily wives and semiretired workers):* While accounting for a relatively small share of total household income, these workers often are dissatisfied with their employment options. In particular, married women pay a steep price for decisions to spend periods out of the labor force. Further, divorced women are at risk of a precipitous fall in their standard of living. Consequently, many communities have responded with programs for displaced homemakers that highlight women's skills and help with the transition back into the labor force. Also, providing better child care facilities can help many women avoid these career interruptions.
- *Workers who are low-earners for limited periods of time:* Often, these workers are on temporary or permanent lay-off. Their transition to a new position may span months of unemployment and temporary employment in low-paying jobs. Unemployment insurance and job search assistance were created to serve these workers.
- *Persistent low-earners who are young but on their own and often have children:* These workers have yet to move up a career ladder or find the best match for their abilities. Many will move out of low earnings, but it may be years before this occurs. Yet many of these same workers are parents, with immediate consequences that must be faced before they can succeed in the future. The Earned Income Tax Credit is particularly useful for this group, supplementing income during low-income periods.

- *Adults who are persistent low-earners and are the primary source of household income:* As chief earners in their families, their failure to find better employment affects their children. These workers often have few marketable skills and are unlikely to have time to enroll in educational or training programs. The Earned Income Tax Credit is helpful, but a preferable solution would be to get these individuals into better working situations, through either promotion or new jobs with bigger, more successful companies.

NOTES

1. We also divided jobs into one of three tiers: elite (managerial and professional workers), good (supervisors, skilled blue-collar, technicians, police, and clerical), and less skilled (factory workers, laborers, salesclerks, and personal and food service workers). Since 1959, as the workforce has become more educated, the less-skilled share has declined while the share of workers in elite jobs has increased.

2. We used the Panel Study on Income Dynamics (PSID), which has been conducted by the Survey Research Center at the University of Michigan since 1968.

3. We use annual earnings, rather than hourly wages, as the defining characteristic of low earning. Some workers have relatively high wage rates but low hours. These workers cannot adequately support a family without other sources of income.

4. The cut-offs of $25,000 and $50,000 were somewhat arbitrary but correspond to what the Bureau of Labor Statistics formerly called "low budget" ($25,000) and "high budget" ($50,000) for a family of three.

5. Elderly workers were an exception: A high percentage of these workers had hourly wages greater than $8.50.

6. For a more detailed discussion of this procedure, see Carnevale and Rose (1998).

7. The earnings distribution of these different jobs validated the employment categories. Only 10 percent of managers, business professionals, and high-tech workers earned below $15,000 (just under 40 percent earned over $50,000). For less-skilled sales and service employment, 58 percent were low-earners. In terms of all low-earners, just under 60 percent were employed in less-skilled manual, sales, and service employment, even though these jobs accounted for just over one-third of all jobs. Another 26 percent of low-earners were employed in good jobs, leaving 14 percent of low-earners employed as managers, professionals, or high-tech workers.

8. We classified members of the clergy, who are highly educated, as professionals even though most have low earnings.

9. When compared with the previous analysis based on the yearly Current Population Survey, the PSID had many advantages but also disadvantages. First, there were fewer survey participants, limiting the number of categories for certain analyses. Second, it has labor market information only for heads of households and marital partners, if present. However, children who left home at any time were always considered to be a household head, even if they moved back in with their parents. As a result, the PSID is not representative of the entire labor force, although it is reasonably reflective of workers over 30. The limitation of the data should be kept in mind when tracing the transition of young workers.

10. Unfortunately, these are the last complete available years in the PSID. While this is unfortunate, we believe that the underlying fundamental relationships have not changed significantly. Due to the strong expansion, there are probably fewer workers in the low-earnings categories. However, if we compare single-year data from the same time period to the multiyear year data from 1988 to 1992, the relationship between short- and long-run conditions should be similar today.

11. Rose (1995a) showed that approximately 10 percent of workers in any given year were having unusually bad years from which they immediately bounced back to higher earnings.

12. Rose (1995b) showed that almost 40 percent of prime-age families would be eligible for the EITC at least once over a 10-year period. Most of the spells were concentrated among families with low average income over the 10 years, but many families with reasonably high average incomes had a single bad year.

13. The way to understand the data in table 3.9 is to read across the rows. The row label depicts the starting conditions of workers in 1982, 1987, or the combined years of 1983–1987. The columns represent the

ending position of those working in either 1992 or the combined years of 1988–1992. Thus, the meaning of the "32" in the upper left cell is that 32 percent of male workers who earned less than $15,000 in 1987 also earned less than $15,000 in 1992.

REFERENCES

Carnevale, Anthony P., and Stephen J. Rose. 1998. *Education for What? The New Office Economy.* Princeton, N.J.: Educational Testing Service.

Rose, Stephen J. 1994. *On Shaky Ground: Rising Fears about Incomes and Earnings.* National Commission for Employment Policy Research Report 94-02. Washington, D.C.: Government Printing Office.

———. 1995a. *Declining Job Stability and the Professionalization of Opportunity.* National Commission for Employment Policy Research Report 95-04. Washington, D.C.: Government Printing Office.

———. 1995b. "Long-Term Eligibility for the Earned Income Tax Credit." Research Report No. 95-05. Washington, D.C.: National Commission for Employment Policy.

4

Employers in the Low-Wage/ Low-Skill Labor Market

Paul Osterman

The dynamics of the low-wage labor market have emerged as a central policy issue. This is driven in part by the surge of inequality, which is a stain on the booming labor market. In addition, welfare reform, by pushing large numbers of people into work, has transformed antipoverty policy from a transfer issue to a jobs issue. The "working poor" are now a larger group than before, and it becomes all the more urgent to understand their circumstances.

Along some dimensions, there appears to be less to worry than would have been the case a few years ago. The long expansion has driven down unemployment rates for all groups, including those who traditionally work in bad jobs. Extensive anecdotal evidence suggests that employers are eagerly recruiting in this sector. Substantial numbers of former welfare recipients appear to have successfully found work.

In short, the low-wage labor market has expanded in tandem with the rest of the job market. But it is far from clear how extensively the quality of these jobs has improved, or whether the mobility prospects of people in them have been enhanced. Wage gains have been modest, particularly when viewed from the perspective of the entire business cycle, and the rate of increase in 1999 actually fell compared with 1998. As a result, much of the growth in family incomes was due to longer hours of work. While evidence on career mobility is sparse, what there is does not suggest that jobs at the bottom are a very powerful springboard into the higher reaches of the labor market.

This chapter begins with a discussion of the boundaries of the low-wage/low-skill labor market. The distinctives of this segment of the labor market are laid out and an estimate of its size is also provided. The characteristics of the labor market from the perspective of employers are then described. This discussion takes up skill requirements, recruiting patterns, differences in treatment of employees based on race, and mobility (or lack thereof) of careers over time. The second part examines policy, again from the employer or demand side. Four broad strategies are identified and discussed: standard setting, union organization, creating labor market intermediaries, and incentives for employers to provide better opportunities for employees.

THE BOUNDARIES OF THE LABOR MARKET

What do we mean when we speak of the low-wage/low-skill labor market? Where is the line drawn? Most researchers follow one of two alternatives. Some focus on skill and define the labor market as those jobs for which only a high school diploma is required and/or which entail very little training. Others emphasize wages, and set the boundary at those jobs which pay below a given standard. Each perspective captures an essential aspect of this labor market, but each also is incomplete.

Focusing on the educational and training requirements of jobs is attractive on its face because it emphasizes the intrinsic characteristic of the work. For example, Lerman, Loprest, and Ratcliffe (1999) define the low-skill labor market by identifying occupations that require less than 12 months of training and then, for each, determining the fraction of employees with a high school diploma or less. These two criteria together are used to define a low-skill job, and the authors find that in 20 metropolitan areas in 1997, low-skill jobs made up between 21 percent and 37 percent of employment.

Although appealing, the difficulty of the education and training approach is that the demarcation of jobs may be sensitive to changes in labor supply. A surge in the availability of college-educated workers, for instance, could lead them to take jobs previously held by high school graduates. In this case, the classification of the job would shift without altering its content. The question is whether it is possible, using only skill-based criteria, to identify low-skill jobs independently of the characteristics of the employee.

Pryor and Schaffer (1999) attempt to accomplish this by classifying jobs by the average education of their incumbents in 1971, and then asking about the size distribution of these jobs in 1996. On the assumption that the job titles mean the same thing in the two years (an assumption that seems doubtful given the pace of technical change and organizational innovations in firms), they compare the growth rate of low-skill jobs with changes in the supply of educated labor. They find that over this period, jobs "requiring" a high school degree or less grew at an annual rate of 1.9 percent while the supply of high-school-or-less labor increased at only 0.2 percent a year. By contrast, jobs "requiring" more than a high school diploma grew at an annual rate of 3.8 percent, while the qualified labor supply increased at a rate of 5.3 percent. These figures imply that over this time college labor was increasingly taking "high school jobs."

The weakness of the education and training approach is that it tends to ignore outcomes. Consider, for example, hotel cleaning staff. In many cities, this is a job that should be considered in a study like this. The job itself can, and frequently is, done by someone with a high school education or less, and while there are skills involved, they can be learned reasonably quickly. In addition, the job often pays poorly. For example, in New Orleans, room cleaners earn near the minimum wage. However, there are exceptions. In Las Vegas, where most of the large strip hotels are unionized, room cleaners earn roughly double the minimum wage and also have access to training for other, more lucrative, employment in the hotels. This suggests that it may make more sense to ask about outcomes rather than skill requirements.

Using 1997 data, Gregory Acs (1999) mapped the low-wage labor market. He defined a low-wage job as one which, in 1997, paid less than $7.50 an hour, a rate 45 percent above the then-minimum wage and 30 percent below the median wage for all workers. He found that 27.9 percent of all workers were low-wage according to this definition (a figure quite close to the Lerman et al. figure cited above). However, many of these were probably teenagers or other secondary workers whose family circumstances were comfortable. To deal with this, he defined a low-income family as one whose total income was $24,000 or less—that is, 150 percent or less than the poverty level for a family of four. Combining the two criteria, he found that 9.6 percent of all workers were low-wage employees who lived in low-income families. Adding children to the mix, he reported that 5 percent of employees were low-wage/low-income with children.

Acs' data also demonstrate the difficulties in using a purely educational criteria for defining the low-wage/low-skill labor market. Among the low-wage/low-income individuals with children, 22 percent had more than a high school diploma.

Another approach is to look at the earnings of full-time employees. In 1998, among people between age 25 and 64 who worked full-time and full-year, a total of 9,772,000 persons, or 11.3 percent of the total, earned less than $8.50 an hour.[1] This, of course, is an underestimate of the size of the low-wage/low-skill labor market because it excludes part-time workers; however, it does have the virtue of controlling for age (eliminating young workers) and labor supply (i.e., people's decisions about how many hours to work).

The wage-based approach, however, suffers from its own set of conceptual difficulties. One issue is the relatively straightforward one of where to draw the line. Acs arbitrarily uses $7.50 an hour (in 1997). However, that is essentially equivalent to the poverty level for a family of four, and many people would argue that any reasonable standard should be higher. A related issue concerns benefits. A $7.50-an-hour job with health insurance is very different than one without it, yet the standard discussions typically omit this consideration. Finally, there is an even more difficult question about whether the job comes with training or is attached to a job ladder that promises a better future. In principle, any determination about whether a job is "good" or "bad" should take into account the long-term prospects the position offers.

The bottom line is that we will have to be flexible and somewhat imprecise about drawing boundaries around the low-wage/low-skill labor market. While perhaps unfortunate, this ambiguity accurately reflects the multidimensional nature of jobs, substantive debates about alternative definitions of adequacy, and the incomplete character of available data.

EMPLOYERS IN THE LOW-SKILL/LOW-WAGE LABOR MARKET

It is convenient, but misleading, to speak of the low-skill labor market as if it were all of one piece. Consider, for example, the differences between a suburban movie theater with ticket-taker jobs, a garment industry sweatshop, a hospital staffing its orderly positions, a downtown department store, and a factory hiring unskilled laborers. Each of these employers may well pay in the $8-an-hour range, yet the working conditions, mobility prospects, skill requirements, and characteristics of the employees differ substantially.

At one end of the low-wage labor market are jobs that operate below the level of prevailing labor standards. These are often held by the estimated 6 million undocumented migrants living in America (Uchitelle 2000). The *New York Times* recently reported, "The Labor Department estimates that in the San Francisco area more than half the 2,000 garment shops violate wage laws. And New York City has more than 3,000 apparel sweatshops with more than 50,000 workers, according to a General Accounting Office study. In El Paso, Los Angeles, and Seattle, sweatshops are often common" (Echaveste and Nussbaum 1994). Building-cleaning contractors follow a similar pattern. According to Howard Wial (1999), 4.3 percent of all wage and salary workers earned less than the minimum wage in 1997 (although Wial also reports that the majority of these cases involve inadvertent and relatively minor violations).

Other employers in the low-wage/low-skill labor market, such as fast-food restaurants or movie theaters, operate well within the law and frequently hire young workers for part-time jobs after school or full-time jobs in the summer. The mobility prospects of these jobs may be limited, but most of the employees are only passing through, and it is not clear that there are substantial public policy concerns.

Intermediate between these extremes are the large number of low-wage employers, ranging from manufacturing to retail to services such as health care aides, who hire adults, pay at or just above the minimum wage, and offer work for their employees that may well be viewed as a long-term trap.

This variation within the low-wage/low-skill labor market is important, but unfortunately is not well captured in national data sets or surveys. We will return to the more-textured view when we take up policy, but for now we will rely on the cruder survey data.

The most straightforward way to describe the low-wage/low-skill labor market is by comparing the occupational and industrial distribution of low-wage workers with the labor market as a whole. Tables 4.1 and 4.2 reproduce the analysis generated by Acs. These data demonstrate that low-wage workers are represented in all occupations and in all industries. There is no sector of the economy, at least at this broad level of aggregation,

TABLE 4.1   Occupational Distribution of Low-Wage Workers and Entire Labor Force, 1997

	Low-Wage/Low-Income with Children (%)	All Employees (%)
Executive and professional	6.8	27.8
Technicians and related support	1.1	3.3
Sales	14.7	12.3
Administrative support, including clerical	10.7	14.2
Private household and protective service	3.1	2.4
Service, except private household	29.6	12.1
Farming, forestry, and fishing	6.0	2.1
Precision production, craft and repair	8.7	10.9
Machine operators, assemblers, inspectors	8.7	6.1
Transportation and material moving	2.9	4.0
Handlers, equipment cleaners, helpers, laborers	7.6	4.2

Source: Acs (1999).

TABLE 4.2 Industrial Distribution of Low-Wage Employees and Entire Labor Force, 1977

	Low-Wage/Low-Income with Children (%)	All Employees (%)
Agriculture, forestry, and fisheries	3.9	2.0
Mining and construction	5.2	7.2
Manufacturing	10.0	15.6
Transportation, communications, and utilities	3.5	7.0
Wholesale trade	2.3	3.6
Retail trade	32.6	17.9
Finance, insurance, and real estate	3.5	6.3
Service	37.1	35.8
Public administration	1.9	4.7

Source: Acs (1999).

that provides an absolute shield against poor earnings. At the same time, there are also clear patterns in the data. Low-wage workers are disproportionately found in service occupations and the retail industry. They are also, although less dramatically, employed in the lower end of blue collar work and in the agricultural (and presumably rural) arena.

GROWTH PROJECTIONS

An important question is the future growth of low-skill jobs. In the labor market as a whole, the skill requirements of jobs are increasing. Indeed, Bureau of Labor Statistics (BLS) projections indicate that while jobs that require an associate's degree or more accounted for 25 percent of all jobs in 1998, they will account for 40 percent of job growth between 1998 and 2008 (Braddock 1999). However, it is important to note that this also implies that a very substantial fraction of job growth, indeed the majority, will be in occupations that require only a high school diploma or less.

Another way of seeing this is to classify jobs by the amount of training they require. The BLS has done this, and its lowest category is "short-term training," which refers to jobs that can be learned after a short demonstration or a month or less of training. These jobs are overwhelmingly in the low-wage labor market: More than 90 percent earn less than the median pay, and more than 55 percent have earnings in the lowest quartile. In 1998, these jobs accounted for 39 percent of employment, and this is not projected to change by 2008. Of the job openings generated during this period, due both to job growth and replacement, these low-training jobs are expected to count for 23 million or 43 percent of the total (Braddock 1999). Among the 30 occupations with the largest projected job growth, the low-training occupations accounted for 16 of the job titles. The occupations on this list are retail sales, cashiers, truck drivers, office clerks, personal care and home health aides, teacher assistants, janitors, nursing aides, receptionists, waiters and waitresses, guards, food counter workers, child care workers, laborers, hand packers, and adjustment clerks.

SKILLS

A central issue for assessing the prospects of workers in the low-wage labor market is the skill requirements of employers. First, what are the requirements of low-wage/low-skill jobs? Second, on the assumption that we are ultimately interested in promoting mobility out of this sector, what is the nature of the skill trajectory in the labor market in general?

Even what appears to be the lowest of the noncollege jobs requires some skill. Katherine Newman (1999), for example, vividly describes work in a fast-food restaurant, with skills including understanding how to operate the food machinery, inventory management, remembering the sequence of orders, making change, working effectively with a team of fellow employees, and dealing with abrasive customers. The picture she paints is convincing, but it is also important to remember that fast-food establishments seem to do quite well by hiring 16-year-old high school students, and hence, in the end, the skills cannot be very daunting. What can we say about skill requirements in the noncollege market as a whole?

A good source of data on the skill requirements of jobs that do not require a college degree is the employer survey conducted by the Multi-City Study of Urban Inequality (Holzer 1996). The survey interviewed 800 employers in Atlanta, Boston, Detroit, and Los Angeles between 1992 and 1994. Data were collected on the most recently filled job in each firm. For the noncollege jobs, average hourly wages ranged from $7.94 to $9.53.

Table 4.3 shows the frequency with which employees in these noncollege jobs were required to perform different tasks. For example, 54.9 percent of the jobs required the daily reading of at least a paragraph. These data show a fairly sharp bifurcation in the noncollege jobs. Somewhat over half require frequent use of computers and arithmetic and nearly half require frequent writing. On the other hand, the remainder, which is also close to half, seem very unskilled. This is further evidence of the diversity in this segment of the labor market.

The survey also explored the screening or hiring requirements for noncollege jobs. A characteristic is counted in table 4.4 only if the employer said that it was "absolutely necessary" or "strongly preferred."

TABLE 4.3 Frequency of Task Performance on Noncollege Jobs

Deal with Customers	Daily	Once a Week	Once a Month	Not at All
In person	.581	.068	.024	.326
On the telephone	.531	.070	.020	.379
Read paragraphs	.549	.206	.071	.175
Write paragraphs	.299	.168	.096	.436
Do arithmetic	.649	.122	.042	.182
Use computers	.510	.052	.023	.415

Source: Holzer (1996), p. 49.

TABLE 4.4 Hiring Requirements for Noncollege Central City Jobs

High school diploma	76.1%
General experience	72.2
Specific experience	66.7
References	73.5
Vocational or other training	41.7

Source: Holzer (1996), p. 55.

There may be some exaggeration in these requirements, particularly given that hiring criteria are likely to be adjusted over the business cycle. To check, Tilly and Moss (2000) report the results of a study in which they linked a subset of the employer interviews, on which table 4.4 is based, with interviews with the actual workers in those jobs. They found that 4.9 percent of the workers lacked the educational credentials that the employer had said it required, 27.6 percent lacked the training background, 4.6 percent lacked the general experience, and 28.8 percent lacked the specific experience. The employer statements are clearly more right than wrong, and very much on target with respect to education, but there is also considerable flexibility in some areas.

Are skill requirements rising in the low-wage labor market? Tilly and Moss report that just under 40 percent of the noncollege employers in the multicity survey say skill requirements have risen. Thus, in this low-end segment of the labor market, growing skills, while not the rule, are far from unusual. The employers who do report an increase split evenly between those pointing to higher requirements for basic reading, writing, and numeracy and those who point to social and verbal skills. Computers are widely cited as a source of change, but organizational innovations are cited with equal frequency.

SOFT SKILLS IN THE NONCOLLEGE LABOR MARKET

The literature concerning skills makes a loose, but important, distinction between hard and soft skills. Hard skills refer to abilities such as operating a machine or a computer, knowledge of a specific organizational process, or the capacity to analyze a problem. Soft skills refer to the motivation and personality of the employee and include the ability to work effectively with coworkers, to respond to the boss, and to relate to customers. Tilly and Moss (2000) in their interviews with employers found that many firms, particularly in retail, place a very high value on these soft skills. In the multicity telephone interviews, employers were asked about the qualities they looked for in an entry-level (noncollege) employee. Hard skills were cited by 24.8 percent, while interaction skills were cited by 39.2 percent and motivation by 36.0 percent. Clearly soft skills are important in this market.

TABLE 4.5 Importance of Soft Skills in Noncollege Jobs

Physical appearance/Neatness	55.5%
English/Verbal skills	78.4
Politeness	81.1
Motivation	75.3

Source: Holzer (1966), p. 59.
Note: These are the percentages of central-city employers who said the characteristic was "very important" or "somewhat important."

Further information along these lines is provided by Holzer (1996). Table 4.5 provides a breakdown of the importance of soft skills.

It seems clear from the foregoing, as well as from the comments employers frequently make regarding motivation and behavior, that soft skills are important. Nonetheless, they should be viewed with some skepticism because there is some reason for worrying that an overemphasis on soft skills can be a signal the job is not very good. One example is a recent survey of 500 establishments that hire entry-level (noncollege) workers (Regenstein, Meyer, and Hicks 1999). The survey was aimed at understanding the job prospects of former welfare recipients. From a list of 12 characteristics, the employers were asked to identify the three most important. The dominant responses (cited by more than 65 percent of firms) were a positive attitude and reliability. The next three were work ethic, punctuality, and friendliness. Having the necessary training was last. The authors draw optimistic conclusions about the job prospects of unskilled workers, but consider the wages: The median pay was $5.50 an hour, 46 percent of the jobs were part-time, and 26 percent provided no benefits, while those that did typically had long waits for eligibility. These patterns suggest that jobs requiring only positive personal characteristics may be a mixed blessing.

Another qualification regarding skill requirements is that they can shift over the business cycle. Firms have a variety of adjustment mechanisms, and there is evidence that when the job market tightens, employers often reduce their hiring standards and compensate by increasing the amount of training they provide (Osterman 1983). As a result, job requirements are not as rigid as they might seem, and the additional implication is that if companies can make this adjustment when times are good, they may also be able to make it throughout the cycle, particularly if they are provided with the appropriate incentives.

SKILLS IN THE BROADER LABOR MARKET

It is clear from the foregoing that many employers in the noncollege labor market require a nontrivial level of skills, both hard and soft. This general pattern is broadly consistent with tendencies throughout the labor market. Whereas an earlier generation of scholars was concerned that the labor market was moving in the direction of "de-skilling," most researchers today would accept the view that firms are increasingly demanding a higher level of skill from their employees. (There is debate about whether increasing skill demands can explain the growth of wage inequality. That is, however, a different question.)

Increased skill demands come from a variety of sources, but the two most notable are the spread of computers and the increased use of new systems of work organization, frequently termed "high performance work systems." High performance work systems involve work teams, as well as quality programs, and their successful implementation involves interpersonal skills ("soft" skills), as well as the ability to engage in the kind of statistical charting techniques employed by quality systems. Surveys of employers are consistent in finding that skill requirements are rising (Osterman 1995; Frazis et al. 1998).

Even so, it is important not to exaggerate skill requirements. To put matters into perspective, consider one of the hiring vignettes provided by Murnane and Levy (1996). They described the hiring process at Honda Motors for blue-collar work. By any measure, these are good jobs for noncollege workers, and Honda is clearly among the most technologically sophisticated employers in which noncollege workers could hope to land. Honda put substantial effort into testing prospective employees for interpersonal or soft skills, and it also administered math and reading tests. However, the academic skills tests aimed to learn if the applicants could perform at the 10th-grade level. If they could, then they were acceptable. The lesson is that while the noncollege labor market requires skills, these skills should be within the grasp of a very wide range of people. If they have not learned them in school, then it is not hard to imagine that well-designed training programs can provide them.

RACIAL ISSUES

What roles do race and ethnicity play for employers in the low-skill labor market? This is an important question, but difficult to answer with certainty. A good start is to look at labor market outcomes by race. Table 4.6 provides earnings data. The table controls for education level, and for one of the groups of most concern—high school graduates with no further education—one column also controls for hours of work, looking at those employed full-time, year-round.

It is apparent that there are considerable racial differences in outcomes, even after controlling for education and labor supply. However, these differences are most pronounced for men. In general, black and Hispanic women do much better relative to white women than do minority men relative to white men. It is also clear that men in general earn more than women.

Holzer, in his analysis of the multicity survey, provides a variety of useful information on how outcomes differ by race, ethnicity, and gender. Table 4.7 shows how hiring patterns vary by skills. These data show that outcomes vary across different groups. However, there is one constant: Black and Hispanic men are consistently less likely than white men to hold skilled jobs. White females are consistently more likely

TABLE 4.6 1999 Median Earnings, People 25 Years and Over

	All	9th–12th Grade Nongraduates	High School Graduates, Including GEDs	Full-Time and Full-Year High School Graduates, Including GEDs	College Graduates, No Advanced Degrees
Men					
Non-Hispanic white	$37,298	$22,939	$31,352	$34,839	$51,884
Black	27,253 (.73)	17,901 (.78)	24,710 (.78)	27,404 (.78)	37,572 (.72)
Hispanic	21,899 (.58)	17,979 (.78)	22,530 (.71)	25,291 (.72)	37,886 (.73)
Women					
Non-Hispanic white	22,170	11,725	17,441	22,468	30,710
Black	20,742 (.93)	10,829 (.92)	16,571 (.95)	20,609 (.91)	31,461 (1.02)
Hispanic	15,544 (.70)	11,092 (.94)	15,856 (.90)	19,923 (.88)	27,490 (.89)

Source: Money Income in the United States, 1999. U.S. Bureau of the Census, P60-209, Table 10.
Note: Figures in parentheses are the ratio to the appropriate non-Hispanic white group.

than not to be in skilled positions. The patterns are mixed for white men and for black and Hispanic women, but black women do appear more likely than black men to be in skilled positions.

Greater insight into these patterns can be gained from more-nuanced field work. One source is the Urban Poverty and Family Life study that was conducted in Chicago in 1987 and 1988 (Wilson 1996). The project interviewed nearly 2,500 persons in poor neighborhoods and 179 employers in the city. Wilson reports that "many [employers] consider inner city workers—especially young black males—to be uneducated, unstable, uncooperative, and dishonest" (Wilson 1996, 111). Indeed, 74 percent of the employers held negative views regarding inner-city black workers. Among the employ-

TABLE 4.7 Race and Gender of New Hires by Skills, Noncollege Jobs

	White Men	Black Men	Hispanic Men	White Women	Black Women	Hispanic Women
All jobs	.260	.096	.089	.341	.102	.067
Talking to customers	.232	.081	.057	.412	.114	.066
Reading/Writing	.260	.086	.073	.363	.098	.068
Arithmetic	.283	.079	.072	.374	.090	.057
Computers	.193	.064	.039	.465	.117	.071

Source: Holzer (1996), p. 81.
Note: The fractions sum to approximately 1 across the rows. To compare skills, note that black men, for example, hold 9.6 percent of all jobs but 8.1 percent of jobs that require talking to customers.

ers who expressed negative views, the opinions were evenly split between those who pointed to skill deficiencies and those who emphasized attitudinal issues, such as work ethnic, dependability, attitude, and interpersonal skills (Wilson 1996, 118).

The weight of employer antipathy appears directed toward inner-city black males. As Wilson notes, "In an overwhelming majority of cases in which black males and females are compared, the employers prefer black women" (Wilson 1996, 122). The interviews also seem to suggest that employers prefer Hispanic immigrants to black males. The consequence of these patterns, according to Wilson, is that, even within the low-skill sector, black men are excluded from the "better" jobs, frequently the manufacturing jobs, and find themselves in low-skill service jobs, which paid in the $5.00–$6.00 range and had turnover rates between 50 and 100 percent a year (Wilson 1996, 142).

Racial distinctions appear to be maintained by the recruiting practices of employers. Wilson reports that 40 percent of the employers did not advertise entry-level jobs in metropolitan newspapers, and that two-thirds of the employers who did use newspapers used neighborhood or ethnic papers in order to shape their labor supply. Employers also tended to avoid hiring from city public schools, preferring to focus on private and Catholic institutions.

Tilly and Moss (2000) also report a variety of employer comments from interviews, some of which point to various forms of discrimination. However, the story that emerges from the multiemployer telephone survey is more mixed. Generalizations about groups seem to be moderate: 18.1 percent of employers were willing to state that one gender was better than another at some set of jobs, while 4.3 percent were willing to make a similar statement with regard to race or ethnicity. Tilly and Moss argue that "political correctness" plays an important role in these responses, and, in fact, more narrow questions elicit a wider scope for racial/ethnic attitudes. Between 19 and 23 percent of employers report that other employees and customers prefer dealing with members of their own racial or ethnic group. With respect to assessment of skills, table 4.8 below shows fairly widespread race and ethnic labeling.

In general, it is very hard using the kind of data described above to disentangle the effects of discrimination from genuine skill differences across races or ethnic groups. There is, however, some evidence that discrimination plays at least some role. Audit studies, in which seemingly identical black and white "applicants" seek work, find that blacks—particularly in retail jobs—are hired at a lower rate than whites (Darrity and Mason 1998). In addition, Holzer and Ihlanfeldt (1998) find that the racial composition

TABLE 4.8 Percentage of Employers for Noncollege Jobs Reporting Attitudes about Particular Groups

	Blacks	Hispanics	Asians
Have lagging hard skills	20.3	5.4	1.7
Have lagging interaction skills	14.6	1.1	0.6
Have lagging motivation skills	33.4	5.4	0.3

Source: Moss and Tilly (2000) from multiemployer survey.

of customers affects who gets hired, and that this effect is particularly troublesome for the hiring prospects of blacks.

RECRUITMENT AND HIRING

The standard story about recruitment and hiring is the trade-off between personal networks and more formal recruitment mechanisms. It is widely thought that informal personal contacts, particularly so-called "weak ties," lead to the best jobs (Granovetter 1973). Another element of the standard view, particularly with regard to the low end of the labor market, is that groups that have difficulty because, for example, they face discrimination or live some distance from jobs, are forced to rely on less-effective formal mechanisms such as schools, the employment service, and job training programs.

Consistent with the view that the worst jobs are found through formal means, the multicity survey shows that firms in the low-wage labor market rely upon a variety of recruiting mechanisms. Referrals from current employees account for only about one-quarter of referrals, with advertising (newspapers and "help wanted" signs) another quarter, and various institutions (the employment service, agencies, schools, and unions) accounting for about 20 percent (Holzer 1996).

A relatively new development in the low-wage labor market is the emergence of temporary-help firms. The explosive growth of these institutions is by now well known and widely commented upon. One striking characteristic is that they span the labor market, from the highest reaches (e.g., firms that provide highly skilled electronic engineers to Silicon Valley) to the low-wage sector. In the low-wage labor market, anecdotal evidence suggests that in some respects these firms are replacing the street corner and are shaping up as the preferred hiring mechanism. Temporary-help firms are used to provide casual labor in a range of low-wage industries. In this sense, they help organize and provide structure to the labor market.

CAREER MOBILITY

There are two alternate images one might have of low-wage jobs. In one case, these jobs, while perhaps not desirable on their own terms, are the first step on a ladder leading to better things. Low-wage employment might provide valuable training, or perhaps the experience of working will pay off over time. In the second image, these jobs are dead ends, and adults who find themselves in them are trapped. This debate is about mobility over the course of the careers of people who begin as adults in the low-wage/low-skill labor market.

Unfortunately, there is little research on this topic. In the youth labor market, several studies have used the National Longitudinal Surveys to ask if there are negative consequences for young people who begin their careers milling around in low-wage/low-skill jobs (Osterman 1994; Klerman and Karoly 1994; Gardecki and Neumark 1998). The broad conclusion is that while there are some young people who fail to settle down successfully, early unstable labor market experience per se is not at fault.

The problem with studying youth to learn about the consequence of holding bad jobs is that the natural trajectory of youth employment is to begin in the low-wage/low-skill labor market and then move on (Osterman 1982). The real question is what happens to adults who work in this sector. The most useful sources of data are various studies using the Panel Survey on Income Dynamics. These enable researchers to compute mobility rates over reasonably long stretches (unlike the Current Population Survey rotation groups, which limit studies to one-year intervals), and are representative of the entire population. Researchers working with these data come to generally similar conclusions. For example, Osterman (1999) found that 49.2 percent of men who were in the bottom earnings quintile in 1979 remained in that quintile in 1995. Although there is clearly mobility, this is a long period for nearly half the group to remain at the bottom. McMurrer, Condon, and Sawhill (1997) report five-year mobility rates out of the bottom quintile of 47 percent for the period 1979–86. Gottschalk (1996) reports that, between 1968 and 1991, 53.3 percent of those in the bottom quintile moved up (and hence 46.7 percent did not). Of those who did, nearly half moved only to the second quintile.

SUMMARY

The foregoing material paints a complicated picture of the low-wage/low-skill labor market. It is clear that, while ill defined, the scope of the market is quite substantial and shows no sign of contracting. Some jobs in the market require real skills, which may be out of reach for some people, while other jobs are much simpler and, at most, require interpersonal soft skills. Race clearly plays a continuing role in this labor market, although it is difficult to pin down the relative contributions of skill and attitudinal deficits, stereotypes, and discrimination. For a great many people, the low-wage/low-skill labor market is not simply a staging area for career mobility but, rather, appears to be a trap from which escape is difficult.

At the same time, there is an incomplete quality to our knowledge and understanding. We lack a coherent theory of the structure and dynamics of this labor market. Some 30 years ago, dual labor market theory (Doeringer and Piore 1972) was widely popular as a way to understand bad jobs. In this view, the secondary labor market was characterized by the absence of well-defined internal job ladders, and it existed either because the jobs required little in the way of human capital, and hence there was no need for long-term attachment, or because the firms in the secondary labor market provided buffer output, expanding and contracting with the ebb and flow of the core labor market. Employees in the secondary labor market moved from job to job with very little payoff to long-term attachment in any one location.

In many respects, this conceptualization remains useful. However, ultimately it does seem defeated by the diversity in the labor market as a whole and in the low-wage/low-skill labor market in particular. The emergence of high-end, contingent jobs shows that buffer or flexible employment need not imply bad jobs. The fact that hotel workers in Las Vegas have good jobs while those in New Orleans have bad ones demonstrates that factors beyond the job per se are important. Nor is it clear what sweatshops have in common with hotel employment or fast-food jobs. In addition, the numerous low-wage jobs in very large hospitals undermine the standard image of the low-wage/low-skill employer.

These complexities suggest that dual labor market theory needs to be reconsidered and updated. As things stand now, there is something unsatisfactory about the ad hoc quality of our understanding of the low-wage labor market. Academic researchers have some way to go in providing a more complete account of this labor market. But until they do, we will have to remain satisfied with the facts summarized above.

POLICY OPTIONS: CHANGING EMPLOYER BEHAVIOR

A fundamental characteristic of the low-skill labor market is that it is shaped by public policy. Minimum wage laws and other labor standards establish the bottom and exercise a substantial impact on the wage structure even above the bottom. Immigration policy influences labor supply, as do the actions of the public schools (given the substantial number of young people who work in low-skilled jobs). Welfare reform has also had a major impact upon the supply of labor. And, of course, a great deal of federal and local job training policy has aimed at this labor market.

A broad range of policies is intended to deal with the low-wage/low-skill labor market. A partial list would include: (a) improving the human capital of people who find themselves trapped at the bottom; (b) creating public jobs to provide employment to people unable to find work; (c) attacking spatial mismatch either by encouraging job creation where poor people live or improving the access of poor people to where jobs are; (d) altering the supply of labor to the low-wage labor market via immigration or school policy; (e) subsidizing work via the earned income tax credit; and (f) influencing the behavior of employers in the low-skill labor market along a range of dimensions (e.g., hiring practices, wages, working conditions, career ladders, and training).

Outside of transfer payments, the bulk of public policy has historically been directed toward improving the human capital of low-wage workers. There is no question that this is important. First, there is a clear relationship between formal education attainment and labor market outcomes. Second, more direct measures also suggest that skills are an issue. For example, the National Adult Literacy Survey found that 60 percent of low-wage men and 45 percent of low-wage women scored in the bottom two (out of five) levels (Lerman 1999). A focus on skills and training is also comfortable in that it does not force policymakers to enter the relatively unfamiliar terrain of how to work with firms to alter their practices.

While improving the skills of low-wage workers is clearly important, it is also insufficient. First, as the Literacy Survey results suggest, a substantial number of low-wage workers score *above* the bottom two levels, yet remain poor. Second, it is important to pay attention to the demand side as well as the supply side of the market. For these reasons, and because other chapters take up the skills and personal characteristics of low-wage workers, the remainder of this chapter focuses on the possibilities for influencing employers in the low-skill labor market.

There are four broad possible ways to influence employers in the low-wage labor market: standard setting; union organization; building new labor market intermediaries; and providing incentives for firms to improve opportunities for their employees.

Standard Setting

The low-wage/low-skill labor market is heavily impacted by government standards, notably minimum wage legislation, hours laws, and health and safety legislation. If deemed desirable, the government could raise the standards and enforce them in a manner that would improve conditions.

There is considerable controversy about the desirability of pushing up standards via legislation. The classic debate revolves around the minimum wage. The debate has become more heated in recent years, with new evidence emerging that employment losses are not very significant. (See Houseman 1998 for a review of the literature.) Although no clear consensus has emerged among economists as to the employment consequences of the minimum wage, it would be fair to say that at current levels these consequences seem minimal. At the same time, the declining value of the minimum wage has been an important culprit in the worsening of wage levels at the bottom of the labor market; hence its restoration would shore up conditions of the working poor (DiNardo and Lemieux 1997). It is true that the minimum wage is a somewhat blunt tool with respect to poverty (in recent years, most adults in poverty do not work, although welfare reform may be changing this), and there is some leakage (many minimum wage workers are in families above the poverty level). Nonetheless, the minimum wage hits its target more than not and is an essential tool for pushing up standards.

A broader way to think about the minimum wage is to conceive of an integrated regulatory strategy that would include not only the minimum wage but also other labor market standards (Piore 1999; Wial 1999). The argument here is that federal regulatory policy in the low-wage labor market has been too much driven by complaints and too little driven by a strategic vision of how to coordinate the range of regulations (e.g., minimum wages, hours, health and safety). This is a policy approach aimed at firms that are out of compliance, and they represent only a minority of low-wage employers. Nonetheless, it is an argument worth considering.

A different regulatory strategy that is gaining increased popularity is the living wage campaign. Living wage ordinances, which have been enacted in over 40 cities, take a variety of forms. Some are directed at contractors that do business with the city; others aim at city employees; and yet others (none of which have been passed) establish a city-specific minimum wage. Living wage campaigns have two logics, one economic and one political. The economic logic is that the campaigns seek to establish a new baseline, "going" wage for adults in the community that is above the federal or state minimum wage. It may be acknowledged that the minimum wage may be acceptable for youth and other people with casual labor market attachment, but it is held unacceptable for adults whose earnings are important for family support. The possibility of establishing the new living wage as the going wage lies partly in legislation—for example, requirements that city contractors pay the living wage—and partly in shifts of expectations. A long line of research on wage settings shows that such expectations can play an important role in local labor markets.

The direct impact of living wage ordinances is limited, usually affecting no more than a few thousand employees in any given city. However, in principle their impact is broader, both because of the expectations effect and because they are a strategy for encouraging public debate about wage levels. For community groups, living wages are also an important organizing tool. First, the beginning of a campaign provides a venue for people to research their local economy and learn about its wage structure. Second, establishing the initial ordinance provides a goal around which considerable energy can be mobilized. Third, once living wages have gained a foothold—for example, via the ordinance—then it is possible to approach a new group of workers and ask them whether they realize they are not being paid the living wage. This provides an ongoing basis for organization.

A final regulatory strategy is vigorous enforcement of equal employment opportunity laws. The material presented earlier suggests that discrimination persists in the labor market, particularly against less well educated black males. Other reviews of the evidence reach similar conclusions (Holzer 1998). The pattern of the results implies that medium to small establishments and suburban establishments with a largely white clientele are particularly a problem. The politics of this issue are obviously difficult, but as a pure policy proposition, new enforcement strategies should be considered.

Union Organization

The most direct way to improve jobs in the low-wage/low-skill labor market is union organization. The earlier comparison of the economic well-being of hotel workers in Las Vegas and New Orleans illustrates this point. Recent union organizing drives have been successful for some classically low-wage occupations, such as home health care workers in Los Angeles and janitors in a number of cities.

Broadly speaking, whether or not a firm is unionized is a decision best made among the private parties. However, several public policy issues are potentially quite important. First, should public authorities wish to encourage organization in the low-wage sector, they can be helpful in a variety of ways. The case of the home health care workers in Los Angeles illustrates this: To succeed, the union needed to establish an employer of record for what was previously a widely dispersed group of seemingly self-employed individuals. Legislation was required to establish a public home health care agency that could serve as a central bargaining agent.

Political leaders, through their rhetoric, could bolster sentiment for organizing low-wage employees. Beyond this, it is widely acknowledged that labor law is not functioning effectively to establish a so-called "level playing field" with respect to union organization and elections. This is a topic that has been widely discussed both in general (Kochan 1998) and with respect to low-wage employers (Wial 1999). It is clearly important if the goal is to enhance the chances of organization in the low-wage sector.

Intermediaries

A third approach is to attempt to transform the nature of career paths in the low-wage/low-skill labor market. The objective is to create pathways that move employees into firms providing higher-quality jobs.

There are a variety of promising programs throughout the country to create new pathways. What is distinctive about them is that they link job training—a longstanding component of antipoverty programs—with a sophisticated understanding of how to work with employers, and provide a range of intermediary services that ease mobility. A good example is Project QUEST, in San Antonio, Texas, which was created by two community organizations affiliated with the Industrial Area Foundation (IAF), a national network of community-based organizations.

At the core of the QUEST model are several distinctive features. The program began with a commitment from firms of jobs for the graduates (and the IAF's power in San Antonio was obviously central to obtaining this). The program worked closely with employers to identify promising job openings and to design training curricula. The training was long-term (lasting about one-and-a-half years), and while full stipends were not provided, various forms of financial support were available, as was intensive counseling and support of various kinds. The support and counseling were essential elements for keeping people in the program and, along with the length of the program, distinguishing it from the typical Job Training Partnership Act (JTPA) effort. The training itself took place in community colleges, and QUEST worked with the community colleges (again drawing upon the power of the IAF organizations) to redesign their curricula and remediation efforts in various ways.

A 1996 evaluation demonstrated that QUEST led to substantial gains for its participants (Osterman and Lautsch 1996). The estimated annual earnings gain was between $4,900 and $7,500, with the expected payoff of costs being a very short three years.[2]

It is very important to note that although the gains for individual clients are clearly important, Project QUEST thinks of itself in more ambitious terms than a traditional employment and training program. In a traditional program, the nature of the external environment—the behavior of firms, the surrounding educational institutions, and the community itself—are taken as given, and the program simply seeks to place clients successfully in that environment. Project QUEST became an active actor in the San Antonio labor market and education system, and obtained institutional change. One example is that it bargained with employers to raise the wages of entry-level workers and to create job ladders attached to some entry-level jobs.[3] Its ability to do so was a reflection of its power in the market. Second, it pushed hard on the community colleges and led them to adopt innovative programmatic, curricular, and scheduling changes, all of which have subsequently been made available to all students, not just those from QUEST.[4]

The program design described above, while in some respects distinctive to Project QUEST, includes the key elements of what has come to be seen as best practice in this area. Effective programs work closely with employers in identifying openings and in designing training. They provide support to trainees and relieve firms of many of the burdens of dealing with the complicated personal circumstances of low-wage workers. They frequently (but not always) work with community colleges. And they pay careful attention to the quality of the jobs and the firms in which they place people.

There are a number of other well-known and effective programs for connecting low-wage employees to better firms. The Regional Training Partnership in Wisconsin has built a network of firms, one component of which is to create a mobility channel for low-wage workers in Milwaukee. The Center for Employment and Training in San Jose runs customized training for high-tech firms in the area. Focus Hope in Detroit has had success in placing low-wage, inner-city workers into the region's automobile industry.

Incentives to Improve Employee Opportunities

The fourth strategy is to improve the nature of the jobs provided by low-wage employers. Obviously, this is also the objective of standard setting and unionization, but here incentives are examined. At the core of this strategy is the view that firms have choices in how they organize work, and that it is possible to influence these choices. This perspective finds justification in the business school human resources literature, which points to firms in the same industry, say Southwest Airlines and American Airlines, that have quite different philosophies about employment practices. There is also a strand of economic theory that argues that employers can choose a high-wage/low-turnover option or a low-wage/high-turnover approach, each of which can be profitable.

One strategy is to reorganize work in ways that lead to better outcomes. This approach is currently characterized in the field as "sectoral" programs. A widely cited example is Cooperative Home Care Associates (CHCA) in New York City, a worker-owned organization that has upgraded what has been traditionally very poorly paid jobs. By providing greater-than-average training of and investment in home care workers, CHCA is able to convince payers to improve pay and working conditions. According to Elliot and King (1999), similar strategies are being followed by programs working with day laborers in Tucson and paraprofessional health care workers in New Hampshire. A less ambitious but related effort is the attempt to encourage firms to upgrade jobs and provide internal ladders. This has had some success in hospitals under collective bargaining (frequently cited cases are the Cape Cod Hospitals as well as agreements in New York and Philadelphia). Pindus et al. (1999) cite other nonunion examples in the health and hospitality industry. Another example is the Garment Industry Development Corporation, which provides technical and marketing assistance in a traditionally low-wage industry and also a range of training opportunities for employees.

Another approach is to provide incentives to employers to provide more training to their low-wage workers. There is evidence, at least with respect to hiring, that well-designed financial incentives can influence the hiring practices of firms (Katz 1998), and it is reasonable to believe that the same is true of training. An example is an incumbent-worker training program in Michigan in which the state influenced companies to expand their training (Holzer et al. 1993). In terms of low-wage/low-skill workers, it is widely recognized that firms offer very little in the way of basic education training even though the needs appear to be substantial. Lerman (1999) cites a survey that found that less than 5 percent of medium-sized firms offered basic-skills training, although about 37 percent of their workforce needed it. The challenge is to design incentives to overcome this gap. One approach is to build financial incentives for individual firms, either though the tax system or direct grants. The alternative is to provide incentives for consortia of firms to develop common solutions, perhaps with a local community college as a hub.

CONCLUSION

The low-wage/low-skill labor market is large and diverse. Both characteristics offer an analytical and policy challenge. The analytical challenge is that no single perspective captures the essential characteristics of the market. In this chapter, the role of skills (hard and soft), work organization, recruiting patterns, and race in the low-wage/low-skill labor market have been examined. Each is important in understanding how the market operates. The problem, of course, is that each also implies a different approach to policy. As a result, a range of policies, including standard setting, union organization, intermediaries, and incentives for firms to transform their employment practices have also been reviewed. Each has a role to play.

The size of the low-wage/low-skill labor market poses a challenge of a different kind. Everyone who works in employment and training knows of well-performing programs. But the hard fact is that when added up, none of them, not even all taken together, achieves the scale necessary to impact the labor market as a whole. This suggests that policies need to be assessed not simply in terms of their impact on their clients or target group, but also with respect to their potential for broader impact. From this perspective, the standard setting and union organization approaches seem more promising than traditional job training efforts. However, if job training or sectoral initiatives are conceived as part of a broader organizing strategy that seeks to improve the functioning of other labor market institutions, such as community colleges, then they, too, may achieve scale.

The final lesson is that while our understanding is incomplete, it is nonetheless substantial, both with respect to the nature of the problem and in terms of imaginative and potentially successful policy interventions. This suggests is that if resources were forthcoming, a great deal could be accomplished.

NOTES

1. This is calculated from the March 1999 Current Population Survey. The figures are arrived at by summing the number of people age 25–64 who worked full-time and full-year and who earned less than $17,499 a year. The $8.50 figure is based on the assumption that a full-time/full-year worker works for 2,080 hours a year. For the data, see http://ferret.bls.census.gov/macro/031999/perinc/new06_000.htm.

2. The evaluation we conducted showed that Project QUEST participants earned more than $7,000 a year more after participation than before. This estimate is based upon a pre/post-design; there was no control group available. Hence, there is a possibility of selection bias. However, we carefully studied the intake procedures, read folders of a randomly selected sample of participants, and concluded that people who had enrolled did in fact suffer from serious barriers to employment that would have been difficult to overcome in the absence of the program. The pre/post-design is also vulnerable to what is termed the "Ashenfelter dip," i.e., the tendency of participants to experience a temporary decline in earnings just prior to enrolling in a program. There was evidence of such a dip in the data, but it was not nearly large enough to explain away gains of the magnitude we found.

3. QUEST insisted that jobs pay at least $7.50 an hour. In several cases, it succeeded in raising wages. In other cases, it convinced employers to transform low-paying jobs into entry steps on a job ladder.

4. For example, it convinced the community colleges to establish a Remediation Academy for entering students to prepare them for Texas admissions tests. In other cases it modified curricula to allow for open-entry/open-exit designs.

REFERENCES

Acs, Gregory. 1999. *A Profile of Low-Wage Workers.* Washington, D.C.: The Urban Institute.

Braddock, Douglas. 1999. "Occupational Employment Projections to 2008." *Monthly Labor Review* (November): 51–77.

Darrity, William, and Mason, Patrick. 1998. "Evidence of Discrimination in Employment: Codes of Color, Codes of Gender." *Journal of Economic Perspectives* 12 (2): 63–90.

DiNardo, John, and Lemieux, Thomas. 1997. "Diverging Male Wage Inequality in the United States and Canada, 1981–1988: Do Institutions Explain the Difference?" *Industrial and Labor Relations Review* 50 (4): 629–51.

Doeringer, Peter, and Michael Piore. 1972. *Internal Labor Markets and Manpower Analysis.* Lexington, Mass.: D.C. Heath.

Echaveste, Maria, and Karen Nussbaum. 1994. "Viewpoints: 96 Cents an Hour: The Sweatshop Is Reborn." *New York Times,* 6 August.

Elliott, Mark, and Elisabeth King. 1999. *Labor Market Leverage: Sectoral Employment Field Report.* Philadelphia: Public/Private Ventures. Winter.

Frazis, Harley, Maury Gittleman, Michael Horrigan, and Mary Joyce. 1998. "Results from the 1995 Survey of Employer-Provided Training." *Monthly Labor Review* 121 (6): 3–13.

Gardecki, Rosella, and David Neumark. 1998. "Order from Chaos? The Effects of Early Labor Market Experience on Adult Labor Market Outcomes." *Industrial and Labor Relations Review* 51 (2): 299–322.

Gottschalk, Peter. 1996. "Notes on 'By Our Own Bootstraps.'" Mimeo. Boston College, Chestnut Hill, Mass.

Granovetter, Mark. 1973. "The Strength of Weak Ties." *American Journal of Sociology* 78 (6): 1360–80.

Holzer, Harry. 1996. *What Employers Want: Job Prospects for Low-Educated Workers.* New York: Russell Sage Foundation.

———. 1998. "Employer Hiring Decisions and Anti-Discrimination Policy." In *Generating Jobs: How to Increase the Demand for Low-Skill Workers,* edited by Richard B. Freeman and Peter Gottschalk. New York: Russell Sage Foundation.

Holzer, Harry, and Keith Ihlanfeldt. 1998. "Customer Discrimination and Employment Outcomes for Minority Workers." *Quarterly Journal of Economics* 113 (3): 835–67.

Holzer, Harry, Richard Block, Marcus Cheatham, and Jack Knott. 1993. "Are Training Subsidies for Firms Effective? The Michigan Experience." *Industrial and Labor Relations Review* 46 (4): 625–36.

Houseman, Susan N. 1998. "The Effects of Employer Mandates." In *Generating Jobs: How to Increase the Demand for Low-Skill Workers,* edited by Richard B. Freeman and Peter Gottschalk. New York: Russell Sage Foundation.

Katz, Lawrence. 1998. "Wage Subsidies for the Disadvantaged." In *Generating Jobs: How to Increase the Demand for Low-Skill Workers,* edited by Richard B. Freeman and Peter Gottschalk. New York: Russell Sage Foundation.

Klerman, Jacob Alex, and Lynn Karoly. 1994. "Young Men and the Transition to Stable Employment." *Monthly Labor Review* 117 (8): 31–48.

Kochan, Thomas. 1998. "Labor Policy for the Twenty-First Century." *Journal of Labor and Employment Law* 1 (1): 117–31.

Lerman, Robert, with Felicity Skidmore. 1999. *Helping Low-Wage Workers: Policies for the Future.* Washington, D.C.: The Urban Institute.

Lerman, Robert, Pamela Loprest, and Caroline Ratcliffe. 1999. *How Well Can Urban Labor Markets Absorb Welfare Recipients?* Washington, D.C.: The Urban Institute.

McMurrer, Daniel, Mark Condon, and Isabel Sawhill. 1997. *International Mobility in the United States.* Washington, D.C.: The Urban Institute.

Moss, Philip, and Chris Tilly. 2000. *Stories Employers Tell: Race, Skills, and Hiring in America.* New York: Russell Sage Foundation.

Murnane, Richard, and Frank Levy. 1996. *Teaching the New Basic Skills.* New York: Free Press.

Newman, Katherine. 1999. *No Shame in My Game: The Working Poor in the Inner City.* New York: Knopf.

Osterman, Paul. 1982. *Getting Started: The Youth Labor Market.* Cambridge, Mass.: MIT Press.

———. 1983. "The Mismatch Hypothesis and Internal Labor Markets." *Proceedings of the Industrial Relations Research Association.* Spring.

———. 1994. "Is There a Problem with the Youth Labor Market and If So How Should We Fix It? Lessons for the U.S. from American and European Experiences." In *Poverty, Inequality, and the Future of Social Policy: Western States in the New World Order,* edited by Katherine McFate, Roger Lawson, and William J. Wilson. New York: Russell Sage Foundation.

———. 1995. "Skill, Training, and Work Organization in American Establishments." *Industrial Relations* 34 (2): 125–46.

———. 1999. *Securing Prosperity: How the American Labor Market Has Changed and What to Do about It.* Princeton, N.J.: Princeton University Press.

Osterman, Paul, and Brenda Lautsch.1996. *Project QUEST: A Report to the Ford Foundation.* MIT Sloan School of Management, Cambridge, Mass. January.

Pindus, Nancy, Darly Dyer, Caroline Ratcliffe, John Trutko, and Kellie Isbell. 1999. "Industry and Cross-Industry Worker Mobility; Experiences, Trends and Opportunities for Low-Wage Workers in Health Care, Hospitality, and Child Care." Washington, D.C.: The Urban Institute.

Piore, Michael. 1999. "The Low Wage Labor Market." Task Force on Reconstructing America's Labor Market Institutions. MIT Sloan School of Management, Cambridge, Mass. August.

Pryor, Frederic, and David Schaffer. 1999. *Who's Not Working and Why: Employment, Cognitive Skills, Wages, and the Changing U.S. Labor Market.* Cambridge, U.K.: Cambridge University Press.

Regenstein, Marsha, Jack Meyer, and Jennifer Dickemper Hicks. 1999. *Job Prospects for Welfare Recipients: Employers Speak Out.* Washington, D.C.: The Urban Institute.

Uchitelle, Louis. 2000. "I.N.S. Is Looking the Other Way as Illegal Immigrants Fill Jobs." *New York Times,* 19 March, A1.

Wial, Howard. 1999. "Minimum-Wage Enforcement and the Low-Wage Labor Market." Task Force on Reconstructing America's Labor Market Institutions. MIT Sloan School of Management, Cambridge, Mass. August.

Wilson, William Julius. 1996. *When Work Disappears.* New York: Alfred Knopf.

PART 2

Program and Policy Priorities

Strategies to Help Low-Wage Workers Advance

5

Staying On, Moving Up

Strategies to Help Entry-Level Workers Retain Employment and Advance in Their Jobs

Anu Rangarajan

Now more than ever, the path to self-sufficiency for most welfare recipients is one of maintaining employment and moving ahead in their jobs. The time limits imposed by the Personal Responsibility and Work Opportunity Reconciliation Act (PRWORA) of 1996 significantly raise the stakes of not being employed. Most states have adopted a "work-first" strategy in an effort to get individuals to move toward becoming economically independent. This strategy focuses on encouraging welfare recipients to seek employment and become attached to the labor force as quickly as possible. It has contributed to increases in the number of low-skilled individuals entering the labor market, typically to take entry-level jobs that offer low pay and few fringe benefits.

To make their way out of welfare and remain above the poverty level, it is important that these individuals maintain employment and advance to jobs providing incomes that are high enough to enable them to maintain a decent standard of living. However, many individuals now entering the labor market are unused to the world of work and, at the same time, must resolve difficult personal or family situations. Many welfare recipients quickly lose the jobs they find, and most have difficulty advancing beyond the entry level. These individuals must make honest efforts to overcome challenges as they attempt to make the transition to work, but external assistance and support may help them overcome some of the barriers.

To assist the efforts of individuals to maintain employment, many states are attempting to help current and former welfare recipients who have found work to retain employment and advance in their jobs. However, job retention and advancement strategies are of fairly recent origin, and established and proven practices have yet to be developed. Thus, many agencies are likely to have difficulty conceiving of and implementing effective job retention and advancement programs.

The Post-Employment Services Demonstration (PESD) was the first federally funded, large-scale demonstration that tested ways to promote job retention for current and former welfare recipients. The demonstration services themselves did not prove to be effective: Rigorous estimates of program impacts based on a random-assignment design showed statistically insignificant results. However, the study provides valuable implementation and program design lessons for agencies considering providing job retention services. This chapter documents and summarizes broad strategies related to retention and advancement.[1]

The following factors are important for programs that focus on job retention and advancement:[2]

- *Many job retention services can be integrated into preplacement, job preparation activities.* Too often, agencies view job placement, job retention, and job advancement activities as separate program components. They turn to job retention and advancement services only after individuals have been through preplacement services and found a job. Although many people use the terms postemployment and job retention synonymously, job retention services need not start after employment. Many job retention services (e.g., contingency planning, soft-skills training, teaching workplace behavior, teaching techniques to deal with unsupportive families and friends) can and should be integrated into job clubs and life-skill training workshops at the time of job search and placement. These and other services can continue to be provided after job start.
- *Initial job placement can be an important factor in helping promote retention and advancement.* The "work-first" strategies that most states rely on, and the pressures imposed on agency staff to place clients, often lead program staff to encourage or pressure people to find jobs as quickly as possible. In so doing, these staff may fail to focus on whether clients and their jobs are well matched. However, research shows that people whose initial jobs are high paying and offer good benefits are more likely to retain their jobs and advance in them or move on to better ones (Rangarajan, Schochet, and Chu 1998; Scrivener et al. 1998). In addition, clients are likely to make the extra effort to keep jobs in which they are interested and jobs in which they like the location, hours, and other characteristics. Thus, if sustained employment is a main program goal, it will be important for programs to pay attention to matching people with appropriate jobs.
- *Programs should consider sustained employment, rather than simply placement, to be their goal for most recipients.* If agency goals are sustained employment, programs may more readily be able to integrate retention services into preplacement strategies, and they may also seek better initial placements. This unified strategy can convey clearly to program staff and clients that sustained employment and career advancement are important. At the same time, programs should recognize that such a long-term goal may not be appropriate for all, especially for the hard-to-employ population. For such individuals, programs may want to focus on helping individuals enter the labor market; retention and advancement strategies may come later.
- *Programs should recognize that individuals are diverse, and broadly tailor services to reflect clients' differing needs.* Too often, programs have the same goals and expectations for all, regardless of each client's abilities, and provide a uniform set of services, regardless of clients' possibly differing needs. Some individuals, especially those who have low education levels or other limitations, may need services that are more inten-

sive and delivered over a longer period. In addition, some individuals are capable of taking only very small steps at a time, so the goal might be to ensure they make an effort to work on mitigating their barriers, while trying to maintain some low level of employment.[3] Those who are less disadvantaged might need fewer or different types of services. They could strive for sustained employment and career advancement.

- *Many options are available for designing job retention programs and services. Choices depend on program goals and resources and the target population.* As discussed below, agencies can choose from a broad menu of options for all or any of the following: what types of services to provide, who will receive these services, who will provide the services, and what the schedule for providing services will be. In designing programs, therefore, state and local agencies should consider carefully the service needs of the target population as well as services currently available. Only then should agencies consider additional types of services to cover gaps.

This chapter focuses on helping current and former welfare recipients with retention and advancement, but welfare recipients and other low-skilled individuals entering the labor market face similar issues, and the broad retention and advancement strategies described here apply to other low-skilled workers as well.

THE NATURE OF THE JOB RETENTION PROBLEM

Although many welfare recipients finding work keep their jobs, a significant number lose those jobs fairly quickly. For example, only three-fifths of a sample of 1,200 welfare recipients in four cities who found jobs in 1994 and 1995 were employed continuously in some job during the year after job start, while 40 percent experienced job turnover within the year and 30 percent were not employed in any job at the end of the year (Rangarajan 1996).[4] These findings are broadly consistent with more recent data from studies on those who leave Temporary Assistance for Needy Families (TANF): Between 29 and 44 percent who left cash assistance were not employed at the time of the follow-up survey, usually 12 to 18 months after welfare exit (Loprest 1999; U.S. General Accounting Office 1999; Brauner and Loprest 1999; Rangarajan and Wood 1999).

Some researchers argue that job mobility is good and to be expected as individuals try to find better job matches and follow a career path they have defined for themselves. If welfare recipients who find jobs do experience wage growth over time because of progression in the same job or a move to a better one, then employment itself should lead to advancement. However, a study based on National Longitudinal Survey of Youth data examined earnings experiences of welfare recipients who had found jobs and were employed five years later; it provided only weak support for these findings (Rangarajan et al. 1998). Although nearly 70 percent did experience a one-third increase in earnings during the five-year period, the increases were driven largely by an increase in hours worked, rather than an increase in hourly wages. Furthermore, between 30 and 40 percent of the welfare recipients who found employment were working in lower-paying jobs or had lower earnings five years after initial employment.[5]

These findings suggest that improving the chances for increasing wages for many may depend on conscious wage-progression strategies developed by states.

Often, the reasons for losing a job are complicated. Focus groups with welfare recipients, discussions with case managers, and surveys conducted with welfare recipients who found jobs reveal the breadth of issues that can affect welfare recipients' ability to remain employed (Rangarajan 1998). These issues include problems both outside and in the workplace. Many individuals (70 percent) have problems *outside work* that make it difficult for them to keep their jobs (table 5.1). For example, most can obtain only low-paying jobs but still must pay for work-related expenses, such as child care, transportation, and appropriate clothes and shoes. Many must cope with a reduction in other forms of social support, such as housing subsidies and, perhaps, food stamps and medical benefits.[6] Nearly 40 percent work nonstandard hours; obtaining child care and transportation during these times can be difficult.[7] Others must confront more severe issues, such as substance abuse, their own or other family members' mental or physical health problems, or previous incarceration that makes it difficult to find jobs. Many receive limited personal or social support and find the transition from welfare to work overwhelming and stressful.

A large number of welfare recipients (41 percent) face problems *at work* that make it difficult to keep their jobs (table 5.2). Because they have had little, if any, prior work experience, many have unrealistic work expectations, and some quit their jobs when these expectations are not met. These jobs also are more likely to be temporary jobs or jobs found through a temporary agency, and neither employer nor employee tend to invest much in them, leading to high rates of turnover. Furthermore, interviews indicate that many employers mainly value clients' "soft" skills, such as getting along in the workplace, knowing what to expect from a job, and so on. However, many welfare recipients do not have these types of skills. Twenty-eight percent of all sample members (more than two-thirds of those who reported any work-related problem) reported

TABLE 5.1 Problems *Outside of Work* That Made Maintaining a Job Difficult

Problem	Clients Reporting Problems (%)
Any problem	70
Child care	34
Transportation	25
Finances/budgeting	33
Housing	19
Family problems	29
Health/pregnancy	18
Physical abuse	6
Other	19

Source: PESD surveys conducted in 1996 with 1,200 newly employed welfare recipients approximately one year after job start.

TABLE 5.2 Problems *At Work* That Made Maintaining a Job Difficult

Problem	Clients Reporting Problems (%)
Any problem	41
Supervisor or coworker	28
Disliked job	10
Work schedule	6
Other	11

Source: PESD surveys conducted in 1996 with 1,200 newly employed welfare recipients approximately one year after job start.

a problem getting along with coworkers or supervisors. The combination of poor basic skills, little soft skills, and pressure to quickly take any job make it difficult for many welfare recipients to maintain sustained employment.

FINDINGS AND LESSONS FROM PESD

PESD, the first large-scale demonstration program to examine the effectiveness of providing job retention services, was initiated by the Administration for Children and Families of the U.S. Department of Health and Human Services in 1993. The demonstration arose in response to the increasing focus on work in state welfare reform initiatives established under waivers to the Job Opportunities and Basic Skills Training (JOBS) program. The demonstration was designed to obtain systematic information on employment paths out of welfare and to test ways to promote job retention among welfare recipients. Programs were fashioned broadly on the approach used in Project Match.[8]

Between spring 1994 and fall 1996, four sites operated demonstration programs under grants from the Administration for Children and Families. Welfare recipients who had participated in the states' JOBS programs and had found employment between March 1994 and December 1995 were identified soon after job start and enrolled in the demonstration. The sites enrolled between 800 and 1,500 welfare recipients who had recently found jobs during this period.[9] Clients were randomly assigned to receive program services or to a control group that continued receiving regular services available to employed welfare recipients in their states.

Case management was the cornerstone of PESD programs. Program guidelines required PESD case managers to contact all clients assigned to them and to inform them about the availability of program services. Case managers were to serve all clients, because it would not be clear up front who did and did not need program services. Program guidelines also required the case managers to maintain regular contact with all clients. Clients assigned to the program group could receive PESD services for at least six months; some could receive services for longer periods. Programs handpicked case managers who had 15 to 20 years of experience, typically serving welfare recipients in JOBS or other employment-oriented programs.

PESD case managers provided five key services to program participants: counseling and support, job search assistance, help resolving eligibility and other benefit issues, service referrals, and support services payment for work-related expenses. Case managers maintained a flexible, less bureaucratic approach to service delivery by adopting an informal and minimally officious approach. They provided individualized services to clients and stressed personal and informal communications. For example, they attempted to maintain regular contact, sent clients cards and newsletters, and held meetings at times and places that were convenient for the clients. To more easily reach clients who worked during the day, case managers sometimes worked evenings or weekends. To make it easy for clients to contact them at various times, they used beepers, cellular phones, or similar devices or had telephone answering machines or voice mail systems in their offices.

The evaluation of the PESD programs found that with extensive outreach and rapid follow-up, case managers managed to reach most clients and establish prompt communications with them. Most clients received counseling and support services during the first six months after program enrollment. Yet despite the delivery of these services, and although clients liked the services and appreciated the case managers' effort and interest, the programs did not affect outcomes; that is, they did little to increase earnings, reduce welfare, or promote a move toward self-sufficiency.[10]

Two factors that may have contributed to the lack of program impacts relate to program design and implementation:

- *The programs, which were experimental and evolved over time, could not benefit from lessons learned from previously developed job retention, service delivery models.* PESD was the first large-scale program of job retention services set in the context of state welfare programs. Case managers had to understand the program, learn how to select appropriate services, and determine how to deliver services without being able to learn from the experiences of other similar case-manager-based approaches to job retention. Although they had latitude with respect to service delivery, they received little guidance on how to serve different clients with different levels of needs, how to decide which clients to serve themselves and which to refer to other agency staff, or how to form links with employers. Furthermore, because the programs were new and unfamiliar to clients, case managers had to spend time contacting and informing clients of the availability of program services. Many clients were suspicious of the PESD case managers whom they did not already know. Finally, program staff had anticipated that case managers would have manageable caseloads, but caseloads remained high because large numbers of clients were losing jobs or continued to need services over time. The higher-than-expected caseloads could also have affected the case managers' ability to contact and provide services to all their clients.
- *Clients' service needs varied, but the PESD programs did not target clients with different levels of needs for different types of services.* The demonstration guidelines specified that job retention services focus on case management, and that all clients assigned to the programs be given case management services. Therefore, although

case managers tried to contact and serve all clients assigned to them, it was not clear that all clients who found jobs needed or wanted the more intensive type of case management services, or that the services helped to improve employment outcomes in every case. For example, in two sites, clients enrolled in the demonstration were more job ready than the average welfare recipient in those sites. In addition, many control group members maintained employment in all sites; it is likely that similar clients in the treatment group would also have been able to keep their jobs with little additional assistance. For these clients, intensive case management services may have had little value. In contrast, individuals with multiple or severe barriers may have had many factors affecting their ability to retain their jobs; the morale-boosting and counseling aspect of case management alone may have been insufficient to help them maintain employment. Providing all clients with the same types of counseling services—and the failure to distinguish among types of clients—may have prevented case managers from concentrating services on the neediest.[11]

Lessons Learned from the PESD Experience[12]

- Program staff can spend valuable time resolving bureaucratic issues related to post-TANF payments, such as child care and food stamps, or correcting errors in TANF benefit amounts. Simplifying service delivery mechanisms so clients can more easily access these benefits can free up case management resources so that case managers can focus more on service coordination issues and meet clients' needs more efficiently.
- Employment retention services must be seamlessly integrated into job search and other preplacement activities. Job retention services must start at the time of preplacement services and must continue after placement.
- Program staff should clearly and consistently convey their expectations about job retention and advancement to clients.
- Basic, broad-based, case management services may help clients feel better about themselves and facilitate the welfare-to-work transition somewhat, but without additional enhancements, they are unlikely to have large effects on retention and advancement.
- Programs should try to identify the needs of clients and provide appropriate levels and types of services.
- Given the wide range of issues that employed clients face, program staff must have access to services or provide service referrals to other agencies. Therefore, close integration of staff from various agencies is important.
- The PESD programs did not involve much interaction with employers or much employer involvement. Involving employers and using employer mediation is important, because many client issues are related to the workplace.
- Programs considering adding job retention assistance to their services should assess carefully the services they offer and make changes to fill gaps.

PROGRAM STRATEGIES AND OPTIONS

Agencies that are considering setting up programs to help clients maintain employment should note two things.

First, placement, retention, and advancement services are often thought of as discrete strategies that follow a sequential pattern—placement, followed by retention, and finally advancement. However, as discussed above, it is important to unify and integrate job retention strategies with preplacement efforts from the outset. Also, the appropriate job placement may facilitate retention and advancement. Individuals who obtain jobs that are good matches, pay well, and offer good benefits are more likely to try to retain these jobs than if they respond to pressures from program staff by taking any job quickly.

The motivation for separating these strategies in the ensuing discussion stems from the fact that individuals have different abilities and goals and may benefit from differing forms of assistance, depending on their needs. Thus, programs must think about "who needs what." For example, although relatively job-ready individuals may benefit from some elements of job retention strategies, it may be critical to focus on initial placement and, possibly, help them with career advancement strategies. Other individuals may face so many barriers that they will benefit only from some type of supported-work strategy, and may have more modest goals of finding employment while performing other activities that attempt to mitigate some of their barriers.

Second, most of the approaches discussed here have not been tested for effectiveness in the public sector; rather, the strategies are designed to address various needs of clients who are making the transition from welfare to work. Some strategies are based on lessons learned in studies of job retention and advancement programs, while others are based on advice and input from individuals who implement these programs or from studies of what the private sector does to retain employees. Rigorous evaluations of various approaches must be conducted to add to the body of knowledge on the effectiveness of retention and advancement strategies.[13]

Initial Placement

Initial job placement can be quite important and can influence the efforts of individuals to maintain jobs. Initial placement activity should consist of a thorough assessment of a client's skills, abilities, and potential barriers to employment. Program staff can use these assessments to help individuals set employment goals and obtain jobs that are consistent with those goals. Because employees often value job quality, program staff should also consider such factors as location, clients' ability to handle the job, and the clients' level of comfort with the job requirements and work hours. Even work-first approaches, which require individuals to quickly find jobs without considering alternative training or basic skills programs, may benefit from trying to make the initial placement a good job match.

For instance, in contrast to many employment-focused programs, the Portland JOBS program encouraged participants to find "good" jobs that were full-time, paid above the minimum wage, offered benefits, and had the potential for advancement.

The evaluation found that this program led to a large increase in employment and earnings (and larger than other work-first strategies) among those in the program relative to those in the control group (Scrivener et al. 1998).

Provide soft-skills training and other basic technology-related training.

The characteristic valued most by employers of low-skilled, entry-level workers is what is loosely termed as "soft skills." Soft skills include the workers' preparation for the world of work, understanding of appropriate work behavior, level of motivation, punctuality, and ability to balance work and home responsibilities. In addition to soft skills, employers also value more advanced skills that reflect an increasingly technology-based work environment. Even people in clerical jobs must have some knowledge of technology.

Agency staff can accomplish two goals by making soft-skills training and basic, technology-related training formal components of customized training programs. First, they can raise their clients' awareness of appropriate work behaviors and methods for resolving work-related issues, and they can equip clients with the basic technological tools used in the workplace. Second, requiring clients to participate in a workshop daily for two to four weeks can help agency staff observe whether clients can be punctual and regularly attend the workshop. Those who do not regularly attend are likely to have similar difficulty on the job. Program staff can help these clients address such issues before they become workplace issues.

Provide career placement assistance as part of job search programs.

Job search assistance under the work-first approach often consists of helping clients write resumes and identify job listings, and requiring clients to apply for a certain number of jobs each week. If retention and advancement are the primary program goals, it will be important to provide clients with additional career placement assistance. For example, program staff may conduct in-depth assessments of their clients. They also may ask clients to take tests designed to identify better career matches, determine the appropriate placement level, and help identify long-term and short-term career plans. This longer-term perspective on clients' employment prospects and career opportunities can provide advice and support in developing interim strategies. In addition, career placement counselors can help clients move along the path for which they are most ready, and also determine whether some clients might benefit from additional vocational training.

Provide basic skills and vocational training in rapidly growing occupations and in areas of high demand.

Even though many clients may be able to find entry-level jobs relatively easily, training may help some clients obtain considerably better jobs that have career paths. Programs may consider providing short-term vocational skills and related basic skills training in decently paying occupations that are in areas of high market demand. The time invested in such human capital may improve rates of retention and advancement. For example, an evaluation of the Center for Employment Training (CET) program, which combines vocational training in high-demand industries with related basic skills training, provided long-term payoffs for participants (Zambrowski and Gordon 1993). Given the work requirement limits imposed by TANF, it will be important that the training be short term, such as six to nine months, and focused on growing industries so those who complete the program can immediately find relevant jobs.

Try to place clients in jobs with employer-sponsored training and opportunities for advancement.

Although most employers do not provide substantial, on-the-job training for low-skilled workers, some offer fairly intensive training (e.g., Marriott and the United Parcel Service [UPS]). Furthermore, the current economic environment, characterized by low unemployment rates and high costs of replacing workers, has encouraged some employers to include retention and development strategies in their training packages. These programs often include job-specific and soft-skills training. Trying to identify such employers, forming ties with them, and placing workers in such jobs can provide clients with valuable training in a context that is relevant.

Retention Strategies

Job retention strategies include a wide range of options, from providing minimal supports to assist retention to much more intensive services. Most of the strategies discussed below have not been rigorously tested; rather they reflect strategies now being attempted by agencies, as well as lessons from PESD and other programs promoting employment and job retention. Agencies that are considering establishing job retention programs should identify their clients' needs, then choose program elements that most seem to fit them. Finally, they should attempt to evaluate the programs rigorously.

Increase the accessibility of support-service payments and services.

Programs can mitigate the costs of employment by helping clients with some of the additional costs of work, such as child care, transportation, and health insurance. Most states offer some version of these support services, but such factors as administrative complexities, lack of knowledge about the availability of benefits, and reluctance to interact with the welfare system have kept utilization rates low.

To the extent that many welfare recipients are unaware of the availability of these benefits or do not know how to access them, it will be important to inform them periodically (prior to job start) about support services available to them. To the extent that low usage is driven by difficulty in accessing services, agencies may want to consider simplifying the systems. Programs can conduct focus groups with former welfare recipients who are employed, including those who are using the benefits and those who are not, to better understand the factors explaining lack of use.

Programs may also want to provide resources to help people access services. For example, clients may need access to child care referral agencies to learn more about child care options near their homes. In addition, because many work in jobs at nonstandard hours, backup child care and transportation can be more difficult to find. Helping these clients find alternative arrangements will be important.

Provide initial employment expenses for work-related payments, such as clothing and tools, and provide other one-time emergency payments.

The first few weeks after job start are a critical period. Employees may have up-front expenses, yet not receive their paychecks for several weeks. Initial payments for employment-related expenses can help clients for a short period. One-time payments for emergencies, such as car repairs or car insurance, can also help. Many states provide emergency payments for certain expenses, but it may be useful to broaden this category so clients can use these (or similar funds) for a wider range of emergencies that might otherwise become barriers to work.

Include job retention components in preplacement workshops.

Job retention services should be offered as soon as clients begin their job placement efforts. This is important for two reasons. First, for many not used to the world of work, it is important to start learning early about the importance of communication, appropriate workplace behavior, getting along with others, dealing with job-related issues, and thinking about career advancement, as well as issues such as accessing transitional supports and the importance of back-up plans. It will also be important to inform clients about all the postemployment services the program offers, providing a sense of the resources and the supports that are likely to be available.

Second, many clients fail to inform their case workers that they have left welfare when they have found jobs. It is difficult to maintain contact with and provide follow-up services for some of these clients. Therefore, informing them about the availability of postemployment services early is a means of ensuring that clients are fully aware of the types of supports to which they may be entitled and how they can access them.

Provide enhanced case management and counseling.

A case-management-based approach is a common, job retention strategy that many agencies use to serve clients who have found jobs. Some individuals, especially those who have multiple problems and little previous work experience, may benefit from having an advocate who can help them navigate the system and facilitate the transition from welfare to work. For example, case managers can help clients with childcare and transportation by helping them find subsidized slots, providing help with child care paperwork, and encouraging and helping those with tenuous arrangements develop back-up plans.

Case managers can also help clients manage their money and budgets, obtain other benefits, and resolve personal problems that might impede sustained employment. In addition, case managers can try to anticipate problems facing new workers or workers who frequently change jobs; they can discuss these clients' work experiences and give them guidance or refer them to a human resources counselor, who may be able to help resolve the workplace issue.

Because case managers must deal with so many issues, it is important that they have access to a wide range of support services—especially specialized services, such as substance abuse and mental health counseling—to which they can refer clients. In addition to providing clients with referrals to providers, they must be able to follow up and work with the other counselors to help clients.

Attempt group meetings with participants.

With high caseloads, it may be difficult for case managers to have one-on-one meetings with clients regularly and frequently. One way to deal with the large caseload issue is to have group meetings. For instance, the Pathways program has monthly group meetings with clients. Two facilitators meet with each group of about 50 to 60 participants scheduled to a "permanent" group that meets the same day each month, with two sessions a day to accommodate clients' schedules (Herr and Wagner 1998).[14] The goal of the monthly meetings is to formulate participants' employability plans for the month; at the same time, the meetings enable participants to set priorities and isolate tasks, receive benefit from supports and peer pressure, and have a place to get and give social support.

Create opportunities for effective mentoring or job coaching.

Some agencies are considering mentoring strategies to promote job retention. Mentors could be employees in the workplace, community volunteers, or peers, such as former welfare recipients. A workplace mentor who understands the work environment can orient the client to workplace customs and practices and provide moral support and counseling. An employee who has a workplace mentor might also feel more vested in the job. In addition, the mentor might be able to encourage the employee to stay with the job during rough times. Peer support groups, including small community support groups of former recipients, could also serve a mentoring role. Individuals would be able to talk to their peers or others who have had similar experiences.

It is important that agencies select mentors who are likely to succeed in this role, and who have the time and desire to make the necessary commitment. In general, the agencies should provide the mentors with some training and try to maintain ongoing supervision of them.

Make work more attractive by providing wage supplements or other subsidies so that low-income earners can have more cash in hand.

Because many low-skilled workers find entry-level jobs in low-paying occupations, work often does not seem to pay. As a result, many welfare recipients do not believe that work represents an improvement over their current situations. Some programs provide earnings supplements to bring the earnings of low-income individuals near or above the poverty level. These programs have helped individuals stay employed, at least in the short run (Bos et al. 1999; Rust 1999). While states often use earnings disregards to increase the attractiveness of work, these policies may lead individuals in high-benefit states to remain on welfare. In today's welfare environment, these individuals may exhaust time limits too quickly. Other strategies include promoting awareness of the federal earned income tax credit (EITC) and advanced-pay option, which is underutilized by employed welfare recipients.[15] Similarly, the expansion of state tax credits or similar benefits can increase the attractiveness of work by implicitly raising hourly wages to provide a decent standard of living.

Consider using financial or nonfinancial incentives to affect behavior or short-term outcomes.

Incentives can encourage individuals and service providers to attain certain outcomes or goals. In the performance-based contracting world, some agencies financially reward service providers that achieve certain benchmarks, such as full-time employment of clients for a certain period (e.g., six months or a year).

These strategies seem appealing but may sometimes be difficult to implement. Agencies must ensure that service providers actually receive the number of referrals promised. In many cases, because of falling caseloads, intermediaries are not sent all the referrals that have been promised, potentially placing them in difficult financial situations if they hold slots open for agency clients (Paulsell and Wood 1999; Pavetti et al. 2000).

Furthermore, programs must pay attention to goals and incentive structures when devising an incentive scheme. For instance, if programs set unrealistic targets for incentives, such as no more than a one-week period of nonemployment between jobs for a one-year, job retention goal, it may be difficult for service providers to help clients who have become unemployed find jobs as quickly as required. Moreover, it may be difficult to monitor such targets.

In addition to giving financial incentives to service providers, programs have become interested in giving individual incentives to remain employed. These incentives or rewards may promote short-term outcomes, such as punctuality over a one- or two-week period, or promote certain behaviors, such as attending a workshop or making contingency plans (Hill and Pavetti 2000). These incentives can be financial or nonfinancial.

Encourage employer involvement and try to tailor services and programs to meet employers' needs.

Because many job difficulties occur in the workplace, agencies may find it helpful to encourage employer involvement. Placement staff may maintain regular contact with employers to learn more about their clients and more about the types of skills and employee characteristics that employers are seeking. However, many welfare clients do not want their employers to know about their links with welfare, so this type of involvement may be difficult to achieve, especially because some clients will find jobs on their own or with the help of case managers or other staff who do not have links with the employers.[16] Some state strategies include specialized training for line supervisors to improve their ability to supervise welfare recipients and respond to potential problems. This training may also make line supervisors aware of the types of support available to entry-level workers and enable the supervisors to contact the case managers to discuss appropriate issues. Finally, program staff can work with employers to learn what strategies private-sector employers use to promote retention and advancement.

Encourage the formulation of community teams and workplace-liaison programs.

Other strategies include forming teams of individuals to bring in members from community colleges, Private Industry Councils, Workforce Development Boards, and other relevant agencies to work with employers and employees to foster retention and advancement. These teams would work with local employers to assess the workplace skills of employees and develop skills acquisition plans and issue career transcripts that track participants skills and development over time (Packer and Siberts 1998). These teams would include a workplace liaison, who would work with both employees and supervisors to engage them in a learning-rich development process to improve skills, while helping employers select, develop, and retain high-quality workers. The goal of these programs would be to develop high-performance workplaces, and the workplace liaisons would work to foster increased productivity and reduced turnover, while helping participants get on a career ladder and move toward self-sufficiency.

Provide funding for EAP programs.

Some state agencies are trying to promote the formation of Employee Assistance Programs (EAP) for small businesses that hire welfare recipients and other low-skilled workers and may not be able to afford their own EAPs. These programs typically offer hotlines that enable employees to obtain information on a wide range of issues, such as work-related problems, personal finances, substance abuse problems, child care problems, and legal problems. The agencies often provide service referrals to providers who specialize in these services. To the extent that EAPs serve all entry-level workers, they can mitigate the stigma associated with receiving EAP services because of welfare receipt. EAPs can serve several small businesses and take a proactive role in helping resolve workplace conflicts.

Ensure easy access to job search assistance and placement.

Many low-skilled workers find jobs only to lose them; others may want better, higher-paying jobs. Individuals who have left welfare for employment must continue to receive job search assistance without having to return to welfare to obtain these services. Moreover, job search placement centers must be accessible to those who work during the day, possibly through extended hours or some weekend hours.

Advancement Strategies

Just as programs have thought about retention strategies in recent years, so, too, are they beginning to consider advancement strategies. Unfortunately, little is known about advancement strategies, partly because they are new and therefore little studied, and partly because they may be more difficult to implement.

Provide opportunities for skill enhancements.

Because many low-skilled workers obtain low-paying, entry-level jobs, additional vocational or basic-skills training while working could help them advance. To this end, some agencies provide financial support and incentives to enable workers to seek further training outside or at the workplace while maintaining employment. Training outside the workplace often is in the form of classes at community colleges or other vocational training programs, with the agencies possibly subsidizing the cost of participation. However, programs usually find that participation rates are very low, primarily because employed single mothers often do not have time for another major activity. Agencies can mitigate these difficulties somewhat by keeping training programs short and focused; giving clients useful information on the types of programs and some career counseling on choosing the right courses; and providing other support, such as child care and transportation subsidies.

Alternatively, employers can provide job-specific or on-the-job training in the workplace or additional vocational education or training located in or near the workplace. Because employers generally provide little on-the-job training or other training in the types of jobs that many low-skilled workers obtain, agencies can give employers financial incentives or matching funds to train low-skilled employees. Such workplace training may also help increase employee retention.[17]

In conjunction with groups of employers, agencies might also design customized training programs that are short term, targeted to meet the employers' needs, and offered near the workplace. Third-party intermediaries may be able to help structure work-based learning opportunities.

Consider sectoral strategies and job laddering.

Agencies are considering sectoral initiatives that offer structured career advancement or "job ladders" by facilitating employee movement between firms. The basic goal of such initiatives is to create career pathways for individuals by clustering employers around common workforce development needs. In this strategy, low-skilled workers in entry-level jobs develop some labor market experience and good work behaviors. After they have established some labor market credibility, the workers attempt to obtain better, higher-paying jobs. The strategy depends on the formation of multiple-employer consortia, with the moves to different employers initiated by employment counselors who work with the consortia. Individuals can be provided with training to move ahead, and firms may be more likely to provide training if they can share the cost. This strategy would also involve creating industry skills standards to be used by workers and employers as benchmarks for employees to move across jobs.

STRATEGIES FOR THE HARD-TO-PLACE

As caseloads fall, it is likely that many who remain on welfare will be difficult-to-employ clients who have multiple or serious barriers to work, including their own or their families' physical and mental health problems, learning disabilities, and drug and alcohol addiction. In addition, some may have had interactions with the criminal justice system; people with felony convictions often find it very difficult to get jobs. The kinds of placement, retention, and advancement strategies discussed above are unlikely to work for this group.

A variety of programs are geared toward special needs populations (e.g., supported-employment programs, programs for learning-disabled populations, programs for non–English speakers, and so on). Rather than describe the programs or strategies for these groups, the purpose of this discussion is to emphasize that some individuals will have special needs and that these needs must be considered in setting goals for this population.[18]

Four points are worth noting. First, programs must conduct careful, detailed assessments with clients to identify any special needs and to develop appropriate goals and strategies. Second, the special needs population is diverse, so programs or strategies to meet the range of needs must be identified. Third, special needs groups are likely to require more intensive support for longer periods of time. Fourth, programs may have to be flexible in how they define activity or participation for some individuals in these groups. For example, individuals with special needs might have the short-term goal of trying to combine community work with other activities, or participating in programs or activities that help address some barriers, even though these activities may not meet program placement requirements for agencies.[19]

DESIGNING POLICIES

As agencies start to design programs aimed at promoting retention and advancement, they will have to consider the broad context in which they will be operating. For example, many programs operate in a work-first environment, with pressure for welfare recipients to find a job as quickly as possible. Given the strong economic conditions and seemingly plentiful unskilled entry-level jobs, it is relatively easy for many welfare recipients to find jobs quickly. However, many are likely to lose these jobs quickly and to have to find others.

Before selecting elements of retention or advancement strategies for inclusion in their programs, agencies must think about the target population and its needs. The choice of strategy and target population goes hand in hand and will have to be made simultaneously. Different programs may choose different strategies depending on the needs of the population. For example, an agency that primarily serves job-ready clients may want to focus largely on placement and advancement strategies, with some retention support. However, an agency that primarily serves highly disadvantaged clients who face multiple barriers may want to include more intensive, case management components and to focus largely on strategies for the hard to employ.

This chapter concludes with two design elements: (1) targeting services to meet the needs of clients; and (2) choice of a service delivery mechanism the agency intends to use.

TARGETING SERVICES: IDENTIFYING WHO NEEDS WHAT

Research shows that welfare recipients, even those who find jobs, are a diverse group. Programs that plan to provide retention or advancement services should consider the needs and resources of welfare recipients who are looking for jobs or finding them. They should set targets or goals for people that match their abilities; setting unrealistic goals is likely to lead to failure. Some clients are relatively more job ready and able to sustain employment independently. They will require little assistance or only short-term assistance to meet specific needs. Some clients may benefit from short-term vocational training to reach this point. Clients who have serious or multiple needs may have a difficult time holding on to jobs or advancing and will likely require on-going assistance.

Identifying clients who are likely to need little assistance and those who are likely to need ongoing assistance could be a challenging task. Research on targeting strategies suggests that it may be possible to identify people and job characteristics (e.g., education level, health status, starting wages, availability of fringe benefits) as guides to help identify people likely to have stable employment outcomes and those likely to have poor employment outcomes (Rangarajan et al. 1998). However, given the complexity of people's lives and characteristics not easily observed in the data, programs will have to supplement these formal targeting tools with assessments by case workers and placement counselors that help identify individual needs, set goals, and determine the types of services to be provided.

Agencies considering providing job retention strategies often focus on current recipients who are working. Agencies have some leverage with these individuals and can require them to use certain job retention services, such as attending workshops. However, programs may want to provide and promote the use of certain job retention and advancement service more broadly to all low-skilled, entry-level workers. These workers need the same types of supports as do welfare recipients. Furthermore, offering supports to all low-income workers can minimize the stigma that may arise if services target only welfare recipients.

CHOOSING DELIVERY MECHANISMS

As programs select strategies, they will also have to consider who can best provide the services. Different agencies or groups, or a combination of agencies and groups, can provide placement, retention, and advancement services and strategies. Because employer involvement may be vital in designing training strategies, employers and workforce agency staff will have to work together to determine what training programs can best meet retention and advancement goals.

Many agencies use intermediaries to provide preplacement, placement, and retention services. These intermediaries will have to work with case managers to ensure that clients use the available public supports—and that the intermediary agency and the case manager work toward the same goal for the client. Similarly, the intermediary agencies may have to maintain contact with employers, so that any work issues can be detected early on.

Finally, welfare agency staff often act as brokers between different players. To the extent that multiple players are likely to be involved, it will be important to ensure coordination among them, so clients do not fall through the cracks. It will also be important for all agencies and players to have the same goal for clients, and to give clients clear, consistent messages about their goals and expectations.

NOTES

1. This chapter focuses largely on broad retention strategies. Operational details and examples of strategies currently being implemented can be found in Rangarajan (1998), Brown et al. (1998), Fishman et al. (1999), and Strawn and Martinson (2000). In this book, Strawn and Martinson address the issue of advancement in greater detail.

2. Throughout, this chapter draws on the lessons learned from PESD program implementation, site visitors' and program staffs' observation of elements that did and did not work well, and newly employed clients' service needs and experiences identified through focus groups and surveys. It also draws on findings from other employment-related demonstration programs that aimed at sustained employment, as well as observations from other job retention programs.

3. In Project Match's Pathways System, each month the caseworker and the participant choose from an activities menu to create an individualized employability plan, with activity goals based on participants' abilities and needs (Herr and Wagner 1998).

4. According to studies that used national data prior to welfare reform, between 25 and 40 percent of women who left welfare for work returned to welfare within a year, and a larger number experienced job turnover within one year. See, for example, Gritz and MaCurdy (1992), Pavetti (1992), Rangarajan et al. (1998), and Cancian and Meyer (1997).

5. In addition, those who were not employed five years after initial job start were considerably more disadvantaged than were those who were, and the former are likely to have experienced lower earnings growth if they had worked.

6. Although many who leave welfare may be entitled to Medicaid, food stamp benefits, and child care subsidies, utilization rates of these benefits are low (Rangarajan and Wood 1999; Loprest 1999; Dion and Pavetti 2000).

7. Among those working nonstandard hours, nearly half prefer these shifts, often because of child care or other reasons, while half would prefer a different shift (Rangarajan and Wood 1999).

8. Project Match is an intensive, supportive employment-oriented program providing services to residents of the Cabrini-Green Community in Chicago. It was one of the first programs to recognize the importance of continuing to help welfare recipients after they begin their jobs (Olson et al. 1990).

9. The PESD programs are demonstration programs, and clients did not know about the availability of these services (in other words, they did not volunteer to be in this demonstration), nor did they know about the service until program staff told them.

10. For a more detailed description of the findings from this evaluation, see Rangarajan and Novak (1999).

11. Although not related to program factors, strong economic conditions and the types of services available to control-group members may also have influenced the magnitude of estimated program effects (Rangarajan and Novak 1999).

12. These lessons are drawn from program implementation experiences, study team and program staffs' observations of elements that did and did not work, and clients' needs identified through focus groups and surveys.

13. The Administration for Children and Families recently sponsored a rigorous evaluation of employment retention and advancement strategies; it will provide more definitive results on alternative employment retention and advancement strategies in a few years.

14. While these numbers may seem high, participants are divided between the two sessions; moreover, some may not show up, for legitimate or nonlegitimate reasons.

15. For instance, fewer than one in five of the PESD sample members took advantage of the advanced-pay option (Rangarajan and Novak 1999).

16. Employees tend to be less resistant if the case managers are also the ones placing individuals in jobs or if the job counselor calls the employees.

17. See Brown et al. (1998) for more details on strategies to promote state-employer ventures to provide training.

18. Dion et al. (1999) and Johnson and Meckstroth (1998) describe a variety of programs and strategies adopted specifically to meet the needs of those with different types of severe employment barriers.

19. The Pathways program discussed earlier is a good example of a program in which participants and case managers work together to help participants set customized monthly goals based on their circumstances and what they can realistically hope to achieve (Herr and Wagner 1998).

REFERENCES

Bos, Johannes, et al. 1999. "New Hope for People with Low Incomes: Two-Year Results of a Program to Reduce Poverty and Reform Welfare." New York: Manpower Demonstration Research Corporation.

Brauner, Sarah, and Pamela Loprest. 1999. "Where Are They Now? What States' Studies of People Who Left Welfare Tell Us." Washington, D.C.: The Urban Institute.

Brown, Rebecca, et al. 1998. "Working Out of Poverty: Employment Retention and Career Advancement for Welfare Recipients." Washington, D.C.: National Governors' Association.

Cancian, Maria, and Daniel R. Meyer. 1997. "Work after Welfare: Work Effort, Occupation, and Economic Well-Being." Draft paper presented at APPAM, October.

Dion, M. Robin, and LaDonna Pavetti. 2000. "Access to and Participation in Medicaid and the Food Stamp Program: A Review of the Recent Literature." Washington, D.C.: Mathematica Policy Research.

Dion, M. Robin, et al. 1999. "Reaching All Job-Seekers: Employment Programs for Hard-to-Employ Populations." Washington, D.C.: Mathematica Policy Research.

Fishman, Michael E., et al. 1999. "Job Retention and Advancement among Welfare Recipients: Challenges and Opportunities." Falls Church, Va.: The Lewin Group and Johns Hopkins University.

Gritz, R. Mark, and Thomas MaCurdy. 1991. "Patterns of Welfare Utilization and Multiple Program Participation among Young Women." Washington, D.C.: U.S. Department of Health and Human Services.

Herr, Toby, and Suzanne L. Wagner. 1998. "Moving from Welfare to Work as Part of a Group: How Pathways Makes Caseload Connections." Chicago: Project Match, Erikson Institute.

Hill, Heather, and LaDonna Pavetti. 2000. "Using Incentives to Promote Job Retention and Advancement: Guidance from the Performance Improvement Industry." Washington, D.C.: Mathematica Policy Research.

Johnson, Amy, and Alicia Meckstroth. 1998. "Ancillary Services to Support Welfare to Work." Princeton, N.J.: Mathematica Policy Research.

Loprest, Pamela. 1999. "Families Who Left Welfare: Who Are They and How Are They Doing?" Washington, D.C.: The Urban Institute.

Olson, Lynn, Linnea Berg, and Aimee Conrad. 1990. "High Job Turnover among the Urban Poor: The Project Match Experience." Center for Urban Affairs and Policy Research, Northwestern University, Evanston, Il.

Packer, Arnold H., and Melissa Siberts. 1998. "The Career Transcript System: A National Demonstration for Welfare-to-Work." Submitted to U.S. Department of Labor, Employment and Training Administration. SCANS 2000 Center, Institute for Policy Studies, Johns Hopkins University, Baltimore, Md.

Paulsell, Diane, and Robert G. Wood. 1999. "The Community Solutions Initiative: Early Implementation Experiences." Princeton, N.J.: Mathematica Policy Research.

Pavetti, LaDonna A. 1992. "The Dynamics of Welfare and Work: Exploring the Process by Which Young Women Work Their Way off Welfare." Cambridge, Mass.: Harvard University.

Pavetti, LaDonna A., et al. 2000. "The Role of Intermediaries in Linking TANF Recipients with Jobs." Washington, D.C.: Mathematica Policy Research.

Rangarajan, Anu. 1996. "The Transition from Welfare to Work: An In-Depth Look at Employment Patterns and Barriers to Job Retention." Paper presented at RAND Conference on Welfare Research, September.

———. 1998. "Keeping Welfare Recipients Employed: A Guide for States Designing Job Retention Services." Princeton, N.J.: Mathematica Policy Research.

Rangarajan, Anu, and Tim Novak. 1999. "The Struggle to Sustain Employment: The Effectiveness of the Postemployment Services Demonstration." Princeton, N.J.: Mathematica Policy Research.

Rangarajan, Anu, and Robert G. Wood. 1999. "How WFNJ Clients Are Faring under Welfare Reform: An Early Look." Princeton, N.J.: Mathematica Policy Research.

Rangarajan, Anu, Peter Schochet, and Dexter Chu. 1998. "Employment Experiences of Welfare Recipients Who Find Jobs: Is Targeting Possible?" Princeton, N.J.: Mathematica Policy Research.

Rust, Bill. 1999. "'Above Average' Welfare Reform: The Minnesota Family Investment Program." *Advocasey* 1 (2): 4–11.

Scrivener, Susan, et al. 1998. "Implementation, Participation Patterns, Costs, and Two-Year Impacts of the Portland (Oregon) Welfare-to-Work Program: Executive Summary." New York: Manpower Demonstration Research Corporation.

Strawn, Julie, and Karin Martinson. 2000. "Steady Work and Better Jobs: How to Help Low-Income Parents Sustain Employment and Advance in the Workforce." New York: Manpower Demonstration Research Corporation.

U.S. General Accounting Office. 1999. "Welfare Reform: Information on Former Recipients' Status." Washington, D.C.: GAO.

Zambrowski, Amy, and Anne Gordon. 1993. "Evaluation of the Minority Female Single Parent Demonstration: Fifth-Year Impacts at CET." Final report submitted to the Rockefeller Foundation. Princeton, N.J.: Mathematica Policy Research.

6

Promoting Access to Better Jobs

Lessons for Job Advancement from
Welfare Reform

Julie Strawn and Karin Martinson

As unemployment reached record lows in recent years, many policymakers began to shift their attention away from the jobless and toward those who were working but still struggling to make ends meet. Increasingly, the question was: How can we best aid low-income workers to advance to better jobs? While the slowing economy in 2001 has renewed recession fears, unemployment remains low, and policymakers are still focused on aiding low-wage workers.

There is little hard research available to guide decisionmaking in the area of job advancement. Nevertheless, some insights can be found in the wealth of research on the experiences of women who have left welfare for work and in the rigorous evaluations of the employment programs that serve them.[1] While the research findings are complex, broadly speaking they suggest that:

- Steady work alone is not a path to substantially higher wages;
- Where someone starts in the labor market—her initial wages and occupation—matters for her future success; and
- Postsecondary education or training is a key factor in who advances over time.

Further, welfare-to-work programs have shown that it is possible to help low-income people move into better jobs—with higher pay and benefits, compared with what they would have found on their own—even within a relatively short time frame. However, workforce development policymakers and practitioners probably cannot replicate this success without making important changes in the way services are currently delivered. Probably the most critical tasks are to involve employers in the design and delivery of services, to make occupational training accessible to those with low skills and to those who are working, and to connect shorter-term training with opportunities to earn postsecondary degrees.

KEY FACTORS FOR LABOR MARKET SUCCESS

Past research on the experiences of women who leave welfare suggest that most become employed but at low wages, typically above minimum wage but below the poverty level. Job loss is high, especially in the first four to six months after leaving welfare. Few of the women manage to work steadily over time; in one study, for example, only 5 percent of those who left welfare managed to work year-round and full-time in each of the five years after leaving. By contrast, 60 percent never worked year-round and full-time in that period (Cancian and Meyer 2000). On average, women who leave welfare do earn substantially more over time because they work an increasing amount, but their hourly wages grow very modestly (by less than 8 cents per year, in the same study). More recent studies indicate somewhat higher wage growth—perhaps as much as 4 percent annually. Given the low initial wages of women leaving welfare, however, even these higher estimates are unlikely to make a substantial difference in whether families leaving welfare escape poverty (Corcoran and Loeb 1999; Gladden and Taber 2000a, b).

Women who have received welfare are a diverse group, however; this overall picture reveals little about who among them succeeds in the labor market or why. Several recent studies have tried to take a closer look and isolate the personal, family, and job factors that predict how welfare recipients entering the labor market do over time. One important observation from this research is that helping people work steadily over time and helping them move up to better jobs may be somewhat different tasks, with different factors important for each.[2]

KEY FACTORS FOR STEADY WORK

- *Working steadily initially is linked to sustaining employment over time, other job and personal factors being equal.* Women who worked more in the first year after leaving welfare were more likely to be employed four and five years after leaving welfare, although not necessarily at the same jobs. This was especially true if they worked full-time throughout the first year after leaving welfare (Cancian and Meyer 2000).
- *Starting out in jobs with higher wages is linked to sustaining employment over time.* Holding education levels and other job and personal factors equal, women in one study who began working at higher wages worked more weeks over a five-year period (Rangarajan, Schochet, and Chu 1998). Another study of women who left welfare for work found that those with higher wages were more likely to stay employed (Rangarajan, Meckstroth, and Novak 1998). This is consistent with recent evaluation research (Freedman 2000) and with earlier labor market studies (Bartik 1997; Lidman 1995; Slaughter et al. 1982).
- *Starting out in jobs with employer-provided benefits is linked to sustaining employment over time, again holding other personal and job factors equal.* One study found that those who began jobs that offered paid vacation stayed employed for an average of 12 months at a time, compared with 7 months among those without such leave. Similarly, those who began working in jobs that offered health insurance worked 77 per-

cent of the following two years, compared with 56 percent of the time for those without insurance (Rangarajan et al. 1998).

- *Starting out in certain occupations may be linked to sustaining employment over time.* One study found that among women who began working in sales in the first year after leaving welfare, 73 percent worked at some time in the fourth and fifth years. By contrast, among women who started in other common occupations, such as private housekeeping, building cleaning or maintenance, clerical, and private-sector care (which includes health care and formal child care), 83 to 95 percent worked in the fourth and fifth years after leaving welfare (Cancian and Meyer 2000).[3] Two other studies also found a relationship between initial occupations and future employment; a third did not.[4]

- *Among those who find work, personal characteristics, such as educational attainment and basic skill levels, are only weakly linked to sustaining employment over time.* Research has found little relationship between the initial basic skills and educational attainment of women who have received welfare and how much they sustain employment over a five-year period. This may reflect in part the fact that those with the lowest basic skills are much less likely to be working at all. In addition, studies find little relationship between other personal characteristics—such as number or age of children or housing status—and sustaining employment over time (Olson and Pavetti 1996; Rangarajan et al. 1998; Strawn and Martinson 2000).

KEY FACTORS FOR MOVING TO BETTER JOBS

- *Working steadily initially at any job—even over several years—does not lead to substantially higher wages later on.* One study found that women who worked full-time and/or all year in the first year after leaving welfare did not have higher wages in the fourth and fifth years than those who had worked part-time for only part of the year. Similarly, women who worked more months in the first three years after leaving welfare did not have higher wages in the fourth and fifth years than those who had worked less (Cancian and Meyer 2000). Another study found similar results (Rangarajan et al. 1998). However, some recent research suggests that full-time work may lead to higher wages than part-time work (see chapter 7 in this volume; Corcoran and Loeb 1999).

- *Switching jobs periodically can be a path to higher wages later on.* One study found that among welfare recipients in four cities who found work, 40 percent changed jobs within the first year, with two-thirds moving to jobs with higher wages and one-third moving to jobs with the same or lower wages (Rangarajan et al. 1998). Another study reached similar conclusions (Cancian and Meyer 2000). Other research has found that changing jobs can be a path to higher wages among low-skilled workers but only in moderation: One voluntary job change a year is linked to higher wages but any more are associated with lower wages, as are involuntary changes (Gladden and Taber 2000b).

- *Starting out in higher paying jobs is linked to higher wage growth over time.* The initial wages of women leaving welfare are strongly linked to future wages (four or five years later), even after controlling for other work history and job and personal factors. In one study, the hourly wages of those in the top one-fourth of the wage distribution grew significantly over five years, from $7.90 to $8.84. By contrast, the average wages of those in the bottom one-fourth did not increase at all (Cancian and Meyer 2000).[5] Several earlier studies found similar patterns (Bartik 1997; Burtless 1997). Similarly, an earlier analysis found that only about half of those whose wages were below $4.50 (in 1992 dollars) in the first year after leaving welfare had incomes above the poverty level in the fifth year, compared with three-fourths of those whose initial wages were $7.50 an hour or more (Cancian and Meyer 1997).

- *Starting out in certain occupations is linked to higher wages later on.* One study found that compared with those who began working in sales, women who started in clerical positions earned 22 percent more an hour five years later, those in production and manufacturing or building cleaning and maintenance earned 17 percent more, and those in private care (which includes health care and formal child care) earned 15 percent more. Different initial occupations were also associated with differing poverty rates in the fifth year (Cancian and Meyer 1997).
- *Higher basic skills, especially education beyond high school, are strongly linked to higher wages later on.* The same study found that those with basic skills test scores in the top three-fourths of all scores earned about 8 percent more an hour in the fourth and fifth years than those with scores in the bottom one-fourth. Interestingly, whether someone had a high school diploma mattered little for wage growth after controlling for other factors, such as basic skills level, how much individuals worked, and at what kinds of jobs. However, education beyond high school was strongly linked to higher wages later on (Cancian and Meyer 1997).

The implications of the research presented here for policy are complex. Broadly speaking, they point in these directions:

- Helping low-income people retain their initial jobs or quickly become employed again may also promote steady work in later years.
- Promoting steady work alone is unlikely to lead to higher-paying jobs for many low-income workers; other policies and services are needed.
- Helping low-income people find better jobs initially—higher-paying jobs or ones with benefits—may promote both steady work and further job advancement in later years.
- Over the long term, better access to postsecondary education and training is likely to be an important piece of the solution to promoting access to better jobs.
- Despite job advancement policies, it is likely that most low-income people will continue to work at low-wage jobs. If poverty reduction is a goal, then wage supplements and other antipoverty policies will be needed.

THREE STRATEGIES FOR JOB ADVANCEMENT

Understanding which factors are important for labor market success is a critical first step toward choosing strategies that enable low-income workers to move up to better jobs. But knowing that a factor is important is not the same as knowing how to change it. The remainder of this chapter discusses research findings and emerging best practices for three job advancement strategies: connecting to better jobs directly, upgrading skills while unemployed, and upgrading skills while working.

In recent years, policymakers in the welfare reform arena have increasingly recognized that focusing on job placement alone is not enough; lasting success for an employment program depends upon its ability to help people stay employed and advance to better jobs. The most common policy response has been to add postemployment retention services—typically case management and supportive services—to existing preemployment welfare-to-work services, which rely primarily on job search.

The research suggests that this response will not be enough. First, there is no hard evidence that retention services make a difference; in fact, two rigorous evaluations of postemployment case management found it had no impact on how long welfare recipients kept jobs or how much they earned (Rangarajan and Novak 1999; Strawn and Martinson 2000). Second, even if retention services were to prove effective, working steadily alone does not appear to bring substantially higher wages over time.

A handful of states has moved beyond postemployment case management, creating other postemployment benefits or services aimed at job advancement, such as individual development accounts, tuition aid, and child care for those in education or training. In the few states with some years of experience, though, few parents appear to have used these benefits. More proactive efforts to create advancement services tailored to working, low-income parents have been launched recently. Participation may be higher than in the more laissez-faire types of aid, but still remains a small proportion of the target population.

These issues do not argue against providing low-income workers with job advancement services, but they do suggest that policymakers who want to have a real impact in this area will need to combine pre- and postemployment strategies to promote access to better jobs. Specifically, they should consider taking these steps:

- *Connecting people directly to better jobs:* Build a job advancement focus into *preemployment* services by making direct placement in better jobs a key program goal for those low-income people whose skills and credentials are already good. Support this goal with detailed information on the labor market, strong relationships with employers, and substantial staff training on assessment, career guidance, and job development.
- *Upgrading skills while unemployed:* Build a job advancement focus into *preemployment* services by making skills training available and accessible to the unemployed, especially those with lower skills or who lack credentials. While this might seem to go against the prevailing "work-first" philosophy, a growing number of states are choosing to do it. To support skill upgrading, think beyond traditional welfare or workforce development programs—such as, how well do student aid and the higher education system function for the working poor?
- *Upgrading skills while working:* Form partnerships with employers to provide *postemployment* advancement services at or near the work site, both to newly employed low-income people and to incumbent workers. Participation is likely to be much higher than for other postemployment services provided outside work

hours, and the training will be closely connected to employer needs. As this approach will necessarily be limited by the extent of employer interest, supplement it with evening and weekend job advancement services at other locations and with financial aid to support individual advancement efforts.

Connecting People Directly to Better Jobs

One of the most cost-effective strategies that states and communities can pursue for helping low-income people advance in the workforce is to connect those who already have work experience, solid basic skills, and a high school diploma or GED with better-paying jobs that offer benefits. Programs that serve the unemployed can use initial job placement as an opportunity to begin working with people on career development issues, goal setting, resolution of personal and logistical challenges to sustaining employment, and placement in a better job that fits into a longer-term career plan. Because a person's initial position in the labor market appears likely to affect future opportunities for advancement, helping low-income people connect to better jobs initially may bring future as well as immediate benefits.

For those who are already working, postemployment services at the worksite or elsewhere in the community can provide similar opportunities for career development, goal setting, barrier resolution, and placement in a better job. Many of the tasks are the same as for the unemployed; however, service delivery for low-wage workers is complicated by competing work demands—and, often, parenting demands as well.

What the Research Says

Evaluation research shows it is possible to connect some low-income people to better jobs directly, without increasing their access to skill upgrading. After two years of follow-up, Steps to Success—Portland, Oregon's Job Opportunities and Basic Skills (JOBS) training program—helped those who entered with high school diplomas or GEDs increase their hourly wages by almost $1 and gain greater access to full-time jobs with health benefits. For those with recent work experience, the wage increase was even higher—$1.56 more than similar parents not in the program. Portland also helped parents find more stable employment, increasing the percentage who worked all of the second year of follow-up (Freedman et al. 2000).[6]

Portland achieved this without significantly increasing education and training for high school graduates beyond what they would have obtained on their own. About one-third of these parents did pursue postsecondary education or training, but this was also true for members of the control group, who did not have similar wage gains.[7] Nationally, a significant percentage of low-income parents already possess the skills to enter jobs with better pay and career potential (Carnevale and Desrochers 1999).

Begun in 1984, Steps to Success, a welfare-to-work program run by Mt. Hood Community College and Portland Community College and involving a host of other partners, annually provides a wide range of services to about 14,000 welfare recipients and applicants. At the time it was evaluated (1994–1996), Steps to Success emphasized rapid employment, but balanced this against its goal of placing recipients in full-time jobs paying above minimum wage with benefits and potential for advancement. The first activity for parents varied according to their basic skill levels, work history, and the presence of personal or family challenges to employment.

High school graduates or GED holders in Portland's program who had work experience typically first entered a job club, which emphasized finding full-time jobs with benefits that paid above minimum wage. Those without work experience typically entered life skills class, followed by education or training. About 10 percent were involved in unpaid work experience or on-the-job training. The work experience was unusual in at least two ways: It involved placements with private employers, and parents were carefully matched to placements that fit their skills and career interests. Everyone who entered the program was assessed for job readiness, including basic skills, substance abuse, mental health, and domestic violence issues. Case managers also took work history and personal goals into account when making assignments to activities or job placement (Scrivener et al. 1998).

Lessons for Policy and Practice

If policymakers want workforce development programs to help low-income people find better jobs than they would on their own, then the state or locality has to communicate in concrete ways the importance of this goal. In addition, programs have to create strong, ongoing relationships with employers; gather good formal and informal labor market information; have internal performance incentives and training for staff; provide a comprehensive set of work supports; and define goals clearly.

- *Set performance measures for welfare and workforce development agencies and their contractors that emphasize job quality.* State-set performance standards may have been a key factor in Portland's success in placing welfare recipients in better jobs. The standards included a wage-at-placement target well above the minimum wage (Scrivener et al. 1998). Similarly, among the performance measures Utah uses for its consolidated workforce development services—whether for welfare recipients, dislocated workers, or others—are percentage increase of an individual's wage after receiving services, longevity of labor force attachment (job retention and job duration), and welfare caseload reduction due to increased income (Materials from Utah Department of Workforce Services). The state of Washington recently developed a cash bonus system for welfare caseworkers who help parents find high-wage jobs with good benefits, with larger bonuses if recipients stay employed over time (Tweedie, Reichert, and Steisel 1999).
- *Train front-line staff on career development strategies and tools so they can craft individual paths to obtaining better jobs.* Training is needed to help staff use labor market information to make good matches of jobs with individuals' skills, interests, and short- and long-term goals. In Utah, training for employment counselors includes career counseling; job development; assessment; employment plan development; job connection resources; and a component on human behavior, communication, and interviewing skills. Staff also receive training on other issues that might interfere with a person's success in employment, such as domestic violence. Training is guided by

the overall goal of delivering services based on a holistic view of each person's needs, not on what particular funding streams allow (Materials from Utah Department of Workforce Services).

- *Help parents develop short- and long-term career goals.* Whether a program's clients are unemployed or working, career exploration and planning are critical elements in any job advancement strategy. Career exploration typically includes opportunities for individuals to assess their interests and skills and explore various occupations by hearing employers talk about what they seek in workers, by visiting work sites, and through job shadowing and internships.[8] Portland's Steps to Success, Salem, Oregon's Up With Wages, and the state of Rhode Island all develop career advancement or income improvement plans with parents to help them think about goals and how to reach them. Postemployment services are then critical for revising and updating these plans as people gain work experience and skills.

- *Develop assessment tools to help staff match skills needed in particular jobs with the skills of low-income people.* While some tools for job matching do exist (e.g., Work Keys), practitioners typically say that existing assessments are problematic for those with limited English proficiency or low skills. This forces programs to use a mix of imperfect formal assessments and more subjective, informal assessments of individuals' skills.

    In the long term, this problem may be ameliorated by the availability of assessments and credentials that are under development. These include ways to certify mastery of work-related basic reading, writing, and math skills; "soft skills," such as problem solving, conflict resolution, and working in teams; and skills needed in specific occupations.[9] Other elements of a good job match include making sure the job location fits well with transportation and child care needs and that the person's work style is well suited to the job itself.

- *Maintain close and continuous contact with local employers.* This is critical for identifying better-paying, full-time jobs with benefits that do not require specialized training. To understand the specific skills needed in particular jobs, staff have to develop relationships with the immediate supervisors. Full-time job developers, such as those used by Steps to Success, are one way to ensure ongoing interaction between local programs and employers. Local Workforce Investment Boards under the federal Workforce Investment Act could help coordinate these efforts across programs. In some states, Unemployment Insurance wage data on employment and earnings can be used to understand which industries and individual employers have a track record of successful outcomes for low-income people (Lane et al. 1998).

    In addition, more in-depth local analyses could guide staff efforts by identifying promising industries and the skills and credentials needed for advancement in them. For example, a detailed analysis of employment opportunities, entry-level requirements, and training programs in Chicago's health care industry led to a guide for city residents on job opportunities in health care and on choosing health career training in the city.[10]

- *Create mechanisms for identifying up-front potential logistical, personal, or family challenges to employment.* This is critical for helping low-income people succeed once placed, as well as for preserving credibility with employers. For example, programs do not want to send someone with a substance abuse problem to employers who require a drug test for employment without taking steps to address that issue. These mechanisms can be formal (e.g., pen-and-paper screens for substance abuse or learning disabilities) or informal (e.g., peer group discussions) (see Dion et al. 1999).

Upgrading Skills while Unemployed

While better job matching and an emphasis on job quality can help some low-income people enter better jobs directly, many will need to upgrade their skills to compete effectively. The key ingredients in helping low-income people find better jobs through preemployment skill development appear to be strong leadership in making job quality a central objective of the program, reinforced with incentives for caseworkers, and access to high-quality job training as part of a comprehensive, employment-focused program.

What the Research Says

Evaluations of welfare-to-work programs find that those focused on job search have consistently helped low-income parents work more, but they generally have not changed the quality of the jobs people find (Bloom 1997; Strawn 1998). Long-term studies find that, with few exceptions, impacts in job search–focused programs fade entirely within five years (Friedlander and Burtless 1995).[11] Yet education-focused programs have not done better. Despite the prevalence of low basic skills among welfare recipients, basic education–focused programs have not helped recipients find better jobs and have not been as consistently successful as a job search in increasing employment and earnings (Hamilton et al. 1997; Pauly and DiMeo 1995).

The most effective welfare-to-work strategy is flexible and individualized, and mixes job search, work, high-quality job training, and employment-focused basic education. Quick employment strategies can help people find better jobs if services are restructured to fit into a shorter time frame and the program emphasizes finding better jobs. Again, the Steps to Success program provides a good example. At the end of two years of follow-up, Portland increased employment rates by 43 percent, and among those employed, increased hourly wages by 13 percent and the percentage who found jobs with health insurance by 19 percent. Portland also increased by 46 percent the proportion of parents earning more than $10,000 annually (Freedman et al. 2000).

Portland placed a strong emphasis on helping low-income parents find better jobs through a mix of job search, work-focused basic education, and occupational and life skills training. Portland did stress moving into the workforce quickly, but this was not a "work-first" program in that the first activity for each person varied, depending on skills, work history, and other factors. The result was a program unusually balanced between skill upgrading and job search, with correspondingly well-balanced outcomes: Among 11 sites in a national evaluation, Portland increased employment and earnings by more than three "work-first" programs, and yet also increased receipt of occupational licenses or certificates and GEDs by as much as seven education-focused sites (Freedman et al. 2000).

Portland's results are consistent with earlier research on Baltimore Options, San Jose's Center for Employment Training, the Alameda County and Butte County GAIN programs, and other programs that stressed better jobs and also used education and training in addition to job search activities (Friedlander and Burtless 1995; Riccio, Friedlander, and Freedman 1994; Zambrowski and Gordon 1993). Portland's results also show that it is possible to help a range of welfare recipients find better jobs, not just the most educated. Over two years of follow-up, the program increased hourly wages for nongraduates who were employed by nearly 60 cents an hour and for graduates by almost 90 cents. Typically, welfare-to-work programs help one group or another find better jobs, but not both.[12]

Access to occupational training for those without high school diplomas or GEDs may be a key to helping these welfare recipients find better jobs. In a national evaluation of 11 welfare-to-work programs, the three sites that most increased hourly pay for nongraduates—Columbus, Detroit, and Portland—also boosted participation by this group in postsecondary education or occupational training. Only Portland, however, substantially increased receipt of occupational licenses or certificates: Nongraduates in the Portland program were four times more likely to receive a trade license or certificate than those not in it (Freedman et al. 2000).

These results showing the ability of nongraduates to benefit from occupational training are consistent with an earlier evaluation of San Jose's Center for Employment Training (CET) (Zambrowski and Gordon 1993).[13] However, job training more generally has not proven consistently effective; it appears that how training is designed and implemented matters a great deal in terms of how well it succeeds (Grubb 1996; Orr et al. 1996; Pindus and Isbell 1997).

Lessons for Policy and Practice[14]

The critical tasks for making preemployment skill upgrading a successful job advancement strategy are improving the quality of job training and work-related basic education, and making job training more accessible to those without high school diplomas or GEDs.

- *Start by targeting 5 to 10 local employers who can offer jobs with higher-than-average wages, benefits, and potential for advancement.* Market program services (screening, training, and postemployment follow-up) to these employers and obtain their input on program design. Developing training for an entire sector rather than one business can help ensure that training does not narrowly benefit one firm.
- *Give participants an opportunity to learn about different career options before choosing a training program.* This may be especially important for helping low-income people envision themselves in careers that few of their peers are in. It could include tours of employers, training programs, and short internships.
- *Assess student strengths and goals, as well as supportive service needs, to ensure a good fit between individuals and training and to arrange for necessary supports.* San Jose's Center for Employment and Training and its affiliates around the country are notable for using no testing in determining admission to training programs, but they

do use testing after entry to determine a starting point for basic education services. Other programs use such testing to determine whether someone could benefit from a short, targeted pretraining class to bridge critical gaps in skills (see below, *Create short-term "bridge" training . . .*).

- *Use a curriculum based on mastering specific competencies developed in partnership with employers, as well as broader skills.* Involving both technical and personnel staff from employers is key to developing up-to-date training curricula and an in-depth understanding of hiring decisions. Hiring or borrowing front-line supervisors as training instructors is also an effective way to ensure that training mirrors actual job tasks.

- *Train on job content ("hard skills"), workplace skills ("soft skills"), life skills, and basic education skills (including English language proficiency).* For example, Portland's electronics manufacturing course includes training in electronics and semiconductors, as well as workplace communication, industrial math, keyboarding, and technical career progress. Life skills are woven into these components; for example, the math teacher begins with having participants develop a family budget.

- *Provide training in employer facilities or in a job-like setting, using a mix of instructional methods.* If training is provided in a work-like setting, then a variety of issues that might later interfere with employment may surface during training instead. At CET, people attend 35 hours per week and punch a time clock; those who do not show up are called or visited at home. Instructional methods should minimize lectures and workbooks and include, for example, practicing real job tasks on actual employer equipment, working on group projects, and role playing.

- *Develop links to community partners—such as substance abuse, mental health, and vocational rehabilitation agencies—for other services that enable individuals to succeed in training and employment.* Both CET and Steps to Success have community resource staff whose job is to find resources outside the program that their participants need. Chicago Commons Employment Training Center has many of these partners on-site at its center. In these programs, as well as in others—such as Utah's welfare reform program—training staff meet regularly with staff from other services so they can work as a team in helping individuals toward sustained employment.

- *Offer college credit for training and link shorter-term training with opportunities for further skill upgrading.* To promote long-term job advancement, shorter-term training should end in an occupational certificate or other recognized credential, offer transferable credits, and be articulated with degree programs. For example, CET is an accredited higher education institution whose programs end in an occupational certificate and whose students typically receive Pell grants; some of its training is articulated with community college degree programs. Seattle's Shoreline Community College has a continuum of short-term training connected to longer-term degree programs. Minnesota's Pathways training initiative offers college credit for many of its courses.

- *Integrate basic education and English as a Second Language (ESL) into occupational training, or at least provide it concurrently and in the context of real work and life tasks.* Doing this allows CET to have no entry requirements and to serve many people with low skills and/or little English. Its training lasts an average of just six months, because it offers training on a full-time, year-found, open-entry/open-exit basis and weaves in basic skills needed for an occupation.[15] Other providers, such as El Paso Community

College, teach basic education and ESL concurrently with training (Strawn 1998). Steps to Success created a "fast-track," six-week GED course that helped people with solid basic skills obtain a GED quickly and move on to training.

- *Create short-term "bridge" training designed to open up training opportunities, either with employers or service providers, to individuals who might not otherwise gain entry.* One alternative to integrating basic skills instruction into job training is to develop pretraining or "bridge" programs that prepare those with low skills or limited English proficiency to succeed in mainstream training programs. Chicago Commons Employment Training Center's bridge training prepares women with third- to sixth-grade skills to enter programs in auto mechanics, woodworking, skilled industrial trades, and health care. The bridge training for manufacturing, for example, includes job-specific skills, such as blueprint reading, as well as more general workplace skills, such as reading, writing, and math. Bridge training can also help people gain access to employer-provided, in-house training. Steps to Success offers Steptronics, six weeks of bridge training that prepares people to enter employer-sponsored training in the semiconductor industry and other electronics manufacturing.

- *Compress existing occupational certificate and degree programs so that low-income people can enter training year-round and complete it quickly.* Low-income people typically need and want to be back in the workforce as soon as possible. Many certificate and degree programs can be shortened by meeting for 30–35 hours each week, rather than the 12 hours typical of traditional college schedules. This allows students to enter a program throughout the year and complete it more quickly. Washington State reinvested $7 million of Temporary Assistance for Needy Families (TANF) savings in 1998–1999 in local college, business, and agency partnerships that provide short-term training to welfare recipients, customized to business needs.

- *Divide training into "chunks" that can be completed at different points in time.* The Washington Aerospace Alliance and Shoreline Community College have developed training for Computerized Numerical Control machine operators. The entry-level training is a 10-week (300-hour) certificate course that was shortened from an existing year-long program. The advanced-level training, which leads to an associate's degree, is broken into eight modules that can be completed one at a time when the workers' schedules allow.

Upgrading Skills while Working

States and communities that provide postemployment job advancement benefits and services are using three main approaches: (1) creating public-private partnerships with employers to do training at the work site; (2) redesigning existing employment and training services to make them more accessible to workers; and (3) providing financial support for low-income workers to upgrade skills on their own.

As noted earlier, participation appears very poor when it is left up to low-income workers to pursue job advancement services entirely on their own. With restructured evening and weekend services, participation appears higher but still rather low. Work-site services seem to achieve the best participation, but the scale of this approach will be limited by the extent to which employers can be persuaded to do it. No matter which approach is taken, the best practices in the previous section for improving the quality of training should also be incorporated here.

What the Research Says

Work-based employment programs for welfare recipients typically have raised employment and earnings; some have also increased hourly wages. On-the-job training produced significant increases in annual earnings for welfare recipients in 16 Job Training Partnership Act–funded programs, as well as in welfare-to-work demonstrations in Maine and New Jersey. However, on-the-job training has typically been reserved for the most employable welfare recipients and operated on a very small scale (Gueron and Pauly 1991; Orr et al. 1996; Plimpton and Nightingale 2000).

Other kinds of work-based training have proven effective, though, with more disadvantaged welfare recipients in two national demonstrations. The AFDC Homemaker-Home Health Aide demonstration and the National Supported Work demonstration raised long-term employment and earnings, with some of the sites also raising hourly earnings (Bell, Burstein, and Orr 1987). Less rigorous research suggests that state-funded, employer-focused training for existing workers can raise earnings and job retention; however, until recently, such programs rarely included low-income people.

Other research further suggests that postsecondary education can increase the hourly wages of low-income individuals. Participation in programs at both community colleges and four-year institutions produces large hourly earnings gains, according to a study tracking nearly two decades of earnings for participants in postsecondary education. This research, which attempted to control for differences in ability and family background between those who go to college and those who do not, found that women who received an associate's degree earned hourly wages 19 to 23 percent higher than similar women without such a degree. Similarly, women who obtained a bachelor's degree earned 28 to 33 percent more than their peers (Kane and Rouse 1995). Other studies have found that each year of postsecondary education generates increased earnings in the range of 6 to 12 percent, with even larger earnings gains for individuals from families in which their parents did not have any postsecondary education.[16]

However, undergraduates who work more hours are less likely to persist in educational programs than similar students who work fewer hours. Longitudinal research by the U.S. Department of Education finds that hours of work relate strongly to how often students report that work limits their school schedules or negatively affects their performance (Horn and Malizio 1998).

Lessons for Policy and Practice

Given low participation in postemployment services, more experimentation is needed with a variety of strategies. The lessons here are broken down into three sections:

- Public-sector/employer partnerships for training provided at or near the work site;
- Evening and weekend job advancement services; and
- Financial aid and supportive services for workers to upgrade skills on their own.

CREATING EMPLOYER-FOCUSED TRAINING[17]

The key to creating effective public-private partnerships for employer-based training is understanding how to meet employers' bottom-line needs, while ensuring that training benefits workers who would not likely obtain it otherwise. While employer-based training can be very effective, the implementation challenges are substantial. Partnering with existing state customized training agencies could speed efforts to open such training to low-income people. These agencies are experienced in creating the public-private partnerships central to customized training. Some states already use customized training agencies to help low-income workers advance in the labor market: California, Iowa, Minnesota, New Jersey, and North Carolina. Two of these agencies, Minnesota's Job Skills Partnership (MJSP) and California's Employment Training Panel, have large efforts to deliver customized training to welfare recipients or former recipients.

These and other customized training efforts suggest a number of key lessons:

- *Fund training with contracts or grants, not tax credits or subsidies.* Employers appear to view tax credits and subsidies as less effective than direct grants or contracts for training because the subsidies and credits are too diffuse, helping the businesses' overall financial picture without being directly applied to training costs (Simon 1997). In addition, public agencies may be better able to leverage private resources—such as release time, use of employer facilities for training, and employer staff time for job coaching—if they can offer in exchange direct funding through a grant or contract. TANF savings are one possible source of funding; the Workforce Investment Act is another.
- *Provide training at or near the work site and require release time for training.* The most successful incumbent worker training programs involve easy access to training, particularly on-site training; direct links between training and job tasks; and a shared investment of time and costs by employers and workers. Offering training at or near the work site during work hours helps overcome one of the most difficult implementation challenges in this area—the difficulty of engaging low-income workers in after-hours training—especially if they are single parents.
- *Customize curriculum, but only for skills that are transferable within an industry.* Public funding can help firms organize around common training needs, ensuring that people are trained for the skills actually in demand but not subsidizing training that is useful to only one employer.
- *Include upgrade training for the existing workforce.* Minnesota is combining Pathways grants, which fund customized preemployment training for welfare recipients, with its existing Job Skills Partnership upgrade training for existing workers in the same workplaces. The state's goal is to create career pathways that allow existing workers to advance, thereby freeing up entry-level jobs for unemployed, low-income parents who can in turn advance. In addition to preemployment and postemployment job training, this initiative includes supervisor training to promote further learning on the job. This pairing of entry-level and upgrade training is also a feature of some of the California Employment Training Panel's welfare-to-work projects.

- *Create career pathways through local partnerships of employers and training providers.* The local education, business, and social service partnerships that receive Minnesota's Pathways grants must develop long-term career and educational pathways for a particular industry sector. Similarly, a partnership of 34 employers and six community colleges in the Seattle area has formed the Tri-County Job Ladder Partnership Project to create career and educational pathways in four sectors: manufacturing, customer relations, information technology, and health services. The goal is to develop individualized career plans that identify job and training opportunities across participating employers and colleges.
- *Link customized training to postsecondary education.* As with other types of shorter-term training, customized training is most useful to workers if it is for college credit and is articulated with degree programs. Georgia is beginning to link its state HOPE scholarships to certified training developed by its technical institutes for specific industries or industry clusters (Regional Technology Strategies 1999).

REDESIGNING EXISTING SERVICES FOR LOW-INCOME WORKERS[18]

- *Recruit through agencies serving the working poor and by targeting past participants in preemployment services.* Staff who see low-wage workers for TANF, food stamps, Medicaid, and other benefits could help refer people to job advancement services, but would need training and incentives to do so. Another way to reach low-wage workers might be to target those who found jobs through an agency's preemployment services.
- *Offer services during evenings and weekends and supplement classroom services with distance learning.* Steps to Success offers advancement services two evenings a week and from 9 a.m. to 3 p.m. on Saturdays. ASAP, an advancement initiative in New York City for graduates of STRIVE, offers training from 6 p.m. to 9 p.m. twice a week and from 9 a.m. to 1 p.m. on Saturdays. Distance learning can supplement and extend what is covered in the classroom and be a vehicle for career counseling and mentoring. Some providers, such as Shoreline Community College in Seattle, are exploring ways to lend or make affordable work stations for their low-income students.
- *Creatively package services for the whole family by brokering job development and advancement services for other entities' services for children and youth.* Steps to Success has found that other programs, such as Head Start, are willing to offer their activities and services at the same times and locations as its postemployment services if Steps to Success provides job development and advancement services to the other agencies' customers. As a result, the program's evening and Saturday workshops now include everything from free child care and meals, to science and computer activities for older children, to adult education, ESL, vocational rehabilitation services, career planning, computer training, job placement, and 12-step activities for the parents.[19] Steps to Success has found that this whole-family approach results in a much greater willingness by busy parents to participate.
- *Set a reasonable time frame for training.* Training can be "chunked" or divided into short modules of 35 to 40 hours each. A single module can then be completed in a week for people who are not working or can take time off; for other workers, it can

be completed in, for example, six Saturday sessions of six hours each. People complete modules as they find the time, and ultimately receive a training certificate or degree when they complete all modules. Part of the redesign efforts in Washington State's technical and community colleges involve creating such modules. ASAP's training can be completed in 10 to 24 weeks of evening and weekend classes.

- *Offer worksite job advancement services that are open to all employees.* Rhode Island's placement, retention, and advancement unit for TANF recipients and former recipients has found employers receptive to on-site workshops, if the sessions are open to all employees. In addition to making it easier for low-income people to attend, such on-site workshops provide opportunities to develop closer working relationships with employers. Salem, Oregon's Up With Wages also does on-site advancement workshops.

SUPPORTING ADVANCEMENT EFFORTS OF LOW-INCOME WORKERS

- *Federal student financial aid, such as Pell grants, may be an option for some.* For low-income workers to obtain Pell grants, they must be in certificate or degree programs and typically must be enrolled for at least six credits (two courses).[20] Yet women who leave welfare for work are typically working more than 30 hours a week and may find it difficult to take more than one course a semester in a training or education program.

- *Support skill upgrading through tuition assistance or waivers at state-supported schools.* Georgia targets its HOPE scholarships toward working adults who can only attend school part-time. The program is open to state residents who enroll in a degree or certificate/diploma program and covers basic skills remediation. For those attending state universities or branches of the Department of Technical and Adult Education, there are no minimum hours of enrollment. The flexibility of HOPE scholarships supports the state's overall emphasis on credentialing incremental skill development (Regional Technology Strategies 1999). Washington State makes funds for tuition and books available to working low-income parents and to other low-wage workers. This tuition aid is designed to help those who have not yet applied for Pell grants or who are ineligible for Pell grants. The reasons for ineligibility vary but include lack of a high school diploma or GED, previous default on federal student loans, enrollment for too few credits, or enrollment in programs that are too short to qualify. As of June 1999, about 4,200 people had enrolled in the program, approximately half current or former welfare recipients. Michigan and Ohio have recently created similar programs to support some types of skill upgrading for low-income families who do not receive TANF cash assistance.

- *Individual development accounts (IDAs) can be used to support skill upgrading, and may include state and employer matching contributions in addition to the worker's savings.* The 1996 federal welfare law opened the door for broader use of individual development accounts for welfare recipients. Such accounts are intended to allow low-income parents to accumulate savings for specific purposes, including education and training. Of the 26 states that allow IDAs for postsecondary education and training, 11 provide matching contributions. Iowa, Minnesota, and some other states make IDAs available to other low-wage workers, not just families. Outside of welfare reform, Pennsylvania is piloting individual learning accounts that involve state, worker, and employer contributions, and are "portable" when an individual switches jobs. However, the state is finding little interest among employers in investing this way in low-wage employees.

- *Use the Workforce Investment Act's new authority to aid incumbent workers.* Under the Workforce Investment Act, federal workforce development programs may provide training to employed, low-income people, provided they have first sought federal student financial aid. Unlike past federal training efforts, the act requires that training for adults generally be provided through individual vouchers rather than through contracts with training providers.[21]

- *Accompany financial aid with career counseling.* Regardless of the funding source, aid to individuals for education and training may be more effective if accompanied by career counseling and help in choosing a provider. While there has been little research on vouchers, Pell grants, or similar aid to low-income individuals for education or training, available evidence suggests that unfettered choice may not produce the desired results in terms of higher employment and earnings. In particular, people often lack good information on what jobs are in demand (Barnow 1999).

KEY CHALLENGES AHEAD

The experience of states and local programs that have pursued one or more of these job advancement strategies suggests that significant challenges lie ahead. These include:

- *Broadening the focus of welfare reform efforts—particularly at the front-line staff level—from caseload reduction to supporting work and job advancement.* In recent years, financial and political incentives have stressed placing people in jobs quickly and reducing welfare caseloads. If the system is to take on a new mission of job advancement and poverty reduction, there will need to be concrete leadership, staff development, and specific rewards for making this shift. In states that have launched job advancement efforts without an accompanying shift in incentives to front-line staff, the result has been a low rate of referrals to job advancement services.

- *Engaging employers in job advancement efforts.* Employer involvement is critical to the success of any workforce development effort. It is especially important for postemployment job advancement services. The logistical obstacles to combining work and learning are most easily overcome when skill upgrading can take place at or near the work site and during work hours. Employers typically have been willing to partner in this way on skill upgrading when the training was related to specific workplace needs and involved mid- or upper-level employees. It has been less clear that employers were willing to invest in training for entry-level employees, especially when training did not directly relate to carrying out jobs (e.g., GED preparation or other basic skills). There are encouraging signs that the tight labor market may be changing employers' views on this in some communities.

- *Engaging low-income workers in job advancement services.* Combining work and learning can be a daunting proposition for many people, especially single parents who frequently lack good transportation and child care options. In addition, there can be real short-term financial trade offs between working additional hours or leaving time for school, even though skill upgrading may increase wages in the long term. Finally, many low-income people have had poor experiences with the education system in the past, do not see themselves as successful learners, and may not be able to envision a different career and educational path in the future. These issues may all contribute to the low participation that a number of providers have experienced when they offered evening and weekend job advancement services to low-income workers.

- *Increasing access by low-income workers to mainstream postsecondary education and training.* To date, job advancement services in welfare reform typically have been provided as "add-on," contract-funded services outside the certificate and degree-granting programs of community colleges and other postsecondary institutions. This allows states and localities to get services up and running quickly, yet, over the long term, there are important reasons for trying to improve access to mainstream postsecondary programs. First, when a community-based organization or community college provides short-term training but without college credit, the worker cannot apply this toward a longer-term educational goal, such as an associate or bachelor's degree. Second, current funding for job advancement services—primarily TANF—may not be a stable source over the long term; in contrast, federal and state postsecondary financial aid is not subject to the political and fiscal vagaries of welfare reform. Third, financing job advancement with welfare funds raises equity arguments as to why certain low-income workers—namely single parents—should gain access to such services while others are denied them. However, low-income workers seeking access to postsecondary education face a number of financial, logistical, and educational barriers. These arise from a complex array of policies in individual colleges, states, accreditation bodies, and federal student aid programs. Resolving these issues will be a long-term task—but one that is necessary to creating a permanent infrastructure of job advancement services for low-income workers.

NOTES

This chapter is a summary of selected sections of *Steady Work and Better Jobs: How to Help Low-Income Parents Sustain Employment and Advance in the Workforce,* by Julie Strawn and Karin Martinson, June 2000. The full paper can be obtained from Manpower Demonstration Research Corporation, (212) 532-3200, http://www.mdrc.org/reports2000/SteadyWorkGuide/pdf.

1. An important caveat to this body of research is that it predates implementation of the 1996 welfare law.

2. It should be kept in mind that while this research did control for many observable differences between those studied (e.g., education, work history, wages), unobservable differences (e.g., motivation, interpersonal skills) are also likely to be important and are not captured in these analyses.

3. The researchers created their own, more narrow, occupational groupings than those in the NLSY data set.

4. Vartanian and Gleason (1999) and Bartik (1997) found the relationship; Rangarajan, Schochet and Chu (1998) did not.

5. Wages expressed in 1996 dollars. It is worth noting that wages for low-skilled women generally have recently begun to rise after years of decline, so the picture for the bottom quartile may be changing.

6. Hourly wage comparisons between program group members and the control group are not true experimental findings as they are only for those in the sample who were employed. The $1,371 is an aver-

age for all parents who entered the program with a high school diploma or GED, including those who were not working. The actual increase in earnings of those who were working is substantially higher.

7. Portland targeted education and training to those without high school diplomas or GEDs and did increase their participation in training and attainment of training credentials (Freedman et al. 2000).

8. According to a recent publication from the National Center for Research on Vocational Education (see NET Gain No. 24: Career Resources at http://ncrve.berkely.edu/NetGain/), there are several good resources on the Internet on career development. Cornell University has an especially good site where people can try out various career exploration tools: http://www.explore.cornell.edu.

9. For example, the National Institute for Literacy's Equipped for the Future initiative developed content standards for work-related basic educational skills. Johns Hopkins University is developing the Career Transcript System, an assessment and curriculum to help workers develop and credential "soft skills." The National Skill Standards Board, along with a myriad of state efforts, is developing credentials for specific occupations or occupational clusters.

10. The study, entitled *Picture of Health: Best Practices in Training and Employing Chicago's Entry-Level Health Care Workforce,* included focus groups with employers and a survey of over 180 health care training programs (Shenoy 1998). The guide is called *Picture Yourself in a Health Career* (Shenoy 1998). To obtain a copy, contact CJC at 332 S. Michigan Avenue, Suite 500, Chicago, IL 60604.

11. The exceptions are two counties in the study of California's GAIN program, Riverside and San Diego. Both programs focused on quick employment but used a mix of job search, education, and training services. See Freedman et al. (1996).

12. For example, in the National Evaluation of Welfare-to-Work Strategies (NEWWS), only 1 other of the 11 sites increased hourly pay significantly for both groups—the Atlanta employment-focused program—and its impacts were about half the size of Portland's. The other sites increased hourly pay either for graduates or for nongraduates but not both (Freedman et al. 2000). Previously evaluated programs have typically been able to find high school graduates better jobs but not nongraduates (Bloom 1997; Friedlander and Burtless 1995).

13. However, it is important to note that while CET had raised employment and earnings among both graduates and nongraduates after two-and-a-half years of follow-up, the impacts for nongraduates had disappeared at the five-year follow-up point.

14. This discussion draws from numerous interviews with practitioners (see Strawn and Martinson 2000) and from Badway and Grubb (1997); Grubb et al. (1999); Pavetti (1997a, b); and Strawn (1998).

15. Rigorous evaluations of CET have found that it is effective in increasing the employment and earnings both of minority, single parents and of disadvantaged youth (Zambrowski and Gordon 1993).

16. For a summary of other research on the economic outcomes of postsecondary education for low-income parents, see Clifford M. Johnson and Esther Kaggwa, *Work Study Programs for Welfare Recipients: A Job Creation Strategy That Combines Work and Education* (Washington, D.C.: Center on Budget and Policy Priorities, August 18, 1998) and the U.S. Department of Labor's review of the economic impacts of employment and training programs, *What's Working and What's Not,* January 1995.

17. This discussion is drawn from interviews with practitioners (see Strawn and Martinson 2000) and from Simon (1997); Regional Technology Strategies (1999); and Strawn (1998).

18. This discussion is drawn from interviews with practitioners (see Strawn and Martinson 2000).

19. Materials from Portland's Steps to Success program and correspondence between author and Kim Freeman, regional codirector of Steps to Success. For further information, contact freemanK@mhcc.cc.or.us.

20. Individuals enrolled in education or training less than half-time are technically eligible for Pell grants, but in practice find it difficult to qualify.

21. See Savner (1999).

REFERENCES AND ADDITIONAL READINGS

Badway, Norena, and W. Norton Grubb. 1997. *A Sourcebook for Reshaping the Community College: Curriculum Integration and the Multiple Domains of Career Preparation.* Berkeley, Calif.: National Center for Research in Vocational Education. Available online at http://vocerve.berkeley.edu.

Barnow, Burt S. 1999. "Vouchers for Government-Sponsored Targeted Training Programs." In *Vouchers and the Provision of Public Services,* edited by C. Eugene Steuerle, Robert Reischauer, Van Doorn Ooms, and George Peterson. Washington, D.C.: Urban Institute Press and Brookings Institution Press. Available online at http://www.urban.org.

Bartik, Timothy J. 1997. *Short-Term Employment Persistence for Welfare Recipients: The "Effects" of Wages, Industry, Occupation, and Firm Size.* Kalamazoo, Mich.: W. E. Upjohn Institute for Employment Research. Available online at http://www.upjohninst.org.

Beder, Harold. 1998. "Lessons from NCSALL's Outcomes and Impacts Study." *Focus on Basics* 2 (D). Cambridge, Mass.: National Center for the Study of Adult Learning and Literacy. Available online at http://gseweb.harvard.edu/~ncsall.

Bell, Stephen H., Nancy R. Burstein, and Larry L. Orr. 1987. *Evaluation of the AFDC Homemaker–Home Health Aide Demonstrations: Overview of Evaluation Results.* Bethesda, Md.: Abt Associates Inc.

Bloom, Dan. 1997. *After AFDC: Welfare-to-Work Choices and Challenges for States.* ReWORKing Welfare: Technical Assistance for States and Localities Series. New York: Manpower Demonstration Research Corporation. Available online at http://www.mdrc.org.

Brown, Rebecca, Evelyn Ganzglass, Susan Golonka, Jill Hyland, and Martin Simon. 1998. *Working Out of Poverty: Employment Retention and Career Advancement for Welfare Recipients.* Issue Brief. Washington, D.C.: National Governors' Association. Available online at http://www.nga.org.

Burtless, Gary. 1995. "Employment Prospects of Welfare Recipients." In *The Work Alternative: Welfare Reform and the Realities of the Job Market,* edited by Demetra Smith Nightingale and Robert H. Haveman. Washington, D.C.: Urban Institute Press.

———. 1997. "Welfare Recipients' Job Skills and Employment Prospects." *The Future of Children: Welfare to Work* 7 (1): 39–51. Available online at http://www.futureofchildren.org.

Cancian, Maria, and Daniel R. Meyer. 1997. *Work after Welfare: Work Effort, Occupation, and Economic Well-Being.* Draft paper prepared for the annual meeting of the Association for Public Policy Analysis and Management, Washington, D.C.

———. 2000. "Work after Welfare: Women's Work Effort, Occupation, and Economic Well-Being." *Social Work Research* 24(2): 69–86.

Cancian, Maria, Robert Haveman, Thomas Kaplan, and Barbara Wolfe. 1999. *Post-Exit Earnings and Benefit Receipt among Those Who Left AFDC in Wisconsin.* Special Report No. 75. Madison, Wis.: Institute for Research on Poverty. Available online at http://www.ssc.wisc.edu/irp.

Cancian, Maria, Robert Haveman, Thomas Kaplan, Daniel Meyer, and Barbara Wolfe. 1999. "Work, Earnings, and Well-Being after Welfare: What Do We Know?" *Focus* 20 (2): 22–25. Available online at http://www.ssc.wisc.edu/irp.

Carnevale, Anthony P., and Donna M. Desrochers. 1999. *Getting Down to Business: Matching Welfare Recipients Skills to Jobs That Train.* Princeton, N.J.: Educational Testing Service.

Cave, George, Hans Bos, Fred Doolittle, and Cyril Toussaint. 1993. *JOBSTART: Final Report on a Program for School Dropouts.* New York: Manpower Demonstration Research Corporation.

Corcoran, Mary, and Susanna Loeb. 1999. "Will Wages Grow with Experience for Welfare Mothers?" *Focus* 20 (2): 20–21. Available online at http://www.ssc.wisc.edu/irp.

Dion, Robin M., Michelle K. Derr, Jacquelyn Anderson, and LaDonna Pavetti. 1999. *Reaching All Job-Seekers: Employment Programs for Hard-to-Employ Populations.* Princeton, N.J.: Mathematica Policy Research, Inc. Available online at http://www.mathinc.org.

Dresser, Laura, and Joel Rogers. 1997. *Rebuilding Job Access and Career Advancement Systems in the New Economy.* Briefing Paper. Madison, Wis.: Center on Wisconsin Strategy. Available online at http://www.cows.org.

Fishman, Michael E., Burt S. Barnow, Karen N. Gardiner, Barbara J. Murphy, and Stephanie A. Laud. 1999. *Job Retention and Advancement among Welfare Recipients: Challenges and Opportunities.* Research Synthesis. Washington, D.C.: Lewin Group. Available online at http://www.lewin.com.

Freedman, Stephen. 2000. *Four-Year Impacts of Ten Programs on Employment Stability and Earnings Growth.* Washington, D.C.: U.S. Department of Health and Human Services and U.S. Department of Education. December.

Freedman, Stephen, Daniel Friedlander, Winston Lin, and Amanda Schweder. 1996. *The GAIN Evaluation: Five-Year Impacts on Employment, Earnings and AFDC Receipt.* Working Paper 96.1. New York: Manpower Demonstration Research Corporation.

Freedman, Stephen, Daniel Friedlander, Gayle Hamilton, JoAnn Rock, Marisa Mitchell, Jodi Nudelman, Amanda Schweder, and Laura Storto. 2000. *Evaluating Alternative Welfare-to-Work Approaches: Two-Year Impacts for Eleven Programs.* Washington, D.C.: U.S. Department of Health and Human Services and U.S. Department of Education. June.

Friedlander, Daniel, and Gary Burtless. 1995. *Five Years After: The Long-Term Effects of Welfare-to-Work Programs.* New York: Russell Sage Foundation.

Gladden, Tricia, and Christopher Taber. 2000a. *The Relationship between Wage Growth and Wage Levels.* JCPR Working Paper 173. Chicago: Joint Center for Poverty Research.

———. 2000b. "Wage Progression among Less Skilled Workers." In *Finding Jobs: Work and Welfare Reform,* edited by David Card and Rebecca M. Blank. New York: Russell Sage Foundation.

Greenberg, Mark. 1999. *Beyond Welfare: New Opportunities to Use TANF to Help Low-Income Working Families.* Washington, D.C.: Center for Law and Social Policy. Available online at http://www.clasp.org.

Greenberg, Mark, and Steve Savner. 1999. *The Final TANF Regulations: A Preliminary Analysis.* Washington, D.C.: Center for Law and Social Policy. Available online at http://www.clasp.org.

Greenberg, Mark, Julie Strawn, and Lisa Plimpton. 1999. *State Opportunities to Provide Access to Postsecondary Education under TANF.* Washington, D.C.: Center for Law and Social Policy. Available online at http://www.clasp.org.

Grubb, W. Norton. 1996. *Learning to Work: The Case for Reintegrating Job Training and Education.* New York: Russell Sage Foundation.

———. 1999. "From Isolation to Integration; Occupational Education and the Emerging System of Workforce Development." *Centerpoint* 3. Berkeley, Calif.: National Center for Research in Vocational Education. Available online at http://ncrve.berkeley.edu. March.

Grubb, W. Norton, Norena Badway, Denise Bell, and Marisa Castellano. 1999. *Community Colleges and Welfare Reform: Emerging Practices, Enduring Problems.* Berkeley, Calif.: National Center for Research in Vocational Education.

Gueron, Judith M., and Edward Pauly. 1991. *From Welfare to Work.* New York: Russell Sage Foundation.

Hamilton, Gayle, Thomas Brock, Mary Farrell, Daniel Friedlander, and Kristen Harknett. 1997. *Evaluating Two Welfare-to-Work Program Approaches: Two-Year Findings on the Labor Force Attachment and Human Capital Development Programs in Three Sites.* Washington, D.C.: U.S. Department of Health and Human Services and U.S. Department of Education. Executive Summary available online at http://www.mdrc.org.

Henderson, Anna. 1998. *Making "Welfare-to-Work" Work for the Hard-to-Employ: Strategies from the West Side.* Chicago: Chicago Commons Employment Training Center.

Hershey, Alan M., and LaDonna Pavetti. 1997. "Turning Job Finders into Job Keepers." *The Future of Children: Welfare to Work* 7 (1): 74–86. Available online at http://www.futureofchildren.org.

Horn, Laura, and Andrew G. Malizio. 1998. *Undergraduates Who Work: National Postsecondary Student Aid Study, 1996.* NCES 98-137. Washington, D.C.: National Center for Education Statistics, U.S. Department of Education, Office of Educational Research and Improvement. Available online at http://www.nces.ed.gov/pubsearch.

Isbell, Kellie, John W. Trutko, Burt Barnow, Demetra Nightingale, and Nancy Pindus. 1997. "Involving Employers in Training: Best Practices." Washington, D.C.: U.S. Department of Labor. Available online at http://www.doleta.gov.

Johnson, Clifford M., and Esther Kaggwa. 1998. *Work Study Programs for Welfare Recipients: A Job Creation Strategy That Combines Work and Education.* Washington, D.C.: Center on Budget and Policy Priorities. Available online at http://www.cbpp.org.

Kane, Thomas J., and Cecilia Elena Rouse. 1995. "Labor-Market Returns to Two- and Four-Year College." *American Economic Review* 85 (3): 600–614.

Lane, Julia, Jinping Shi, and David Stevens. 1998. *New Uses of Administrative Records in Welfare-to-Work Policy and Program Management Decisions: Employer Hiring and Retention of Former Welfare Recipients.* Working Paper. Chicago: Joint Center for Poverty Research. Available online at http://www.jcpr.org.

Lazere, Edward. 2000. *Welfare Balances after Three Years of TANF Block Grants: Unspent TANF Funds at the End of Federal Fiscal Year 1999.* Washington, D.C.: Center on Budget and Policy Priorities. Available online at http://www.cbpp.org.

Lidman, Russell M. 1995. *The Family Income Study and Washington's Welfare Population: A Comprehensive Review.* Olympia, Wash.: Washington State Institute for Public Policy. Available online at http://www.wa.gov/wsipp.

Loprest, Pamela. 1999. *Families Who Left Welfare: Who Are They and How Are They Doing?* Discussion Paper 99-02. Washington, D.C.: The Urban Institute. Available online at http:www.newfederalism.urban.org.

Martinson, Karin, and Daniel Friedlander, 1994. *GAIN: Basic Education in a Welfare-to-Work Program.* New York: Manpower Demonstration Research Corporation. Available online at http://www.mdrc.org.

Mikulecky, Larry. 1997. "Too Little Time and Too Many Goals: Suggested Remedies from Research on Workplace Literacy." *Focus on Basics* 1 (D). Cambridge, Mass.: National Center for the Study of Adult Learning and Literacy. Available online at http://gseweb.harvard.edu/~ncsall.

Minnesota Job Skills Partnership. 1999. *Interim Pathways Report.* St. Paul, Minn.: Minnesota Job Skills Partnership.

Moore, Richard W., Daniel R. Blake, and G. Michael Phillips. 1995. *Accounting for Training: An Analysis of the Outcomes of California Employment Training Panel Programs.* Northridge School of Business Administration and Economics, California State University, Northridge, California.

Murnane, Richard J., and Frank Levy. 1996. *Teaching the New Basic Skills.* New York: Free Press.

Murphy, Garrett, and Alice Johnson. 1998. *What Works: Integrating Basic Skills Training into Welfare-to-Work.* Washington, D.C.: National Institute for Literacy. Available online at http://www.nifl.gov.

Olson, Krista, and LaDonna Pavetti. 1996. *Personal and Family Challenges to the Successful Transition from Welfare to Work.* Washington, D.C.: Office of the Assistant Secretary for Planning and Evaluation and Administration for Children and Families, U.S. Department of Health and Human Services.

Orr, Larry L., Howard S. Bloom, Stephen H. Bell, Fred Doolittle, Winston Lin, and George Cave. 1996. *Does Training for the Disadvantaged Work? Evidence from the National JTPA Study.* Washington, D.C.: Urban Institute Press.

Pauly, Edward, with Christina Di Meo. 1995. *The JOBS Evaluation: Adult Education for People on AFDC— A Synthesis of Research.* Washington, D.C.: U.S. Department of Education and U.S. Department of Health and Human Services, Office of Assistant Secretary for Planning and Evaluation.

Pavetti, LaDonna. 1997a. *Against the Odds: Steady Employment among Low-Skilled Women.* Washington, D.C.: Urban Institute Press. Available online at http://www.urban.org.

———. 1997b. *How Much More Can They Work? Setting Realistic Expectations for Welfare Mothers.* Washington, D.C.: Urban Institute Press. Available online at http://www.urban.org.

Pavetti, LaDonna, and Gregory Acs. 1997. *Moving Up, Moving Out, Moving Nowhere? A Study of the Employment Patterns of Young Women and the Implications for Welfare Mothers.* Washington, D.C.: Urban Institute Press. Available online at http://www.urban.org.

Pindus, Nancy, and Kellie Isbell. 1997. *Involving Employers in Training: Literature Review.* Washington, D.C.: U.S. Department of Labor. Available online at http://www.doleta.gov.

Pindus, Nancy, Daryl Dyer, Caroline Ratcliffe, John Trutko, and Kellie Isbell. 1997. *Industry and Cross-Industry Worker Mobility: Experiences, Trends, and Opportunities for Low-Wage Workers in Health Care, Hospitality, and Child Care.* Washington, D.C.: Urban Institute Press. December. Available online at http://www.urban.org.

Plimpton, Lisa, and Mark Greenberg. 1999. *TANF Policies in Nine States: Implications for Microenterprise Initiatives.* Washington, D.C.: Center for Law and Social Policy. December. Available online at http://www.clasp.org.

Plimpton, Lisa, and Demetra Smith Nightingale. 2000. "Welfare Employment Programs: Impacts and Cost-Effectiveness of Employment and Training Activities." In *Improving the Odds: Increasing the Effectiveness of Publicly Funded Training,* edited by Burt S. Barnow and Christopher Tiking. Washington, D.C.: Urban Institute Press.

Rangarajan, Anu, and Tim Novak. 1999. *The Struggle to Sustain Employment: The Effectiveness of the Postemployment Services Demonstration.* MPR Reference No. 8194-620. Princeton, N.J.: Mathematica Policy Research, Inc. Available online at http://www.mathinc.com.

Rangarajan, Anu, Peter Schochet, and Dexter Chu. 1998. *Employment Experiences of Welfare Recipients Who Find Jobs: Is Targeting Possible?* Princeton, N.J.: Mathematica Policy Research, Inc. Available online at http://www.mathinc.com.

Regional Technology Strategies, Inc. 1999. *A Comprehensive Look at State-Funded, Employer-Focused Job Training Programs.* Washington, D.C.: National Governors' Association. Summary available online at http://www.nga.org/workforce/jobtrainingprograms.asp.

Riccio, James, Daniel Friedlander, and Stephen Freedman. 1994. *GAIN: Benefits, Costs, and Three-Year Impacts of a Welfare-to-Work Program.* New York: Manpower Demonstration Research Corporation. Available online at http://www.mdrc.org.

Savner, Steve. 1999. *Key Implementation Decisions Affecting Low-Income Adults Under the Workforce Investment Act.* Washington, D.C.: Center for Law and Social Policy. Available online at http://www.clasp.org.

Scrivener, Susan, Gayle Hamilton, Mary Farrell, Stephen Freedman, Daniel Friedlander, Marisa Mitchell, Jodi Nudelman, and Christine Schwartz. 1998. *The National Evaluation of Welfare-to-Work Strategies: Implementation, Participation Patterns, Costs, and Two-Year Impacts of the Portland (Oregon) Welfare-to-Work Program.* Washington, D.C.: U.S. Department of Health and Human Services and U.S. Department of Education. Executive Summary available online at http://www.mdrc.org.

Shenoy, Pratibha. 1998. *Picture of Health: Best Practices in Training and Employing Chicago's Entry-Level Healthcare Workforce.* Chicago: Chicago Jobs Council.

Simon, Martin. 1997. *Investing Public Resources to Support Incumbent Worker Training.* Issue Brief. Washington, D.C.: National Governors' Association. Available online at http://www.nga.org.

Slaughter, Ellen, Gale Whiteneck, and Edward Baumheier. 1982. *Post Placement Services to WIN Clients: Final Report of a Denver WIN Research Laboratory Project.* New York: Manpower Demonstration Research Corporation.

Stein, Sondra. 2000. *What Adults Need to Know and Be Able to Do in the 21st Century.* Washington, D.C.: National Institute for Literacy.

Strawn, Julie. 1998. *Beyond Job Search or Basic Education: Rethinking the Role of Skills in Welfare Reform.* Washington, D.C.: Center for Law and Social Policy. Available online at http://www.clasp.org.

Strawn, Julie, and Robert Echols. 1999. *Welfare-to-Work Programs: The Critical Role of Skills.* Washington, D.C.: Center for Law and Social Policy.

Strawn, Julie, and Karin Martinson. 2000. *Steady Work and Better Jobs: How to Help Low-Income Parents Sustain Employment and Advance in the Workforce.* New York: Manpower Demonstration Research Corporation. June.

Tweedie, Jack, Dana Reichert, and Sheri Steisel. 1999. *Challenges, Resources, and Flexibility: Using TANF Block Grant and State MOE Dollars.* Washington, D.C.: National Conference of State Legislatures.

Tyler, John H., Richard Murnane, and John B. Willett. 1999. *Do the Cognitive Skills of School Dropouts Matter in the Labor Market?* NBER Working Paper No. W7101. Cambridge, Mass.: National Bureau of Economic Research.

U.S. Department of Health and Human Services, Administration for Children and Families, Office of Family Assistance. 1999. *Helping Families Achieve Self-Sufficiency: A Guide on Funding Services for Children and Families through the TANF Program.* Washington, D.C.: U.S. Department of Health and Human Services. Available online at http://www.acf.dhhs.gov/programs/ofa.

U.S. Department of Labor. 1995. *What's Working (and What's Not).* Washington, D.C.: U.S. Department of Labor. January.

Vartanian, Thomas P., and Philip M. Gleason, 1999. *Income and Job Market Outcomes after Welfare.* Working Paper. Washington, D.C.: Joint Center for Poverty Research.

Washington State Board for Community and Technical Colleges, Education Division. 1999. *Preparing Welfare and Other Low-Income Adults for Work and Better Jobs: A Report on Low-Income Students Enrolled in Colleges and the Start-Up of Work First Programs.* Research Report No. 99-6. Olympia: Washington State Board for Community and Technical Colleges. December.

Zambrowski, Amy, and Anne Gordon. 1993. *Evaluation of the Minority Female Single Parent Demonstration: Fifth-Year Impacts at CET.* Princeton, N.J.: Mathematica Policy Research, Inc. December.

7

Sustained Employment and Earnings Growth

Experimental Evidence on Earnings Supplements and Preemployment Services

Charles Michalopoulos

W e know how to get low-income people to go to work: Build a strong and growing economy filled with jobs; make work pay through generous tax credits and welfare programs that allow working people to keep more of their benefits; and implement programs with employment and training services and time-limited welfare benefits. However, we know little about the types of policies that will help people stay employed and increase their earnings over time.

This chapter seeks to help fill that gap by pulling together recent evidence on how preemployment services and earnings supplements can promote sustained employment and earnings growth. It describes results from 13 programs, all begun since the early 1990s, that share three important characteristics:

- Each program tested a policy designed to help or encourage single-parent welfare recipients to work.
- Each program has enough information to assess whether it promoted sustained employment and growth in hourly wages or quarterly earnings.
- Each program was studied by the Manpower Demonstration Research Corporation (MDRC) using a rigorous, experimental research design that gave reliable information about the effects of new policies.[1] In these studies, people were assigned at random to either a *program group,* which required them to participate in an employment and training program or offered an earnings supplement, or a *control group* that did not.

In other ways, the 13 programs are quite diverse. They operated in a number of places: Atlanta, Georgia; Columbus, Ohio; Detroit, Michigan; Grand Rapids, Michigan;

Portland, Oregon; Riverside, California; seven counties in Minnesota; and the Canadian provinces of British Columbia and New Brunswick. Most were part of state welfare-to-work programs funded under the Job Opportunities and Basic Skills Training (JOBS) program of the Family Support Act of 1988 (FSA). But one was a Canadian federal demonstration to test the effects of supplementing the earnings of long-term welfare recipients, and one began as a test of a change to the now-defunct welfare program, Aid to Families with Dependent Children (AFDC).

Most important, the programs used different methods to help or encourage parents to find work. Two relied solely on supplementing the earnings of people who went to work, 10 used employment and training services such as job search assistance or adult basic education, and one combined earnings supplements with employment and training services.

Because of this diversity, the studies as a group provide useful information on sustained employment and growth in earnings. Their key lessons include the following:

- *Earnings supplements promote sustained employment.* Three programs supplemented the income of people who went to work. Each increased the number who worked, and all three increased the number who stayed employed for a year or longer. This makes sense: By providing families with extra income, the programs provided a reason to keep working and financial resources to weather temporary crises, such as child care or transportation problems.
- *Preemployment services focused on getting people to work quickly can promote sustained employment, but not all programs are equally effective.* To help people find jobs, four programs used preemployment services, such as a job club. Of these, two were more effective at promoting sustained employment. The two less-effective programs emphasized job search and work experience almost exclusively. The two more effective programs used a broader mix of job search and adult basic education. In addition, the most effective program operated in a strong economy, and its staff urged people to wait for "good" jobs that paid more than the minimum wage, were full-time, and offered opportunities for advancement.
- *Programs that emphasize building skills through adult basic education can promote sustained employment, but most programs studied had small effects.* Six programs required people to enroll in adult basic education or vocational training to increase their employability. The programs generally had modest effects on employment overall and sustained employment. However, there is some evidence that requiring all people to enroll in basic or vocational education is as effective at promoting sustained employment as requiring all people to look for work initially. In two sites, programs ran side-by-side, one requiring most people to look for work initially and one enrolling most people initially in adult basic education or vocational training. The two approaches increased the number of people who went work and stayed employed by about the same amount.
- *Sustained full-time work may be the key to increasing hourly wages.* One program supplemented the earnings of people who worked full-time (30 hours or more a week) but did not reward part-time work. Therefore, people who went to work because of

the earnings supplement worked full-time, and many sustained their full-time employment. In this program, wages were more likely to increase for people who were offered the earnings supplement than for people who were not.

- *Preemployment services focused on getting people to work can result in earnings gains over time, but growth in earnings may be more closely linked to sustained employment.* Programs that used preemployment services to encourage immediate work increased the number of people whose earnings increased over time. However, programs that had the largest effects on sustained employment were also the most likely to result in earnings that increased over time.

The story is complex and somewhat speculative. There is no one way to increase retention, earnings, or wages. Earnings supplements appear consistently effective, but employment and training services are also effective in some settings.

DESCRIPTION OF PROGRAMS STUDIED

Of the programs studied here, 10 were evaluated as part of the National Evaluation of Welfare-to-Work Strategies; two were versions of the Minnesota Family Investment Program (MFIP); and the last was Canada's Self-Sufficiency Project (SSP).[2]

Earnings Supplements in Minnesota and Canada

Programs studied in Minnesota and Canada supplemented the earnings of people who went to work. The Minnesota program allowed working welfare recipients to keep more of their welfare benefit than they could under AFDC.[3] For example, a mother of two who worked 20 hours a week and earned $6 an hour received almost $250 a month more in income under the new policy than under AFDC. In addition, the Minnesota program required people who received welfare for 24 or more months over a three-year period to either work or prepare for work through job search or education. To understand the effects of the program's earnings supplement alone, some individuals were assigned to a program (called MFIP Incentives Only) that offered the earnings supplement but did not require participation in employment and training services.

The Canadian program offered a monthly cash payment to single parents who had been on welfare for at least one year and who left welfare for full-time work (30 hours or more a week) within a year of entering the program. While collecting the supplement, a single parent's total income before taxes was about twice her earnings.

Job-Search-First Programs in Atlanta, Grand Rapids, and Riverside[4]

These programs required most participants to look immediately for work, usually through a job club that lasted from one to three weeks. People who completed job search without finding a job were often then enrolled in adult basic education, vocational training, or work experience.

Education-First Programs in Atlanta, Grand Rapids, Riverside, Columbus, and Detroit[5]

These programs required most participants to enroll initially in education and training programs, particularly vocational training for high school graduates and adult basic education for others.

Mix of Job Search and Education in Portland, Oregon

This program required people who were considered ready to work to look for work, but required people who were thought to need more skills to enroll initially in short-term adult basic education or vocational training before looking for work. As in the job-search-first programs, staff in Portland emphasized to clients that the goal of the program was to get a job. Unlike those programs, however, the Portland program encouraged participants to wait until they found "good" jobs that paid more than the minimum wage, were full-time, and offered opportunities for advancement.

EVIDENCE ON SUSTAINED EMPLOYMENT

Lesson 1: Earnings supplements promote sustained employment.

The Canadian SSP and Minnesota MFIP Incentives Only programs did nothing but supplement earnings. Minnesota allowed welfare recipients to keep more of their welfare benefits when they went to work, and Canada provided them with a supplement outside the welfare system, if they left welfare to work full-time. The full MFIP program combined an earnings supplement with mandatory services designed to help people move into work. All three programs increased employment, and all three also increased sustained employment.

Evidence on the effects of earnings supplements is presented in table 7.1. As in all the tables here, results are based on *experimental comparisons*. That is, this study compared average outcomes for the entire program group with average outcomes for the entire control group. Consequently, when the table refers to the proportion of people who did something, it refers to the proportion of *all* people who were assigned to a program group or a control group; it does not refer merely to the people who ever worked.

The first three rows of table 7.1 show the effects of the Canadian program on full-time employment and on *sustained* full-time employment.[6] As the first row indicates, 42.5 percent of the program group worked full-time early enough in the follow-up period that we could determine whether they stayed employed for a year or longer. During the same period, only 27.3 percent of the control group worked full-time. The difference indicates the effect of the program. In this case, the Canadian program increased the proportion of people who ever worked full-time by 15.2 percentage points, a 55.6 percent improvement over what the control group did without the supplement offer.

People who ever worked full-time can be divided into two groups: those who stopped working full-time quickly and those who did not. The next two rows of

TABLE 7.1 Effects of Programs with Earnings Supplements on Sustained Employment[7]

Employment Outcome	Program Group (%)	Control Group (%)	Effect (Difference)	Change (%)
Canadian SSP				
Ever worked full-time	42.5	27.3	15.2***	55.6
Left full-time work quickly	21.6	17.0	4.6***	27.4
Stayed employed full-time for a year or more	20.9	10.4	10.6***	101.8
Minnesota MFIP Incentives Only				
Ever worked	44.4	39.2	5.2	13.3
Left work quickly	12.2	13.5	−1.3	−9.6
Stayed employed for a year or more	32.2	25.7	6.5***	25.3
Minnesota Full MFIP				
Ever worked	50.5	39.2	11.4***	29.1
Left work quickly	16.3	13.5	2.8	20.7
Stayed employed for a year or more	34.2	25.6	8.6**	33.6

Source: Calculations from 18-month and 36-month follow-up survey data in SSP and 36-month follow-up survey data in MFIP.
Note: Statistical significance levels are indicated as: * = 10 percent; ** = 5 percent; *** = 1 percent.

table 7.1 report composite outcomes for: (1) the proportion of the program and control groups that found full-time jobs but stayed employed full-time for *less than* a year, and (2) the proportion that found full-time jobs and stayed employed full-time for *a year or more.*

How should these measures be interpreted? At one extreme, all people encouraged by the Canadian program to work full-time might have stopped working quickly (after less than a year). In that case, the program's effect on the proportion who worked full-time for a year or more would be zero, and its effect on the proportion who worked full-time for less than a year would be as large as its effect on full-time employment overall (15.2 percentage points).

At the other extreme, all people encouraged by the Canadian program to work full-time might have done so for a year or more. In that case, the effect on full-time employment that lasted a year or more would be the same as its effect on full-time employment (15.2 percentage points), and the effect on full-time employment that lasted less than a year would be zero.

Neither extreme occurred. Most, but not all, of the initial full-time employment generated in the Canadian program lasted at least a year. In particular, more than twice as many people in the program group as in the control group found full-time jobs and stayed employed full-time for a year or longer—20.9 percent compared with 10.4 percent.

Table 7.1 shows similar results for people who were offered Minnesota's earnings supplement but not required to participate in its employment services.[8] While 39.2 percent of the control group worked at some point, 44.4 percent of the program group did, an increase of 5.2 percentage points. Like the Canadian program, Minnesota's earnings supplement primarily increased sustained employment: The earnings supplement increased employment of a year or more by 6.5 percentage points, even more than it increased employment overall.

Finally, table 7.1 shows similar results for people who were both offered the Minnesota program's enhanced earnings disregard and required to participate in its employment services. Combining the two policies appears to be somewhat more effective than offering the earnings supplement alone. The full Minnesota program increased employment overall by more than 10 percentage points and increased sustained employment by nearly 10 percentage points.

The three programs that tried to make work pay produced consistent results. All three increased employment, and all three increased sustained employment much more than they increased temporary employment. Earnings supplements in Minnesota and the Canadian program were available every month, giving people a reason to keep their jobs or find new ones when they lost work, and also giving them financial resources to weather crises such as problems with child care or transportation.

Lesson 2: Preemployment services focused on getting people to work quickly can promote sustained employment, but not all programs are equally effective.

Table 7.2 shows results on sustained employment for four "employment-focused" programs that required people to participate in preemployment services designed to help them go to work quickly. As noted, the job-search-first programs in Atlanta, Grand Rapids, and Riverside required almost all participants to enroll initially in job search, most commonly in job clubs lasting from one to three weeks. In Portland, only people considered job ready had to look for work, while those considered most in need of basic skills could enroll in adult basic education or vocational training.

The four employment-focused programs had quite varied results, both in terms of how much they encouraged people to find work and how much they increased sustained employment. The most successful program at increasing employment overall was Riverside, which increased employment by 10.6 percentage points. At the other extreme, Atlanta's program increased employment by only 3.5 percentage points.

The programs also differed substantially in whether they led to sustained employment. In Portland and Atlanta, the increase in sustained employment was as big as or bigger than the increase in employment overall. For example, Portland increased employment overall by 7.0 percentage points and increased sustained employment by 6.7 percentage points. Atlanta increased sustained employment by 5.9 percentage points even though it increased employment overall by only 3.5 percentage points. In contrast, Grand Rapids and Riverside increased primarily short-term employment.

It is not clear why the programs had such different effects on sustained employment. Three possible explanations are the mix of education and job search used in the different programs, attitudes of staff about the effectiveness of the job-search-first approach, and economic conditions.

Atlanta and Portland used a broader mix of job search and adult basic education than Riverside and Grand Rapids. In Portland, this mix was an explicit part of the program. Although Atlanta required nearly everyone initially to look for work, it made

TABLE 7.2 Effects of Employment-Focused, Welfare-to-Work Programs on Sustained Employment

Employment Outcome	Program Group (%)	Control Group (%)	Difference (Effect)	Change (%)
Job-search-first				
Atlanta				
Ever worked	74.6	71.1	3.5**	4.9
Left work quickly	36.8	39.3	−2.5	−6.3
Stayed employed for a year or more	37.8	31.9	5.9***	18.6
Grand Rapids				
Ever worked	85.1	79.6	5.5***	6.9
Left work quickly	51.3	47.8	3.4*	7.1
Stayed employed for a year or more	33.9	31.8	2.1	6.6
Riverside				
Ever worked	66.6	55.9	10.6***	19.0
Left work quickly	35.4	28.7	6.7***	23.3
Stayed employed for a year or more	31.1	27.2	4.0***	14.6
Mix of job search and education (Portland)				
Ever worked	80.1	73.4	7.0***	9.5
Left work quickly	37.6	37.4	0.3	0.8
Stayed employed for a year or more	42.7	36.0	6.7***	18.5

Source: Calculations from employment reported to state unemployment insurance systems.
Note: Statistical significance levels are indicated as: * = 10 percent; ** = 5 percent; *** = 1 percent.

substantial use of adult basic education for people who looked for work without finding it. In contrast, Riverside required many people who failed to find work to continue looking, and Grand Rapids placed much of this group into unpaid work experiences. This does not imply that relying primarily on adult basic education is a key to sustained employment, but rather that the mix of job search and adult basic education may be important. This, perhaps, because programs that use both job search and education can target each strategy at people who would benefit from them.

Atlanta and Portland also differed from Riverside in the services that case managers thought would best help welfare recipients move to work. In both the Portland and Atlanta programs, twice as many staff preferred human capital development to quick job entry as a strategy for moving clients to work. In Riverside's program, in contrast, nearly all case managers preferred labor force attachment to human capital development.

The state of the local economy is a third possible explanation for the larger increases in sustained employment in Atlanta and Portland. Between 1993 and 1998, employment grew in all four sites, but Riverside's unemployment rate was the highest by far, particularly in the early part of the program. When Riverside moved people to work quickly, it was in a poor economy that might have provided short-term, temporary, or undesirable jobs. The economy was strong in Grand Rapids, suggesting that more than a favorable economic environment is needed to ensure that employment services will generate increases in sustained employment.

The fact that the Riverside program increased short-term employment more than it increased sustained employment should not necessarily be viewed as negative. The primary goal was to help people go to work, and Riverside was the most effective of the four employment-focused programs in accomplishing it. However, it does suggest that a program that tries to get people to work as quickly as possible may need other features, such as postemployment services, to help them stay at work and advance.

Lesson 3: Programs that encourage most people to build skills through adult basic education or vocational training can also increase retention, but most of these programs had small effects.

Another major approach to encouraging welfare recipients is by increasing their skills, thereby increasing their attractiveness to employers and their ability to earn a living wage. Table 7.3 presents results on sustained employment for six programs that required most people initially to enroll in adult basic education or vocational training. Overall, these programs did not promote much sustained employment. Nevertheless, focusing on basic education appears to be as effective as focusing on job search in encouraging sustained employment.

In general, these education-focused programs had fairly small effects on employment, ranging from 2.7 percentage points in the Columbus Traditional program to 6.5 percentage points in Riverside. They also had fairly small effects on sustained employment. Only Atlanta and the Columbus Integrated program significantly increased the number of people who went to work and stayed there for a year or longer.

It would be a mistake to conclude that adult basic education is less effective than job search at promoting sustained employment, because most of the education-focused programs operated in different sites with different people from the employment-focused programs shown in table 7.2. Fortunately, results from Atlanta and Grand Rapids present a rare opportunity to compare the job search and adult basic education approaches. Both sites randomly assigned people to the job-search-first programs shown in table 7.2 and the education-first programs shown in table 7.3.[9] As a result, any differences in the effects of the two programs can reliably be attributed to differences in the programs. While there were a number of differences in implementing the two types of programs, the primary difference was in the self-sufficiency approach: The job-search-first programs asked most people to look for work initially; the education-first programs asked most people to enroll in adult basic education or vocational training.

When results for the Atlanta and Grand Rapids job-search-first programs in table 7.2 are compared with the education-first programs in table 7.3, the two approaches appear equally effective (or ineffective) at encouraging sustained employment. The Atlanta job-search-first program increased sustained employment by 5.9 percentage points, but the Atlanta education-first program increased sustained employment by 5.5 percentage points. Likewise in Grand Rapids, neither program significantly increased sustained employment. Thus, something about the site—for example, the state of the economy, the people enrolled in the programs, or other local policies—appears to be more

TABLE 7.3 Effects of Education-First, Welfare-to-Work Programs on Sustained Employment

Employment Outcome	Program Group (%)	Control Group (%)	Difference (Effect)	Change (%)
Atlanta				
Ever worked	74.2	71.1	3.0**	4.3
Left work quickly	36.8	39.3	−2.5	−6.3
Stayed employed for a year or more	37.4	31.9	5.5***	17.3
Grand Rapids				
Ever worked	82.9	79.6	3.3**	4.1
Left work quickly	49.0	47.8	1.2	2.4
Stayed employed for a year or more	33.9	31.8	2.1	6.6
Riverside				
Ever worked	55.7	49.2	6.5***	13.2
Left work quickly	31.7	27.6	4.2**	15.1
Stayed employed for a year or more	24.0	21.7	2.3	10.7
Columbus Integrated				
Ever worked	81.8	78.2	3.6***	4.6
Left work quickly	38.1	38.3	−0.1	−0.3
Stayed employed for a year or more	43.6	39.9	3.7**	9.3
Columbus Traditional				
Ever worked	80.8	78.2	2.7**	3.4
Left work quickly	38.7	38.3	0.4	1.1
Stayed employed for a year or more	42.2	39.9	2.2	5.6
Detroit				
Ever worked	75.8	72.4	3.4**	4.7
Left work quickly	46.6	45.3	1.3	2.9
Stayed employed for a year or more	29.1	27.1	2.1	7.6

Source: Calculations from employment reported to state unemployment insurance systems.

Note: Statistical significance levels are indicated as: * = 10 percent; ** = 5 percent; *** = 1 percent.

responsible than the self-sufficiency approach for increases in sustained employment in these programs.

EVIDENCE ON GROWTH IN HOURLY WAGES AND QUARTERLY EARNINGS

Prior evidence has not made it clear that low-skilled workers earn higher hourly wages over time. In looking at five years of information for a group of women who had left welfare, Maria Cancian and colleagues at the University of Wisconsin-Madison (Cancian et al. 1999) found that average hourly wages gradually increased. In the year after leaving welfare, the median worker earned $6.36 an hour. Four years later, the median person earned $6.73 an hour. Although hourly wages increased on average, the increase was quite slow: about 1 percent a year.

Cancian and colleagues found more promising news about annual earnings. In the year after leaving welfare, the average person in the sample earned $7,668. By the fifth year after leaving welfare, she earned $10,942 on average, an increase of more than 40 percent over four years. Even among people who earned the least, earnings increased about 60 percent over four years, although this group continued to earn very little. Since hourly wages rose very slowly, the large earnings increases mean that people were working more hours or working more often over time.

Two recent studies provide more hope that welfare recipients can increase their hourly wages. The key may be steady, full-time work. Tricia Gladden and Christopher Taber (1999) suggest that wages increase as much for low-skilled workers as for high-skilled workers when they increase their work experience by similar amounts. Because high-skills workers typically work full-time all the time, this suggests that low-skills workers would also see substantial increases in their wages if they could work full-time all the time. Mary Corcoran and Susanna Loeb (1999) found that former welfare recipients who worked full-time had substantially higher wage growth than those who worked part-time.

Although these findings are interesting, they are not based on rigorous, random assignment evaluations. There is evidence, though, on how the Canadian SSP program affected growth in hourly wages and how the programs with mandatory employment services affected growth in quarterly earnings. Growing wages and earnings may indicate advancement in careers, even if indirectly.

Lesson 4: Full-time work may be the key to increasing hourly wages over time.

Of the studies summarized here, only the Canadian study, which encouraged a substantial number of people to work full-time and stay there, collected information on hourly wages over time. Table 7.4 indicates that the program also resulted in growing hourly wages for a substantial number of people.[10]

The first row indicates that hourly wages decreased for 5.7 percent of the control group and 6.7 percent of the program group between the end of the first year after random assignment until the end of the third year. In other words, few people had wages

TABLE 7.4 Effects of Canada's Self-Sufficiency Project on Wage Growth between End of Year 1 and End of Year 3 after Random Assignment

Employment Outcome	Program Group (%)	Control Group (%)	Difference (Effect)	Change (%)
Employed and hourly wage decreased	6.7	5.7	1.1	19.3
Employed and hourly wage increased	21.0	13.4	7.6***	56.5

Source: Calculations from 18- and 36-month follow-up survey data in SSP.
Note: Statistical significance levels are indicated as: * = 10 percent; ** = 5 percent; *** = 1 percent.

that decreased over time, and there was little difference between the two groups, even though the program had a substantial overall effect on employment.

This suggests that the program's main effect was to encourage people to take jobs in which their wages increased. This is confirmed in the next row. While 13.4 percent of the control group took jobs in which their wages increased, 21.0 percent of the program group did. Thus, the Canadian program increased the number of people in jobs with growing wages by more than half.

Results from the Canadian program are more encouraging than results described by Cancian et al. (1999), but are consistent with the findings of Gladden and Taber (1999) and Corcoran and Loeb (1999) that working full-time and working regularly may be keys to growing wages. This makes sense. A full-time worker spends more time gaining valuable skills through on-the-job training than a part-time worker, perhaps because employers are more willing to invest in full-time workers. Likewise, someone who is working in most months can gain on-the-job skills faster than someone who works sporadically; someone who is in and out of work may lose skills while looking for new employment.

Lesson 5: Preemployment services focused on getting people to work quickly can result in earnings gains over time, but growth in earnings may be linked to sustained employment.[11]

Table 7.5 shows the impact of the four employment-focused programs (Portland and the job-search-first programs in Atlanta, Grand Rapids, and Riverside) on quarterly earnings.[12] Each of the programs caused more people to experience earnings growth. However, variation across the programs in their ability to increase people's

TABLE 7.5 Effects of Programs with Employment Services on Earnings Growth over Four Years

Employment Outcome	Program Group (%)	Control Group (%)	Difference (Effect)	Change (%)
Job-search-first				
Atlanta				
Employed and earnings did not increase	32.9	31.6	1.2**	3.8
Employed and earnings increased	32.0	28.3	3.7**	13.1
Grand Rapids				
Employed and earnings did not increase	39.3	35.2	4.2**	11.9
Employed and earnings increased	38.0	34.2	3.8**	11.1
Riverside				
Employed and earnings did not increase	35.0	25.1	9.9***	39.4
Employed and earnings increased	24.4	20.0	4.4***	22.0
Mix of job search and education (Portland)				
Employed and earnings did not increase	33.5	30.1	3.3***	11.0
Employed and earnings increased	36.9	30.1	6.8***	22.6

Source: Calculations from state unemployment insurance systems.

Note: Statistical significance levels are indicated as: * = 10 percent; ** = 5 percent; *** = 1 percent.

earnings was similar to variation in their ability to promote sustained employment. This may suggest that the two outcomes are linked.

The first two rows show the impact of the Atlanta job-search-first program on people's earnings over time: 32.9 percent of the program group worked at some point but did not have their earnings increase over time. This group is actually composed of three smaller groups. Some people went to work and had their earnings decrease over time, some went to work and had constant earnings, and some worked too sporadically to determine reliably whether their earnings increased or decreased. During the same period, only 31.7 percent of the control group worked but did not have their earnings increase. The difference in outcomes between the two research groups indicates that the Atlanta program had little effect on the proportion of people who went to work and then did not have their earnings increase.

The second row indicates that the Atlanta job-search-first program increased the number of people with earnings that grew over time. While 32.0 percent of the program group worked and had their earnings increase, 28.3 percent of the control group worked and had their earnings increase.

Each of the other three programs also increased the number of people with growing earnings. Like Atlanta, the job-search-first programs in Grand Rapids and Riverside increased the proportion of the sample that went to work and had increased earnings by about 4 percentage points. The Portland program had an even larger effect on the number of people with increasing earnings.

The results on earnings growth are similar to results on sustained employment. The job-search-first programs in both Grand Rapids and Riverside increased sustained employment less than they increased short-term employment, and they increased the number of people with increasing earnings less than the number of people with stagnant or falling earnings. On the other hand, the programs in Portland and Atlanta both promoted sustained employment and increased the number of people with earnings that increased over time. These results may provide further evidence that sustained employment is important in helping people increase their earnings over time. Alternatively, some factors in Portland and Atlanta—such as use of both adult basic education and job search, an education-friendly staff, and strong economies—may have simultaneously promoted sustained employment and growing earnings.

THE IMPLICATIONS FOR PUBLIC POLICY

These studies provide information on policies that promote sustained employment, but they are not perfect. First, the programs included only welfare recipients and, therefore, cannot indicate how certain strategies would affect a broader group of low-skill workers. Second, their primary objectives were to get people to go to work; none of the programs used postemployment strategies to help people stay employed or advance.[13] Third, they did not collect information on the types of jobs people held, so they cannot directly tell us whether people who went to work because of these programs advanced in their jobs. In addition, only one of the studies has information on hourly wages over time, so that little can be said about these programs' effects on growth in hourly wages. Finally, researchers studying the programs used a short-term measure of sustained employment; it is impossible to know at this time whether the programs will help people stay employed for long periods of time.

Despite these drawbacks, patterns across the programs point to some possible recommendations about using preemployment programs to promote sustained employment and wage or earnings growth.

Offer and Market Earnings Supplements

Most of us work for pay. It makes sense, then, that making work pay for low-income families through earnings supplements, welfare earnings disregards, or earned income tax credits would encourage people to stay employed. In addition to providing incentives, these incentives also provide extra income that might help low-income families weather short-term crises (e.g., car problems) that might otherwise keep them from working. Are earnings supplements a credible option today? Not only are they credible, they are available to all working poor families through the federal earned income tax credit. A number of states have similar credits. In addition, more than 40 states allow working welfare recipients to keep more of their welfare benefits than they did prior to welfare reform. Even if new earnings supplements cannot be offered, it is important to make sure that low-wage workers know about and use the ones they can receive.

Encourage Full-Time Work

There is growing evidence that full-time work is a key to both employment retention and advancement. There may be a number of reasons for this. Employers are less likely to hire a full-time worker to fill temporary needs. Full-time work is more likely than part-time work to come with health insurance and other fringe benefits that provide an additional incentive to continue working. Full-time, steady work provides people with more work experience that can be marketed to future employers.

Of course, full-time work has potential drawbacks. Some parents with low skills might not be able to find full-time work, thus limiting the number of families who benefit from programs that help only full-time workers. Full-time work will increase the need for child care, possibly cutting into take-home pay and possibly affecting children's psychological and social development. In the New Hope project—a program that offered an array of earnings supplements, medical insurance, and child care subsidies to low-income parents who worked 30 hours or more a week—there was no evidence that children were hurt when their parents went to work; there was evidence that some children benefited (Bos et al. 1999). Likewise, in the Canadian Self-Sufficiency Project, elementary school–age children appear to have benefited from their families' increased income even though an earnings supplement encouraged many parents to begin working full-time (Morris and Michalopoulos 2000). Nevertheless, programs that encourage full-time work may also need to invest more in child care, either by increasing child care subsidies or developing after-school programs.

Job Search Alone Is Not Enough

Requiring people to look for work and helping them look are effective in getting them to work. Keeping them at work requires more, however. Of the job search programs described here, one combined job search with earnings supplements, two allowed many people to build basic skills through adult basic education or vocational training, and one encouraged people to wait for jobs that have fringe benefits or pay more than the minimum wage. Because job search can be so effective in getting people to work, combining job search with postemployment services or education may also be a good way to encourage retention and advancement. It is still not clear what types of services would achieve this goal.

Basic Education Alone Is Not Enough

Requiring all people to enroll in adult basic education or vocational training is no more effective at promoting sustained employment than requiring all people to look for work. Again, a broad mix of the two approaches may be most effective. This is not to say that education more generally will not promote retention and advancement. None of the programs used long-term education or community college, for example, as ways to build skills that might help people get better jobs. These strategies remain possibilities that should be examined in the future.

More Is Needed

Although some strategies discussed here appear to promote sustained employment and wage growth, many people never work, and many who do cannot sustain their employment. In other words, the strategies have been effective to a point, but much more is needed. Many states and localities have begun to address such problems as substance abuse, domestic violence, and depression. Many programs are also trying postemployment services to give people advice on how to get promoted, help them identify educational opportunities that might help them advance, and so on. At this time, there is no credible information on how much these approaches help. Fortunately, the U.S. Department of Health and Human Services recently launched the Employment Retention and Advancement initiative to use random assignment evaluations to test the effectiveness of a variety of approaches. In several years, much better information will be available on what works to promote retention and advancement.

NOTES

Results for this chapter came from the National Evaluation of Welfare-to-Work Strategies (NEWWS), the Self-Sufficiency Project (SSP), and the Minnesota Family Investment Program (MFIP). I wish to thank the U.S. Department of Health and Human Services for permission to use results from the NEWWS evaluation, the Minnesota Department of Human Services for permission to use results from the MFIP evaluation, and the Social Research and Demonstration Corporation for permission to use results from SSP. I also wish to thank Stephen Freedman for thoughtful research on sustained employment and earnings growth in NEWWS and Cynthia Miller and the MFIP team at MDRC for work on sustained employment in MFIP.

1. A number of other studies have done research on sustained employment and earnings growth, but have not used the rigorous, random-assignment method. For a summary of this research, see the MDRC how-to guide on sustained employment (Strawn and Martinson 2000) or chapter 6 in this volume.

2. For more details on data sources and the way that sustained employment and earnings growth were defined, contact the author. Results described here come from three recent or forthcoming reports: Michalopoulos et al. (2000) on the Canadian program, Miller et al. (2000) on the programs in Minnesota, and Freedman (2000) on programs in Atlanta, Columbus, Detroit, Grand Rapids, Riverside, and Portland.

3. MFIP is also the name of the Minnesota welfare program implemented statewide in response to the federal welfare reform of 1996. The statewide program is a substantially modified version of the pilot MFIP program described here; it has time limits on receipt of welfare, a less-generous earnings supplement, more stringent requirements for participating in employment and training services, and a greater emphasis on job search.

4. The Riverside programs discussed here are not the Riverside GAIN program studied by MDRC beginning in 1988. That program had some of the largest effects on employment seen in a random-assignment evaluation of a welfare-to-work program. Like the program in Portland discussed below, Riverside GAIN emphasized employment but allowed people in need of basic education to enroll in adult basic education before looking for work. Results on sustained employment were not calculated for the Riverside GAIN program and are, therefore, not presented here. The program and its results are described in Riccio, Friedlander, and Freedman (1994).

5. Oklahoma City also ran an education-first program that was studied in NEWWS. However, too little follow-up information was collected to show its effects on sustained employment or earnings growth.

6. Researchers of the Canadian program looked only at sustained full-time employment because full-time employment was the goal of the program. Because some people in the Canadian program were employed part-time but never worked full-time, employment rates or the Canadian program are somewhat lower than in the other studies discussed here.

7. In each table, two-tailed t-tests were applied to differences between the outcomes for the program and control groups.

8. Results for the Minnesota program are limited to long-term welfare recipients in urban counties, because this is the only group for which sustained employment was calculated by the program's evaluators.

9. In each site, the education-first program was also called a "human capital development" or HCD program, and the job-search-first program was also called a "labor force attachment" or LFA program. Riverside also ran programs of both types. Only people in need of basic education were assigned to Riverside's education-first program, however. Because results are not available for members of the job-search-first program group in need of basic education, results for the two programs cannot be directly compared.

10. Wage growth can be meaningfully measured only for people working at the beginning and end of a fairly long period of time. In the Canadian study, wage growth was calculated only for people who were working at the end of the first year and at the end of the third year after entering the evaluation. Note that wage growth could not be calculated for most people using these criteria.

11. Evidence on earnings growth is also available for the education-focused programs discussed earlier. Only one of the six programs significantly increased the number of people with growing earnings, so results are not shown in this paper. Results on wage growth and earnings growth are not available for the Minnesota programs.

12. Hourly wages were not available over time in these studies. Results therefore indicate growth in quarterly earnings rather than hourly wages.

13. To learn more about experimental evaluations of postemployment services, see the reports on the Postemployment Services Demonstration or PESD (Rangarajan and Novak 1999) and the Self-Sufficiency Project Plus (Quets et al. 1999), two projects that used postemployment services to try to increase employment among ex-welfare recipients but that failed to do so. Results on sustained employment and wage or earnings growth were not available for these two evaluations, so they are not discussed in this chapter. In this volume, Rangarajan (chapter 5) describes lessons culled from PESD on advancement and retention.

REFERENCES

Bos, Hans, Aletha Huston, Robert Granger, Greg Duncan, Tom Brock, and Vonnie McLoyd. 1999. *New Hope for People with Low Incomes: Two-Year Results of a Program to Reduce Poverty and Reform Welfare.* New York: Manpower Demonstration Research Corporation.

Cancian, Maria, Robert Haveman, Thomas Kaplan, Daniel Meyer, and Barbara Wolfe. 1999. "Work, Earnings, and Well-Being after Welfare: What Do We Know?" *Focus* 20 (2): 22–25.

Corcoran, Mary, and Susanna Loeb. 1999. "Will Wages Grow with Experience for Welfare Mothers?" *Focus* 20 (2): 20–21.

Freedman, Stephen. 2000. *National Evaluation of Welfare-to-Work Strategies: Four-Year Impacts of Ten Programs on Employment Stability and Earnings Growth.* Washington, D.C.: U.S. Department of Health and Human Services, Office of the Assistant Secretary for Planning and Evaluation and Administration for Children and Families, and U.S. Department of Education. Prepared by Manpower Demonstration Research Corporation.

Gladden, Tricia, and Christopher Taber. 1999. "Wage Progression among Less-Skilled Workers." Working Paper 72. Chicago: Joint Center for Poverty Research.

Michalopoulos, Charles, David Card, Lisa A. Gennetian, Kristen Harknett, and Philip K. Robins. 2000. *The Self-Sufficiency Project at 36 Months: Effects of a Financial Work Incentive on Employment and Income.* Ottawa: Social Research and Demonstration Corporation.

Miller, Cynthia, Virginia Knox, Lisa A. Gennetian, Martey Dodoo, Jo Anna Hunter, and Cindy Redcross. 2000. *MFIP Adult Report: The Minnesota Family Investment Program.* New York: Manpower Demonstration Research Corporation.

Morris, Pamela, and Charles Michalopoulos. 2000. *The Self-Sufficiency Project at 36 Months: Effects on Children of a Program That Increased Parental Employment and Income.* Ottawa: Social Research and Demonstration Corporation.

Quets, Gail, Philip K. Robins, Elsie C. Pan, Charles Michalopoulos, and David Card. 1999. *Does SSP Plus Increase Employment? The Effect of Adding Services to the Self-Sufficiency Project's Financial Incentives.* Ottawa: Social Research and Demonstration Corporation.

Rangarajan, Anu, and Tim Novak. 1999. *The Struggle to Sustain Employment: The Effectiveness of the Postemployment Services Demonstration.* Princeton, N.J.: Mathematica Policy Research.

Strawn, Julie, and Karin Martinson. 2000. *Steady Work and Better Jobs: How to Help Low-Income Parents Sustain Employment and Advance in the Workforce.* New York: Manpower Demonstration Research Corporation.

8

Achieving Economic Self-Sufficiency through Asset Building

Opportunities for Low-Income Workers

Colleen Dailey and Ray Boshara

Individual asset building is gaining recognition as a promising approach to alleviating poverty and promoting self-sufficiency for the millions of working poor Americans. Based on the theory that increased income alone is unlikely to move individuals and families permanently out of poverty, asset-building strategies promote and reward savings and empower individuals to make economic choices that provide long-term benefits for themselves, their families, and their communities. While not targeted exclusively to the working poor, asset-building initiatives now being implemented appear particularly promising for helping low-income workers develop financial skills and participate more fully in the nation's economy as savers, producers, and entrepreneurs.

This chapter reviews asset-building strategies for the poor, based on research and policy work conducted by the Corporation for Enterprise Development (CFED) and by the Center for Social Development (CSD) at Washington University as of May 2000. It discusses asset development theory, summarizes what community-level initiatives are demonstrating about the impact of asset building on the lives of the working poor, and offers policy recommendations for creating a universal, asset-building system that will reduce inequality and help all Americans achieve economic self-sufficiency.

THE EMERGENCE OF ASSET DEVELOPMENT AS SOCIAL POLICY

For the past six decades, America's public and private sectors have spent billions of dollars on the poor in the form of income support and safety net programs. While preventing the vast majority of poor families from falling through the bottom, the prevailing New Deal framework has rarely led to investments that enable or encourage the poor to build wealth or participate in the economy in any way other than as recipients of its excesses. To the contrary, income-based policy often discourages, and in some cases prohibits, asset accumulation.

Asset development for the poor began to emerge as an alternative to New Deal strategies in the early 1990s. In *Assets and the Poor,* Michael Sherraden (1991) made a strong case for asset development as the "missing piece" in antipoverty initiatives. Prior to that, a handful of social policy researchers had focused on asset distribution and its contribution to increasing inequality, but the issue had not gained currency as an antipoverty strategy.[1] Although many American politicians expressed concern over the growing concentration of wealth, the notion of addressing the wealth gap through asset development rarely entered policy discussions.

In recent years, sociologists, economists, and politicians have begun to pay more attention. For example, a number of research studies have documented the positive impacts of asset ownership on individuals, families, and communities. These impacts include (Boshara et al. 1998):

- Promoting greater household stability;
- Improving self-esteem;
- Increasing knowledge and experience in money management;
- Fostering long-term thinking and planning;
- Providing a foundation for risk taking;
- Increasing social status and social connectedness;
- Increasing community involvement and civic participation; and
- Enhancing children's well-being and educational prospects.

Other studies have pointed out that asset-building policies to support home ownership, retirement savings, and investment have benefited nonpoor Americans tremendously, while hardly benefiting the poor at all. For example, in 1999, 71 percent of the $53.4 billion in mortgage interest deductions on federal taxes went to households with annual incomes greater than $75,000 (U.S. Congress 1999); in 1998, 91 percent of the $47 billion in expenditures went to households with incomes greater than $50,000 (Sherraden 1998). Tax expenditures for retirement are also highly regressive: In 1998, 67 percent of retirement benefits went to households with annual incomes greater than $100,000, and 93 percent went to households earning more than $50,000.[2]

Recognition of, and discomfort with, this gross inequality has led to two types of strategies to extend comparable asset-building policies to the poor. The first aims to initiate asset accumulation at birth; the second tackles the more politically challenging task of bringing the poor and disadvantaged into the economic mainstream.

Consistent with growing political support for improving the lives of children, proposals to institute universal asset accounts at birth have been more common. For example, Robert Haveman (1998) has proposed $10,000 "human capital accounts" granted at age 18; Richard Freeman (1999) favors "starting gate" wealth endowments funded at birth; and Bruce Ackerman and Anne Alstott (1999) introduced a proposal to create $80,000 "stakeholder" accounts for all Americans. In the political arena, legislative proposals for children's asset accounts have come from both the right and left.

Senators Lieberman (D-CT) and Kerrey (D-NE) introduced the first major piece of legislation, KIDSAVE, in 1995; Representative Amo Houghton (R-NY) introduced a more comprehensive proposal, the Children's Financial Security Act, in 1997 (Curley and Sherraden 1998).

Despite their political appeal, these proposals to benefit children have made little progress. Shifting the focus away from future generations and toward the poor of today requires a different strategy—one that takes into account the many obstacles that currently come between the poor and saving. In *Assets and the Poor,* Sherraden proposed the idea of Individual Development Accounts (IDAs) as an innovative private-public strategy to bring low-income individuals and families into the economic mainstream. These accounts were conceived as optional, interest-bearing, tax-benefited savings accounts, similar to Individual Retirement Accounts (IRAs), and restricted to designated purposes, such as home ownership, small business development, and postsecondary education or training. Although available to all Americans, these accounts would be subsidized for the poor and designed to attract creative financing through the private sector.

No longer an untested concept, IDAs are now available in at least 250 communities throughout the United States, and upwards of 5,000 low-income individuals are saving in IDAs for long-term asset goals (primarily home ownership, microenterprise development, and postsecondary education and training). Since 1996, 28 states have included IDAs in their Temporary Assistance for Needy Families (TANF) plans, and 27 have passed some form of IDA legislation. At the federal level, the Assets for Independence Act of 1998 established a five-year, national IDA demonstration that is expected to reach an additional 30,000 to 40,000 working poor by 2003. In 1999, IDAs were included in the Senate-passed tax bills, which proposed nearly $1 billion in federal tax credits to encourage financial institutions to match IDAs. This legislation was expanded and reintroduced in 2000 by Senators Lieberman (D-CT), Santorum (R-PA), and others under the Savings for Working Families Act of 2000 (S. 2023), a proposal to make IDAs available to all U.S. citizens or legal residents age 18 or older and living at or below 80 percent of area median income. A companion bill, H.R. 4106, was introduced by Representatives Joseph Pitts (R-PA), Charles Stenholm (D-TX), and others. In addition, the Clinton administration registered support for IDAs and asset-building strategies in its proposals for Universal Savings Accounts, First Accounts, and Retirement Savings Accounts (Boshara 2000). Most recently, as a presidential candidate, George W. Bush registered support for asset building by proposing $1 billion in IDA tax credits as part of his "New Prosperity Initiative."

With an explicit focus on helping poor individuals and families achieve self-sufficiency, IDAs are a policy tool whose time has come. Politicians on both the right and left are affirming this, and the building momentum could lead to substantial improvements in the lives of millions of working poor Americans and their families.

INDIVIDUAL ASSET ACCOUNTS IN THE NEW ECONOMY[3]

Individual Development Accounts and other asset-building strategies should be viewed in the context of larger changes in domestic policy and community development. More than just a new program, IDAs are part of a fundamental shift from "welfare states," based predominantly on income support, toward a more empowering, more flexible domestic policy, based on asset building. Top-down categorical programs have been the primary strategy of the industrial era, but as we progress into the information age, policy is shifting to strategies and mechanisms that emphasize control by individuals and families. Families with resources in asset accounts are making more decisions about education, job training, homes, businesses, financial investments, health care, and retirement security.

This shift toward individual asset accounts began in the 1970s, with the dramatic change from defined-benefit retirement plans (with regular benefit payments each month) to defined-contribution retirement plans, such as 401(k)s, 403(b)s, Thrift Savings Plans, IRAs, Roth IRAs, and the possible shift to individual accounts for some portion of Social Security. In addition to retirement, policies and proposals for other uses of asset accounts are becoming more common, such as Super IRAs for home ownership and education (like Roth IRAs), Medical Savings Accounts, Educational Savings Accounts, Individual Training Accounts, and Children's Savings Accounts. Some of these accounts are public and some private, yet even the private-sector plans are typically defined by public policies and receive generous subsidies through the tax code.

There is every reason to believe that this trend toward asset accounts will continue. Asset accounts could become a primary domestic policy instrument within a few decades. The most frequently discussed reason for this change will be the coming fiscal strain in entitlements. However, it seems the more fundamental reason is that portable asset accounts may be more suited to the economy and labor market dynamics of the information technology age. In the industrial era, mass labor markets and stable employment called for categorical programs and income protection policies; in the information era, rapidly changing labor markets will require household flexibility and control over investments in family well-being.

The great danger in the expansion of asset-based policy is that the poor may be excluded. There are two reasons for this concern. First, the poor often do not participate in current asset-based policies, in part because they lack access to the institutions and information that facilitate participation. Second, asset accounts operate primarily through tax benefits, which tend to be more regressive than social insurance.

In this broad policy context, IDAs are not simply another new idea or one more option in the community development tool kit. Rather, IDAs are an effort to connect the poor to a major domestic policy transition of our time. In the absence of IDAs or other progressively funded, asset-building strategies for the poor, domestic policy is likely to move toward asset accounts, while leaving the poor behind with even fewer economic opportunities.[4]

INDIVIDUAL ASSET ACCOUNTS AS AN EMPLOYEE BENEFIT

Ensuring that asset-building policies are inclusive is a critical goal, but only the first step. Once asset accounts are established for the poor, the challenge will be to provide adequate outreach and education to ensure that those who *could* benefit from them *will*. We cannot expect millions of low-income Americans, particularly those in the estimated 20 percent of households that do not have a checking or savings account, to take advantage of individual asset accounts of their own accord (Gale and Carney 1999).

This being the case, maximizing the outcome of a universal asset account system will require a wide range of "intermediaries," connecting individuals with programs. The list of potential intermediaries includes financial service providers, community development organizations, faith-based organizations, housing organizations, state and local government agencies, and employers. Depending upon the capacity of the intermediary and its relationship with asset account holders, its role will vary, but may include such responsibilities as marketing and outreach, enrollment, counseling, and raising private-sector matching funds.

As a key point of contact for low-income workers, employers could play an important role in providing information about and access to individual asset accounts. Consistent with their role as the primary intermediary for 401(k)s, pension plans, and IRAs, employers could also serve as a "storefront" for individual asset accounts. And there is reason to believe that businesses could increase their bottom lines by making IDAs available to employees, if they do so strategically. By providing low-income workers with an opportunity to improve their economic stability, increase their skills, and improve their self-esteem, businesses will ultimately be rewarded with a more stable, more skilled workforce.

Although this is yet to be demonstrated on a large scale, experience with Lifelong Learning Accounts (LiLAs) and IDAs suggests that the employer-accountholder relationship can be mutually beneficial. Moreover, the data on these two types of accounts points to how they might affect the development of, and interact with, a third type— the Individual Training Accounts (ITAs) that form an important feature of the Workforce Investment Act of 1998.

Lifelong Learning Accounts

Lifelong Learning Accounts are an asset-building tool developed by the Center for Adult Experiential Learning (CAEL), a national nonprofit committed to expanding lifelong learning opportunities for adults. Similar to IDAs, LiLAs are individual asset accounts established on behalf of employees, but they focus solely on postsecondary education and training. LiLAs function as an alternative financing-and-delivery system for providing job training and lifelong learning opportunities, and they are designed to serve the interests of both employers and employees. By reducing administrative burdens and demonstrating a return on investment, LiLAs facilitate employer investments in education and training; at the same time, they provide valuable consumer information and counseling to enable individuals to make informed decisions about the future. Experience with LiLAs has demonstrated that employees become more motivated to learn, more productive in the workplace, and better able to adapt to and integrate new work practices. Employers benefit through a tax exemption for contributions to employee training, cost reductions due to improved performance, increased productivity and customer satisfaction, and lower turnover resulting from increased employee morale (CAEL 2000).

Since 1984, CAEL has worked with dozens of companies to make tuition assistance policies easier to administer, easier to participate in, and complementary to businesses' overall learning strategy. CAEL has also worked with a number of government agencies, universities, and colleges to facilitate the creation of stronger public/private partnerships to promote lifelong learning, and it is consulting for 30 companies in 21 states. In one of its largest and most successful projects, CAEL established 18 education and training centers prior to the closing of 22 Levi Strauss plants in the South and Southwest. Over 12,000 dislocated Levi Strauss employees participated between 1998 and 1999, and many went on to start their own businesses.[5]

Having demonstrated the success of LiLAs for individual firms, CAEL is planning a multiregional demonstration to explore how LiLAs could be made available more broadly, particularly to low-income workers. A major goal of this effort will be to gather more information about the role of public policy in facilitating a universal, lifelong learning system that increases individual choice. The outcomes of this demonstration will have relevance to the pursuit of a universal asset-building system to accommodate multiple goals.

Individual Development Accounts

In practice at the community level for nearly a decade, IDAs gained greater recognition in September 1997 when CFED launched a 2,000-account, 13-site, multiyear demonstration. With generous support from 11 foundations, the American Dream Demonstration (ADD) was the first demonstration of IDAs as a social and economic development tool for low-income and low-wealth households. ADD IDA programs are operated by community-based organizations and community development credit unions in partnership with local banks, education providers, and a wide array of public and nonprofit agencies.

Nearly three years into this five-year effort, ADD data show that low-income people, particularly low-income workers, can and do save when given incentives and institutional support. In June 1999, the Center for Social Development (2000) compiled and analyzed savings data for 1,326 accounts opened under ADD.[6] These data indicate that:

- Accountholders saved $378,708 and leveraged $741,609 in matching funds (based on a typical match rate of 2 : 1).
- The mean monthly savings rate was $33, and it was not affected by income.
- Accountholders saved 71 cents for every dollar that could be saved and matched.
- Very low-income accountholders (those at or below 50 percent of the federal poverty level) saved 8 percent of their annual income, while those with higher incomes (at or above 150 percent poverty) saved 2 percent.
- Out of 92 approved withdrawals, 33 percent were for microenterprise development, 47 percent for home purchase or improvement, and 20 percent for postsecondary education.

Demographic data for these accountholders suggest that gender, location of residence, income, and possession of other assets have no significant effect on saving patterns. Participant profiles indicate that 60 percent of accountholders are employed full-time and 25 percent part-time. Former welfare recipients saved $6 a month *more* on average than participants who had never received welfare.

These findings and success stories around the country have generated a higher level of public- and private-sector interest in IDAs. In the private sector, a small but growing number of employers are looking to IDAs as a recruitment and retention tool. Whether for housing, education, or job training, employers are beginning to see IDAs as a benefit that can serve worker and business needs simultaneously. For example:

- Childspace Cooperative Development in Philadelphia offers IDAs as a benefit for day care workers.
- The Community Development Technology Center—CD Tech—in Los Angeles has recruited five manufacturing plants to offer IDAs to employees through its Worker Income Security Program, which also offers financial education, English language instruction, and job training.
- In a modified IDA approach, Massachusetts and Oregon are using TANF funding to subsidize the wages of welfare-to-work clients by requiring employers to deposit $1 for every hour worked into savings accounts restricted to education and job-training uses.
- The Northland Foundation is recruiting Duluth, Minnesota, employers to participate in a five-year, business-assisted, IDA demonstration that will offer high-yield money market accounts to eligible employees.

This rising interest among private-sector employers is encouraging and suggests that businesses might play an important role in large-scale IDA implementation. If a universal asset account system is created, employers will be key in providing outreach to low-income workers. Also, employers can simplify the transaction side of IDAs by offering automatic payroll deduction transfers to savings accounts, providing additional match funding as a business investment, and promoting the use of IDAs for job-related education and training.

This latter role is especially important. Job training has been the least popular use of IDAs to date: Only 2 percent of ADD accountholders identify it as an intended use, and 3 percent of actual withdrawals were approved for that purpose (Center for Social Development 2000). While research has not identified the reasons for this underutilization, ADD data suggest that a sponsoring agency's capacity to provide information about and access to job-training services is an important factor. Thus, there is a need for increased capacity in this area, and employers can bridge this gap.

Individual Training Accounts

In compliance with the Workforce Investment Act (WIA) of 1998, states are making provision for a third type of asset account to promote education and training: Individual Training Accounts. The new ITA system is intended to improve the performance of federally funded job training and employment-related services by offering individuals greater control and a wide range of options in selecting among service providers.

ITAs are being implemented in conjunction with a One Stop delivery system that aims to decrease fragmentation in employment services and maximize results for employers and employees. Together, the ITA/One Stop system represents an effort to streamline services, empower individuals, provide universal access to employment-related information, enhance customer choice, increase the accountability of training providers, and give states and localities more flexibility in implementing comprehensive and innovative workforce investment systems (U.S. Department of Labor 1999).

Given this ambitious agenda, ITAs' potential to transform the field of workforce development is huge. At best, they could be the central funding mechanism for an inclusive asset-building/workforce investment system; at worst, they could be an underfunded voucher for last-resort assistance to WIA clients. It will be primarily up to local workforce investment boards to determine what ITAs will achieve in practice.

In March 2000, the Department of Labor made grants totaling $6.4 million to 13 states and localities that will serve as laboratories for ITA implementation as part of a national demonstration.[7] During the first year, sites will receive technical assistance from the department and its contractors, and the department will disseminate lessons from the sites to aid in the development of ITAs in other locations. Given the range of innovations being explored, the results of this demonstration could go a long way toward the development of a viable workforce development system to benefit the majority of workers and employers. Furthermore, given that Individual Development Accounts have been opened in all but one demonstration state (Nebraska), the potential for linking ITAs with IDAs is high.

In the absence of actual data on ITA implementation, we can only speculate as to how they might fit into a universal asset-building system. If carefully designed, ITAs could build on the experience of LiLAs and IDAs quite well. The combination of an asset account with consumer information services is an extension of the LiLA model, improving upon it by offering information on a wider range of services across a broader geographical area. Thus, it would be ideal if employees participating in LiLA programs could take advantage of the consumer information provided by One Stop systems. Similarly, IDA accountholders wishing to use their savings for postsecondary education and training could benefit greatly from well-functioning One Stop centers. And if the list of eligible trainers provided by the centers includes those offering money management courses and microenterprise training, the potential would exist for *all* IDA accountholders to seek training and channel funds through One Stop centers.

The big challenge will be ensuring that the One Stop system is staffed and implemented to meet the needs of a broad population of job seekers and those looking to advance in the workforce, not just those who are income eligible for intensive services. If this is not achieved, millions of low-income workers could be left without access to the education and training they need to advance economically. However, steps can be taken to ensure that ITAs can be an integral part of a universal asset-building system.

CREATING A UNIVERSAL ACCOUNT SYSTEM: KEY ISSUES AND CHALLENGES

Based on the high level of academic, foundation, and political support that Individual Development Accounts have received in recent years, it seems likely that the idea of matched savings for the poor will play a central role in a progressive policy for asset building. The field is at an exciting and hopeful place, yet we've only just begun to think about how to translate the success of hundreds of small IDA initiatives into a multi-billion-dollar account system that can work for all Americans. Creating an asset-building policy that is "inclusive, progressive, simple, participant-centered, and enduring" presents a long list of challenges, both political and practical.[8] We focus here on two categories:

- Broad issues associated with achieving scale; and
- Issues specific to increasing employer involvement and linking asset-building policy to a workforce development system.

Moving from Small Scale to Large Scale

Issues of scale are inextricably linked to issues of inclusion, and the major question that remains is: Can the nation create an asset-building system that benefits everyone? The difficulty lies not only in providing access but also in allowing for asset purchases that are appropriate and relevant for all participants in the system. At present, for example, there is significant debate about what types of IDA asset purchases qualify under the "big three" (home ownership, microenterprise, and postsecondary education and training) and whether to expand the list to include other uses, such as transportation and retirement. With additional federal funding will undoubtedly come greater scrutiny and concern about fraud, so it seems likely that a universal system will be more restrictive, which some may legitimately see as counter to the goal of inclusion.

Another important question relates to the issue of inclusion: What is the definition of the poor? Neither the federal poverty level nor guidelines for earned income tax credit eligibility would be broad enough to include many of the poor who are currently saving in IDAs. If the definition is broader, where will the match funding come from? It is worth noting that conservative support for the "pro-family/pro-work" earned income tax credit (EITC) has waned as federal funding has increased from $1 billion to $30.5 billion over the past 25 years. Is it possible to generate equivalent support for a policy that is less closely tied to work? If so, how can we ensure that the nonworking poor will be able to access the system?

Finally, a series of questions will need to be addressed in determining how to administer a universal asset-building policy. Should administration and asset management be centralized? Ideally, rather than creating a whole new level of bureaucracy, the goal will be to build on asset-building programs for the nonpoor to create a universal system that works for the poor as well. For example, if it proves desirable to retain the basic structure of IDAs in a universal system, it seems that the IRA (or possibly Roth IRA) would be a good starting point for determining how best to administer universal asset accounts for restricted uses. Research and analysis recently conducted by Michael J. Graetz et al. (1999) demonstrated how President Clinton's complicated Universal Savings Account proposal, aimed at helping American workers build retirement savings, could be shaped into a workable policy to benefit the poor, if combined with existing IRAs. A similar examination would need to be undertaken in proposing a model structure for universal asset accounts.

Answers to these questions will ultimately determine the key players in a universal asset-building system. For example, if savings accounts are replaced by IRA-like accounts in a universal system, this will significantly change the role of financial institutions and credit unions, two central players in current IDA initiatives. The role of community-based organizations currently operating IDA programs also will be altered. If freed from the burden of administering IDAs, they will likely focus attention on offering financial education and training, credit counseling, and other auxiliary services needed to support a universal system.

Increasing Employer Involvement: Linking Asset Building and Workforce Development

Given rising employer interest in IDAs, what obstacles have served to discourage employer support of IDAs? The most prominent relate to at least four concerns:

- *Equity concerns:* Nondiscrimination statutes make it difficult for employers to provide benefits to one class of employees while denying others the same or equal benefits.
- *Tax treatment:* Current law treats employer contributions to IDAs as wages, and subjects them to FICA withholding. As a result, employees don't receive a true dollar-for-dollar match. Furthermore, they must pay taxes on interest earned on employer match funds. (However, match funds provided by anyone other than an employer are treated as a tax-exempt charitable contribution, benefiting both the donor and the IDA saver.)
- *Administrative burdens:* The special tax status of employer contributions places additional accounting and reporting burdens on the employer or sponsoring agency.
- *Self-interest conflicts:* Some employers are uncomfortable with the notion of portable accounts and/or supporting microenterprises as a qualified use. They fear that employees will leave, compromising employers' return on their investment.

Any policy in support of a universal asset-building system should mitigate or eliminate these obstacles to employer participation. For example, the Clinton administration's Retirement Savings Account proposal provided for tax deductible employer contributions with offsetting tax credits (White House 2000). Absent such incentives for employers, private-sector participation in a universal asset-building system will be limited; as a result, the benefits to the larger community will be diminished.

Turning that argument around, employers could play a role in substantially increasing the benefits to society by facilitating a strong link between a universal asset-building system and a national workforce development system. Research conducted by CAEL and others indicates that many workers don't pursue employment-related education and training because they don't know what opportunities are available and what resources they can leverage to pursue those opportunities. In other words, without appropriate motivation and guidance, low-skilled workers fail to develop their potential, leading to adverse outcomes for employees and their employers.

Employers who understand this dynamic can take a proactive role in improving the skills of their labor force. This can be accomplished by:

- Funding training or bringing trainers into the workplace, as a growing number of high-tech companies are doing;
- Providing employees with information on education and training resources that are available and relevant to their occupations; and
- Partnering with other employers, training providers, and state agencies to craft a workforce development strategy to benefit the entire region.

In any of these scenarios, the universal asset account would be the funding mechanism for education and training services, effectively channeling private, public, and individual funding into workforce development. This linkage would aid in the creation of a sustainable, workforce development system that is truly a public-private partnership.

SUMMARY AND POLICY RECOMMENDATIONS

This chapter has touched on a few aspects of asset-building policy for the poor, with a focus on the potential that asset-building strategies hold for low-income workers and employers in today's labor market. It bears repeating that the goal of inclusiveness is paramount in the universal asset-building policy agenda, and emerging asset-building strategies have the potential to benefit all Americans, regardless of race, class, education level, employment status, and so on.

Having said that, the following policy recommendations extend the issues addressed here. Based on current asset-building policy and what we know about the working poor, we advocate several steps toward constructing a system that enables low-income workers to better their economic prospects through saving and investment:

Build on Existing Policy for the Working Poor

- Ensure that contributions to asset accounts will not interfere with eligibility for EITC and other benefits for low-income workers.
- Directly link the EITC and other transfer payments (e.g., TANF, SSI) with asset accounts to facilitate increased saving.
- Encourage local workforce investment boards to link ITAs to IDAs, LiLAs, and other types of asset accounts to increase utilization of One Stop employment and training services centers.
- Allow for and encourage multiple sources of funding for ITAs (including WIA funds, Pell grants, Stafford loans, EITC refunds and contributions from employers, foundations, individuals, etc.).

Encourage Employers to Promote Asset-Building Programs and Policies

- Offer tax credits for employer contributions to asset accounts, similar to those for defined-contribution plans.

- Grant tax exemptions for *all* match funding for asset accounts, regardless of the source, when used for qualified asset purchases.
- Ensure that all federally created asset accounts are compatible with, rather than competitive with, other asset-building plans (e.g., 401[k]s, IRAs, pension plans).
- Ensure that federally created asset accounts are easy for employers to administer.

Address the Needs of All Low-Income Workers

- Enact the Savings for Working Families Act 2000 and create Retirement Savings Accounts matched by federal dollars for the poor, per the Clinton administration's 2000 proposal.
- Provide adequate information about education and training opportunities to maximize individual choice.
- Improve access to financial education, possibly by linking asset-building strategies with current initiatives to increase the national savings rate.
- Ensure that traditional workers, temporary workers, self-employed individuals, and unemployed individuals alike can take advantage of federally created asset accounts.

Large policies are rarely, if ever, put into place all at once. Thus, these recommendations are intended to serve as guidelines on the intersecting paths to a more effective, workforce development system and a more equitable asset-building system. We believe that, when possible, attempts should be made to coordinate and integrate these separate but related agendas.

We close with a cautionary statement: There is much to be learned about asset building and its potential as a poverty reduction strategy. As more data become available on the impacts of IDAs, LiLAs, and ITAs on the working poor, thinking about how to create a universal asset-building policy is sure to evolve. Likewise, there is much more to be done in designing and implementing a comprehensive, workforce development system.

Our foremost recommendation, then, is for policymakers to be mindful of the connections between these two policy agendas, so that progress in one reflects and reinforces progress in the other. The common goals of expanding opportunities for low-income workers and helping them achieve self-sufficiency will thus be more effectively advanced.

NOTES

1. Most notable were Edward N. Wolff's research in the late 1980s on wealth inequality in the United States, and Melvin Oliver and Thomas Shapiro's studies of asset inequality.
2. President Clinton cited these figures during an April 14, 1999, speech at the White House on his Universal Savings Accounts proposal.
3. The ideas in this section were contributed by Michael Sherraden and first appeared in "IDAs in the Big Picture," *Assets: A Quarterly Update for Innovators,* Summer 1998.
4. We should acknowledge here that Clinton administration proposals for Universal Savings Accounts (USAs) and Retirement Savings Accounts (RSAs) were more inclusive than existing asset-building policies. Nonetheless, the challenge to guarantee inclusiveness for asset-building policies on the whole is major. For more information about these proposals, see http://www.cfed.org/individual_assets/ida/policy_initiatives.html.
5. Sam Leiken, CAEL vice president for public policy and government relations, provided this information in a telephone conversation on April 20, 2000.

6. Although the demonstration began in September 1997, the median age of these accounts was nine months.

7. The sites are in California, Connecticut, Georgia, Indiana, Maryland, Michigan, Missouri, North Carolina, Nebraska, Ohio, Oregon, Pennsylvania, and Texas.

8. This vision for a universal asset-building system was developed by CFED and CSD with input from members of the Growing Wealth Working Group at a brainstorming meeting on asset building, Washington, D.C., February 2000.

REFERENCES

Ackerman, Bruce, and Anne Alstott. 1999. *The Stakeholder Society.* New Haven: Yale University Press.

Boshara, Ray. 2000. "Federal and State IDA Policy Overview." Washington, D.C.: Corporation for Enterprise Development.

Boshara, Ray, Edward Scanlon, and Deborah Page-Adams. 1998. *Building Assets for Stronger Families, Better Neighborhoods and Realizing the American Dream.* Washington, D.C.: Corporation for Enterprise Development.

Center for Adult Experiential Learning. 2000. http://www.cael.org/serveemp/live_se.html.

Center for Social Development. 2000. *Saving Patterns in IDA Programs.* St. Louis: Washington University.

Curley, Jami, and Michael Sherraden. 1998. "The History and Status of Children's Allowances: Policy Background for Children's Savings Accounts." Center for Social Development, Washington University, St. Louis, Mo.

Freeman, Richard B. 1999. *The New Inequality: Creating Solutions for Poor America.* Boston: Beacon Press.

Gale, William G., and Stacie Carney. 1999. "Asset Accumulation in Low-Income Households." Paper prepared for the Ford Foundation symposium, *Benefits and Mechanisms for Spreading Asset Ownership in the United States.* New York University, December 1998; revised May 1999.

Graetz, Michael J., Armando Gomez, and Zoe Neuberger. 1999. "Universal Savings Accounts: The Clinton IRA." Tax Analysts Document No. 1999-19782. Available at http://www.tax.org/About/aboutf.htm.

Haveman, Robert. 1988. *Starting Even: An Equal Opportunity Program to Combat the Nation's New Poverty.* New York: Simon and Schuster.

Sherraden, Michael. 1991. *Assets and the Poor: A New American Welfare Policy.* Armonk, N.Y.: M.E. Sharpe.

———. 1998. "IDAs in the Big Picture." *Assets: A Quarterly Update for Innovators* (Summer).

U.S. Department of Labor. 1999. Employment and Training Administration. *ITA/Eligible Provider Demonstration Briefing Book.* Lansing, Mich.: Public Policy Associates, Inc.

White House. 2000. "President Clinton's Tax Agenda for Community, Opportunity, and Responsibility." Press release. White House Office of the Press. January 27.

9

Stepping Up

*State Policies and Programs Promoting
Low-Wage Workers' Steady
Employment and Advancement*

Carol Clymer, Brandon Roberts, and Julie Strawn

I t's about 5:30 in the evening. We are traveling on North West 14th Avenue in Liberty City, a Miami neighborhood where the riots of 1980 occurred. The street is quiet. We stop to pick up dinner for several women we are driving to meet and talk with about their experiences getting off welfare and going to work. In the restaurant, our presence is noticed. Not only have we made other customers wait in line for more than 15 minutes to place their orders, but also our bill comes to $87.53. This is unusual, one customer comments. We are questioned about the reasons for the large quantity of food. A woman who says she'd love to have that much money suggests we should've checked with her first. She would have cooked us a much better meal for that price. Everyone seems interested in our order. As we leave, the conversation continues.

We pull into Liberty Square Community Center. Five women ranging in age from 24 to 45 welcome us. They are employed in jobs that pay $6.00 to $10.50 an hour. Each woman has attended a year's worth of weekly group meetings designed to help them keep their jobs and get promoted. They talk with us freely.

Their stories are similar. Each is a single parent who has been on and off welfare. For the most part, none likes being in the "system." They have had good and bad experiences with social workers. They are conflicted: Sometimes they feel they will beat the system by working; sometimes they feel that, by their working, the system will beat them. They all try to better themselves. They struggle, yet have hope:

> *I'm scared of the [welfare] system. It's like a swimming pool you can't get out of because it's 10 feet deep and you've been swallowed all the way in. That's how I feel. It's like they're making it like a hole because you're like so dependent upon it, you know, because you can't get this without this, you can't get this without that. And they make you dependent upon them. You know what I mean?*

Because it's like a circle, you know. Your rent goes up because you're making too much money. And then you feel like you've just got to go back to [welfare] because you can't afford to pay that rent, you know. That's too much money.

Continuing education is a goal for each woman. One completed a computer training program but couldn't get a job in that field. Another likes sewing and wants to make gowns, but needs more training. She hasn't been able to secure the $5,000 she needs for tuition to design school. One woman wants a degree in accounting or computer programming. She would like a computer so she can work at home, be with her children, and go back to school.

When I was younger, you know, we could get assistance, we could get all that free money and all those loans. And now I'm in default on my student loans.

Each is learning on the job and in the weekly support group:

They help us with self-esteem, try to get a better job, better attitude towards things, you know. When I first started the program, I had a nasty attitude.

Some find ways to stay in unpleasant jobs until better ones come along; they discover strengths they didn't know they had:

You sit in there and it's like 2:00 in the morning and it's like 50 degrees in there. And there is no chance for advancement. And they were like coming to me, God, you stuck in that for a long time. Because I think I was strong-willed. And the reason why I did that was because I had a goal, and I wanted to stay at that job until at least I finish school and then maybe, you know, I'll be able to move on.

They confront their fears:

But it's like dealing with these new people every day, I was afraid. I was like I was hoping that I don't make a mistake. But [the facilitator] was always there for me. She would call me in my unit, "how is it going?"

Each woman has barriers that prevent getting ahead:

Even when I was working full-time, I was still struggling because it's just so many things, and then so many things happen with your children, and emergencies with your car. And if you don't have backup or somebody there for you, it will just wipe you out.

The government offered 20 houses within the inner-city area of Miami. But only 30 people could qualify. This was my first question: How you gonna select these people, what are the criteria? If it's credit, I'm out, you know, don't even apply.

Back in the '80s I got myself in trouble, I was a bad girl back then. I was in jail for sticking my nose in my sister's problem. I wanted to fill out an application. I'm in school, I graduated school, I'm in college, I have a job. And I'm doing everything. Just because of my background, they wrote me a letter, mailed it off: I'm sorry, it's your background. They don't see the fact I'm in school now. And it happened five years ago, five years ago. They don't see that. They just see the fact that I went to jail.

THE CHALLENGES OF STEADY WORK AND BETTER JOBS: FROM WELFARE TO THE LOW-WAGE WORKFORCE

While the 1996 federal welfare reform legislation, the Personal Responsibility and Work Opportunity Reconciliation Act, gave states more funding and flexibility to provide financial assistance to needy families, it also limited the length of time people could receive assistance. Many states responded with "work-first" policies that required individuals to find jobs—either by diverting them from welfare altogether or by enacting stricter time limits on welfare assistance than the federal legislation required. After five years, a key question for "work first" is: Can individuals who move from welfare to work keep their jobs and advance?

Although the issues of low-wage work are broader than welfare reform, research regarding individuals moving from welfare to work also provides important insights about the working poor in general. Thus far, the evidence suggests that finding jobs with both decent pay and benefits and opportunities for job advancement is a significant challenge. While most women who have left welfare in recent years are employed, they typically find jobs that pay near the minimum wage—not enough to move their families above the poverty level. For example, the most recent national data show that among families who left welfare between 1995 and 1997, 61 percent of parents were working, earning an average $6.61 an hour. Fewer than one-fourth had access to employer-sponsored health insurance (Loprest 1999).

Policymakers and the public have become more aware that women who leave welfare for work struggle to stay employed. National studies from the mid-'90s have found that only about half those who leave welfare for work are still working one year later. Many of those who lose jobs do not find new ones quickly. In fact, spells of unemployment between jobs last as long as the jobs themselves, so that over the long term, women who had received welfare tend to spend as much time out of work as employed (Hershey and Pavetti 1997). This may be changing with the strong economy and the shift to a work-focused welfare system, but early data suggest that job loss continues to be common, especially during the first three to six months of employment.

Over the long term, women who leave welfare gradually work more each year, but many find job advancement an elusive goal. Wages remain stubbornly low even after years of work, particularly for those who start out in low-wage jobs. For example, a national study of women who left welfare voluntarily found that their median hourly wages barely increased over five years, from $6.36 to $6.73 (Loprest 1999).[1] And women whose starting wages were in the bottom one-fourth for the group saw no increase at all.

The experiences of women who leave welfare for work have much in common with those of other low-wage workers: erratic employment, persistently low pay, lack of access to job benefits, and occupations that offer few opportunities for advancement. Both groups have markedly lower skills and educational attainment than the population as a whole (Loprest 1999).

Public/Private Ventures, the National Governors' Association, and the U.S. Department of Health and Human Services have launched state initiatives to test ways to help individuals, like the women in Miami and other low-wage workers, retain jobs and gain skills needed to support their families. This chapter, while it is not about these specific initiatives, draws heavily on the experience of some of the states involved in them and of other states that have taken extra steps to assist low-wage workers.[2]

In particular, this chapter reviews the efforts of several states that have taken advantage of devolved federal authority and the flexibility of the welfare reform legislation to create new state policies and strategies in support of low-income individuals as they work. It includes information on:

- Opportunities for and key elements of supporting steady employment and job advancement for low-income workers;
- Examples of state policies and programs that enable low-income workers to retain employment and advance on the job;
- The challenges of designing and implementing job retention and advancement strategies for low-income workers; and
- Policy and program ideas for moving ahead.

Although it is too early to know the outcomes of state efforts, current data on the income gap suggest that it continues to widen. Too many individuals who work full-time remain in poverty. And although individuals are getting off of welfare in unprecedented numbers, those who do still do not earn enough to support their families.

Unquestionably, states are charting new and difficult territory. The difficulty of narrowing the income gap is considerable for several reasons, even in this robust economy. For one, our political system does not support significant tampering with the economy. Many believe it is best to allow market forces to operate relatively unfettered, and if those who can work do, poverty will decrease. This view argues that although many people in this country are poor, our system historically has provided better incomes for more people than any other in the world. Consequently, there is limited economic or social policy experience, and less programmatic expertise, aimed at helping low-income individuals work their way out of poverty. Not surprisingly, there are more challenges than successes, but the experiences of the pioneering states are still illuminating. And the current alignment—a healthy economy, the need for skilled labor, welfare savings, flexible funding, and workforce development legislation that enables states to provide assistance to the working poor—offers an unusual opportunity to narrow the income gap via social policies and interventions.

IMPROVING THE ODDS FOR LOW-WAGE WORKERS

Little research or program experience aids policymakers and program operators as they decide which services and benefits might be most important to help the working poor work steadily and move up to better jobs. However, several recent studies have added important insights by attempting to separate the influences of different personal, family, and job factors on labor market outcomes.[3]

Among the themes that emerge are:

- Working steadily initially after leaving welfare is linked to being employed in later years but not to higher hourly wages in later years, holding other work history, job, and personal factors equal.
- Starting out in better jobs—ones with higher hourly wages or better benefits—is linked both to being employed and to having higher wages in later years, holding other work history, job, and personal factors equal.
- Education skills and credentials—especially postsecondary education—are strongly linked to obtaining better jobs.
- Both the chances of working steadily initially and of finding better jobs initially are likely related to other factors that are more difficult to observe, such as motivation, social skills, and differing labor market opportunities.

This research has important implications for the policies and services needed to help low-income workers work steadily and advance. In particular, it underscores the critical importance of workforce development services to help low-income families move up to better jobs.

In sum, available research[4] regarding the impact of different strategies on job retention and advancement finds that:

- *"Work first,"* when it relies on job search services and does not include substantial access to other activities, helps low-income parents work more in the short but not the long run. Job search does not produce lasting impacts, because it typically does not help individuals find better jobs than they would on their own. It also fails to help the most disadvantaged individuals.
- *Mixed strategies* for preemployment services can be as effective as "work first" in increasing short-run employment, are more likely to produce long-term success, and can improve the quality of jobs that participants find. Successful, mixed-strategy programs support a clear employment goal with a range of services, such as job search, work experience, and education and training. The Portland, Oregon, Job Opportunities and Basic Skills Training (JOBS) program is the best recent example of this approach. JOBS welfare recipients increased their hourly wages and found more stable employment, even if they entered the program without a high school diploma or GED. Access to training for the latter may have been a key ingredient.
- *Work-based strategies,* such as supported work for the harder-to-employ or on-the-job training for more employable workers, have been consistently effective in increasing employment and earnings. In particular, the National Supported Work Demonstration sustained participant earnings impacts even eight years later and was most effective with the most disadvantaged recipients (Gueron and Pauly 1991; U.S. Department of Labor 1995).[5] Some of these programs also helped people find higher-paying jobs.

Based on these findings, effective workforce development strategies might include:

- Greater attention to barriers to steady employment through access to needed support and retention services;
- Greater emphasis on skills upgrading through access to postsecondary education, worksite training, or other opportunities for on-the-job learning, such as coaching and mentoring; and
- Wider use of combinations of work and learning, such as partnerships with employers to create coordinated part-time work, part-time school arrangements, or campus work-study.

THE OPPORTUNITY TO CHANGE STATE POLICY

Declining caseloads, new regulatory flexibility, and substantial federal resources have provided states with a rare opportunity to invest in job retention and advancement strategies. This opportunity exists because welfare caseloads have fallen by more than half in recent years, and states can use the resulting federal and state welfare savings to create or expand these services.

Welfare Reform

Funding of the Temporary Assistance for Needy Families (TANF) block grants— $16 billion annually in federal funds and an additional $10 billion in state maintenance-of-effort funds—dwarfs other workforce development resources.[6] Cash assistance is just one possible use of these funds; indeed, less than half of total federal and state TANF funds are being spent on traditional welfare aid.

Combined with TANF surpluses, the sweeping flexibility of the final TANF regulations issued in April 1999 creates many new opportunities for states and localities to adopt policies and provide services to support steady work and access to better jobs. Federal TANF funding can be used to assist all low-income parents, regardless of whether they have custody of their children. Federal TANF funds can even be used to help those who are not yet parents, if the services or benefits provided might help prevent out-of-wedlock pregnancies.[7] In addition, TANF-funded workforce development services do not carry TANF time limits, work requirements, or other conditions applying to TANF cash assistance. This makes it possible for states and localities to use TANF to support a wide range of workforce development services, whether or not the services meet federal work requirements for TANF cash assistance.

Workforce Investment Act[8]

The Workforce Investment Act (WIA) offers approximately $1 billion annually to support workforce development services for adults. While not as flexible as TANF, WIA affords states and localities more options than in the past for using these federal funds, especially to expand services beyond the unemployed to include low-wage workers.

WIA provides significant new ways for states to promote longer-term employment retention and advancement for low-wage workers. For example, the infrastructure of employer-led workforce boards and One Stop career centers could provide low-income workers with greater access to workforce development services. In contrast to its predecessor, the Job Training Partnership Act (JTPA), WIA asks states and localities to track longer-term outcomes for employment retention and wage progression. Moreover, underscoring the importance of advancement, WIA funds can be used to provide workforce development services to incumbent workers. Funds for serving adults can support a broad array of pre- and postemployment services. These include individualized job preparation services, skills training, work-related basic education and English as a second language (ESL), case management before and after employment, paid and unpaid work experience, on-the-job training, incumbent worker training, customized training, supportive services, and needs-related payments. Finally, WIA allows states to engage in unified planning for a group of related federal employment and education programs.

Integrating Workforce Development Services

TANF and WIA each create opportunities to provide postemployment services to individuals. But the services available through TANF could be augmented if states and localities integrate—not just co-locate or coordinate—workforce development services through WIA. Integration of services across state and federal funding streams is not easy, and WIA largely leaves categorical funding roadblocks in place (e.g., federal employment training funding available through TANF, food stamps, HUD, voc rehab, Carl Perkins, etc.). Nevertheless, where integration can be achieved, seamless delivery of workforce development services provides clear benefits to employers and workers.

States and localities may find it difficult to focus on improving the overall quality and effectiveness of workforce development systems while they are still absorbing the sweeping changes made by welfare reform, and are creating the new infrastructure of WIA-mandated Workforce Development Boards and One Stop career centers. Yet the redesign of multiple systems also presents an important opportunity to break with past practices. And better integration of workforce development services could address in part some difficult issues inherent in helping low-income parents and other low-wage workers retain jobs and advance to better ones. Equitable access to services; better articulation of basic education, job training, and postsecondary degree programs; assessment and referral to specialized support services; and continuity of services exemplify ways to help individuals move from unemployment to work and from job to job.

A recent study of 12 localities suggests that service integration or close coordination results in participants receiving more comprehensive and individualized services, a key characteristic of effective workforce development programs (Pindus et al. 2000). In sites where services were integrated or closely coordinated across welfare and workforce development programs, participants benefited in concrete ways that included:

- Referral to more services and to a wider range of services;
- Greater intensity of services to clients;

- Simplified referral processes;
- The convenience of having some or all agencies in one location; and
- Improved case management as staff across agencies worked jointly to manage cases.

While true service integration is rare, Utah illustrates the possibilities.[9] The state has unified all its workforce development services, including those for welfare recipients, in one department. Performance measures are set for the entire department across funding streams, and funding sources are invisible to front-line staff and customers. All customers go to the same employment centers and are served primarily by generic employment counselors (although social workers are also on staff for those with the most serious barriers to employment). Employment counselors provide assessment, career planning, job placement, follow-up, and job advancement services. Each counselor stays with an individual throughout the time he or she needs services, both before and after becoming employed, and whether or not the person is receiving other benefits, such as cash assistance.

A wide array of services can be provided, including career counseling, job placement, classroom training, on-the-job training, postsecondary certificate or degree programs, adult basic education, supportive employment, and life skills and self-esteem courses. Customers fill out a single application for all workforce development services. They can also sign up for food stamps, Medicaid, and other benefits at the centers, where centralized staff determine eligibility for all benefit programs statewide. The state envisions workforce services that are compassionate, individualized, employment focused, and provided in a professional environment, with zero waiting time.

Of course, better coordination or integration of services does not automatically mean higher quality. In particular, improving adult education and job training services is an urgent, critical task for states and localities seeking to create an effective workforce development system.

WHAT STATES AND LOCALITIES CAN DO OUTSIDE THE TANF CASH ASSISTANCE PROGRAM TO AID LOW-WAGE WORKERS[10]

With Federal TANF Block Grant Funds

- Provide services and benefits without having to apply the conditions intended for cash assistance recipients, such as time limits, work and participation requirements, and child support assignment rules. Examples of "nonassistance" services and benefits include:
  - Refundable earned income tax credits for working families;
  - Child care for working families;
  - Transportation for working families;
  - Wage subsidies (payments to employers or to third parties to cover the cost of wages, benefits, supervision, and training);
  - Individual Development Accounts;
  - Nonrecurrent, short-term benefits designed to deal with a specific crisis or need, not intended to meet ongoing needs, and not extending beyond four months; and
  - Services that do not provide basic income support (e.g., education and job training, case management).

- Provide services and benefits specifically mentioned in the rules by creating work expense allowances for employed welfare recipients during the initial months of employment. For example, Kentucky offers a nine-month allowance to families who leave welfare for work. Former TANF recipients who work 35 hours a week are eligible to receive $500 every three months for a total of nine months. Such allowances are considered "nonassistance," as long as the amount is related to actual work-related expenses, and are not meant to meet basic living costs.[11]
- Make services available to more low-income people than are eligible for TANF cash assistance by setting financial eligibility for these services and benefits higher than for TANF cash assistance, such as at 200 percent of the federal poverty level.
- Create a range of supports for working low-income families, such as child care and transportation help, wage supplements or work expense allowances, career counseling, job training, or education.
- Make different categories eligible for these TANF-funded workforce development services; for example, noncustodial parents and youth who are not yet parents.

With Maintenance-of-Effort Funds

To receive their full federal TANF block grant, states must maintain a certain level of state spending—known as maintenance-of-effort (MOE)—on cash assistance, services, or other aid to low-income families. As with federal TANF funds, though, states are not required to spend MOE funds within the TANF cash assistance program itself. The MOE obligation can be satisfied by spending state funds in a non-TANF program, referred to in TANF rules as a "separate state program." Important aspects of MOE funds include:

- They are exempt from such TANF conditions as time limits and work participation requirements, regardless of the types of benefits they support. Therefore, they can pay cash-like benefits, such as living stipends for people in long-term education or training, or wage subsidies to individuals.
- Only low-income families (e.g., 200 percent of the poverty level) may be helped with state MOE funds, not noncustodial parents or low-wage workers without children.
- They can be used for services and benefits to support job advancement, such as student aid for low-income parents, as exemplified in Maine's Parents as Scholars. This program provides scholarships to cover living expenses for low-income parents enrolled in two- or four-year postsecondary education degree programs.

STATE POLICY ACTIONS TO INCREASE THE INCOME OF LOW-WAGE WORKERS

The alleviation of poverty will require more than expanded workforce development strategies that help individuals maintain steady employment and advance on the job. As noted by the women we quoted above, achieving economic stability is a formidable challenge. It is important to recognize that a range of support is necessary, including wage supplements, expanded and accessible child care, and health care subsidies. Significant resources and more flexible federal laws governing welfare and workforce development afford the opportunity for states to create these supports.

A small but growing number of states has initiated policies to help workers sustain employment and increase income. By focusing on policy actions to reduce poverty, these states are moving beyond caseload reduction and job placement as goals for welfare reform and workforce development. Their efforts can be grouped into three categories:

- Make work pay;
- Reduce barriers to employment; and
- Expand postemployment efforts.

Make Work Pay[12]

Efforts to make work pay primarily involve supplementing the earnings of low-wage workers. States are taking several actions to compensate for low-wage employment so recipients are appropriately rewarded for work:

- *Income disregards* ensure that welfare recipients have more income from work than from public assistance.[13] In most states, individuals become ineligible for assistance when income surpasses 75 percent of poverty, but seven states allow recipients to earn up to 100 percent of poverty. For the last six years, Minnesota has operated the Minnesota Family Investment Program (MFIP), allowing recipients to receive welfare payments until their income reaches 200 percent of poverty. An evaluation by the Manpower Demonstration Research Corporation found that MFIP increased employment 35 percent and earnings 23 percent compared with a control group (Knox, Miller, and Gennetian 2000).
- *State earned income tax credits* complement the federal earned income tax credit by reducing the state tax burden on the working poor. Eleven states have some form of earned income tax credit. Many also provide a refundable credit for low-income families with little or no tax burden. Credits that exceed foregone tax revenues can be paid with TANF or MOE funds.
- *Child support payment passthroughs* provide more cash assistance to working single parents, and serve as an incentive for noncustodial parents to fulfill their child support obligations. Currently, most states capture child support payments to current and former welfare recipients to reimburse for public assistance payments. Connecticut passes through all child support payments to the TANF recipient. It also disregards up to $100 of this payment against a family's TANF income.
- *Individual Development Accounts* (IDAs) help low-income families accumulate financial assets that would enable them to purchase a home, attend school, or start a business. Over half the states allow for some type of IDA; however, only a few make IDAs available statewide and provide funds to match a family's contribution. Arkansas makes its IDA program available to all working families with incomes up to 185 percent of poverty; it uses TANF funds to match family contributions at a rate of $3 of state funds for every $1 in family contribution. It also encourages other indi-

viduals and corporations to contribute to a nonprofit that sponsors IDAs by allowing a state credit against income tax liability equal to 50 percent of the contribution.

Other policies and tools designed to increase a working family's income include increasing the minimum wage, worker stipends, increased cash benefits, and short-term aid for emergencies, such as paying the electric bill. All these efforts are directed at helping families meet their financial needs, while reinforcing the concept that work is the most direct way out of poverty.

Reduce Barriers to Steady Employment

States are increasing the number of support services that can facilitate workers' continued attachment to work, as well as expanding eligibility for these services to the working poor (sometimes to a level as high as 200 percent of poverty).

- *Child care* is an area in which most states have taken significant steps to expand coverage and reduce costs for recently employed welfare recipients and the working poor.
- *Health care* coverage is a critical issue for low-income workers. A few states are expanding Medicaid coverage for the working poor. Wisconsin retains Medicaid coverage for working parents and children up to 200 percent of poverty, while other states (e.g., California, Missouri, Rhode Island) offer coverage to families earning between 100 and 150 percent of poverty.
- *Transportation* is often provided to help welfare recipients obtain and keep employment. Services range from transport subsidies to financing for car ownership. A limited number of states, including Kansas, Nebraska, Pennsylvania, and Michigan, provide cash assistance for welfare recipients to purchase a car. Arkansas offers such assistance to all workers making less than 185 percent of poverty. In addition, Arkansas IDA accounts can be used to purchase or repair cars.
- *Housing assistance* provided through TANF funds helps recently employed welfare recipients offset reductions in housing subsidies that result from increased earned income. Connecticut, New Jersey, and several other states offer vouchers to cover rental costs that exceed 40 and 45 percent of family income, respectively.

States can do even more to enhance the supports available to working families. For example, they can subsidize the purchase of employer-provided health care, expand employee assistance programs, and extend domestic violence services. Increasingly, states understand that failure to address personal issues is often the reason workers leave jobs and return to public assistance. In addition, many states are more closely examining the effect of wage income on other assistance provided to sustain employment, so individuals are not unintentionally penalized for working.

Expand Postemployment Efforts

A few states are taking other policy and organizational steps that can foster retention and advancement efforts. Four types of action are noted: redirecting resources, establishing performance measures, engaging business, and expanding eligibility to the working poor.

- *Redirecting resources* to support retention and advancement initiatives represents a clear signal that state policymakers have made these a priority. This is the case in Florida and Oregon: State leaders have moved to ensure that local welfare reform emphasizes and supports efforts to sustain employment and help people increase income.

  Oregon requires its 15 Adult and Family Service Districts to spend 25 percent of their TANF employment and training funds (more than $5 million annually, excluding support services) on job retention and career advancement activities. As a result, each district has developed a range of approaches to work with participants after they are employed. In some districts, recipients receive up to a year of comprehensive, case-managed retention services, training in occupations with career ladders, and on-site job coaching.

  Florida invested $25 million of its welfare funds to support Retention Incentive Training Accounts—RITAs—for currently or recently working welfare recipients. RITAs provide financial support for workers to obtain skills upgrading or additional education. The funds can pay for training as well as the ancillary services needed, such as child care, transportation, and career counseling.

- *Establishing performance measures* is another way that states can encourage better retention and advancement outcomes. Essentially, it means observing the maxim: "What gets measured is what gets done." At this point, only a few states collect performance data on retention and advancement of low-wage workers. Although WIA requires states to collect this information, retention data will not include the vast majority of welfare clients who make the transition to work, because so few states have opted to include TANF in a unified WIA plan. On their own, some states have enacted performance measures that push beyond simplistic measures of caseload decline and initial job placement.

  Alaska developed and applied performance measures to its TANF program in 1998. This gives attention to participant outcomes, not to the processes of delivering services. The state sets performance goals not only for its overall operations but also for the operations of key district offices. Retention at 12 months and increases in earnings are key measures that drive the delivery of local services. In fact, Alaska will undertake an efficiency study of local operations, seeking to determine whether certain service delivery activities can be eliminated if they do not contribute to participant outcomes.

  Washington State has moved to help low-income workers move out of poverty. Its WorkFirst Reinvestment Program directs almost $31 million of welfare savings to a job-training-for-wage-progression strategy. A key element of this statewide effort is the establishment of performance measures and standards. By continuously measuring outcomes related to intended enrollments, placements, retention, and earnings, Washington monitors performance and makes adjustments accordingly. In the first year, for example, the state learned that its effort to provide tuition assistance to help recently employed recipients improve their education and skills fell short of enrollment targets. Efforts are now underway to encourage local welfare offices to actively recruit employed former welfare recipients to participate in skills-upgrade training.

- *Engaging business* to play a role in retention and skills-upgrade activities is an under-developed area. While many states appoint businesspeople to welfare reform advisory or policy boards—WIA *mandates* their participation—few states actually seek to incorporate firms into substantive programmatic activities. Several states are breaking new ground in this area.

    California and *Minnesota* are using their traditional, state-supported, customized training programs to target retention and skills-upgrade services to newly employed welfare recipients. Historically seen as an economic development tool for high-skill, high-wage jobs, these programs now recognize that firms' competitive positions are also influenced by the availability and quality of the low-wage workforce, particularly the ability of that workforce to sustain employment and advance. Both states offer firms significant resources for providing welfare recipients with skills that enable them to pursue career pathways within a firm and elsewhere. (See "Key Elements of Retention and Advancement Programs" below and the appendix for more details.)

    Florida has taken an unusual approach to help firms better manage, retain, and train the entry-level workforce. In 1999, the state WAGES Board, now Workforce Florida, Inc. (WFI), supported a program with the Orlando Chamber of Commerce to educate and assist 1,000 local firms on these issues. In the third year of its effort, the Chamber will deliver a day-long training program to firms on such issues as how to reduce turnover and how to obtain local assistance for skill upgrading. WFI is extending the initiative to four new communities.

- *Expanding eligibility to the working poor* is an opportunity afforded under TANF, as noted earlier. The rationale is twofold. First, recipients do not automatically drop their need for retention and skill-upgrading assistance when their incomes exceed eligibility standards. For most, the path to economic security is an extended one, with many challenges along the way. Second, many working poor have never been on public assistance, yet they remain unable to work their way out of poverty. Many need assistance to move ahead.

    Some states have recognized both participant needs and the opportunity that TANF resources provide to expand state-supported retention and advancement services. Washington's Work First Reinvestment Program is designed to serve low-income working adults earning up to 175 percent of poverty, far above the state's eligibility standard for TANF assistance. Oregon offers job retention services to individuals until they reach 185 percent of poverty. Ohio and Indiana both recognize that stable employment and advancement depend upon personal factors: Ohio offers many services, including drug and alcohol abuse programs, for families earning up to 200 percent of poverty; Indiana offers short-term services or benefits, including emergency housing aid, to help families earning up to 250 percent of poverty stay employed.

Overall, states and localities can take a number of steps to promote an agenda directed at moving people toward sustainable employment and economic self-sufficiency. These policy and organizational actions do not substitute for the programmatic efforts discussed in the next section; rather, they complement and reinforce them.

KEY ELEMENTS OF RETENTION AND ADVANCEMENT PROGRAMS

While few retention and advancement programs include all the elements below, many include some. Key to retention programs are strong relationships with participants, preemployment services, follow-up support, and workplace assistance. Although efforts to help individuals advance on the job are scarce and slow to develop, a few approaches are emerging. These fall into two broad and intersecting categories: career planning/advancement services and skills-upgrade training. Elements include:

- *Development of strong relationships:* At the heart of successful retention programs are relationships that help individuals learn new skills, build self-confidence, and deal with workplace problems. At Vocational Foundation, Inc., an employment training program for economically disadvantaged young people in New York City, the relationship that develops between career advisors and participants is central to the retention strategy. This relationship is built by fostering a climate of high expectations and mutual responsibility throughout training, placement, and postemployment support. After two years in the program, 63 percent of those placed in jobs retained those jobs (Proscio and Elliott 1999).
- *Preemployment services:* Retention and advancement programs often begin with preemployment training. Job search services, life skills classes, and employability assessment and training are important features of preemployment strategies that can contribute to the success of postemployment services.
- *Follow-up support:* Maintaining contact with an individual to lend needed support after employment is accomplished through routine "checking in," case management, and replacement services. Routine checking in to see how things are going, identify problems at home or at work, and help with immediate problem solving usually triggers more substantive, longer-term follow-up sessions, largely involving case management.

Case management takes many forms, but it is fundamentally counseling to facilitate access to support services, income enhancements and disregards, and career guidance and education. Case management sessions frequently include information sharing, goal setting, and making plans and decisions necessary for accomplishing employment goals. Case management might involve several different people who help individuals obtain services, especially given acute employment barriers, such as substance abuse, domestic violence, or criminal records. Sometimes, the case management process involves family members or friends who have a role in the worker's continued employment.

Reemployment services are also a critical component of follow-up. The pattern of rapid and frequent job loss suggests that helping individuals find other employment quickly is essential, but continued attention to the issues that impede steady employment and increase wages is equally important.

Workplace assistance helps individuals deal with personal and work-related challenges that surface after employment begins. Support groups, job skill workshops, coaching and mentoring, employer liaison services, and incentives for participation are among the workplace assistance activities common in many retention programs. These activities can happen individually or in groups, at the workplace, or off the job. Improving supervisors' abilities to manage and train new workers so they better adjust to and understand the work environment is also increasingly evident.

Career planning and advancement services help individuals think about short- and long-term employment goals. Rapid attachment to the workforce often obliges people to take jobs they have neither the interest nor skill to perform proficiently. Even if a person has the ability to keep a job, she or he is not always in a position to advance in it. Getting "stuck" in jobs is partially due to lack of knowledge regarding the availability of more rewarding work and how to get it. Lack of experience with work and the nature of different occupations is obviously an issue for many individuals with limited and sporadic work histories. Thus, career advancement efforts begin with thoughtful career planning: learning about different jobs and what people actually do in them; setting goals for short- and long-term employment; and using labor market information to explore the viability of goals. As a person forms goals, the career advancement process is propelled by matching goals, skills, and personal circumstances to the requirements of another available job.

Skills-upgrade training provides opportunities for workers to increase basic or technical skills, build self-confidence, and apply learning to the job. Viable training programs are accessible, and help workers target jobs with opportunities for increasing income (Stillman 1999). Training is often short-term and combines basic and technical skills for occupations that need workers.

Skills training can be provided off or on the job. Off-the-job strategies are often initiated by the individual worker, taking advantage of Individual Training Accounts (ITAs) or other tuition assistance. On-the-job upgrade strategies are typically driven by the employer, who takes advantage of external funds or uses company training dollars to provide services that enable workers needing specific occupational or literacy skills to advance (Gruber 2000).

It is also important to provide support services and case management to help workers complete training: child care and transportation, if training is not during work hours; counseling to help deal with personal issues; and continued career guidance to capitalize on advancement opportunities.

RETENTION AND ADVANCEMENT: WHAT'S HAPPENING

Moving individuals from welfare to work is no small undertaking. Enabling those who are not earning enough to support their families is even more challenging. The few states that have earmarked funds for retention and advancement initiatives for at least three years—California, Minnesota, Oregon, Rhode Island, Texas, Virginia, and Washington—are in the early stages of developing their approaches; performance data are often unavailable. Funding ranges from $5 million in Minnesota to $31 million in Washington. Among these states, Oregon and Washington target the working poor as well as those moving from welfare to work. The other five make services available primarily to those moving from welfare to work.

While there is considerable agreement among policymakers and local practitioners about the importance of creating ways to help low-wage workers stay employed and
increase earnings to support their families, strategies are just beginning to take shape.
For the most part, practitioners are honing retention services, and only starting to
think about ways to help individuals advance. Employer involvement is increasing, but
participation in sponsoring and shaping strategies is still limited. Not surprisingly,
these programs are too new to be definitive about what works and what does not.
Nevertheless, what is being tried and learned can inform future efforts.

California: Employment Training Panel

The Welfare-to-Work program of California's Employment Training Panel (ETP)
requires participants to work 20 hours a week and complete 40 hours of training, customized for skills needed to succeed on jobs guaranteed by employers. For service
providers to be fully paid, participants must retain full-time employment (30 hours or
more) for at least 90 out of 120 consecutive days after completing training, with no more
than three ETP-eligible employers. Individuals receive time off or pay while in training.

Two very different ETP programs are Employment Success, operated by Lockheed
Martin in San Diego, and Jewish Vocational Services in San Francisco.

- *Employment Success* is a mentoring/on-the-job training strategy. It requires a total of
  60 hours of mentoring during the first month of employment: 20 hours by a Lockheed
  Martin staff member and 40 hours by another employee at the business where the participant is placed. Activities can include assistance with the skills required for the job
  (e.g., customer service, computer training, office procedures, safety), workplace literacy and numeracy skills, or soft skills (e.g., getting along with others). The employer
  receives $2,000 per employee if the individual receives on-the-job mentoring, demon-
  strates competency in skills, and stays employed for 90 days.
- *Jewish Vocational Services* provides retention services by combining resources: ETP,
  WIA, and Welfare-to-Work. Services include follow-up support, one-on-one coaching, employer support and mediation, 24-hour crisis counseling, preemployment
  training, and, if needed, reemployment services. Retention services range from 1 to
  10 hours hour a week per participant, depending on the need. Staff members are in
  the process of planning advancement services and developing short-term skills-
  upgrade training in ESL and customer service.

Minnesota: Pathways Projects

Pathways projects focus on providing skills training for public assistance recipients in
occupations with defined career paths and advancement opportunities. The approach
to training varies. Some projects provide short-term classroom training for five to
eight weeks; others offer training that may take up to six months and involve a combination of classroom work, on-the-job training, and internships. Retention services are optional, as is upgrade training; however, all proposed projects must define available career

paths. In many programs, training is provided for entry-level workers, with upgrade training available for successful completers through Minnesota Partnership Grants.

The Pathways programs provide two examples of retention and advancement approaches:

- *Resources, Inc.,* a nonprofit agency, provides training for computer technicians and case management support for nine months after placement. This support entails routine contact with the employee and employer, with more frequent contact during the first months of placement.
- *Pine Technical College* offers a number of retention services for new hires through a training program it operates for security and building maintenance workers at American Securities Corporation and Marsden Building Maintenance Company. Upon employment, participants receive 12 hours of basic-skills training that emphasizes ways to retain employment and advance on the job. Participants are paid for successfully completing the training. A mentoring program, offered by a local faith-based organization, is also provided for new workers. Other program features include advancement training for incumbent workers (primarily ESL and accent reduction classes). Employees take these classes on their own time during weekends; upon successful completion, they receive hourly wages for the class time.

Oregon: Adult and Family Services Retention and Advancement Efforts

Oregon's approach to retention and advancement begins when individuals apply for welfare. Up-front evaluation and work search services help people avoid public assistance. For those who receive cash assistance, the JOBS program offers a wide range of education, training, and family support services (e.g., drug rehabilitation, domestic violence prevention, family-based case management). Illustrative of Oregon's efforts to address the needs of the hardest-to-serve are waivers that allow individuals to participate in support activities and subsidized employment, rather than running the cash assistance time clock.

Each of Oregon's 15 Adult and Family Services Districts is required to develop strategies for postemployment retention and advancement. Examples include:

- *Medford,* District 8, centers postemployment retention services on Individualized Learning Plans derived from a self-sufficiency assessment. The assessment includes a scale for rating barriers to steady employment. Categories on the scale include: reluctance/desire to participate in the retention program, child care stability, housing arrangements, employment history, partner relationship circumstances, parent education/literacy background, youth risk/resiliency, school attendance, family health issues, substance abuse history, mental health issues, community involvement patterns, level of public assistance, family income, criminal justice involvement, and transportation issues.

  Employment follow-up services—job coaching, employer mediation, and support and career enhancement training—are offered by a postemployment service team staffed by several agencies (e.g., AFS, Job Council, community college personnel, Goodwill). Self-sufficiency assessments and educational plans are carefully monitored for a year.

- *The Lane Workforce Partnership* in Eugene provides case management for several months, a couple of hours a week before and after participants are employed. During sessions, individuals work on developing a positive vision of themselves and their futures by concentrating on goal setting, developing self-esteem and motivation, and creating a network of support. Staff closely monitor client progress through the "Client's Plan for Success," which includes 10 "life domains": family, housing, employment, education/training, legal, medical/physical/emotional/mental, social/recreational, crisis/safety, transportation, and community. Significant time is spent on quality job matching and "checking in" at work or during lunch breaks. Mediating with employers to resolve work-related problems and issues is an important component of the approach.

Texas: Retention and Reemployment Services and Demonstration Grants

Retention and reemployment projects, administered by public and private institutions, have a number of allowable activities: job coaching, job site mentoring, extended case management, direct cash or noncash incentives to meet employment benchmarks, "raise matching" to encourage job advancement, peer-mentoring networks, IDAs connected to job retention, transportation assistance, public transportation enhancement, emergency assistance grants and loans, and ESL.

Projects are funded for one year. Most focus on retention, not job advancement. Participants are referred primarily by local One Stops. Providers also collaborate with a number of local agencies to provide appropriate support services when needed.

Texas has developed a variety of approaches, including:

- *Post-Employment Retention Is Key* (PERK) provides fairly intensive postemployment services for welfare recipients. Developed by Houston Career and Recovery Resources, a community-based organization offering employment services primarily to substance abusers and individuals who have been incarcerated, PERK begins with a two-hour, individual "Client Counseling and Coaching Follow-up Assessment." This is designed to get to know the client's history, circumstances, interests, and needs. Participants also attend four hours of training in customer service and social survival skills in the workplace. The program provides weekly follow-up, job coaching, and access to support services, according to participant needs. Participants commit to these sessions for 12 months. Staff follow up with employers to see how individuals are doing and run interference when needed.
- *The Comprehensive Case Management Project,* operated by the Houston Urban League, began in 1998. It includes a four-week preemployment component with computer skills training and extensive client assessment. Following job placement, staff provide follow-up counseling; subsidized transitional benefits; cash for emergencies; help with tax incentives; additional computer training; reemployment assis-

tance; employer mediation; connections to weekend and evening classes; and workshops on life skills, motivation, and self-esteem.

THE CHALLENGES OF RETENTION AND ADVANCEMENT

Even in states that have made retention and advancement priorities, progress has been slow and implementation uneven. In fact, even in those that emphasize retention and advancement, "work first" and caseload reduction continue to be policy priorities. Not surprisingly, a number of policy and programmatic challenges limit state efforts to assist individuals in achieving economic security.

Policy Challenges

Inadequate and uncoordinated policies: Although some states have taken action to move working adults out of poverty, these efforts are generally fragmented and independent of other initiatives to assist the working poor. No state has a cohesive package that combines policy, organizational, and programmatic actions using a concerted strategy focused on poverty alleviation for those who work. In fact, no state has articulated an overall vision that those who work full-time in this economy should not remain poor.

Inadequate understanding of the labor market: It is important to test and ground actions in the labor market realities of both workers and employers. Too often, policies are enacted without adequate consideration of issues that often cause job loss (e.g., insufficient pay and benefits, work schedules that are incompatible with the family responsibilities of single parents, poor supervision, inhospitable work sites). This lack of understanding underscores the importance of finding ways to engage employers more substantively in these efforts.

Misplaced emphasis on training funds: Attempts to fund training so workers can advance to better-paying jobs with benefits have been made without seriously considering whether individuals will be able to participate in upgrade training. Perhaps the most obvious example involves efforts to establish individual training accounts with TANF employment and training funds so recently employed participants can gain skills to advance to better-paying jobs. In general, participants are not using these training accounts, possibly because single parents new to the workforce find it difficult to work all day, go to school in the evenings, *and* care for their families. In addition, the accounts rely on the individual to get training outside work while, in today's labor market, many businesses are open to providing on-site skills upgrading for groups of entry-level workers. Failure to recognize such realities can lead to policy and program investments that are unused.

Lack of strategic support and accountability: Too often, a lack of capacity to support implementation thwarts the good intentions of program development. Devolution has led to too many instances in which states provide funds for local actions but do not accompany the funding with mechanisms for building technical expertise. Even the most creative policy and program innovations will meet with mixed reactions if they do not have sufficient support and time for program development. And, because little is known about how to implement retention and advancement strategies successfully, it is important to initiate ways for staff to continually monitor, evaluate, and improve efforts as they try new strategies.

Program Challenges

Individuals are eager to abandon connections with the welfare system: Many individuals moving from welfare to work do not want to have anything more to do with a case manager. They do not want to be associated with the welfare system or an agency, especially when they are trying to "fit in" at work. Programs have not responded with appropriate recruitment strategies. Providing information about the requirements and benefits of participation calls for both clarity and sensitivity. For example, the term "retention" provides little information about services, and referring to someone as a "case" is less than engaging.

Overwhelmed new workers: One of the greatest challenges lies in the fact that many entry-level workers are overwhelmed. Getting a new job, the first for some, is stressful. Work and family responsibilities take up most single parents' time. For individuals with low self-esteem or mental health issues, just getting out the door is an accomplishment. Many individuals need and want to take only one step at a time. The first step—getting to work—is about all they can handle. Extra classes and activities, even when beneficial, are impossible for many. Service providers might think more strategically about what can be accomplished during preemployment programs to better equip individuals to learn on the job. It is also important to build strong relationships that connect participants to support and education systems they can access when assistance is needed for job retention or advancement.

The slow response of education and training institutions: The nation's public infrastructure for skills training—community colleges, vocational schools, and specialized skills centers—has not fully adjusted to the realities of the current economy and workforce. Employers and workers need to access specialized skills training that can be offered on a short-term basis and during flexible hours. They also need institutions that are sensitive to and supportive of personal situations that can affect successful participation in training programs. Similarly, postsecondary institutions have been slow to develop and offer training for high-wage occupations at times and in ways that are appropriate, especially for individuals who have not succeeded in traditional education programs.

MOVING AHEAD

While the challenges are great and evidence regarding the impact of existing strategies is limited, the experiences of those exploring new territory is enlightening. For states, several critical policy areas warrant attention if they want to take serious action to reduce poverty by enabling low-wage workers to increase income. Many promising ideas for strengthening postemployment retention and advancement efforts are beginning to emerge.

Policy Actions

As governors' offices and legislatures focus more on the needs of the working poor, a number of policy actions can better equip states to address this matter.

> *Develop an overall state vision and strategy to enable full-time workers to earn incomes above the poverty level.*

As a result of the mandated state plan, WIA may provide impetus for thinking more broadly about how to assist workers in achieving economic self-sufficiency. States have greater flexibility and resources than ever before to address these issues. In addition, as noted by the National Governors' Association (NGA), states need to rethink "old support systems so that they are relevant to workers' needs in today's technology-driven, service-oriented, global economy" (NGA 1999, 1).

This rethinking cannot be done without a firm vision and commitment to helping the working poor achieve economic security. The vision has to encompass not only the vast variety of workforce development resources, but also the other income and social support policies and activities identified earlier. To date, no state has articulated such a vision publicly, although the NGA has recognized the need to help states move in this direction. The NGA recently organized a policy academy, "Expanding Opportunities for Low-Income Families to Advance in the New Economy." State teams from Colorado, Indiana, Kentucky, Michigan, Montana, Ohio, and Washington are engaging in a process that seeks to develop and integrate workforce, welfare, health, child care, income support, and tax policies to address issues of the working poor.

> *Fund and ensure access to services for workers seeking to move from poverty wages to a family-supporting income.*

The evidence that millions of workers, both those moving from welfare and others, are stuck in low-wage jobs indicates a strong need for retention and advancement services and other income enhancements. States could take advantage of the savings from caseload reduction and the flexibility that is allowed with TANF resources to provide greater economic and programmatic support for low-wage workers. They could do so by funding expanded transitional benefits for those moving from welfare to work, wage supplements for the working poor, and retention and advancement services to enable workers to increase earnings on the job. This includes using TANF funds to provide services to other low-wage workers, for example, those at 180 percent of poverty or more. It also includes creating new ways of communicating and delivering services to the working poor, and assuring that those who want services can get them.

> *Use performance measures to emphasize employment retention and wage advancement.*

It is important for states to hold both themselves and those that deliver services locally accountable for helping workers achieve economic self-sufficiency. This means emphasizing performance measures that go beyond simple caseload reduction and initial job placement. Although WIA requires the application of employment retention and wage advancement measures to a state's programmatic efforts, it would be useful to extend these measures to all workers and related assistance efforts. This includes assistance under TANF and other education and training programs not necessarily included under WIA.

Directly support businesses that seek to improve retention, build skills, and provide advancement opportunities for low-wage workers.

In providing overall policy guidance for the use of workforce development resources (e.g., through state plans or strategies), direct involvement of employers in retention and wage progression activities could help make services more accessible. In the current economic climate, employers have a strong vested interest in reducing turnover and increasing worker productivity. Increasingly, employers are open to participating in new approaches that utilize their time, staff, and resources to improve worker performance in entry-level jobs. Such efforts can range from supporting work-based retention specialists to on-the-clock, skills-upgrade training. Such efforts can be enhanced by new partnerships and working relations (e.g., with community colleges) that often require outside guidance and support, a role that states can provide. Further, for employers who invest in strategies to retain and train low-wage workers, it would be useful to provide resources to study their outcomes.

State Program Ideas

As states take action to promote and support retention and advancement efforts at the local level, they should be mindful of several overall program elements.

Provide sufficient time and resources for program development, implementation, and sustainability.

Observation of the few state retention and advancement efforts described here reveals that the cost and time needed to succeed are generally greater than state officials anticipate. Greater consideration of the time and resources it takes for local programs to plan strategies, pilot test them, and make needed modifications would help strengthen efforts. Yet, with so little evidence of what does and does not work, it is essential for states to allow for and fund these kinds of program development, as well as technical assistance costs.

Moreover, states are making short-term investments in retention and advancement without giving enough attention to the time it takes for workers to increase wages. No state has addressed retention and advancement efforts in a comprehensive way. If local programs are to develop strategies that encompass a continuum that includes needed support services at accessible hours (e.g., case management after 5:00 p.m.), it is important for states to consider expanding funding over the course of several years.

Further, the value of convening local organizations to develop these services for the purpose of sharing lessons and experiences should not be overlooked. Oregon schedules monthly meetings of 15 Adult and Family Services district managers to report on progress and attend to issues and challenges. Outside consultants provide expertise to state and local officials, as well as to front-line retention and advancement staff.

Create incentives for education and training institutions to be more responsive to the training needs of workers and employers.

It would be productive for states to encourage and reward education and training institutions that more fully participate in efforts to equip the working poor with higher-level skills. In general, this means engaging the system at the state level and taking actions that tie overall state funding to success in serving the working poor. It also may mean supporting local institutions—community colleges, business associations, community-based groups, workforce investment boards—to advocate and stimulate change at the community level.

Washington's experience illustrates one approach. Through the WorkFirst Reinvestment Program, community and technical colleges are funded to redesign curricula for short-term, pre- and postemployment training in high-wage industry sectors, and to collaborate with human services and employment security offices to provide support services for the retention and advancement of low-wage workers. Community college presidents were reluctant initially to participate, anticipating the cost of customizing curricula for a "work-first" environment (e.g., offering classes on weekends or in the evenings, and meeting with employers and staff in the other organizations, such as the Department of Social Services and Employment Security). Washington's curriculum redesign funding helps colleges cover these costs and become involved in making skills-upgrade training more accessible for low-wage workers.

Develop ways to evaluate and monitor efforts.

In addition to setting statewide performance measures for retention and advancement, states must have ways to monitor the success of local efforts. This means building reliable and effective management information systems. Keeping track of retention rates and wage increases is essential, as is conducting evaluations that determine if participants and employers are receiving the services needed.

Local Program Ideas

There are no precise models for implementing retention and advancement projects at the local level. However, several issues should be considered.

Identify and contract with agencies/providers that can build the trust of participants and make services accessible.

With some exceptions, local welfare agencies are unlikely candidates for this key task. Participants historically have not had good relationships with welfare agencies:

Clients often feel denigrated when they apply for and receive welfare. Although welfare agencies may not intentionally treat individuals this way, it is inherent in the process of determining eligibility. It is simply unrealistic to expect participants to return to welfare agencies to obtain needed services. More is likely to be achieved if welfare agencies contract retention and advancement services to other organizations that are more experienced in developing positive relationships with participants and employers.

For example, in The Dalles, Oregon, the local welfare office contracts with Columbia Gorge Community College to provide short-term credit classes for former welfare recipients who are employed. "Success on the Job" includes six three-hour sessions aimed at building confidence, getting promoted, and succeeding at work. Advice on transitional services, work issues, and employment barriers is provided informally during the evening sessions. A peer-to-peer support group naturally develops during the class. And providing dinner helps make the atmosphere relaxing and social.

"Success on the Job" is a prerequisite for "Introduction to Technology," which is aimed at helping individuals develop computer skills. In class, participants learn computer assembly, basic computer terminology, software installation, and Windows and word processing skills. Participants get a new computer as a reward for completing the class.

Create a decentralized infrastructure that enables workers to obtain needed services through the workplace.

The employment and training infrastructure is too far removed from the business world to effectively provide retention and advancement services. This is not to malign the value of the preemployment training provided by many organizations. But for delivery of services to individuals who are working, the infrastructure simply falls short. Even in the most successful employment training programs, many service providers have minimal connections with the workplace. Local workforce development organizations could fund more programs that operate through human resource and training departments of larger companies or, for smaller employers, through employer associations. And programs need to be available for all low-wage workers.

A Minnesota company uses economic development funding for a new position in the firm: a retention specialist. A 10-month training program for specialists, offered in cooperation with a local technical school, includes instruction on such issues as cultural diversity, team building, communications, mentoring, problem solving, and the local welfare/social support system. Each specialist must be fluent in two languages and familiar with another culture.

In Salem, Oregon, the human resources department of a company was pleased with the job candidates placed through a retention effort operated jointly by Chemeketa Community College and Adult and Family Services. The employer invited a retention specialist to provide on-site support services and assistance with access to ongoing skills training. Skills training is also provided by the customized-training department of the college for all employees. Meetings with the retention specialist and training are completed during company time.

Support organizations whose mission is directly related to retention and advancement.

Retention and advancement services should be provided by organizations and people that can create supportive, productive environments in which both employers and employees feel comfortable, confident, and invested. Staff should be able to perform the following functions: identify what employers need and devise ways for employees with many barriers to meet those needs; look for and try new approaches; offer activities at times that are convenient for working parents; and, most important, provide services that do not perpetuate the stigmas and labels associated with welfare and other obstacles that individuals are trying to overcome.

The Trades Mentor Network in Seattle provides ongoing support and reinforcement for former welfare recipients and other low-income individuals. The program includes a paid, on-the-job training program in which there is a wage increase every six months: $12 an hour to start for most apprentices, going up to $18–$20 an hour. Over three to five years, an apprentice can become a professional and develop portable skills.

Apprentices are assigned a mentor, a journeyman-level person who acts as a guide and a coach—a person committed to bringing new people along. The mentors are all volunteers and receive no additional wages for participation. Five signatory companies are involved, and they guarantee that 15 percent of the work will go to apprentices.

Mentor training is a key component of the effort. Since 1992, 200 mentors and 105 apprentices have been trained. All potential mentors must complete 24 hours of classes and agree to have contact twice a month with their "mentees." Half of apprentices who did not have mentors left the program; 75 percent of those with mentors stayed.

MOVING FURTHER

State and local programs have much to consider in creating policies and shaping strategies to help low-wage workers maintain steady employment and increase wages. Although the current policy environment allows states significant latitude to support the working poor, the political, economic, and social issues to be addressed are numerous and complex. Still, we have an unusual opportunity to support those who are struggling to work their way out of poverty. There are resources to design and implement programs to help individuals retain jobs and advance—and ways to use these resources to provide services and wage supplements to help individuals gain needed skills and increase income. And there are examples of approaches that have the potential to boost individuals' chances of achieving greater economic security. This is a start.

Close to the end of our time in Liberty City, we asked the women if they were earning a living wage. One woman questioned us: "What do you mean by a living wage?" We explained: "Enough money that you feel you're supporting yourself and your family." While a few of the women felt that they were supporting their families, each had hope of earning just a little more—enough to have a car that works, to have savings that aren't wiped out when the kids have to go to the dentist, to turn the lights on whenever they need to, or to buy a treat for their child in the grocery line. One woman's comments illustrate why it might be time to adjust a system that perpetuates the working poor:

> *There would be times when I felt unsure of myself and I'd get frustrated. I'd pick up the phone and I'd call Kathy [the group facilitator], and I'd cry on the phone with Kathy because I need Kathy and I need her support. And I wasn't a faithful member [of the retention group] because of the hours I work. Sometimes I have to work 13 hours, sometimes 10, 12 hours. I just got a raise. And so right now I'm just doing everything on my own. I bought a car from an auction five months ago, and I haven't gotten it on the road yet. I need a transmission seal. And I keep going, faithful, going to work every day, working 13 hours. So by the time I get there [home], it's 8:00 at night. I go home by public transportation, do homework, give her [my daughter] a kiss, and put her to bed. I don't have any benefits right now, but I make a decent salary.*

She made $8.50 an hour.

APPENDIX: STATE INITIATIVES TO PROVIDE POSTEMPLOYMENT SERVICES[14]

California: Employment Training Panel

California's Employment Training Panel (ETP), a joint business- and labor-supported state agency, was created in 1983 as an economic development initiative to retrain incumbent workers. In 1997, ETP began the Welfare-to-Work training program for businesses that hire welfare recipients (CalWORKS participants). Because the criteria for ETP funding require employment, Welfare-to-Work programs can be accessed only after a worker is on the job for at least 20 hours a week. It is anticipated that $5 million will be expended on Welfare-to-Work projects in FY 2000. Since 1997, 19 contracts have been awarded, ranging from $49,000 to $9.5 million. An additional $15 million is targeted for worker training in high-unemployment areas, especially rural areas. The funds are aimed at the working poor, who have not benefited from the economic recovery.

The State Initiative

As an agency established to boost California's economic development, the Employment Training Panel's $70 million FY 2000 budget is earmarked for employers to train new workers and retrain workers in danger of being laid off. Funding comes from 0.01 percent of subject unemployment insurance wages paid by every private, for-profit employer and some nonprofits. Programs historically funded by ETP had to be targeted to high-skill, high-wage jobs. The wage requirement has been softened with the Welfare-to-Work initiative: Wages only have to meet the state or federal minimum wage, whichever is higher.

ETP efforts are moderately connected with the Employment Development Department (EDD). EDD's Job Services Division is responsible for Welfare-to-Work grants and WIA implementation. Through EDD, the state has allocated $1.5 million from the governor's Welfare-to-Work funds to support skills-upgrade projects, to be operated in some of California's One Stop service centers.

The Department of Social Services is responsible for CalWORKS, which is administered by 58 county welfare departments. Each department has considerable control over the expenditure of funds and programming. While postemployment retention and advancement for CalWORKS participants are considered important activities by state officials, there is no focused state effort in this regard.

California is a "work-first" state, and each of these participating agencies is involved in helping low-income residents get jobs and remain employed. Postemployment retention and advancement approaches are still being defined by each agency, and many of the projects are in the early stages of implementation.

Key Elements

ETP participants must be employed and receiving, or have received, TANF assistance within one year of beginning training. At the end of training, participants must retain full-time employment (30 hours a week or more) for at least 90 out of 120 consecutive days, with no more than three ETP-eligible employers. During training, participants must be employed for a minimum of 20 hours a week. Temporary employment is allowed. ETP contracts are performance-based, can continue for two years, and can provide participants training for up to 18 months. Training must last at least 40 hours.

The primary goal is entry-level employment retention, but the funding can be used for advancement training. Skills training is the foremost activity of the contracts, and it includes classroom and on-the-job training in occupational and soft skills for many industries (hospitality, service, transportation, medical, auto repair, manufacturing, communication, business management, information technology, and maintenance). Basic skills, ESL instruction, and mentoring are allowed.

Funding is performance based: 25 percent can be claimed at enrollment, 50 percent at completion of training, and the remaining 25 percent if participants are retained for 90 days. Programs are generally operated by an employment and training service provider and the local department of social services, which identifies potential participants. Contractors include Private Industry Councils, training organizations, employer organizations, employers, and postsecondary institutions (including proprietary schools).

ETP has had difficulty expending the Welfare-to-Work funds. In 1997–98, when $20 million was appropriated, ETP could not attract applicants because of the employment requirements. Many employers did not want the funding because they do not hire many CalWORKS participants and would not apply for funding for a few employees. A second difficulty is related to how the funding is awarded and on what it can be spent. Because it is performance based, many training providers do not want to take on the risk. Further, to use this funding, ETP originally required 40 hours of classroom training, which was largely inappropriate for employees and employers. Now it can be used for on-the-job training.

Goals/Evaluation

The goals of ETP for funding Welfare-to-Work programs are essentially the same as for other full-time, incumbent-worker training programs. The primary goals are to update workers' skills and to keep jobs in California. Contracts are performance based: Participants must complete postemployment training and remain employed for 90 days after training. ETP relaxes the number of hours that participants must work for Welfare-to-Work projects (20 hours a week as opposed to 35 hours) and allows for more total training hours (40 to 200 for other programs, while the upper limit for Welfare-to-Work can be negotiated depending on need). It is expected that these provisions will enable trainees to be successful employees.

Minnesota: Pathways Program

The Pathways Program is a three-year-old initiative designed to equip public assistance recipients with the training and skills to access longer-term, career path positions in the private sector. The program supports customized training and requires partnerships among businesses, education/training institutions, and community organizations. Preference goes to projects that provide employment with benefits and defined career paths, and that offer supports for recipients to attend training and retain employment.

Pathways has supported 19 projects that plan to train more than 2,666 public assistance recipients. Funding of $2.5 million annually is available to finance projects for fiscal years 2000 and 2001.

The State Initiative

Minnesota operates its TANF and JTPA/WIA initiatives under a philosophy of "work first." However, neither of the agencies responsible for TANF (Human Services) or WIA (Employment Security) has focused on sustainable employment and skills training.

The Pathways Program is administered by the Minnesota Jobs Skills Partnership (MJSP), which operates under the direction of an independent board. MJSP is housed in the Minnesota Department of Trade and Economic Development, formed in 1983, and promotes worker training through joint efforts by business and educational institutions. The state considers MJSP a tool for economic development and a catalyst for encouraging educational institutions to develop the capacity to meet the training needs of business.

MJSP's primary training effort is the Partnership program, which supports training for new or existing employees, with no focus on the trainee's economic status. The Partnership program has a budget of about $15 million annually for 2000 and 2001. The Pathways program was added in 1997 to serve public assistance recipients specifically.

MJSP has strong support from the Minnesota legislature and, historically, has been funded with general state revenues. The first two years of Pathways funding ($3.5 million) came from general revenues. Pathways funding for the second two years (a total of $5 million) combines state general revenues, a dedicated employment tax, and $3 million of state TANF funds.

Minnesota operates welfare through the Department of Human Services (DHS), which contracts with the state's 87 counties to deliver welfare and social services. For the most part, county, not state, agencies operate the programs. The Department of Employment Security (DES) funds 17 service delivery areas or local workforce investment areas. Neither DHS nor DES nor, for that matter, any other state agency is considered a formal collaborator in the Pathways program.

Key Elements

The central theme of MJSP training activity is the direct involvement of private employers in preparing and implementing education and training. MJSP believes that education and training programs that involve employers from the beginning have the best chance of success in achieving both quality training and actual job placements. While MJSP seeks to fund training programs that will address immediate industry needs, it also intends to serve as a catalyst in the development of long-lasting relationships between education and industry—relationships that will continue beyond individual project duration.

MJSP can support programs that involve more than one employer. Training may take place at the educational institution, the workplace, or a location acceptable to the two parties. MJSP encourages innovative, creative, and effective models of interaction between education and business. The goal is to target training for full-time employment in the growth sectors of the state's economy. While participating employers are not required to commit themselves to hiring all trainees, high rates of placement and retention are expected.

Each Pathways project can be funded to a maximum of $400,000 (the limit was $200,000 during the first two years). Pathway funds support the cost of instruction, instructional development, training, materials, supplies, equipment, and related costs. Funds cannot be used for wage subsidy or tuition reimbursement.

Public and private education and training institutions within the state are eligible for the funding. A 1 : 1 match is required from participating businesses. The match may be in the form of cash or in-kind contributions of goods and services.

All Pathways proposals must specifically describe how other community organizations will support the project—by providing recruitment/referral services as well as support services that help recipients participate in training and retain employment. Applicants are expected to document how these services are funded. Proposals must also define educational and career pathways that are associated with the training offered through the project. Applicants are expected to train participants in ways that position them to obtain further training and advance along a defined career path.

Goals/Evaluation

To date, Pathways has focused its concern for outcomes around the number of projects funded, persons receiving training, and projected placements. The program is too new to effectively measure the number of placements, wages at placement, and long-term success; only a few projects have reached the point of completion.

Pathways has engaged the National Results Council (NRC) to conduct an ongoing evaluation. NRC will monitor and assess the projects and seek to measure the impacts of participation. It will conduct the assessment over two years, concluding its work in 2001. During this time, it will survey training participants at enrollment, 120 days after completion, and a year after completion. NRC will measure changes in participants' employment status, including income, hours worked, benefits, training, promotions, and job changes. Information will also be sought on participants' continued use of public benefits, access to support services, and barriers to work. NRC will conduct qualitative analyses of the development and operations of Pathways projects.

Oregon: Adult and Family Services Retention and Advancement Effort

Oregon has a long history of building an infrastructure to support the efforts of low-income families to gain economic self-sufficiency. Despite a strong emphasis on rapid attachment to the workforce, state policy and programs focus on helping individuals find and keep jobs and advance to better employment. Support services and programs aimed at assisting working individuals are available for those who fall below 185 percent of poverty. The state enacted legislation allowing TANF savings from caseload reduction to be redirected to support working families by increasing child care assistance, housing subsidies, and retention and advancement services. The 15 Adult and Family Services districts must also spend 25 percent of their TANF budgets on retention and advancement services for individuals who fall at or below 185 percent of poverty. This amounts to more than $5 million a year for activities beyond support services.

The State Initiative

Oregon's approach to retention and advancement begins when individuals apply for welfare. Intensive up-front evaluation and work search services help people avoid public assistance. For those who receive cash assistance, the JOBS program offers a wide range of education, training, and family stability services, such as drug rehabilitation and domestic violence and family-based case management. Waivers allow individuals to participate in support activities and subsidized employment, rather than running the cash assistance time clock, demonstrating Oregon's commitment to addressing the needs of the hardest-to-serve. To support the development of retention and advancement activities, the agency has also provided a series of technical assistance workshops to help regions shape strategies and services.

District managers meet monthly to exchange ideas about their efforts and deal with implementation challenges. Eventually, state officials see the agency as one that focuses on those who are employed, rather then just the unemployed. To this end, district managers are thinking about ways to generate, market, and provide services to working individuals who have never received cash assistance.

The state advertises services for the underemployed in a brochure aimed at "low-income Oregonians. . . . You don't have to be out of work to get services. We can help if you're working but earn a low income. And we might be able to help with a problem that could cause you to go on welfare." Services include help with basic expenses (e.g., money for rent, food, utilities, other emergencies), medical benefits, alcohol or drug treatment problems, getting and keeping a job, help getting a better job, and work-related child care and transportation. Oregon encourages participation in education activities: About 1,450 clients have received their GED during the biennium.

Adult and Family Services (AFS) works closely with other agencies. Collaborative arrangements with community colleges and the One Stops are common throughout the state. For example, many case managers have offices in community colleges even when the college is not the contractor for the One Stop. Further, AFS uses a process called "staffings" for case management. Staffings are group case management sessions at which representatives from various agencies involved in providing services meet with the client as a team to review progress on Educational Development or Income Improvement Plans. A team might include staff from a college, the housing authority, a drug rehab program, Child Support and Enforcement, and AFS.

Key Elements

AFS gives much latitude to districts in designing retention and advancement strategies, and all are strongly invested in case management. Other common services include extended service hours (clients can receive support services in evenings and on

Saturdays), support groups, training activities, and problem solving for employed clients. State officials are seeking additional resources to fund retention and advancement activities and related support services by requesting authority to redirect unspent food stamp allocations.

Retention and advancement services are indicated on clients' individualized plans.[15] Oregon also provides Individual Training Accounts that can be used for upgrade training, although it appears that few clients take advantage of them. Child care and transportation subsidies related to employment are substantial in Oregon, as are work-related education and training.

Although not fully implemented, another key element in Oregon's strategy is to separate the work responsibilities of case mangers. This means there will be two types of case manager: one responsible solely for eligibility issues, the other attending to job retention issues. This is an important change, allowing one person to focus on support services, especially those that are income related, and another to focus on employment and training issues.

Goals/Evaluation

Oregon has several goals in helping families become self-supporting:

- To help people in need get and keep jobs;
- To help families get regular child care; and
- To provide benefits that support those working toward self-sufficiency.

Oregon requires each district to set its own performance measures. For example, the goal for one district is to increase employment income via increased hours, higher wages, income enhancement, or shifts to better jobs. However, with a variety of measures, it is difficult to get a handle on the desired outcomes for the state as a whole.

State reports indicate participation rates and general outcomes. For example, in the 1997–99 biennium, 22,093 individuals were in the JOBS program (employment preparation, training and placement, basic education, life skills, and job search assistance). Of those people in JOBS Plus training slots, 64 percent went on to unsubsidized employment, and 93 percent of clients who found work over an 18-month period were off welfare.

Texas: Retention and Re-Employment Services and Demonstration Grants

The Texas Retention and Re-Employment Services and Demonstration Grants fund was established in 1998 to develop model postemployment retention and advancement strategies for current or former welfare recipients. Projects are diverse and can include any number of services to enable individuals to maintain steady employment. A wide variety of public and private organizations has been funded to provide services. For FY 1999, $3 million was awarded: 23 projects were funded, ranging from $35,000 to $525,000, to serve 3,158 individuals across the state. In FY 2000, $6 million was available, but grants cannot exceed $250,000.

The State Initiative

Texas maintains a "work-first" philosophy, but has combined employment and training funding sources to help welfare recipients "get a job, find a better job, and then develop a career." In addition to the Retention and Re-employment Demonstration Grants, Texas also has appropriated $2 million for innovative projects related to transportation, microenterprises, or training for nontraditional jobs. It also has a $12 million self-sufficiency fund designed to provide customized preemployment training and support services for welfare recipients through local educational organizations, leading to specific jobs made available by employer-partners.

The Texas Workforce Commission, which administers the funds, is a consolidated agency established in 1995, with responsibility for employment security, WIA, and the welfare employment and training program. The commission also administers the Welfare-to-Work Formula and Competitive Grants through its Welfare Reform Division and locally through 28 Workforce Development Boards.

Redirected TANF funding supports the Retention projects, and the effort has strong support from the legislature. Other welfare programs are administered by the Texas Department of Human Services.

Key Elements

The Texas Workforce Commission is interested in promoting innovation with the Retention grants, and places relatively few restrictions on the funding. Funds are used for a broad range of activities: pre- and postemployment case management models, career advancement, direct cash or noncash incentives to meet employment benchmarks, child care, transportation assistance, emergency assistance grants and loans, and basic skills or ESL, for example. Most projects focus on job retention; there is little evidence of job advancement services.

In the second year of funding, Texas made several significant changes in the operational requirements for funding. In FY 1999, grant applicants had to obtain local Workforce Development Board approval. In FY 2000, proposals were submitted by the boards. The name of the program was changed to the Job Retention and Local Innovation Service for TANF Recipients.

During the first year, grants were available to educational institutions, community and faith-based organizations, private for-profit companies, and quasi-governmental organizations. For the second year, local Workforce Development Boards must submit grants on behalf of a partnership with a community- or faith-based organization. These organizations can make contractual arrangements with others to implement projects. Local boards can submit separate proposals for each project, and they can submit an unlimited number.

Originally, grantees had only to recruit participants from Workforce Center operators (One Stops). Now, projects are to be fully coordinated with Workforce Center operators and integrated into the local One Stop service delivery network.

Projects were funded for one year, but many were extended due to recruiting difficulties. In FY 2000, the duration of the projects was negotiated with the Texas

Workforce Commission. Grantees do not have to match funds, although most are using additional resources to provide services.

Goals/Evaluation

The goal of the Job Retention and Local Innovations Grants is to invest in the long-term success of welfare recipients in their transition from welfare to self-sufficiency. The Texas Workforce Commission collects data on the number of individuals served each month and monitors projects to determine if they are meeting stated benchmarks. Grantees submit monthly retention data, including wages, at 6, 9, and 12 months. Projects funded to develop case management models must include an "evaluation of the effectiveness and quality of the case management provided."

Initially, providers had difficulty recruiting participants. In October 1999, 15 projects were not serving their projected number of participants. Two of the programs had not recruited anyone. Eventually, most programs met enrollment goals, and the numbers were fairly high: More than 3,000 participants were enrolled across the state by February 2000. State officials indicated that projects needed more planning time, and recognized that some of the One Stops were less enthusiastic about making referrals than they should have been. Therefore, many changes for the second year of funding were designed to promote coordination among the organizations involved in providing retention services.

Washington: WorkFirst Reinvestment Program

The state of Washington is redirecting TANF surplus dollars to develop new initiatives that help current and former welfare recipients and other low-income adults retain employment and increase wages. As part of a $31 million investment, the state funds each community college to develop a 10- to 12-week training program focused on high-demand career sectors. Programs are designed to give participants a "quick start" in employment and to increase literacy, access further education and training, access needed support services, and improve the ability to advance at work. Services are available for the unemployed and underemployed who fall at or below 175 percent of poverty. In 1998–1999, 6,600 individuals enrolled in WorkFirst Reinvestment Programs, 73 percent of the targeted number.

The State Initiative

Community and technical colleges have the lead role in WorkFirst Reinvestment Programs; however, funding is disbursed through subcontracts from the Department of Social and Health Services (DSHS) to the State Board for Community and Technical Colleges (SBCTC). Funds are available to redesign courses and services and to provide preemployment occupational training, tuition assistance to employed participants, workplace literacy for low-wage entry-level workers, family management skills for working parents, and evening and weekend child care.

The governor, who is very much behind the initiative, has taken steps to see that the key agencies influencing its outcomes work together. The SBCTC, DSHS, Department of Employment Security (DES), and Department of Community, Trade and Economic Development must collaborate and develop joint plans and performance measures.

While Washington is a "work-first" state, it is one of the few that provides retention and advancement assistance for welfare and former welfare recipients as well as low-wage workers. The state also allows welfare recipients to pursue preemployment training courses developed by community colleges in place of the traditional job search programs. In short, the WorkFirst Reinvestment Programs are integral to Washington's intention to promote economic self-sufficiency.

Key Elements

Washington's underlying objective is to make community colleges more accessible to both employers and low-income workers. To this end, community colleges are developing strategies that combine short-term pre- and postemployment training (aimed at jobs in high-wage sectors and opportunities for advancement) with other postemployment retention and support services. Other characteristics include strong employer involvement in curriculum design, training that provides both basic and occupational skills, and clear connections to employment opportunities.

To redesign programs, all 30 community colleges in the state system are working with local partners—from DSS, DES, and employers. Colleges received $109,000 to $149,000, depending on the size of the target population, to develop short-term training courses and hire coordinators to provide direct services, such as career planning, enrollment, support, and connections to other agency services. Examples of occupations for which short-term training is offered include call-center specialists, CNC operators, bus drivers, warehouse forklift operators, office workers, nursing assistants, and automotive technicians.

The Reinvestment program has six components:

- *Program redesign and delivery* provides funding to develop programs and services that make it easier for participants to attend and succeed in college.
- *Tuition assistance* pays for books and tuition because traditional financial aid is not available for short-term programs or for students enrolled in courses with less than 10 credits.
- *Preemployment training* involves short-term courses to build skills in a particular field. Training is developed for employers who commit to giving first consideration to hire those who complete training.
- *Customized literacy training* for specific workplaces is available through Workplace Basics contracts.
- *Families that Work* funding is earmarked for programs that prepare parents with low basic skills for work by combining literacy instruction with family management skills.
- *WorkFirst Work-Study* combines a participant's learning and work by providing employment through colleges.

Goals/Evaluation

This program has several goals:

- Create entry-level employment opportunities at above-average wages;
- Combine literacy and parenting skills training with employment training;
- Improve the basic skills of workers in entry-level jobs; and
- Ensure the availability of financial assistance for training to WorkFirst participants who are employed and to other low-wage workers.

The State Board for Community and Technical Colleges, Education Division, recently released a report on the progress of the program. As of 1999, 2,600 welfare recipients, 1,000 former recipients, and 3,000 low-income workers participated; 4,215 individuals took advantage of tuition assistance; 1,609 enrolled in preemployment training; 753 participated in workplace basics courses; 571 enrolled in the families-that-work programs; and 133 children used child care services. A total of 171 classes were redesigned, and seven colleges provided evening and weekend child care for participants.

During the first year of implementation, the state found, among other things, that developing and implementing programs were more complex than anticipated; participants needed much more assistance accessing and completing training than envisioned; and participation was lower than projected.

NOTES

1. Wages are expressed in 1996 dollars.

2. At least 30 states provided postemployment services as of October 1999, according to data collected through the State Policy Documentation Project, a joint initiative of the Center for Budget and Policy Priorities and the Center for Law and Social Policy. California, Minnesota, Oregon, Rhode Island, Texas, Virginia, and Washington have funded distinct state employment retention initiatives. We visited California, Minnesota, Oregon, Texas, and Washington to learn about their efforts (see appendix).

3. These studies are Cancian and Meyer (1997, 2000) and Rangarajan et al. (1998). All tracked, over five years, a national sample of women in the labor market who had received welfare, and they compare various personal, family, and work characteristics in the initial years after leaving welfare with the women's economic well-being four or five years later. The Cancian and Meyer studies are notable for the wide range of job, personal, family, work history, neighborhood, and labor market variables brought into the models, including measures of changes in employment and education over time.

4. U.S. House of Representatives (2000); Strawn and Martinson (2000); Freedman et al. (2000); U.S. General Accounting Office (1999); Strawn (1998); Bloom (1997); Friedlander and Burtless (1995).

5. These dollar amounts are averages across the entire sample, including those not working.

6. This total does not include an additional $7 billion in unspent federal TANF funds from prior years, which remain available to states. Unless states obligated these funds by October 1, 1999, however, only current and prior-year TANF funds can be used for "nonassistance" services and benefits, such as workforce development.

7. This is especially relevant for using TANF to serve at-risk youth. See Cohen (2000).

8. This discussion is drawn from Greenberg and Savner (1999); see also Greenberg (1999).

9. This description is drawn from Strawn and Martinson (2000).

10. This discussion is taken from Greenberg and Savner (1999); see also Greenberg (1999).

11. See Strawn and Martinson (2000) and Center for Law and Social Policy (1999).

12. Much of this information is drawn from Center on Budget and Policy Priorities (2000).

13. If not structured properly, expanding disregards could have a serious downside: running recipients' time clocks for a small amount of income.

14. These descriptions are based on visits during fall 1999. The authors interviewed state and local officials, visited programs, and reviewed documents for each initiative.

15. Districts have different names for these plans, such as Employment Development, Income Improvement, or Learning Plans.

REFERENCES

Bloom, Dan. 1997. *After AFDC: Welfare-to-Work Choices and Challenges for States.* ReWORKing Welfare: Technical Assistance for States and Localities Series. New York: Manpower Demonstration Research Corporation. Available at http://www.mdrc.org.

Cancian, Maria, and Daniel R. Meyer. 1997. *Work after Welfare: Work Effort, Occupation, and Economic Well-Being.* Draft paper prepared for the annual meeting of the Association for Public Policy Analysis and Management, Washington, D.C.

———. 2000. "Work after Welfare: Women's Work Effort, Occupation, and Economic Well-Being." *Social Work Research* 24(2): 69–86.

Center for Law and Social Policy. 1999. Audio conference with Mike Storrs, Director, Division of Self-Sufficiency Programs, Office of Family Assistance Administration for Children and Families, U.S. Department of Health and Human Services. May 12.

Center on Budget and Policy Priorities. 2000. *Windows of Opportunity: Strategies to Support Families Receiving Welfare and Other Low-Income Families in the Next Stage of Welfare Reform.* Washington, D.C.: Center on Budget and Policy Priorities. January.

Cohen, Marie. 1999. "TANF Funds: A New Resource for Youth Programs." In *Youth Notes* (September). Washington, D.C.: National Youth Employment Coalition.

Freedman, Stephen, et al. 2000. *Evaluating Alternative Welfare-to-Work Approaches: Two-Year Impacts for Eleven Programs.* Washington, D.C.: U.S. Department of Health and Human Services and U.S. Department of Education.

Friedlander, Daniel, and Gary Burtless. 1995. *Five Years After: The Long-Term Effects of Welfare-to-Work Programs.* New York: Russell Sage Foundation.

Greenberg, Mark. 1999. *Beyond Welfare: New Opportunities to Use TANF to Help Low-Income Working Families.* Washington, D.C.: Center for Law and Social Policy. Available at http://www.clasp.org.

Greenberg, Mark, and Steve Savner. 1999. *The Final TANF Regulations: A Preliminary Analysis.* Washington, D.C.: Center for Law and Social Policy. Available at http://www.clasp.org.

Gruber, David. 2000. *We're Education . . . You're Semiconductors.* Philadelphia, Pa.: Public/Private Ventures. January.

Gueron, Judith, and Edward Pauly. 1991. *From Welfare to Work.* New York: Russell Sage Foundation.

Hershey, Alan M., and LaDonna Pavetti. 1997. "Turning Job Finders into Job Keepers." *The Future of Children: Welfare to Work* 7 (1). Available at http://www.futureofchildren.org.

Knox, Virginia, Cynthia Miller, and Lisa Gennetian. 2000. *Reforming Welfare and Rewarding Work: A Summary of the Final Report of the Minnesota Family Investment Program.* New York: Manpower Demonstration Research Corporation.

Loprest, Pamela. 1999. *Families Who Left Welfare: Who Are They and How Are They Doing?* Discussion Paper 99-02. Washington, D.C.: Urban Institute. Available at http://www.newfederalism.urban.org.

National Governors' Association Center for Best Practices. 1999. "State Policy Academy on Expanding Opportunities for Low-Income Families to Advance in the New Economy." Washington, D.C.: National Governors' Association. August.

Pindus, Nancy, Robin Koralek, Karin Martinson, and John Trutko. 2000. *Coordination and Integration of Welfare and Workforce Development Systems.* Washington, D.C.: The Urban Institute for the U.S. Department of Health and Human Services.

Proscio, Tony, and Mark Elliott. 1999. *Getting In, Staying On, Moving Up.* Philadelphia, Pa.: Public/Private Ventures. Winter.

Rangarajan, Anu, Peter Schochet, and Dexter Chu. 1998. *Employment Experiences of Welfare Recipients Who Find Jobs: Is Targeting Possible?* Princeton, N.J.: Mathematica Policy Research, Inc. Available at http://www.mathinc.com.

Stillman, Joseph. 1999. *Working to Learn: Skills Development under Work First.* Philadelphia, Pa.: Public/Private Ventures.

Strawn, Julie. 1998. *Beyond Job Search or Basic Education: Rethinking the Role of Skills in Welfare Reform.* Washington, D.C.: Center for Law and Social Policy.

Strawn, Julie, and Karin Martinson. 2000. *Steady Work and Better Jobs: Helping Low-Income Parents to Sustain Employment and Advance in the Workforce.* New York: Manpower Demonstration Research Corporation.

U.S. Department of Labor. 1995. *What's Working (and What's Not).* Washington, D.C.: U.S. Department of Labor. January.

U.S. General Accounting Office. 1999. *Welfare Reform: Assessing the Effectiveness of Various Welfare-to-Work Approaches.* Washington, D.C.: U.S. General Accounting Office. September.

U.S. House of Representatives. 2000. Committee on Ways and Means. *2000 Green Book: Background Material and Data on Programs within the Jurisdiction of the Committee on Ways and Means.* Washington, D.C.: U.S. House of Representatives.

PART 3

Different Strokes

Overcoming Barriers Facing Particular Groups

10

Increasing Economic Security for Low-Wage Women Workers

Vicky Lovell and Heidi Hartmann

Women low-wage workers face four kinds of problems that are unique to their situation as women.

First, women workers, including low-wage workers, face gender-based discrimination in the labor market: They are more likely to work in low-wage jobs than men with similar qualifications, and low-wage jobs typically held by women offer little opportunity for advancement. Thus, women workers are more likely to be stuck in low-wage jobs for many years.

Second, women workers usually have greater responsibility for the care of family members than male workers. Women are more likely to be custodial single parents than men, and wives spend more time providing family care than their husbands.

A third issue is that women are more likely to be hurt by structural changes in the labor market, such as the growth of low-paid service jobs, contingent employment, and falling wages at the bottom of the labor market. This is because women have a disproportionate presence in low-wage, nonstandard, and service sector employment.

Finally, for two reasons, women may not be able to benefit from the recent growth of educational earnings premiums to the extent that men can. Male and female students still often pursue different courses of study. Also, employers often steer equally qualified women and men into different occupations with different wage structures.

Such problems will not be remedied simply by individuals making different choices about their labor market involvement or moving up a job ladder into higher-paid work. While some women will be able to escape the female job ghetto, which offers low pay and few advancement opportunities, or find a family-friendly employer, most will not. These job structures and widespread gender discrimination will only change as a result of appropriately designed public policies.

Improved federal enforcement of equal employment opportunity laws, including substantial outreach and education to both employers and workers, is an important base for these policy initiatives that would direct more income and earnings to female low-wage workers. Such improvements could reduce race and sex discrimination at all stages of the employment relationship: hiring, on-the-job training, promotion, and wage setting. The role of federal agencies in overcoming institutionalized employment bias through proactive follow-up to legislation and executive orders dating from the 1960s and 1970s is essential for women, particularly women of color, to move toward economic autonomy.

In addition, another kind of enabling legislation would help advance the goal of women's economic viability: strengthening labor laws to make it easier for workers to unionize and easier for unions to protect workers' interests in negotiations with employers. Research has repeatedly shown that unions increase workers' wages, and a study by the Institute for Women's Policy Research (IWPR) demonstrates that unions have an especially important role in raising women's wages (Hartmann, Allen, and Owens 1999). Unions also advocate public policies that would especially benefit women workers. Increased unionization in female-dominated occupations and industries would provide women with a powerful ally in their efforts to achieve economic security.

BARRIERS TO WOMEN'S ECONOMIC SECURITY

Women are becoming much more like men in their employment patterns: 60.2 percent of women are in the workforce (up from 42.7 percent in 1969), as are 74.7 percent of men (down from 79.8 percent in 1969), and 46.6 percent of the labor force is female (U.S. DOL 2001). However, the nature of the employment experience is very different for women and men. Women work fewer hours than men and in different occupations and industries. Women constitute the bulk of part-time workers (63 percent) and remain concentrated in such traditionally female jobs as administrative support, nursing, and teaching: Two of every five working women hold one of these jobs.[1] Women are disproportionately present in the low-wage workforce, representing 60 percent of this group (Mishel, Bernstein, and Schmitt 2001).

If women are eager to work, why are they on different work tracks than men, 30 to 40 years after the Equal Pay Act of 1963, the Civil Rights Act of 1964, the Higher Education Act of 1965, and Executive Order 11246 of 1965 made employment discrimination illegal and opened many educational and employment opportunities to women? One big reason is children and families. Despite women's impressive pursuit of employment, the burden of family caregiving remains unevenly distributed among women, men, and public institutions, imposing an enormous disadvantage on women who wish to combine their labor market and caregiving work. The time and effort required to care for children, physically and emotionally, are not easily reconciled with the demands of employment, particularly when a job requires overtime or when workers do not have flexibility to schedule work around their children's child care or school hours, or to take time off to care for ill children.

Strategies workers use to combine family responsibilities and employment in manageable ways include reducing work hours to less than full-time, taking breaks from employment (e.g., either parental leave at the birth of a child or temporarily dropping out of the workforce), or avoiding jobs that are likely to require work schedules that would be incompatible with caregiving.[2] All these avenues depress earnings. Part-time workers suffer lower hourly wages than their full-time colleagues (Hipple and Stewart 1996); they are also much less likely to be included in employers' benefit plans (U.S. DOL 1999). With 25 percent of employed women working part-time, the impact of caregiving on reducing hours of paid employment is a concern. So are the consequences of temporarily leaving the workforce. It is not surprising that leaving work entirely while caring for children would reduce one's wages on returning to work: Skills may dull during an absence. But parenting has a continuing, depressing effect on earnings during employment, especially for women.

Family care responsibilities also impose direct employment costs on workers, as substitute care must be hired when family caregivers join the workforce. Theoretically, for married parents, the costs of child care are a family expense. In reality, however, whether because men's wages are generally higher than women's (making it more lucrative for fathers to work than mothers) or because social norms still identify men as "primary" breadwinners, parents are likely to view child care expenditures as a corollary to wives' employment decisions. This expense in effect taxes mothers' earnings, reducing earnings and discouraging employment.

This employment penalty takes a sizeable bite out of low-earners' pay: 19 percent of low-income women's earnings and 13 percent of their family income goes to child care expenses. The bite is even bigger for low-income single women: Welfare recipients pay 34 percent of their earnings, and 19 percent of their family income, for child care services (IWPR 1997). Child care expenses have been shown to steer women toward nonemployment and, among workers, toward part-time work. In fact, some research suggests that the negative impact of motherhood on married women's employment operates largely through the cost of care (Powell 1998).

The expense of child care is one way that being a parent affects employment. The challenge of caring for and organizing everything it takes to raise children while working at a job site can be an impossible effort. This is particularly so when employers fail to offer the flexibility needed to care for sick children (or those who may be recovering from an illness but must remain away from school or child care), or to take both healthy and ill children to health and dental appointments. Low-wage workers are much less likely than higher-wage earners to have this crucial flexibility: 36 percent of employed mothers who are former welfare recipients have no sick leave for themselves, compared with 20 percent of mothers who have never received welfare (Heymann and Earle 1999); 63 percent of low-wage workers cannot take time off to care for sick children without losing pay, while only 39 percent of high-wage workers face this obstacle (Galinsky and Bond 2000). Thus, for many working parents, the structure of the low-wage labor market presents an unworkable set of options when a child becomes ill: leave the child home unattended, care for the child and lose pay, or care for the child and lose a job.

Besides unequal caregiving responsibilities, continued discrimination is another big reason for differences between women's and men's pay, work hours, and occupations. The continuing success of the Equal Employment Opportunity Commission and the Office of Federal Contract Compliance Programs in prosecuting claims of gender-based employment discrimination demonstrates that overt bias against women still restrains women's labor market options.[3] Strengthened enforcement would bring more equity for women workers.

Covert, institutionalized bias that socializes women and men to believe there are gender differences in skills and interests may be an even more powerful influence on women's educational and employment opportunities (Brown and Pechman 1987; Reskin and Roos 1990). This structural discrimination contributes to underpayment in female-dominated occupations: that is, the devaluation of work women do, simply because women do it. Job evaluation studies that compare the skills, effort, responsibility, and working conditions of male- and female-dominated occupations consistently find that women's jobs pay less for a comparable level of expertise (England 1992). Even job evaluation systems themselves, which purport to objectively describe job content, often reflect a bias against women's skills, leading to discounted determinations of the value of women's work (Steinberg 1990).

The labor market's wage-setting structure seems to be constructed in such a way that women do not receive the same compensation as men, even with equivalent training and experience. Thus, a 1998 Council of Economic Advisers White Paper found that when researchers analyze pay differences between women and men and identify the elements that contribute to them, only some of the raw wage gap can be explained: A 12 percent gap still remains between what men and women are paid, holding constant education, experience, occupation, industry, and union status—all the available measures of workers' employment value.

POLICIES TO INCREASE THE ECONOMIC SECURITY OF LOW-WAGE WOMEN WORKERS

While women workers face formidable barriers to achieving economic security, a wide array of public policies can help. One set of policies would make it easier for workers with caregiving responsibilities to increase their work hours. Another group would change wage-setting systems or increase women's skills to allow women to advance into higher-paying jobs. Income supplement programs could also target the needs of women workers. And updating collective bargaining laws and enforcing existing equal employment opportunity legislation would shift the balance of power in the labor market toward women, eroding obstacles to women's economic autonomy.

Removing Barriers to Work Attachment

Numerous policies can make it possible for caregivers to work more continuously; work longer hours; and take advantage of training, promotional, and career opportunities. These supports are crucial to women's economic security, especially for low-wage workers and former welfare recipients, who are least likely to have the paid leave and employment flexibility that parents need to increase their employment stability and provide family care (Heymann and Earle 1998).

Policies to Keep Workers on the Job

Access to reasonable leave policies diminishes the disadvantage experienced by workers who meld work and family. All workers, whether employed full- or part-time, need personal vacation and sick leave along with employment breaks to welcome new children into their families; they also need leave to stay home to care for ill children and seriously ill spouses. Workers should be able to take time off to care for frail elderly relatives, too, either in emergencies or simply to help with doctors' appointments for chronic medical needs. Leave policies maintain job attachment and can help ensure that workers have opportunities for wage increases and promotions as their job tenure increases.

Paid leave for women with new babies is one of the most important policies for supporting women's economic security: It increases women's employment tenure (Rönsen and Sundström 1996) and earnings (Joesch 1997). However, while the 1993 Family and Medical Leave Act (FMLA) guarantees covered employees—both women and men—up to 12 weeks of job-protected leave in specified circumstances, including care for a new baby or newly adopted children, it does not require that workers receive any wage replacement during their leave.[4] When leave must be taken, such as to give birth, the FMLA job guarantee is a very important protection for low- and high-wage workers alike, but the absence of wage replacement prevents many workers from taking advantage of the act. Of the 4 million workers who needed to take leave but did not, according to a 1995 survey, 64 percent could not afford to forego their earnings during the leave period (Commission on Leave 1996).

Without an income component, job-guaranteed leave programs help higher-income workers, who are more likely to have either savings or accumulated vacation or sick leave to support them during the leave, but they are not adequate for low-wage workers. Low-earners, African Americans, and Hispanics are more likely to experience a need for leave than higher-wage and white workers, but low-wage workers and African Americans are less likely to be able to take leave (Gerstel and McGonagle 1999).

Recent state-level advocacy efforts, coupled with President Clinton's policymaking, may succeed in mandating some income support for workers with newly born or adopted children. In May 1999, Clinton directed the U.S. Department of Labor to issue regulations allowing states to use their unemployment insurance systems to pay benefits for this select group of workers. Even before the final regulations were promulgated in June 2000, 15 states were considering legislation that would have either offered partial payment for some forms of family and medical leave or required further legislative study of the issue (National Partnership for Women and Families 2000). Although no leave programs were enacted in 2000, both houses of the Massachusetts legislature passed a bill for "Baby UI," as the directive supporting birth and adoption leave has been dubbed. The Republican governor vetoed the initiative (Barbarisi 2000).

While state-level efforts are important, the proposed policies are insufficient to meet the needs of the contemporary workforce. There are two main problems: The wage replacement levels are generally too low to be of adequate assistance for low-wage workers, and some members of the workforce are excluded from coverage. Furthermore, the FMLA's definition of "family," which state legislation is likely to duplicate, reflects cultural biases that favor middle- and upper-class heterosexual white workers, while disadvantaging workers of color and gays and lesbians.[5] For example, the FMLA's concept of family fails to legitimize significant kin (siblings, grandparents, and aunts and uncles) and nonkin ties that are more frequently found in communities of color than among whites (Gerstel and McGonagle 1999). In addition, to truly allow employed parents to participate in all the important aspects of their children's lives, the kind of paid leave that some progressive businesses offer allowing parents to attend parent-teacher conferences and even volunteer in the schools should be expanded to all workers, including those without immediate family needs of their own.

Other employer-specific policies that fall within the rubric "family friendly" make life easier for working parents and increase their employment and earnings as well. Even something as basic as having a supervisor who genuinely supports the concept of a family-friendly workplace makes a difference in the effect of company policies on employee behavior and employment outcomes, making it more likely that women will return to work following childbirth (Glass and Riley 1998). While these policies, when implemented, are typically adopted by individual firms, public policy could support their development by offering tax incentives for these programs, just as employer-paid health insurance and pension plans receive favorable tax treatment now. For example, the 1981 Economic Recovery Tax Act spurred employer support for child and elder care services by granting dependent care status as a nontaxable employee benefit (Friedman and Johnson 1997).

One final aid to parents facing barriers to employment is assurance that all workers have adequate health insurance for themselves and their children. This would obviate the need some pregnant workers succumb to of leaving work in order to qualify for Medicaid coverage of prenatal care (Bond 1992). It would also make it more likely that medical problems would be treated before developing into major illnesses or disabilities that might disrupt employment for substantial periods.

Child Care and School-Work Integration

Subsidized funding of child care is an important method of reducing the costs of working for parents of young children, and it particularly benefits low-earners and women. Public funding assistance can also be expected to increase the supply of child care, making it easier for parents to find the kind and schedule of child care they want (Meyers 1990).

The current policy mix of vouchers and subsidized child care slots for some low-income parents, the dependent care income tax credit, and occasional voluntarily provided employer subsidies is inadequate. To make employment more feasible and increase income, women workers need a more thorough system, covering more workers and a greater percentage of their child care costs.

Public subsidies may be especially important for the development of child care slots for sick children and for care outside usual work hours. In this way, parents needn't always take time off when children are sick, and parents could work evening and night shifts, when most child care facilities are closed.

When children reach the age of compulsory schooling, they no longer require full-time child care, and the cost of their care decreases. However, the typical school day is shorter than the standard workday, so many of these children still need care before or after school. Some school systems provide on-site care, recognizing the costs and logistical difficulties this school/work hours mismatch causes. Many more parents could be helped if public schools would reorient themselves toward schedules that acknowledge that 68 percent of children do not have a parent at home full-time.[6] Even middle school and high school children, who may be mature enough to be home alone, can benefit from a vast expansion of on-site before- and after-school activities, along with improved transportation programs that facilitate their participation in activities at other schools and public facilities.

Policies to Improve Income Supports for Workers Who Are between Jobs

The unemployment insurance (UI) system fails to provide adequate support to women: Only 23 percent of jobless women receive UI benefits, compared with 35 percent of unemployed men (Emsellem, Allen, and Shaw 1999). Women are often vulnerable to requirements that unemployed workers have a certain level of earnings in the 12 months before their job loss, that their employment ended for acceptable reasons, and that they are available for work. Someone quitting a job because their child care arrangements collapsed, because they need to care for an ill loved one, or because they have followed a relocated spouse may not be eligible for benefits. Many states also exclude part-time workers from UI, a policy design that affects many more women than men.[7]

States could also increase the level of UI benefits so this social insurance system would better support workers who are temporarily out of the workforce.[8] Dependent allowances, which provide additional benefits based on a worker's family size, would also make the system's support of low-income families more adequate.

In the past, the welfare system functioned in effect as a UI system for low-income mothers, who typically cycle between low-wage/low-hours work and periods of joblessness (Spalter-Roth et al. 1995). Changes in the welfare system have drastically reduced the availability of this support, but low-wage women are still particularly likely to face unemployment because of the structural barriers that disrupt their work tenure. It is important that this support be rebuilt and even increased.

Because the UI system targets workers with a substantial work history, it does not help people just entering the labor market and seeking employment, such as caregivers returning to work after a stint at home with children. In Canada, income support through UI is available to new labor market entrants, facilitating their search for a job that matches their skills (Malin 1995–1996). A similar policy expansion in the United States would be particularly helpful to women.

Policies to Increase the Quantity of Full-Time Jobs and the Quality of Part-Time Jobs

Because of the fixed costs associated with hiring additional employees, employers sometimes demand overtime of regular employees when workloads increase. Changing labor laws to encourage employers to offer compensatory time off for overtime, in lieu of an overtime premium, would encourage employers to spread work hours among a larger number of employees (Tilly 1996). A lower hours-worked threshold (fewer than the 40 hours currently provided for in the Fair Labor Standards Act [FLSA]) for requiring overtime pay would have a similar effect, as would increasing the current 50 percent wage premium on overtime required for workers covered by the FLSA (Tilly 1996). Mandating a shorter regular workweek—say, 30 or 35 hours instead of 40—would also support job creation.

When firms offer part-time jobs as a way of reducing their labor costs, labor market regulation can ensure that the workers in these short-hours positions are not marginalized, but receive wages and benefits proportionate to those provided to full-time workers: regular earnings, vacation and sick leave, health care insurance, pensions, training opportunities, and promotions and wage increases. If part-time jobs were of similar quality to full-time jobs, only with fewer hours, caregivers could safely use the part-time work strategy to combine caregiving and paid work, with minimal losses to current income and benefits and without jeopardizing future retirement income.

Better Planning for Low-Wage Women Workers' Retirement Security

Economic security for women workers as they move through the life cycle into retirement also requires public policy intervention. The policies discussed here would lead to higher Social Security benefits for women, because measures of lifetime earnings and years of employment are part of the equation for calculating benefits. Encouraging or requiring employers to provide better pension coverage to lower-paid workers would supplement women's Social Security income.

In addition to ensuring that the current Social Security system is not "reformed" in a way that makes older women even more vulnerable,[9] policies specifically focused on women's retirement are also needed. Raising the replacement rate for low-earners, modifying the special minimum benefit (an alternative benefit calculation targeted at long-term low-wage workers), increasing the widow's benefit, and expanding benefits for divorced and disabled women would help many low-income women.

Women who have reduced their years in the workforce to care for their families would also see higher benefits and lower poverty rates in their later years if a family service credit were implemented in Social Security. This policy would incorporate a certain amount, say $5,000 a year, into a lower-earning spouse's (or single parent's) earnings record while the individual was caring for an infant full-time (perhaps for each of the first six years of each child's life, to a maximum of 10 years of credits). Credits could also be given for caring for disabled adult children or dependent adults. Alternatively, individuals could be allowed to exclude a certain number of years with no earnings from their benefit calculation—if the years were spent in caregiving (Task Force on Women and Social Security 2000). Without this kind of progressive government action, older women will continue to face higher poverty rates because of their devotion to their families' needs (Kingson and O'Grady-LeShane 1993).

Increasing the Earnings of Low-Wage Women Workers

Many workers cannot increase their earnings substantially simply by working additional hours, because their hourly pay is too low to produce above-poverty earnings even working full-time. This is a problem faced by more women than men, because women are concentrated in low-wage occupations. Because of discrimination, differences in the focus of women's and men's educational investments, and the institutionalized devaluation of women's job skills, women receive lower pay than men with comparable levels of education. The lack of internal job ladders for many low-wage jobs means that increased time at a job will not lead as a matter of course to higher wages in a different occupation. Workers in the low-wage labor market would benefit from increased government regulation of the wage and employment structure, as well as policies to increase workers' stock of the skills and experience that command higher pay.

Increasing Equal Employment Opportunity Efforts

Equal employment opportunity (EEO) laws and practices are effective in increasing the wages, employment, and occupational status of protected groups (Badgett and Hartmann 1995; Holzer and Neumark 1998). However, EEO policies are enforced by federal agencies, and the intensity of enforcement efforts varies, along with support for EEO goals, among presidential administrations. For example, the Reagan and Bush administrations not only reduced funding of federal EEO agencies but actively sought to roll back legislated and negotiated commitments to the goals of EEO (Conway, Ahern, and Steuernagel 1995). A renewed and continuing commitment to using affirmative action and the power of the Equal Employment Opportunity Commission and the Office of Federal Contract Compliance Programs to increase the quality of women's employment outcomes is an important component of policies to improve women's economic security.

Support for Fair Pay for Women's Work

Equal pay for men and women performing the same job has been a legal requirement since 1963, although violations still occur. A much more pervasive and covert source of sex-based pay inequity is institutionalized through occupational segregation—the tendency of women and men to work in different jobs. Wages in occupations with a disproportionate number of female incumbents are generally lower than those in occupations held primarily by men, even when differences in skill levels are taken into account (England 1992).[10] Although advocates and members of the women's movement have been educating around this issue and proposing initiatives to respond to it for decades, public policies adequate to the problem have yet to be enacted.

One way to overcome inequities based on occupational segregation and sex typing is to use gender-neutral job evaluation systems to identify the value of various skills required in a job and then devise wage-setting structures that reflect these values, not gender-biased social definitions of worth. This strategy of identifying the "comparable worth" of dissimilar jobs can be very effective in counteracting the wage devaluation of women's jobs, raising women's wages and reducing the gender wage gap. In Minnesota, for example, a comparable-worth system that cost the state 3.5 percent of its wage bill closed the gender wage gap by 31 percent (Hartmann and Aaronson 1994).

Comparable-worth programs can be initiated voluntarily by individual private-sector employees, or they can be imposed by legislatures overseeing state civil service systems. They have been undertaken by some smaller government units, such as municipal workers in San Jose, California, and county workers in New Castle County, Delaware. In addition, legislation has been introduced in Congress that would mandate equal pay for work of comparable value.

Some of the benefits of comparable worth can be achieved without undertaking job evaluations or even acknowledging that women's jobs tend to be devalued. Disproportionately raising the wages of low-wage jobs typically benefits women more than men, because women are concentrated at the bottom of the wage ladder. Minimum wage and living wage adjustments have a similar effect of bringing women's earnings closer to parity with men's.

Minimum Wage and Living Wage

Low-wage workers need the security of government policies that ensure that the compensation paid for their labor is reasonable. The minimum wage, which is intended to provide a floor below which workers' wages may not fall, is becoming less effective in providing this guarantee: Its real value has declined substantially over the last 30 years. In 1979, the minimum wage was worth $6.53 in 1999 dollars; in 2001, it still reflects the 1997 increase to $5.15 (Mishel, Bernstein, and Schmitt 2001).

Women need an increase in this wage floor, along with assurance that further increases will occur as inflation eats into their earnings. Thirteen percent of all women workers—about one in eight—would see a direct wage increase if the minimum wage were raised to $6.15. An additional 10 percent who now earn between $6.15 and $7.14 would likely be affected as well, as an upward movement of the entire low-wage labor market would probably follow such a change (Bernstein, Hartmann, and Schmitt 1999). African-American and Hispanic women would benefit from this policy initiative disproportionately, as they are overrepresented in the minimum-wage labor force.

The living wage movement is a newer antipoverty approach that complements efforts to increase the minimum wage. Initiated in Baltimore in 1994, living wage laws require private firms contracting with the city to augment wages for their "working poor" employees. These policies seek to reduce the effect that the privatization of government services may have of lowering the wages of workers who deliver essential public services (Niedt et al. 1999).

Policies to Discourage Substandard Employment

Many women would move into regular, higher-paid employment with new laws forbidding or discouraging the expansion of various forms of contingent employment, such as contract, temporary, and payrolled work,[11] all of which frequently subject workers to low pay and restricted benefit availability. Alternatively, public policies could mandate that contingent employment be compensated at the same level as regular employment. Increasing unionization, as discussed below, should also increase the quality of contingent jobs, because unions typically act to minimize the extent of the secondary labor market (Tilly 1996).

Increasing wages for part-time workers would also benefit low-wage workers. In addition to regulation of wage floors, enacting labor laws to make it easier for full- and part-time workers to form unions could raise the earnings of the low-paid part-time workers (Tilly 1996). Public policies can encourage employers to rethink the way jobs and internal labor markets are organized and provide upward mobility even in lower-skill jobs. Government-sponsored programs to train managers in restructuring jobs and promotional ladders—"designing jobs for people"—would balance the traditional emphasis on increasing workers' skills, while enhancing lower-level workers' opportunities and wages (Lambert 1999).

Improving Accessibility through Transportation

Another way to enhance the earnings of low-wage workers is to make it easier for them to get to higher-paid jobs. Sometimes the simple fact that white, African-American, and Hispanic workers live in different, segregated parts of a community, coupled with the choice of some businesses to locate in suburbs and the poor design of public transportation systems that could connect residential and business locations, creates an obstacle to low-wage workers' access to important segments of the labor market. This is particularly a problem for welfare recipients and other poor women with children (Stoll, Holzer, and Ihlanfeldt 2000). Urban planning policies that make it easier for low-income families to live in the suburbs near suburban businesses, and careful design of public transit systems that allow workers to move easily between urban communities and suburban jobs, would help expand job opportunities for disadvantaged workers.

Support for Skill Development

One of the biggest barriers preventing many low-wage women workers from attaining economic security is their lack of marketable skills. At the most basic level, educational achievement correlates positively with labor force participation for both women and men and for all race/ethnic groups (U.S. Census Bureau 1999). Educational credentials have become increasingly important for achieving economic security as the "education premium" has become a more important factor in wage determination (Katz and Murphy 1992). The realities of the need for education are very stark for women: Women workers with less than a high school education experienced a 2 percent decline in real wages between 1969 and 1994, while those in every other educational category had real earnings growth. College-educated women fared the best, raising their weekly wages 20 percent over this period (Blau 1998).

Programs to keep students in school until they complete secondary education are very important for helping workers move into better-paid employment, and they simultaneously provide the business community with better-trained and more productive employees. For women, part of this effort requires educating girls about the economic prospects that await young women and, in particular, young mothers who are unprepared for the demands of the contemporary labor market. Parents, educators, and counselors should help young women understand the connection between their schooling and their chances of achieving their goals throughout adulthood. Businesses can play a role in this exchange, not only by developing mentorship and apprenticeship programs for high school students but also by improving women's employment outcomes so students will see that investing in school is worthwhile.

Postsecondary educational programs are also needed, along with government assistance (via grants, not loans) in paying tuition and living expenses. Programs that are specifically designed to attract women to nontraditional occupations, including high-paid craft and construction trades and male-dominated science fields, can help women explore and prepare for jobs with better earnings and advancement potential.

As welfare reform moves many low-skilled women into the workplace for the first time or after a long absence, programs must be designed not just to shift women off welfare as quickly as possible but to assist them in developing the skills and behaviors that will start them on jobs with career tracks and higher wages. Postsecondary education, an important component of this assistance, leads to greater labor force attachment and higher wages (Kahn and Polakow 2000).

Supplementing the Earnings of Low-Wage Women Workers

For some workers, the only viable path to above-poverty income is income support, because they are unable to develop the skills that command a living wage or they have too many barriers to successful labor force attachment. Families who are poor despite their work effort need continued expansion of the earned income tax credit (EITC). This kind of progressive, refundable tax credit program that rewards work while reducing the economic disadvantage faced by low-wage workers is especially important for low-wage parents—single mothers are the largest group of EITC recipients.[12] The federal program has been expanded in recent years, making it a better vehicle for helping the working poor than it was when it was enacted. Continued increases in benefits and broader eligibility are still needed.

Additional policy interventions at the state and local level can take this idea further. Fifteen states have enacted EITCs that are based on the federal program, allowing workers to take a credit of between 4 and 43 percent of their federal EITC against their state income tax liability. Montgomery County, Maryland, offers a local version as well (Johnson 2000). Enacting and expanding state EITCs can help reduce poverty among the working poor, including former welfare recipients, and their children, especially if the credit is refundable. EITCs increase the progressivity of the overall tax system so that lower-income individuals pay a smaller portion of their income in taxes than higher-income taxpayers.

Improved and expanded paid family and medical leave and unemployment insurance programs are also important supplements to the earnings of low-wage women workers. In addition, public policy could recognize the value of child rearing to society as a whole, as well as the financial burden it imposes on parents, by instituting the kind of child or family allowance that is common in Europe and Scandinavia (Wennemo 1992). Usually, these payments are not means-tested, but provide a fixed amount of transfer income for each child; they thereby provide proportionately greater value to lower-income families, including single mothers.

Supporting Unionization

Unions can make a big difference in women's attachment to their jobs and in their earnings and fringe benefits. In an overall comparison, unionized women make 38 percent more than nonunionized women. Controlling for human capital, work-related, and demographic differences between unionized and nonunionized women, the union wage premium is 12 percent (Spalter-Roth, Hartmann, and Collins 1994). Unions have been active in fighting for pay equity, both in contract negotiation and by supporting legislative initiatives, and they reduce gender and racial/ethnic wage gaps for their members (Hartmann et al. 1999). The benefits of unionization for women are reciprocated by women's increasingly large role in the union movement: Women are now 42 percent of the unionized workforce,[13] up from 17 percent in 1954 (Cobble 1996).

The benefits of unionization could assist many more workers if U.S. labor law were revised to match contemporary work organizations better. A federal commission appointed jointly by the Departments of Labor and Commerce in 1993 recommended a series of labor law reforms to enhance productivity and labor-management cooperation (Dunlop Commission 1994). Implicitly acknowledging differences between the workplace of the 1950s, when unionization rates peaked, and that of today, the commission advocated for clarifying the right to form employee participation and labor-management partnerships, speeding up unionization elections, strengthening the National Labor Relations Board's use of injunctions during labor disputes, and encouraging the railroad and airline industries to develop new collective bargaining strategies.

Collective bargaining rights should also be offered to domestic and agricultural workers, supervisors, managers, professional workers, and contingent workers. Expanding the coverage of union-negotiated contracts to other employers on an industrial or occupational basis would increase the amount of pressure unions can apply during labor disagreements and put workers in a stronger position when bargaining for higher wages and better workplace benefits; so, too, would allowing the use of certain currently outlawed tactics, such as secondary boycotts (Cobble 1996). The August 2000 ruling of the National Labor Relations Board that temporary workers can organize at their job site with regular employees, without first receiving permission from their temporary employment agency, is a move in the right direction toward easier, broader unionization (Greenhouse 2000).

FAMILIES, WORKPLACES, AND SOCIETY

Women continue to experience the labor market in a very different way than men do, working in different occupations, for a different number of hours a week, and taking more time out of the workforce to care for their families. As a result of this sex-based divergence, women earn less than men during their working lives, and their income is lower when they retire. This outcome does not need to continue. Many effective public policies can mitigate the disadvantage of being female. Designing policies that specifically address women's employment situation is a crucial avenue to economic security for low-wage workers.

In addition, all public policies that affect the labor market and individual workers' employment outcomes, including education, training, minimum wage, and tax policies, should be analyzed in terms of their likely impact on women workers and on low-wage workers. For example, the failure of policymakers to curtail the development of the contingent workforce is not an instance of overt gender bias, but it affects women disproportionately and has the same effect as explicit discrimination. Some policy issues, such as welfare, are clearly important for women; even there, however, policymakers do not always sufficiently recognize the realities of women's work experiences or the obstacles to achieving success in the workforce.

The probable impact of public policies on men's commitment to caregiving should also be considered carefully. Increasing men's experience of the employment constraints associated with caregiving will expand the constituency that demands and institutes labor market changes to provide a more supportive environment for America's families. Congress and state legislatures are good targets of this pressure, but the initiative of individual employers can also make a huge difference—by enacting family-friendly policies that don't marginalize workers with family responsibilities, by pursuing comparable-worth programs, and by training all supervisors in gender-neutral employment practices. Each worker has a part to play, too—by becoming aware of how gender and employment intersect, by examining the values used to evaluate subordinates, by making an extra effort to respect workers' needs to care for their families, and by mentoring women and helping them strategize about their careers.

Women's economic insecurity is not just a women's problem; it's a problem for our families, our workplaces, and our society. We all have individual roles to play in increasing women's economic security. And it is imperative that public policies be directed at the structural barriers that women cannot overcome alone.

NOTES

1. Authors' calculation based on U.S. DOL (2000).

2. Thirty percent of workers who are voluntarily in part-time jobs choose reduced hours to accommodate child care problems or family or personal obligations (U.S. Census Bureau 1999). While most research on the impact of caregiving on employment looks at the effect of having children, caring for elderly parents causes the same changes in work attachment: reduced hours, employment loss, and inability to take advantage of rewarding job opportunities (MetLife Mature Market Institute 1999).

3. Settlements arranged in 1999 involved a wide array of businesses, including Fifth Third Bank, Texaco, Sunoco, and Boeing (Appelbaum 2000).

4. To be eligible for FMLA leave, workers must have worked for their employer for at least 12 months and for at least 1,250 hours in the 12 months preceding the leave, and must work for a firm that employs 50 or more workers at the worker's establishment or within a 75-mile radius thereof. With these limits, the FMLA benefits just over half the workforce. Workers with low family income are the least likely to have FMLA coverage (Commission on Leave 1996)

5. Gays and lesbians may take FMLA parental leave but not FMLA leave to care for an ill spouse (Gerstel and McGonagle 1999).

6. U.S. HHS (1999), Table ES 3.1.

7. Although the Social Security Act of 1935 effectively requires states to provide UI programs, the details of eligibility requirements and benefit-payment structures are almost completely open to state discretion. Massachusetts and some other states have enacted a number of policies that increase access to UI benefits for low-wage workers, including women (Halas 1999). Other states are much more punitive.

8. Although some argue that higher UI benefits make life without a job more pleasant and thus discourage return to employment, research indicates that higher benefit levels actually increase labor productivity. UI may allow workers to take time to search carefully for a job that makes the most of their skills, rather than forcing them to take the first job offered, which may be an offer for underemployment (Acemoglu and Shimer 1999).

9. Making personal social security accounts part of the retirement system and reducing guaranteed benefits would likely reduce women's ability to access their husbands' earnings records for their own retirement income and decrease their monthly payment. Proportionately larger administrative costs on their smaller personal accounts and women's more risk-averse investment strategies would further reduce their retirement benefits (Hill, Shaw, and Hartmann 2000).

10. It has been argued that women are clustered in a small set of lower-paid occupations because those occupations offer more of the flexibility that facilitates work-family balance, which, according to this theory, women choose instead of seeking higher pay. However, research shows that female-dominated occupations do not support women's efforts to combine paid employment and caring work (DeSai and Waite 1991).

11. In payrolled work, paychecks are issued by a firm that specializes in that service and that may hold itself out as the workers' true employer. This practice may deprive workers of the payscales and benefits provided to regular employees.

12. Ed Lazere, Center on Budget and Policy Priorities, personal communication, September 27, 2000.

13. Authors' calculation based on U.S. DOL (2001) (refers to workers represented by unions).

REFERENCES

Acemoglu, Daron, and Robert Shimer. 1999. "Productivity Gains from Unemployment Insurance." NBER Working Paper 7352. Cambridge, Mass.: National Bureau of Economic Research.

Appelbaum, Judith C. 2000. "Testimony before the Committee on Health, Education, Labor and Pensions, United States Senate, on Gender-Based Wage Discrimination." Washington, D.C.: National Women's Law Center.

Badgett, M. V. Lee, and Heidi I. Hartmann. 1995. "The Effectiveness of Equal Opportunity Policies." In *Economic Perspectives on Affirmative Action,* edited by Margaret Simms. Washington, D.C.: Joint Center for Political and Economic Studies.

Barbarisi, Daniel. 2000. "Cellucci Rejects Parental Leave Bill." *Boston Globe,* 11 August, B5.

Bernstein, Jared, Heidi Hartmann, and John Schmitt. 1999. "The Minimum Wage Increase: A Working Woman's Issue." Washington, D.C.: Economic Policy Institute.

Blau, Francine D. 1998. "Trends in the Well-Being of American Women, 1970–1995." *Journal of Economic Literature* 36 (1): 112–65.

Bond, James T. 1992. "The Impact of Childbearing on Employment." In *Parental Leave and Productivity: Current Research,* edited by Dana E. Friedman, Ellen Galinsky, and Veronica Plowden (1–16). New York: Families and Work Institute.

Brown, Clair, and Joseph A. Pechman. 1987. *Gender in the Workplace.* Washington, D.C.: The Brookings Institution.

Cobble, Dorothy Sue. 1996. "The Prospects for Unionism in a Service Society." In *Working in the Service Sector,* edited by Cameron Macdonald and Carmen Sirianni. Philadelphia, Pa.: Temple University Press.

Commission on Leave. 1996. *A Workable Balance: Report to Congress on Family and Medical Leave Policies.* Washington, D.C.: Commission on Leave.

Conway, M. Margaret, David W. Ahern, and Gertrude A. Steuernagel. 1995. *Women and Public Policy: A Revolution in Progress.* Washington, D.C.: CQ Press.

Council of Economic Advisers. 1998. "Explaining Trends in the Gender Wage Gap." http://clinton3.nara.gov/WH/EOP/CEA/html/gendergap.html.

DeSai, Sonalde, and Linda S. Waite. 1991. "Women's Employment during Pregnancy and after the First Birth: Occupational Characteristics and Work Commitment." *American Sociological Review* 56: 551–66.

Dunlop Commission [Commission on the Future of Worker-Management Relations]. 1994. "Report and Recommendations." Washington, D.C.: U.S. Department of Labor and U.S. Department of Commerce.

Emsellem, Maurice, Katherine Allen, and Lois Shaw. 1999. "The Texas Unemployment Insurance System: Barriers to Access for Low-Wage, Part-Time and Women Workers." New York and Washington, D.C.: National Employment Law Project and Institute for Women's Policy Research.

England, Paula. 1992. *Comparable Worth: Theories and Evidence.* New York: Aldine de Gruyter.

Friedman, Dana E., and Arlene A. Johnson. 1997. "Moving from Programs to Culture Change: The Next Stage for the Corporate Work-Family Agenda." In *Integrating Work and Family: Challenges and Choices for a Changing World,* edited by Saroj Parasuraman and Jeffrey H. Greenhaus (192–208). Westport, Conn.: Quorum Books.

Galinsky, Ellen, and James T. Bond. 2000. "Helping Families with Young Children Navigate Work and Family Life." In *Balancing Acts: Easing the Burdens and Improving the Options for Working Families,* edited by Eileen Appelbaum (95–114). Washington, D.C.: Economic Policy Institute.

Gerstel, Naomi, and Katherine McGonagle. 1999. "Job Leaves and the Limits of the Family and Medical Leave Act." *Work and Occupations* 26 (4): 510–34.

Glass, Jennifer L., and Lisa Riley. 1998. "Family Responsive Policies and Employee Retention following Childbirth." *Social Forces* 76 (4): 1401–35.

Greenhouse, Steven. 2000. "Labor Board Makes Union Membership Easier for Temps." *New York Times,* 31 August, A18.

Halas, Monica. 1999. "Memo to Participants in the NELP/IWPR Strategy Forum for Improving Unemployment Insurance Policies to Benefit Women, Low-Wage and Contingent Workers." Boston, Mass.: Greater Boston Legal Services.

Hartmann, Heidi I., and Stephanie Aaronson. 1994. "Pay Equity and Women's Wage Increases: Success in the States, a Model for the Nation." *Duke Journal of Gender Law & Policy* 1:69–87.

Hartmann, Heidi, Katherine Allen, and Christine Owens. 1999. "Equal Pay for Working Families." Washington, D.C.: AFL-CIO and IWPR.

Heymann, Jody, and Alison Earle. 1998. "The Work-Family Balance: What Hurdles Are Parents Leaving Welfare Likely to Confront?" *Journal of Policy Analysis and Management* 17 (2): 313–21.

———. 1999. "The Impact of Welfare Reform on Parents' Ability to Care for Their Children's Health." *American Journal of Public Health* 89 (4): 1–4.

Hill, Catherine, Lois Shaw, and Heidi Hartmann. 2000. "Why Privatizing Social Security Would Hurt Women: A Response to the Cato Institute's Proposal for Individual Accounts." Washington, D.C.: Institute for Women's Policy Research.

Hipple, Steven, and Jay Stewart. 1996. "Earnings and Benefits of Contingent and Noncontingent Workers." *Monthly Labor Review* 119 (10): 22–29.

Holzer, Harry J., and David Neumark. 1998. "What Does Affirmative Action Do?" Institute for Research on Poverty Discussion Paper No. 1169-98. http://www.ssc.wisc.edu/irp/.

IWPR [Institute for Women's Policy Research]. 1997. "Child Care Usage among Low-Income and AFDC Families." Research-in-Brief. Washington, D.C.: IWPR.

Joesch, Jutta M. 1997. "Paid Leave and the Timing of Women's Employment Before and After Birth." *Journal of Marriage and the Family* 59:1008–21.

Johnson, Nicholas. 2000. "A Hand Up: How State Earned Income Tax Credits Help Working Families Escape Poverty in 2000: An Overview." Center on Budget and Policy Priorities. http://www.cbpp.org/4-12-00stp.htm. (Accessed September 5, 2000.)

Kahn, Peggy, and Valerie Polakow. 2000. "Struggling to Stay in School: Obstacles to Post-Secondary Education under the Welfare-to-Work Regime in Michigan." Center for the Education of Women, University of Michigan, Ann Arbor, Mich.

Katz, Lawrence F., and Kevin M. Murphy. 1992. "Changes in Relative Wages, 1963–87: Supply and Demand Factors." *Quarterly Journal of Economics* 107 (1): 35–78.

Kingson, Eric R., and Regina O'Grady-LeShane. 1993. "The Effects of Caregiving on Women's Social Security Benefits." *The Gerontologist* 33 (2): 230–39.

Lambert, Susan J. 1999. "Lower-Wage Workers and the New Realities of Work and Family." *Annals of the American Academy of Political and Social Science* 562: 174–90.

Malin, Martin H. 1995–1996. "Unemployment Compensation in a Time of Increasing Work-Family Conflicts." *University of Michigan Journal of Law Reform* 29 (1 & 2): 131–75.

MetLife Mature Market Institute. 1999. "The MetLife Juggling Act Study: Balancing Caregiving with Work and the Costs Involved." New York: Metropolitan Life Insurance Company.

Meyers, Marcia K. 1990. "The ABCs of Child Care in a Mixed Economy: A Comparison of Public and Private Sector Alternatives." *Social Service Review* 64 (4): 559–79.

Mishel, Lawrence, Jared Bernstein, and John Schmitt. 2001. *The State of Working America 2000/2001*. Washington, D.C.: Economic Policy Institute.

National Partnership for Women and Families. 2000. "State Family Leave Benefit Initiatives: Making Family Leave More Affordable." Washington, D.C.: National Partnership for Women and Families.

Niedt, Christopher, Greg Ruiters, Dana Wise, and Erica Schoenberger. 1999. "The Effects of the Living Wage in Baltimore." Economic Policy Institute Working Paper No. 119. Washington, D.C.: Economic Policy Institute.

Powell, Lisa M. 1998. "Part-Time versus Full-Time Work and Child Care Costs: Evidence for Married Mothers." *Applied Economics* 30:503–11.

Reskin, Barbara F., and Patricia A. Roos. 1990. *Job Queues, Gender Queues: Explaining Women's Inroads into Male Occupations*. Philadelphia, Pa.: Temple University Press.

Rönsen, Marit, and Marianne Sundström. 1996. "Maternal Employment in Scandinavia: A Comparison of the After-Birth Employment Activity of Norwegian and Swedish Women." *Journal of Population Economics* 9:267–85.

Spalter-Roth, Roberta, Heidi Hartmann, and Nancy Collins. 1994. "What Do Unions Do for Women?" Paper presented at the conference "Labor Law Reform: The Forecast for Working Women." Washington, D.C.: Women's Bureau, U.S. Department of Labor.

Spalter-Roth, Roberta, Beverly Burr, Heidi Hartmann, and Lois Shaw. 1995. "Welfare That Works: The Working Lives of AFDC Recipients." Washington, D.C.: IWPR.

Steinberg, Ronnie J. 1990. "Social Construction of Skill: Gender, Power, and Comparable Worth." *Work and Occupations* 17 (4): 449–82.

Stoll, Michael A., Harry J. Holzer, and Keith R. Ihlanfeldt. 2000. "Within Cities and Suburbs: Racial Residential Concentration and the Spatial Distribution of Employment Opportunities across Sub-Metropolitan Areas." *Journal of Policy Analysis and Management* 19 (2): 207–31.

Task Force on Women and Social Security. 2000. "Strengthening Social Security for Women." Washington, D.C.: Task Force on Women and Social Security, National Council of Women's Organizations, and Institute for Women's Policy Research.

Tilly, Chris. 1996. *Half a Job: Bad and Good Part-Time Jobs in a Changing Labor Market*. Philadelphia, Pa.: Temple University Press.

U.S. Census Bureau. 1999. *Statistical Abstract of the United States*. Washington, D.C.: U.S. Government Printing Office.

U.S. DOL [U.S. Department of Labor]. 1999. "Employee Benefits in Medium and Large Private Establishments, 1997." USDL-99-02. Washington, D.C.: U.S. Government Printing Office.

———. 2000. "Highlights of Women's Earnings in 1999." Report 943. Washington, D.C.: U.S. Government Printing Office.

———. 2001. *Employment and Earnings*. Washington, D.C.: U.S. Government Printing Office.

U.S. HHS [U.S. Department of Health and Human Services]. 1999. *Trends in the Well-Being of America's Children and Youth*. Washington, D.C.: U.S. Government Printing Office.

Wennemo, Irene. 1992. "The Development of Family Policy: A Comparison of Family Benefits and Tax Reductions for Families in 18 OECD Countries." *Acta Sociologica* 35:201–17.

11

Career Advancement Prospects and Strategies for Low-Wage Minority Workers

Harry J. Holzer

On average, minorities in the United States earn less than whites. In part, this is due to lower average levels of education and differing regional residential patterns. Yet African Americans and other minorities earn less and are less likely to be working, even when they have comparable levels of education to whites and live in comparable regions.

What accounts for these differences across racial and ethnic groups? Do less-educated or lower-income minorities face special barriers to skill development and career advancement? If so, what are those challenges, and what strategies might overcome them?

This chapter provides some of the evidence on the lower educational attainment of minorities relative to whites, and on their lower relative wages and higher un-employment rates, even at comparable levels of education. It then considers a variety of reasons why these gaps persist, as well as the barriers to career advancement that minorities face, such as differences in the quality of their education, differences in work experience, disadvantages related to residential segregation, persistent labor market discrimination, and other factors.

This chapter further discusses strategies to improve the career advancement prospects of less-educated minority workers. While government policy can play an important role in improving these prospects, private-sector intermediaries and other organizations have a significant part to play as well.

Throughout, this chapter focuses primarily on African Americans and Hispanics, the two largest minority groups in the United States. Data are most readily available on these groups, and these groups also encounter the most serious and persistent labor market difficulties. However, the discussion includes Asian Americans and other U.S. minority groups when the data allow for comparisons.

LOW EDUCATIONAL ATTAINMENT, LOW EMPLOYMENT, LOW EARNINGS

The educational attainment of African Americans and Hispanics continues to lag behind that of whites, clearly contributing to their worse labor market outcomes. During the past two decades, the earnings gap between more-educated and less-educated workers has risen dramatically (Katz and Murphy 1992), with particularly large wage losses for less-educated males. Because blacks and Hispanics are more heavily concentrated than whites among the less-educated, they suffer disproportionately from the earnings losses experienced by less-educated workers in general. On the other hand, recent gains in educational attainment, at least among African Americans (Mare 1995), have likely rendered these losses less severe than they otherwise might have been.

Table 11.1 presents data on educational attainment by race and gender, with the percentages of the relevant populations earning high school diplomas or higher and college degrees or higher. The data cover two age ranges: 25 and older, as well as those age 25 to 34. Data for the narrower age group better reflect more recent trends in enrollment and attainment.

The data indicate that blacks and Hispanics continue to lag behind whites in educational attainment, even in the younger cohorts. While blacks have achieved parity with whites in high school graduation rates, they lag far behind in college (and postgraduate) degrees. More disturbingly, Hispanics lag well behind whites and blacks in graduation from both high school and college. Their lower rates of educational attainment only partly reflect the concentration among Hispanics of less-educated immigrants (U.S. Department of Labor 1999).

Table 11.2, median hourly wages and unemployment rates, indicates the extent to which educational attainment accounts for differences across ethnic groups in labor market success. Clearly, the lower educational attainment of blacks and Hispanics accounts for some, but not all, of their lower wages, while Asian Americans' apparently higher educational attainment more than fully accounts for their higher wages. The

TABLE 11.1 Educational Attainment by Race and Gender, 1998

	Whites (%)		Blacks (%)		Hispanics (%)	
	Male	**Female**	**Male**	**Female**	**Male**	**Female**
Ages 25 and older						
High school graduates	83.6	83.8	75.2	76.7	55.7	55.3
College graduates	27.3	22.8	13.9	15.4	11.1	10.9
Ages 25 to 34						
High school graduates	86.5	89.5	87.1	86.9	59.7	63.7
College graduates	26.7	30.1	15.0	15.6	9.9	12.3

Source: U.S. Department of Commerce 1998.

TABLE 11.2 Labor Market Outcomes by Race/Ethnic Group and Education

	Whites	Blacks	Hispanics	Asian Americans
Median Hourly Wage, 1997				
All workers	$18.20	$12.92	$11.53	$18.66
High school graduates	13.12	10.56	10.62	10.79
College graduates	21.45	16.53	17.37	19.86
Unemployment Rates, 1998				
All workers	3.0%	6.4%	5.5%	n.a.*
High school graduates	3.4	7.4	5.5	n.a.
College graduates	1.7	2.9	3.2	n.a.

Sources: Median wage figures are from Bernstein et al. (1999); unemployment rates are from the U.S. Department of Labor.
*n.a. = Not available

median wages of blacks and Hispanics are roughly 70 percent and 63 percent of those among whites; the wages of Asian Americans *exceed* those of whites. However, among high school graduates only, the median wages of all three minority groups are roughly 80 percent of those of whites; among college graduates, their wages range from 77 to 92 percent of whites.

Unemployment rates tell a similar story. African-American unemployment is more than double that of whites; for Hispanics, the rate is almost double. The differentials are similar among high school graduates, although the rates for blacks with college degrees are closer to their white counterparts than to less-educated blacks. Blacks without high school diplomas suffer the highest unemployment rates in the United States, along with the lowest rates of labor force participation (Juhn 1992).

OTHER CAUSES OF LOW EARNING AND LOW EMPLOYMENT

The lower educational attainment of African Americans and Hispanics clearly contributes to their labor market difficulties. *But it does not fully account for them.* Additional factors include other measures of skill, residential segregation by race and class, persistent racial discrimination, and criminal activity and incarceration.

Other Measures of Skill

Even when levels of educational attainment are similar, differences along a variety of other dimensions of skill might contribute to the labor market problems of minorities relative to whites. For instance, the labor market rewards for cognitive skills have risen in the past two decades (Murnane and Levy 1995) as employer demand for a variety of cognitive tasks on the job has steadily grown (Holzer 1996). In this context, the relative losses experienced by people without these skills may have grown as well.

Recent evidence suggests that, given similar levels of education, the average scores for blacks are lower on tests of cognitive achievement, such as the Armed Forces Qualifications Test (AFQT). While these gaps narrowed significantly during the 1980s, progress has leveled off since then, and substantial differences in performance remain (Grissmer et al. 1998). Differences in cognitive skills account for large parts of the wage gap between young whites and blacks of similar levels of education, but less of the employment gap (Johnson and Neal 1998).

Differences in test scores might reflect differences in the *quality* of education available to different racial and ethnic groups, even when levels of attainment are similar. Certainly, little evidence supports the view that testing differences reflect innate differences in average intellectual caliber, despite suggestions by a few (Herrnstein and Murray 1994). On the other hand, recent literature provides little support for the view that differences on tests largely reflect racial biases in the structure and content of the tests themselves (Jencks and Phillips 1998).

Blacks' lower test scores at least partly derive from family and neighborhood characteristics that limit access to good schooling, factors that Derek Neal and William Johnson (1996) have dubbed "premarket." But, even after accounting for premarket factors, remaining substantial differences in scores may reflect subjective factors, such as differing teacher expectations of performance for white and black students (Jencks and Phillips 1998; Ferguson 1998).

Another dimension along which the skills of whites and minorities might differ concerns "soft skills," encompassing a variety of attitudes toward work, as well as social and verbal skills. Social and verbal skills seem to be particularly important in jobs involving substantial contact with customers or coworkers. Many employers say that black workers lag behind whites in these areas, particularly when it comes to work attitudes (Moss and Tilly 1996).

Of course, employer perceptions are subjective and may reflect prejudices as well as the real skills of employees. On the other hand, William Julius Wilson (1996) notes that many black employers in Chicago report the same concerns about their young black employees as do white employers, raising doubts about whether employer prejudice can fully account for their reported observations.

Minorities also lag behind young whites in terms of early work experience. At very early ages, young blacks (and, to a lesser extent, Hispanics) begin to fall behind young whites in accumulating work experience (Rothstein 1999). While barriers to gaining early work experience may have little to do with relative skills initially, minorities accumulate a history of employment more slowly, contributing substantially to slower wage growth (Taber and Gladden 2000).

The lower accumulation of work experience among young blacks and Hispanics partly reflects their difficulties gaining employment and partly creates difficulties in keeping a job (Ballen and Freeman 1986; Holzer and Lalonde 2000). Yet not all job turnover is detrimental to career advancement and earnings growth. In fact, voluntary job changes—"job-to-job" changes—are far more likely to improve young workers' earnings than are involuntary, "job-to-nonemployment" changes; in fact, job-to-job changes account for a large part of the wage growth that occurs for young people (Topel and Ward 1992). And it is *only* in the job-to-nonemployment category that the rates of job changes among young minorities exceed those for young whites, with detrimental effects on the career earnings prospects of the former.

Finally, the earnings of immigrant groups (and perhaps their children) are often limited not only by low educational attainment but also by a lack of facility with English. In fact, a number of studies show that adjustments for both educational attainment and English language ability eliminate most of the wage differences between native-born whites and a variety of ethnic groups (Reimers 1983).

Residential Segregation

Minorities are especially likely to live in communities with high concentrations of other members of their minority group. Overall, the tendency for minorities to live in poor and/or racially segregated neighborhoods limits their career prospects substantially.

This *residential segregation* may partly reflect the desires and preferences of group members, as well as lower income and wealth levels. However, most analyses of the phenomenon (Massey and Denton 1992; Farley et al. 1997) also attribute residential segregation to continuing barriers to integration in the housing market, from discrimination by landlords and financial institutions to the tendency of whites to flee changing neighborhoods.

Racial segregation between whites and blacks remains much higher than that between whites and any other ethnic group. While such segregation has been declining slowly but consistently over the past several decades, it remains high by any absolute standard. Furthermore, segregation by *class* or income group has been rising, even as racial segregation declines (Jargowsky 1996). Middle-class blacks increasingly relocate to moderately integrated city or suburban neighborhoods, but the tendency is rising for poor blacks and Hispanics to live in predominantly poor neighborhoods, in relative isolation from middle-class residents.

What are the consequences for the career employment prospects of minorities as residential segregation by race and class continues, perhaps even grows? The most serious one is that young people growing up in poor and racially segregated neighborhoods appear to suffer in several ways that likely limit their skill attainment, early work experience, and ability to "keep out of trouble" and maintain future chances for success. They attend weaker, more violent schools; they are influenced by peer groups in which a variety of less positive behaviors (e.g., crime, drug use, teen pregnancy) are more prevalent; and they have less contact with potentially positive role models.

"Neighborhood effects" on educational and employment outcomes have been much debated, but empirical support for their existence and importance has grown in recent years (Brooks-Gunn et al. 1998). And in U.S. cities, residential segregation clearly reduces the educational and employment outcomes of blacks (Cutler and Glaeser 1997).

Related to neighborhood effects are "spatial mismatches." Increasingly, jobs tend to be located in outlying suburbs, while at least some minorities remain concentrated in inner cities. Presumably, residential segregation disadvantages some minorities in the process of seeking suburban employment for at least two reasons: transportation difficulties (especially for people who lack their own automobiles) and limited information about job opportunities in outlying areas. A lack of metropolitan-wide economic development policies often exacerbates the extent and impact of spatial mismatches.

The spatial mismatch hypothesis has been debated for more than 30 years, but most of the recent evidence suggest that this effect limits employment opportunities for inner-city minorities (Ihlanfeldt and Sjoquist 1998). Relatively few opportunities for employment exist within predominantly poor and minority neighborhoods, and a variety of barriers limits employment options for minority and poor individuals in other neighborhoods (Stoll et al. 2000).

While information about job openings may also relate to the geographic location of people and jobs, the career options of poor minorities may be limited more generally by a lack of "contacts" in the labor market, especially contacts with establishments that pay relatively high wages. Large percentages of people find jobs through friends and relatives whose ability to generate good employment for low-income minorities may be limited by their own low rates of employment and concentration in low-wage firms and jobs (Holzer 1987).

Racial Discrimination

The most blatant and overt forms of employment discrimination against minorities have largely disappeared since the passage of the Civil Rights Act of 1964 and the 1965 implementation of President Lyndon Johnson's Executive Order 11256 establishing "affirmative action" requirements for federal contractors. However, do more subtle forms of discrimination in hiring, pay, and promotion continue to limit the career advancement prospects of minorities?

The answer appears to be *yes*. While traditional statistical analyses are not well suited to identifying discrimination as a cause of earnings and employment differences by race and ethnicity—differences in the characteristics of individuals might cause observed disparities by race—a number of other analytical techniques have recently provided strong evidence of persistent discrimination. For instance, in studies that have sent matched pairs of minority and white applicants with apparently equal credentials to apply for jobs, whites routinely get more interviews and job offers than either black or Hispanic applicants (Fix and Struyk 1994). This evidence is consistent with the evidence described earlier that observed differences in education and test scores account for most wage differences between blacks and whites, but not differences in employment rates. Thus, discrimination against African Americans may be most severe at the hiring stage, with less bias occurring once employment is attained.

Other studies indicate that not all types of employers discriminate equally. The worst offenders appear to be small establishments, who mostly hire informally (and therefore are more subjective in evaluating applicants) and who are less visible to law enforcement agencies and potential plaintiffs. Also, suburban employers that serve a predominantly white clientele appear to discriminate against blacks and Hispanics in hiring for jobs that involve significant customer contact (Holzer 1998; Holzer and Ihlanfeldt 1998).

The ability of workers from particular racial or ethnic groups to avoid the effects of discrimination depends on their ability to find enough nondiscriminating employers to avoid the discriminators. Nondiscriminating employers and jobs may be available to Hispanic workers in sufficient numbers for them to avoid the labor market costs of discrimination, but this appears to be less true for blacks (Holzer 1996).

Furthermore, the tighter the labor market, the less the ability of employers to engage in discriminatory behavior. This effect can be strong. Very simply, when employers cannot attract enough job applicants from their most preferred groups to satisfy hiring needs, they tend to consider applicants from other groups. Given the extraordinary tightness of U.S. labor markets at the end of the 1990s, and the difficulties employers are reporting in finding acceptable applicants (Holzer 1999), it seems logical that discrimination in hiring would be relatively less pervasive now.

Furthermore, reduced discrimination may improve the employment prospects of minority candidates over the longer term, as employers learn from their new hiring experiences and as minority employees gain work experience. In fact, previous episodes of minority progress during tight labor markets—World War II and the late 1960s, for example—resulted in long-term improvements in the economic status of African Americans.

Criminal Activity and Incarceration

Another reason that growing up in poor neighborhoods may damage the career prospects of young minorities may be higher exposure to crime and violence. In fact, young men's relatively high rates of criminal activity and incarceration have seriously hurt their labor market prospects.

For one thing, crime has the potential to generate alternative sources of income, making it easier for less-skilled individuals to refuse low-wage work in the regular labor market. But these individuals will also gain less labor market experience, and their wages will grow more slowly. Furthermore, employers may be much more reluctant to hire an individual who has been incarcerated.

Research supports all these hypotheses. More than one-third of all young black men and a majority of young, black, male high school dropouts are involved with the criminal justice system at some point in their lives (Freeman 1992). The fraction of young men who perceive they can make more "on the street" than in legitimate employment certainly rose in the 1980s and early 1990s, partly fuelled by the crack epidemic. Although the crack trade and overall crime rates have fallen significantly in recent years, almost two million individuals are now incarcerated, and the numbers continue to rise.

Furthermore, the vast majority of employers state a reluctance to hire young men with criminal records (Holzer 1996). And a record of incarceration substantially reduces a person's future employment prospects, an effect that persists for at least 10 years (Freeman 1992).

The fear of crime among middle-class whites and blacks alike hurts even young blacks who engage in no illegal activity. A fear of crime drives middle-class residents and employers out of inner-city areas, exacerbating some of the spatial imbalances and the concentration of poor minorities in poor neighborhoods. And employers may tend to penalize an entire class of potential workers (i.e., young black males) because they feel unable to distinguish between those who have criminal records and those who do not.

POLICIES TO ADVANCE THE CAREER PROSPECTS OF LESS-EDUCATED MINORITIES

Less-educated minorities face a wide range of barriers to achieving career success in the labor market. To improve their prospects calls for consideration of policies and strategies that emphasize:

- Improving the basic skills of minorities, their educational attainment, and their early work experience and resulting attitudes toward work;
- Improving physical access to jobs and to safer, more-integrated neighborhoods;
- Providing effective employment and training programs for disadvantaged, out-of-school youth, especially ex-offenders and others with particular needs; and
- Reducing persistent discrimination.

Improving Educational Outcomes and Early Work Experience

Given the large impact of skill deficiencies on minorities' relative earnings, improving the quantity and quality of their education must be the highest priority of strategies to improve their career prospects. But we are somewhat limited in making specific policy prescriptions: We lack a good understanding of why gaps persist in the cognitive skills of young whites and minorities of the same education or family background.

The negative effects of family poverty on early childhood development are known (Duncan and Brooks-Gunn 1998), so a sensible starting point might be to improve the access of poor minorities to high-quality early childhood programs such as Head Start, perhaps making preschool programs universal. And some recent studies suggest that such programs do have positive long-term effects on labor market outcomes for white and Hispanic children—but not for blacks (Currie and Thomas 1995).

Still, the failure of early positive effects to persist among poor young blacks seems at least partly tied to their subsequently attending poor schools and residing in poor neighborhoods. Therefore, a sensible approach would be to make Head Start universally accessible—and to complement it with special tutoring programs at elementary and secondary schools in low-income areas. Some individualized tutoring programs, such as Success for All and Reading One-to-One, appear to be quite cost-effective (Crane 1998).[1] Mentoring programs for youth, such as Big Brothers Big Sisters of America, have generated promising results as well.

For secondary students, improving the links between schools and the job market might be an important way of raising student performance motivation and their early accumulation of work experience. Many questions remain about which "school-to-career" approaches are most successful, although evaluations have shown that a few specific models (e.g., Pro Tech in Boston and Career Academies nationwide) generate positive outcomes.[2] The usefulness of vocational instruction and various kinds of skills credentialing and certification in the schools remains unclear as well, but deserves continued exploration.

Overall, lowering the high school dropout rate is crucial, particularly among Hispanic youth. Indeed, preventive approaches that seek to keep students in school appear to be more successful than the body of "second chance" programs for out-of-school youth (described below) geared to young people who have failed in the educational system. Any of the above approaches that improves the long-term motivation and success of young people within the school system might reduce dropout rates, although these efforts might also be complemented by other programmatic approaches, such as the Quantum Opportunities project.[3] Beyond dropout prevention, encouraging minorities to pursue postsecondary education, perhaps by improving their awareness of and access to Pell grants, should be critically important as well.

Other approaches to improving the overall quality of schools in poor neighborhoods also deserve mention. For one thing, the causal link of student performance to investing educational resources in reducing class size or improving teacher certification continues to be explored, but remains controversial. The use of financial incentives to improve the performance of public schools has been under study, as well, in a variety of contexts.

Finally, all these approaches seek to improve educational outcomes for young minorities within their current schools and neighborhoods, but a variety of recent school choice mechanisms have explored the idea of improving the access of poor young minorities to quality schools beyond their communities. For example, many states have authorized public charter schools, and several U.S. cities, notably Milwaukee and Cleveland, have introduced voucher systems. Parental satisfaction with the latter appears to be high, and at least some improvements in test scores result (Rouse 1997), but little is known about the results—both for those who choose non-neighborhood schools and those left behind—if such systems were implemented on a large scale.

Improving Access to Better Neighborhoods

Another approach to improving the access of young minorities to better schools and neighborhoods seeks to enhance *residential mobility,* using Section 8 housing vouchers and supportive services to help the poor move to middle-income neighborhoods. The Gautreaux program, begun in Chicago in 1976, significantly improved the employment and earnings of parents, as well as children's educational attainment (Rosenbaum and Popkin 1991), although some methodological questions plagued the evaluation. In 1994, the U.S. Department of Housing and Urban Development (HUD) launched the Moving-to-Opportunity pilot in several U.S. cities. In general, parents and children have reported satisfaction with safer schools and neighborhoods in the early program evaluations, but positive effects on earnings or employment of adults have yet to be found (Katz et al. 1998).

Alternatively, efforts can be made to improve the quality of existing low-income communities, either by attracting businesses and jobs or by improving the quality of housing and services. Most state-level "enterprise zone" programs in the 1980s appear to have been quite cost-*in*effective at attracting businesses or creating employment for zone residents: Large amounts of money were spent per new job created (Papke 1993). The current generation of programs, such as the federal Empowerment Zone and Enterprise Community efforts funded by HUD in several dozen U.S. cities and rural areas, focuses more on the quality of housing and services; this approach may yet prove to be somewhat more effective.

Providing Employment and Training for Out-of-School Youth

A variety of "second chance" programs seeks to enhance training and employment outcomes for young people, particularly minority youth, who remain in poor neighborhoods and have left school with weak educational credentials and little work experience.

Many such programs, including those funded by the Job Training Partnership Act (now becoming the Workforce Investment Act, funded by the U.S. Department of Labor but administered by local Workforce Investment Boards) are modestly successful at improving outcomes for adults (particularly women) but quite ineffective among youth (Lalonde 1995). Short-term training that does not deal with the wide range of disadvantages faced by youth in poor neighborhoods appears unlikely to generate improvements.

One approach that appears to be successful is the Department of Labor's Job Corps program: A much more intensive approach, it provides roughly a year of remedial education and skills-related training in more than 100 residential centers throughout the United States. While the residential component greatly adds to the program's cost, it also seems to be a major reason for its relative success. The Department of Labor is currently reevaluating the Job Corps.

The Job Corps takes low-income youth out of their neighborhoods; an alternative is to try to change the neighborhoods themselves, saturating them with a comprehensive array of educational and employment services. Earlier models of such efforts, such as Youth Fair Chance and Youth Opportunities Unlimited, were never carefully evaluated. A much broader effort along these lines is being implemented through Youth Opportunities Grants: The Labor Department is distributing roughly $1 billion to 30 low-income neighborhoods over the next four years.

Training is one type of service that can be provided to disadvantaged minority youth, but private-sector intermediaries that connect employers and job seekers can provide a wider range of services. Other services that can be useful include assistance related to *job search and placement, retention, and mobility.* Job search and placement assistance might help young minorities overcome barriers that are associated with spatial mismatches, particularly limited access to transportation and information about job openings. For instance, in several large cities, HUD's "Bridges to Work" demonstration focuses on the placement and transportation components that improve the mobility of inner-city workers to outlying suburban jobs; many other programs provide job search assistance as well that is generally inexpensive to the funder and cost-effective.

Effective forms of job retention assistance are more difficult to identify. The Post-Employment Services Demonstration, in which individuals employed in private-sector jobs receive support services designed to promote retention, is being evaluated at several sites nationwide. More broadly, labor market intermediaries can help employers improve the quality of worker-job matches or help low-skilled workers achieve career advancement over a sustained period and through mobility across several job placements. Access to affordable child care also promotes job retention for low-income women.

This combination of training with sustained placement, retention, and mobility assistance has been the basis of the success of the Center for Employment and Training (CET) in San Jose, STRIVE, and other well-known programs.[4] Also critical are strong linkages between the labor market intermediary and local employers: This connection ensures that the services provided respond to employer needs and that the intermediary retains its credibility with those employers. An effort to replicate CET's success in other project sites is under evaluation by the Department of Labor. Also deserving further study is the strategy of basing the intermediaries in the neighborhoods themselves, as with the Jobs-Plus effort funded by HUD and the Rockefeller Foundation in several sites.

Finally, *work experience* programs (or "community service jobs") can sometimes effectively provide the disadvantaged with transitional assistance, and also provide low-income communities with needed services. For example, Youth Corps and YouthBuild, which combine education/training with community service jobs, offer promising models of transitional assistance.[5] The National Supported Work Demonstrations, funded by the Department of Health and Human Services in the late 1970s, also generated strongly positive effects on postprogram outcomes for welfare recipients.

Work experience programs may be particularly important for individuals who would have great difficulty finding private-sector employment on their own, even in very tight labor markets. Such individuals would include those with very poor cognitive skills and those with relatively severe disabilities or physical or emotional health problems (Danziger et al. 1998).

For work experience programs to provide a useful transition to private-sector employment might require the development of a credential for those who successfully complete such programs. Alternatively, the "sheltered-workshop" approach to employment might need to be longer term, particularly for those with disabilities. Work experience programs might also be more important during an economic recession when private-sector employment for the unskilled is more scarce.

Finally, the particular labor market problems of young and middle-aged men with criminal records need separate consideration, and this category will include increasingly large numbers of minority men over the next decade or two. Ex-offenders are an important subset of noncustodial, low-income fathers who are eligible for funds under welfare-to-work programs and are the target group for various "fatherhood" efforts.

Poor fathers as a group, especially the ex-offenders among them, tend to suffer from very serious skill deficiencies and a lack of work experience, as well as some major stigmas in the eyes of employers. Efforts to overcome these problems will require combining work experience with remedial education and training, as well as changes in child support rules that encourage both greater work and participation in child rearing. Improving access to wage supplements or eligibility for the earned income tax credit might also be considered.

Further Reducing Discrimination

As noted, hiring discrimination against minorities (particularly African Americans) remains most serious at small establishments and those that mostly serve white customers (presumably in predominantly white, suburban neighborhoods). Yet effective strategies to reduce such discrimination may be difficult to develop: By their very nature, small establishments are difficult to monitor. Moreover, given the "economies of scale" in focusing antidiscrimination efforts at large establishments, it would probably be a mistake to shift significant enforcement resources toward smaller firms. Also, suburban employers often receive few minority applicants, making such efforts even more problematic.

Still, discrimination at small or suburban establishments likely matters enough to contribute to the weaker career prospects of young African Americans. Thus, job placement and transportation strategies, which can deliver more minority applicants to businesses in these areas, might be combined with closer monitoring of employer hiring decisions once these workers apply for jobs. Enforcement practices targeting small establishments or suburbs might also make greater use of "audit" or "tester" studies, using matched pairs of white and minority applicants.

AN AMBITIOUS AGENDA

A variety of problems impairs the career employment prospects of less-educated minorities, but relatively low skills is the most serious. Therefore, our highest priority needs to be a long-term effort to improve the educational attainment, basic skills, and early work experience of these young people.

This priority can be met through two approaches, either or both of which need to be pursued: (1) improve the access of young minorities to high-quality schools or residences outside their neighborhoods; and (2) improve their current schools and neighborhoods. In particular, concerted efforts to raise the basic skills of minority children early on, maintain early progress through tutoring in the elementary schools, and generate work-related skills and other links to the workforce for teens deserve strong support.

For disadvantaged minority youth who are out of school, a better sense of what actually works is also emerging. At a minimum, successful approaches recognize the multiple barriers associated with residence in high-poverty communities, and they address these barriers either by moving individuals from these neighborhoods (as in the Job Corps) or by saturating their communities with a comprehensive array of educational, employment, and training services. Efforts that combine training, job mobility, job placement and retention assistance, and perhaps work experience seem to offer the greatest promise. On the other hand, efforts to prevent educational and labor market failures in the first place are likely to be more effective than "second chance" approaches after the failures have occurred.

Also needing exploration are creative efforts to further reduce discrimination in small or suburban establishments, perhaps combined with improving the access of minority youth to such establishments. And the special needs of low-income fathers, especially the ex-offenders among them, will require a combination of remedial education and training, work experience, income supplements, and child support reforms.

Two factors greatly impede our ability to successfully implement any such ambitious array of strategies: (1) the costs of such investments; and (2) the current limited understanding of what actually works in many contexts.

Regarding the first issue, it is well to consider not only the budgetary costs of the programs but also the enormous costs imposed on society by the failure to address these problems. For instance, Richard Freeman (1996) has estimated that the social costs of crime among nonemployed young men have been as high as 4 percent of GDP in recent years, or roughly $300 billion. Even modestly successful prevention efforts could yield very large social payoffs, although the investment must be made well in advance of reaping the returns. Furthermore, the investment required will likely be much greater than the public sector alone can make: Public funds will have to be leveraged with private-sector matches, through partnerships with foundations, community groups, and other entities.

Regarding the limited understanding of what works, continued experimentation and careful evaluation of diverse approaches must continue as we grope toward a better understanding of effective models. The areas that are most in need of continued experimentation and evaluation include: (1) the different approaches to improving student performance, school quality, and school choice in low-income areas; (2) the school-to-work transition, especially the usefulness of efforts to develop specific job market skills and the credentials of those in school; (3) work experience programs that attempt to generate credentials that private-sector employers might take seriously; and (4) communitywide efforts to improve educational and employment services in very low-income neighborhoods.

NOTES

1. As of 1997, Success for All programs had been implemented in 750 schools nationally and Reading One-to-One in 70 schools. Both are funded primarily through Title I (or Chapter 1) of the Elementary and Secondary Education Act.
2. For general evidence and discussion of school-to-career programs, see Hershey et al. (1997) and the Jobs for the Future Web site: http://www.jff.org. The ProTech program, begun in three Boston high schools, is a youth apprenticeship program that combines classroom learning and internships in specific fields, such as allied health or telecommunications. Career Academies are based on a "school within a school" concept that provides academic and career-oriented instruction in more than 300 high schools nationwide.
3. Originally funded by the Ford Foundation at five sites nationwide, Quantum Opportunities provides a comprehensive range of services to students over a four-year period, including mentoring by an adult.
4. CET has been funded by the U.S. Department of Labor and the Rockefeller Foundation. STRIVE is mostly privately funded. STRIVE began in East Harlem and has since spread to several other sites nationwide, including Chicago and Pittsburgh.
5. Youth Corps programs operate in about 200 sites, with funding from the National and Community Service Act. Participants spend roughly four days a week in community service projects and one day a week in education or training activities. HUD-funded YouthBuild, originating in New York and now operating at about 100 sites, combines remedial education, life skills training, and leadership development with work on housing rehabilitation projects.

REFERENCES

Ballen, John, and Richard Freeman. 1986. "Transitions between Employment and Nonemployment." In *The Black Youth Employment Crisis,* edited by Richard Freeman and Harry Holzer. Chicago: University of Chicago Press.

Bernstein, Jared, Lawrence Mishel, and John Schmitt. 1999. *The State of Working America.* Washington, D.C.: Economic Policy Institute.

Brooks-Gunn, Jeanne, Greg J. Duncan, and Lawrence Aber, eds. 1998. *Neighborhood Poverty.* New York: Russell Sage Foundation.

Crane, Jonathan. 1998. *Social Programs That Work.* New York: Russell Sage Foundation.

Currie, Janet, and Duncan Thomas. 1995. "Does Head Start Make a Difference?" *American Economic Review* 85 (3): 341–64.

Cutler, David, and Edward Glaeser. 1997. "Are Ghettoes Good or Bad?" *Quarterly Journal of Economics* 112 (3): 827–72.

Danziger, Sandra et al. 1998. "Barriers to Employment of Welfare Recipients." Working Paper, University of Michigan, Ann Arbor.

Duncan, Greg J., and Jeanne Brooks-Gunn, eds. 1998. *Consequences of Growing Up Poor.* New York: Russell Sage Foundation.

Farley, Reynolds et al. 1997. "The Residential Preferences of Whites and Blacks: A Four-Metropolis Analysis." *Housing Policy Debate* 8 (4): 763–800.

Ferguson, Ronald. 1998. "Teachers' Perceptions and Expectations and the Black-White Test Score Gap." In *The Black-White Test Score Gap,* edited by Christopher Jencks and Meredith Phillips. Washington, D.C.: The Brookings Institution.

Fix, Michael, and Raymond Struyk. 1994. *Clear and Convincing Evidence.* Washington, D.C.: The Urban Institute Press.

Freeman, Richard. 1992. "Crime and the Employment of Disadvantaged Youths." In *Urban Labor Markets and Job Opportunity,* edited by George Peterson and Wayne Vroman. Washington, D.C.: The Urban Institute Press.

———. 1996. "Why Do So Many Young American Men Commit Crimes and What Might We Do about It?" *Journal of Economic Perspectives* 10 (1): 25–42.

Grissmer, David et al. 1998. "Why Did the Black-White Score Gap Narrow in the 1970's and 1980's?" In *The Black-White Test Score Gap,* edited by Christopher Jencks and Meredith Phillips. Washington, D.C.: The Brookings Institution.

Herrnstein, Richard, and Charles Murray. 1994. *The Bell Curve.* New York: Free Press.

Hershey, Alan, Marsha Silverberg, and Joshua Haimson. 1999. "Expanding Options for Students: Report to Congress on the National Evaluation of School-to-Work Implementation." Princeton, N.J.: Mathematica Policy Research, Inc.

Holzer, Harry. 1987. "Informal Job Search and Black Youth Unemployment." *American Economic Review* 77 (3): 446–52.

———. 1996. *What Employers Want: Job Prospects for Less-Educated Workers.* New York: Russell Sage Foundation.

———. 1998. "Why Do Small Establishments Hire Fewer Blacks Than Larger Ones?" *Journal of Human Resources* 33 (4): 896–914.

———. 1999. "Will Employers Hire Welfare Recipients? Recent Survey Evidence from Michigan." *Journal of Policy Analysis and Management* 18 (3): 449–72.

Holzer, Harry, and Keith Ihlanfeldt. 1998. "Customer Discrimination and Employment Outcomes for Minority Workers." *Quarterly Journal of Economics* 113 (3): 835–67.

Holzer, Harry, and Robert LaLonde. 2000. "Job Change and Job Stability among Young and Less-Educated Workers." In *Finding Jobs: Work and Welfare Reform,* edited by Rebecca Blank and David Card. New York: Russell Sage Foundation.

Ihlanfeldt, Keith, and David Sjoquist. 1998. "The Spatial Mismatch Hypothesis: A Review of Recent Studies and Their Implications for Welfare Reform." *Housing Policy Debate* 9 (4): 849–92.

Jargowsky, Paul. 1996. *Poverty and Place.* New York: Russell Sage Foundation.

Jencks, Christopher, and Meredith Phillips. 1998. *The Black-White Test Score Gap.* Washington, D.C.: The Brookings Institution.

Johnson, William, and Derek Neal. 1998. "Basic Skills and the Black-White Earnings Gap." In *The Black-White Test Score Gap,* edited by Christopher Jencks and Meredith Phillips. Washington, D.C.: The Brookings Institution.

Juhn, Chinhui. 1992. "Decline of Male Labor Force Participation: The Role of Declining Market Opportunities." *Quarterly Journal of Economics* 107 (1): 79–121.

Katz, Lawrence, and Kevin Murphy. 1992. "Changes in Relative Wages, 1963–1987: Supply and Demand Factors." *Quarterly Journal of Economics* 107 (1): 35–78.

Katz, Lawrence, Jeffrey Kling, and Jeffrey Liebman. 1998. Draft Paper Analyzing Moving-to-Opportunity Program in Boston.

LaLonde, Robert. 1995. "The Promise of Public Sector-Sponsored Training Programs." *Journal of Economic Perspectives* 9 (2): 149–68.

Mare, Robert. 1995. "Changes in Educational Attainment and School Enrollment." In *State of the Union,* vol. 1, edited by Reynolds Farley. New York: Russell Sage Foundation.

Massey, Douglas, and Nancy Denton. 1992. *American Apartheid.* Cambridge: Harvard University Press.

Moss, Philip, and Chris Tilly. 1996. "Soft Skills and Race." Working Paper. New York: Russell Sage Foundation.

Murnane, Richard, and Frank Levy. 1995. *Teaching the New Basic Skills.* New York: Free Press.

Neal, Derek, and William Johnson. 1996. "The Role of Premarket Factors in Black-White Wage Differences." *Journal of Political Economy* 104 (5): 869–95.

Papke, Leslie. 1993. "What Do We Know about Enterprise Zones?" Cambridge, Mass.: National Bureau of Economic Research.

Reimers, Cordelia. 1983. "Labor Market Discrimination against Hispanic and Black Men." *Review of Economics and Statistics* 65 (4): 570–79.

Rosenbaum, James, and Susan Popkin. 1991. "Employment and Earnings of Low-Income Blacks Who Move to Middle-Class Suburbs." In *The Urban Underclass,* edited by Christopher Jencks and Paul Peterson. Washington, D.C.: The Brookings Institution.

Rothstein, Donna. 1999. "Work Experience among Youth: A Tale of Two Cohorts." Mimeographed paper. Washington, D.C.: Bureau of Labor Statistics, U. S. Department of Labor.

Rouse, Cecelia. 1997. "Private School Vouchers and Student Achievement: An Evaluation of the Milwaukee Parental Choice Program." Working Paper. Cambridge, Mass.: National Bureau of Economic Research.

Stoll, Michael et al. 2000. "Within Cities and Suburbs: Racial Residential Concentration and the Spatial Distribution of Employment Opportunities across Submetropolitan Areas." *Journal of Policy Analysis and Management* 19 (2): 207–31.

Taber, Christopher, and Tricia Gladden. Forthcoming. "Wage Progressions among Less-Skilled Workers." In *Finding Jobs: Work and Welfare Reform,* edited by Rebecca Blank and David Card. New York: Russell Sage Foundation.

Topel, Robert, and Michael Ward. 1992. "Job Mobility and the Careers of Young Men." *Quarterly Journal of Economics* 107 (2): 439–79.

U.S. Department of Commerce. 1998. *Educational Attainment in the United States: March 1998.* Current Population Reports. Washington, D.C.

U.S. Department of Labor. 1999. *Employment and Earnings.* Washington, D.C. January.

Wilson, William J. 1996. *When Work Disappears.* New York: Alfred Knopf.

12

Latino Low-Wage Workers

A Look at Immigrant Workers

Sonia M. Pérez and Cecilia Muñoz

All low-wage workers face a variety of challenges to advancement in the workforce, yet Latino workers, both immigrants and those born in the United States, face two sets of additional obstacles. The first set is composed of human capital and structural obstacles that characterize the Latino low-wage labor force but are not limited to those Latinos who are immigrants. The second set results directly from immigration law and other policies that target immigrants. These policies have created barriers within the workplace as well as obstacles to obtaining supports, such as access to nutrition and health care programs, that are vital to the low-wage workforce.

Any discussion of changing the dynamics and conditions in the low-wage workforce is incomplete without specific consideration of the barriers faced by Latino workers overall, and immigrant workers specifically. Latino workers, including the substantial share of immigrants among them, represent a large and increasing share of new entrants to the labor force—between 40 and 50 percent by some estimates (*Economist* 1997; Vernez, Krop, and Rydell 1999). Their status links directly to the future health of the nation's economy: Ultimately, the debate over improving the preparation of these workers for jobs with secure wages and benefits is critically important as a key element of the nation's overall economic well-being, not just as a labor force strategy in the new economy.

THE LATINO WORKFORCE

One of the most profound demographic shifts in the United States during the last two decades has been the dramatic increase in the Latino population, driven by both immigration and relatively high birthrates.[1] This shift is reshaping the U.S. labor force: The Hispanic population, calculated at 35.3 million in 2000, now constitutes about 13 percent of the U.S. population—a proportion similar to that of African Americans. Hispanics are expected to become the nation's largest minority group within three to

239

five years. Although Latinos are concentrated in five states (California, Texas, New York, Florida, and Illinois), the Latino population has also grown significantly in other parts of the United States over the past decade, most notably in the South. Moreover, while the immigrant portion of the community receives the bulk of political and policy attention, more than half of Latinos were born in the United States. With the addition of naturalized citizens, about 70 percent of Latinos are citizens.[2] In 1996, one-third of the U.S. Latino population were first-generation Americans (Del Pinal and Singer 1997).

With the growing proportion of immigrants has come an even larger increase of their presence in the labor force, partly because most Latino immigrants are young and in search of economic opportunity. According to the U.S. Department of Labor, the number of foreign-born workers employed in the labor force has grown from 13.4 million in 1996 to more than 15.7 million in 1999, an increase of 17 percent (U.S. Bureau of Labor Statistics n.d.; Greenhouse 2000).

Latinos represent diverse backgrounds, including Cubans, Mexicans, and Central and South Americans. Data indicate that more than four-fifths of immigrant adults from Cuba and Central and South America were first generation in 1996. In particular, Central and South Americans have the largest proportion of recent immigrants. Mexicans, the largest Latino subgroup, also constitute the largest share of Latino immigrants, at 27.2 percent of the total U.S. foreign-born population. The other Latino immigrant subgroups whose presence in the United States has increased over the past decade are Dominicans and Salvadorans; at 2.5 percent and 2.4 percent of the foreign-born population, they represent the third and fourth largest Latino immigrant groups.

The distribution of immigrant workers includes all professions, but immigrants are more likely than natives of the United States to work in low-wage occupations. According to the 1990 Census, foreign-born males were more likely than their native-born counterparts to work as operators, fabricators, and laborers (21.4 percent for foreign-born and 20.1 percent for native-born) or in the service industry (14.5 percent for foreign-born vs. 9.7 percent for native-born). As table 12.1 shows, foreign-born females were also more likely to serve in domestic or service professions than their native-born counterparts (23.2 percent and 16.3 percent, respectively) and as opera-

TABLE 12.1 Occupational Distribution of Foreign-Born and U.S.-Born Workers, 1990

Occupation	Men (%)		Women (%)	
	Foreign-Born	U.S.-Born	Foreign-Born	U.S.-Born
Managerial/Professional	22.3	25.5	22.0	28.4
Tech./Sales/Administrative	18.7	22.0	34.7	44.5
Service occupations	14.5	9.7	23.2	16.3
Precision production/Craft/Repair	17.6	19.1	4.1	2.2
Operators/Fabricators/Laborers	21.4	20.1	14.6	7.9
Farming/Forestry/Fishing	5.5	3.6	1.3	0.8

Source: U.S. Bureau of the Census (1993).

tors, fabricators, and laborers (14.6 percent and 7.9 percent, respectively) (U.S. Bureau of the Census 1993).

During the 1980s, approximately half of male immigrants and more than two-thirds of female immigrants worked in manufacturing, which is associated with unstable employment and low wages (Morales and Ong 1993). Men were especially likely to work in furniture, fabricated metals, machinery, and electrical equipment; women were most likely to be employed in the apparel sector. Overall, 43 percent of foreign-born workers were employed in low-skill jobs in 1997, compared with 29 percent of native-born workers (Grenier and Cattan 2000).

On two fronts, recent developments underscore the significance of the large numbers of immigrant and Latino workers in the low-wage labor force. First, industry groups are increasingly active in advocating for better access to immigrant workers and for legalizing the undocumented portion of their workforces. At the same time, in the wake of major long-term organizing efforts by the Service Employees International Union, the Union of Needletrades, Industrial and Textile Employees (UNITE), and other unions, the AFL-CIO recently established a clear policy that support for immigrant workers is a critical element in the overall strategy to improve wages and working conditions for the U.S. workforce (AFL-CIO 2000).[3]

In this context, three sets of barriers help explain the relatively disadvantaged position of Latinos in the U.S. labor force:

- *Human capital characteristics:* In particular, the low education levels of Latinos are significant determinants of the occupational placement and outcomes of Hispanic workers as a group.
- *Structural and institutional concerns:* The changing dynamics of the U.S. economy have greatly influenced the status of Latino workers.
- *Legal and policy barriers:* Immigration law, discrimination, and related factors play a role in shaping how well Latino workers fare in the U.S. economy.

HUMAN CAPITAL ISSUES

What workers offer the labor market in terms of educational preparation, skills, and transferable experience influences the types of jobs, wages, and economic mobility available to them. For any worker, education is the most significant human capital predictor of earnings and labor market success. The economy's growing emphasis on literacy and numeracy represents a particular challenge for Latino immigrant workers: Latinos, as a group, have the lowest educational levels of all Americans.

An examination of the educational profile of all Hispanics indicates that they are more likely than African Americans and whites to start school later and leave earlier.[4] As Holzer notes (see chapter 11), only slightly more than half of Hispanics age 25 and older completed high school in 1998, compared with three-fourths of blacks and more than four-fifths of whites. Equally troubling is the fact that while more than one in four whites had a college degree, only about one in seven African Americans and 1 in 10 Latinos had graduated from college that year.

Latino immigrants are especially likely to have limited academic preparation. Overall, about 70 percent of U.S.-born Latinos had completed high school in 1996, compared with 42 percent of foreign-born Latinos (Del Pinal and Singer 1997). Specific subgroup data show that while two-thirds of Mexicans age 25 and older born in the United States had completed high school, fewer than 3 in 10 of those born outside the country had a high school diploma. Similarly, 84 percent of U.S.-born Central and South Americans graduated from high school. By contrast, 59 percent of foreign-born Central and South Americans had a high school diploma.

High school completion is one indicator of educational disparities between Latino immigrants and their native-born counterparts; a comparison of overall years of schooling underscores these discrepancies. For instance, in 1996 more than half of foreign-born Mexicans had fewer than nine years of schooling, compared with 16 percent of U.S.-born Mexicans. Thus, not only are immigrants less likely than others to be high school graduates, but the short duration of their schooling in their home countries represents an added barrier in a labor market that rewards advanced education, high skill, and technical training.

With respect to higher education, U.S.-born Latinos are more likely than those born elsewhere to have completed four years of college. However, as del Pinal and Singer (1997) note, the gaps in college attainment are not as great as those for high school attainment between native- and foreign-born Latinos. In 1996, about 12 percent of Latinos born in the United States had college degrees, compared with 8 percent of foreign-born Latinos.

The ability to communicate effectively in English is another skill necessary for the U.S. workplace, particularly for those in growth industries that offer economic mobility. Limited English proficiency represents an employment barrier for a notable proportion of Latino immigrants. Data from the 1990 census (the most recent [not at this writing] national-level data available) show that almost three-quarters of Hispanics in the United States speak English "very well" or "well." By contrast, 26 percent say they speak English "not well" or "not at all." Among foreign-born Mexicans, only 23 percent of men and 21 percent of women reported speaking English "very well" (Chiswick and Hurst 2000).

Several factors underscore the importance of English language proficiency for Latinos. First, the youthfulness of the Hispanic immigrant population suggests that most immigrants are beginning their employment history; lack of English skills can greatly affect job opportunities, paths to improvement, and overall employment prospects. Second, Latino immigrants are concentrated in low-paying, dead-end jobs; without English language fluency, their chances to move into high-wage industries are small. A third issue relevant to language fluency, and to bilingualism in particular, relates to income. A recent University of Miami study showed that families speaking only Spanish had the lowest average income, while those speaking only English had an average income of $32,000. Those with skills in both languages registered the highest family income, $50,376.[5]

English language skills and proficiency are especially important in the case of recent immigrants. Carliner found that wage increases are a worker's reward for speaking English well. Compared with other workers, immigrants earn much less than native-born workers when they first arrive in the United States; over time, this gap narrows. For immigrants who arrived in the 1950s and 1960s, improvements in English language skills contributed to 6 to 18 percent of this narrowing, depending on gender and education levels. Moreover, workers (especially men) with weak English skills are at a serious disadvantage: For example, less-educated men who spoke only English earned 29 percent more than similar men who spoke no English (Carliner 1996).

Two other human capital barriers affect the extent to which Latino immigrants succeed in the U.S. economy: their accumulated labor market experience and their ability to offer specific skills currently in demand. Latino immigrants are industrious and especially likely to begin work at an early age. Indeed, their primary motivation for migrating to the United States is employment potential or economic opportunity. Thus, their pattern of premature entry into the workforce, coupled with high and consistent labor force participation and late retirement, translates into long work histories, especially for Latino immigrant men. However, work experience accumulated over time does not necessarily mean that Latino immigrants acquire the skills in demand by the marketplace, or that they step onto a path of employment mobility. Many Latino immigrants enter at the bottom of the labor market, where human capital and other barriers limit their ability to move into better-paying jobs. In particular, low-wage jobs often do not offer the human capital experience valued by the economy; consequently, while Latino immigrants may consistently work, they may not be able to transfer this experience into more meaningful employment that allows them to reap the rewards of their labor.

Similarly, the labor market demands specific skills for high-paying jobs. In addition to English language fluency, the requirements often include computer literacy, technical skills, and competent levels of overall verbal and mathematical literacy. These factors put Latino immigrants at a disadvantage. Furthermore, given their concentration in the low-wage labor market, Latino immigrants lack opportunities to acquire these skills on the job. Ironically, those jobs that require the highest levels of academic preparation are precisely those that also provide advanced training and other workforce development opportunities for their employees. Conversely, low-skilled sectors, in which Latino immigrants are likely to work, typically do not offer training or skills development opportunities.

Despite their education and skill barriers, especially given the demands of the current economy, Latino immigrant workers have demonstrated both industriousness and tenacity as they incorporate themselves into the workforce. In fact, Central and South American men, as well as Mexican men—most of whom are foreign-born—have the highest labor force participation rates of any group of American workers. This is consistent with the dominant forces that motivate their immigration from Latin America: limited economic opportunity, high unemployment, and poverty.

Ineffective job search techniques and networks further exacerbate the overrepresentation of Latino immigrant workers in the low-wage labor market. Recent research by Meléndez and Falcón shows that Latino workers tend to rely on social networks (family and friends) in searching for employment, as well as on open-market search strategies, such as want ads and walk-ins; these strategies are disconnected from employers' recruitment networks (Meléndez and Falcón 2000).

In part, their job search strategies lead to the perpetuation of Latino workers in low-wage labor markets. While Meléndez and Falcón did not focus specifically on Latino immigrants, their research does suggest that if this is the case for all Hispanics, it would arguably apply more strongly to Latino immigrants. Given Latino immigrants' human capital characteristics, ethnic isolation, and lack of knowledge of employment practices, they probably rely heavily on social networks to find jobs. Indeed, other research has found that, in part because of their limited English ability, Latino immigrants are often employed by firms "where informal employer-employee relations based on ethnic and kinship ties prevail" (Morales and Ong 1993).

STRUCTURAL AND INSTITUTIONAL CONCERNS

Most Latino immigrants come to the United States to work. Relative to their home countries, the U.S. economy offers significant economic opportunity. This is particularly true now, during the nation's longest period of sustained economic growth in history. The economic boom notwithstanding, the U.S. economy has changed dramatically from previous decades; however, the notion of low-skilled immigrants arriving to work their way up the economic ladder is no longer valid.

Decades ago, low-skilled workers and those with limited education could find work in manufacturing and other industries that allowed them to support their families, but in recent years, the bulk of Latino immigrants has entered the U.S. economy at a time of rapid change and shifts in industries. The United States has experienced significant declines in the numbers of manufacturing and low-skilled, blue-collar jobs—once the path to upward mobility for many workers with limited educational preparation, and a sector in which many Latinos, including immigrants, have tended to cluster.

Latino and other immigrants confront a new economic reality, and one that puts them at a disadvantage relative to their counterparts who arrived decades earlier. For example, both the loss of manufacturing jobs and declining wages in this sector have adversely affected entry-level jobs, particularly for Mexican immigrants. Morales and Ong (1993) found that Mexican immigrants have suffered a deterioration in their economic position as well as declining employment opportunities relative to both European immigrants and earlier cohorts of Mexican immigrants.

On the plus side, the economic expansion, coupled with Latino immigrants' strong work ethic, has resulted in low unemployment rates for Latinos as a whole, as well as more opportunities for their economic integration and mobility. However, two trends are noteworthy. First, in general, Americans benefiting from the new economy are doing so by working more hours, not because overall wages have improved significantly. In fact, wages deteriorated in the 1990s, especially among low-wage earners but also among middle-class and college-educated workers (Mishel, Bernstein, and Schmitt 1999). This trend has particularly affected young families. Latino immigrants, who tend to be young and overrepresented among low-earners, have felt the impact of these trends particularly hard.

Second, the economic expansion has masked serious inequities especially relevant for low-wage immigrant, Latino, and other workers, such as high poverty, a growing wealth gap, and the declining power of unions (Collins, Leondar-Wright, and Sklar 1999). Throughout the 1990s, economic growth has emphasized the absolute number of jobs created, not improved wages or overall job quality. As a result, research and data suggest, overall economic well-being has not improved for a significant share of U.S. workers, particularly those at the bottom of the economic ladder. Not only has the gap in wages between skilled and unskilled workers grown over the past two decades, but disparities in other economic indicators (e.g., health and pension coverage) also signify growing inequality in the workforce (Passell 1998).

Moreover, according to the Economic Policy Institute, jobs have become less secure and less likely to offer health and pension benefits (Mishel et al. 1999). This is particularly a concern for Latinos who, in addition to being in low-skilled occupational categories, are especially likely to work in firms with fewer than 25 employees. Job security allows for wage growth over time, the addition of fringe benefits, and a cushion against cyclical economic shifts. The types of jobs in which Latino immigrants are concentrated are less likely to offer health insurance, pension plans, and other benefits that are often considered "extras" but that are critical to the economic well-being of employees and their families. To illustrate, the number of uninsured Hispanics almost doubled from 1987 to 1998 to reach 11.2 million, and more than one in three Latinos lacks health insurance (Quinn 2000). When Latinos are not insured through their employers, they are also less likely than either African Americans or whites to be eligible for publicly funded health insurance programs.[6]

With regard to pensions and retirement plans, there is limited information about the participation and coverage rates of Latino immigrants. Data do show that, as a group, Latino workers are less likely than their African-American or white counterparts to participate in an employer-sponsored pension plan. Moreover, the presence of immigrant workers does not explain the disparities in benefit coverage between Latinos and other workers: There are only modest differences in access to benefits between U.S.- and foreign-born Latinos (Santos and Seitz 2000). With respect to retirement, foreign-born Hispanics appear to have different attitudes from U.S-born Hispanics about saving for their postemployment years.[7]

Another characteristic of the new economy—and the new reality for low-wage workers—is that the pool of entry-level jobs often does not lead to employment pathways into better-paying opportunities. Under the previous economic structure, particularly in manufacturing, job ladders within a firm allowed low-skilled employees to gain experience and advance to positions with better pay and benefits. The bulk of jobs in small firms, as well as in the expanding service industry, does not offer these ladders.

A related structural issue is training. Given their low education and skill levels, as well as limited English proficiency, Latino immigrants stand to benefit enormously from a range of workforce development programs. Such programs include specific skills training, as well as English language instruction. Yet, because Latino immigrants are more likely to work for small firms or in low-quality jobs, this benefit is less often available through their employers.

This leads to an issue of access to workforce development programs operated by community-based organizations or other private agencies. Latinos tend to be underrepresented in such programs, which research has found to be effective in improving wages and employment opportunities for Latinos overall (NCLR 1997).[8] With respect to language instruction programs, the acquisition of English language fluency for Latino immigrants is often hampered by the limited availability of such programs. According to the National Clearinghouse for ESL Literacy Education, the demand is high—and the waiting lists long—for adult, English language training classes. As an example, in 1996 more than 4,000 adults were on waiting lists in San Jose, California; in Massachusetts, 15,000 adults were wait listed.[9]

A final structural and institutional barrier to Latino immigrant employment and labor market success is employment discrimination. Employment discrimination is likely to play a role in concentrating immigrants in the low-wage sector and in limiting their opportunities to work outside of it. While specific types of discrimination emerge directly from immigration policy, immigrant workers are also subject to discrimination based on national origin, a phenomenon they share with their native-born co-ethnics. A 1994 hiring audit conducted by Kenney and Wissoker found that Anglo job applicants had substantially higher success rates in obtaining job interviews and offers than similarly qualified Latinos in every category of the employment search (cited in Chapa and Wacker 2000). Similarly, there is evidence that some employers and industries allocate employment based on racial stereotypes, and therefore concentrate minority workers into low-skill, low-paying jobs.

LEGAL AND POLICY BARRIERS

While low-wage immigrant and nonimmigrant Latino workers face a number of common obstacles, a host of specific barriers to the advancement of this workforce results directly from immigration law and other policies aimed at immigrants. These policies undermine workplace rights and civil rights, as well as access to the safety net services that offer important supplements for individuals and families trying to survive on low wages.

Immigration Laws: Employer Sanctions

The 1986 Immigration Reform and Control Act (IRCA) established a new principle: The workplace would be a major focus of the U.S. strategy to deter undocumented migration. By making it illegal to employ undocumented workers—the first time federal law embodied such a standard—Congress made employers second only to the U.S. Border Patrol in terms of their role in immigration enforcement.

Since the passage of IRCA, employers have been required to use immigration form I-9 to check and record the identity and work authorization documents of all newly hired employees. The Immigration and Naturalization Service (INS) has the authority to check employer records to ensure that all I-9s are properly completed. Employers are liable to fines for incomplete I-9 files, with criminal penalties for a pattern and practice of ignoring IRCA requirements. Moreover, while employers are not liable simply for the presence of undocumented workers in the firm—for example, the employer is not penalized if a worker submits false I-9 documents—they do face fines, and even criminal penalties, for knowingly hiring undocumented immigrants.

Impact on Undocumented Workers

Employer sanctions have established a workplace standard and a set of procedures for employers to follow when hiring new employees, yet they have not achieved the policy's fundamental purpose: to deter undocumented migration by eliminating the job market for undocumented workers. The flow of undocumented immigrants into the United States has continued apace, at a level of 200,000 to 300,000 a year, roughly the same level as before IRCA's enactment.[10]

On the other hand, the workplace standard, with its accompanying penalties for employers, has had a significant impact on the workforce, particularly on undocumented and legal immigrants, as well as on native-born Americans who are mistaken for immigrants.

The most obvious impact has been on undocumented immigrants in the workforce, estimated by the INS to be at about 5 million people, increasing by 200,000 to 300,000 a year. Because the very nature of this workforce is "underground," formal data are difficult to obtain, but the presence in immigration policy debates of trade associations, labor unions, and other representatives of the service, meatpacking, agriculture, and hotel and restaurant industries highlights the concentration of undocumented workers in these occupations.

Undocumented workers in these sectors often bypass I-9 requirements with purchased or borrowed documents, exposing themselves to severe penalties for document fraud under immigration law. Regarding employers who ignore the I-9 requirements, or even assist employees in obtaining false documents, there is evidence that some reduce their undocumented employees' wages to offset the potential cost of employer sanctions. Although U.S. labor law technically protects undocumented employees, these workers are reluctant to report wage and other workplace abuses: To do so would expose them to being revealed to the INS by their employers. The INS is generally aggressive about removing undocumented workers from the United States, even those who have a pending labor law complaint against an abusive employer, and immigration law offers them no reliable protection.

In an environment in which undocumented workers have much to fear if they complain about workplace abuse, the cases that emerge are revealing. Recent lawsuits in various parts of the country have illustrated sexual harassment, violations of worker safety protections, and other abuses. For example, a recently settled lawsuit found that the Holiday Inn Express in Minneapolis, Minnesota, denied undocumented immigrant workers lunch and rest breaks, gave them more rigorous productivity schedules, and denied them promised pay raises at the end of the 90-day probationary period. When the workers complained, Holiday Inn Express called the INS to have some deported. Those who remained filed the lawsuit. In another case, the federal government filed a lawsuit against Quality Art of Gilbert, Arizona, claiming that 27 former workers— undocumented immigrants from Mexico and Guatemala—received lower wages than their colleagues, endured verbal abuse, and suffered sexual harassment, including strip searches for female workers (*USA Today* 2000).

Workplace Discrimination for Other Workers

Increasingly, immigrants are coming forward with complaints, supported largely by labor unions, against abusive employers. However, such cases remain rare, and the immigration status of even successful complainants is uncertain. The recent dramatic shift in AFL-CIO policy highlights the notion that the presence of a large, vulnerable segment of the workforce undermines protections for all U.S. workers; accordingly, the labor movement has taken the position that such workers must be legalized in order to receive full protection under the nation's labor laws (AFL-CIO 2000).

This is a major shift: Throughout its history, the labor federation had tended to support restrictions on immigration, including the employer sanctions policy. The change in policy reflects a change in thinking in a labor movement with a large immigrant presence; the AFL-CIO has formally recognized that legalizing undocumented workers and ensuring that they enjoy full labor rights is more appropriate than supporting new strategies to keep them out of the country.

As the AFL-CIO's policy shift reflects, INS's employer sanctions regime has also engendered new forms of discrimination against immigrant workers legally in the United States, as well as against Americans whom employers mistake for immigrants. Eleven separate studies conducted by government and private agencies in the years immediately following the implementation of sanctions found that the policy engendered a consistent, widespread pattern of employment discrimination (Muñoz 1990). Typical examples included: selectively checking the documents of "ethnic" employees, often based on surname or appearance; asking some employees for more documents based on the assumption that they were immigrants; and avoiding some job applicants altogether because the sanctions policy made them more "troublesome" to hire.

According to a 1990 report by the U.S. General Accounting Office (1990), which was required under IRCA:

- 10 percent of a population of 4.6 million employers discriminated based on "foreign" appearance or accent.
- 8 percent of these employers applied IRCA's verification system only to persons who appeared or sounded "foreign."
- An additional 9 percent of employers responded to the law by discriminating based on citizenship status.
- Discrimination was most extensive in parts of the country with high Hispanic and Asian populations, affecting more than 25 percent of employers in some of these regions.
- In a hiring audit, Hispanic U.S. citizens were three times more likely to encounter unfavorable treatment by employers than white non-Hispanics, who received 52 percent more job offers than equally qualified Hispanics.

More recently, research has confirmed that employer sanctions have contributed to an increase in employment discrimination against all Latinos and, specifically, to a decline in hourly wages of Latino workers in Southwestern border states (Bansak and Raphael forthcoming).

Given the predictable potential for sanctions to engender discrimination, the original IRCA statute included civil rights protections, and established the Office of Special Counsel for Unfair Immigration-Related Employment Practices within the Department of Justice to pursue discrimination claims. In 1990, Congress added a specific protection against "document abuse," responding to evidence that the most common form of discrimination under IRCA was the practice of requiring more or different documents from ethnic employees. However, in 1996, Congress dramatically weakened IRCA's civil rights protections by requiring claimants to demonstrate employers' actual discriminatory intent, a difficult standard to meet, particularly when employers often genuinely believe that the law requires them to selectively check Latino or Asian job applicants.

The collective effect of IRCA and its amendments is a clear willingness on the part of policymakers to undermine the civil rights of a substantial portion of the workforce. And it does so in the name of immigration policies that have proven ineffective in deterring undocumented migration.

Verification, Social Security Numbers, and Low-Wage Workers

The latest development in the regime of employer sanctions emerges not from immigration law but from the intersection of sanctions policies with an agency whose function is unrelated to immigration enforcement: the Social Security Administration. Although its mission is processing worker contributions to the Social Security system and payments to retirees, the Social Security Administration has been drawn into immigration policy because the Social Security number is fast becoming a *de facto* personal identifier, with particular potency in allowing employers and others to determine whether workers are legally in the United States.

As it became clear that a major liability of employer sanctions is the ease with which workers use fraudulent documents, Congress authorized the INS to pilot programs that made it easier for employers to verify that employees were legally authorized to work. However, INS data, even when reliable, only refer to immigrants; the INS cannot, for example, determine the work authorization of native-born U.S. citizens. Birth certificates, which are maintained under more than 50 very different, state record-keeping systems, are also flawed. Thus, the Social Security Administration was in the best position to assist INS with the verification task, using records that closely reflect the native-born and naturalized U.S. workforce.

Although still in the pilot phase, INS's verification efforts have exacerbated the discrimination problem under employer sanctions. They have also heightened the likelihood that some people who are legally authorized to work will have their presence in the workforce questioned because of inferior or incomplete data or other mistakes in the verification system. By providing access to a computer system to check on employees, INS has increased the opportunities for employers to engage in discriminatory practices, including screening out job applicants before the hiring process takes place and dismissing work-authorized employees because of inferior data. The current state of INS and Social Security Administration data makes it highly likely that workers who are legally in the United States, even native-born citizens, will have their ability to work jeopardized because a computer system insists that the employer cannot legally hire them.

In addition to problems with the INS verification system, the Social Security Administration's own efforts to make its data accurate for the purposes of paying out Social Security benefits have led to inadvertent but serious immigration-related problems. These effects have been well-documented among low-wage workers in the meatpacking, service, and other immigrant-dominated industries. In its efforts to clean up its database, the Social Security Administration sends "no-match" letters to employers, who then submit wage deductions to the agencies for Social Security numbers that do not match the federal records. Employers are supposed to review these letters and clarify mistakes in consultation with the worker. However, because the Social Security number is closely identified as an indicator of immigration status, employers frequently dismiss workers when a no-match letter arrives, despite the high likelihood that the problem is unrelated to immigration status, such as interposed numbers, name misspellings, or other common mistakes.

In some cases, employers have ignored the no-match letters unless a union organizing campaign occurs, then used the letters to threaten union supporters. Labor unions have identified the no-match letters as a major obstacle to organizing campaigns in industries with undocumented workers, and immigrants' rights groups have similarly identified them as a major problem in protecting the rights of the immigrant workforce.

In a 1999 initiative based on employer sanctions, INS implemented Operation Vanguard in the meatpacking industry in Nebraska and Iowa. It subpoenaed all the personnel records of the region's industry, covering some 40,000 workers. INS compared the information in these records against its own data and the Social Security Administration database, arriving at more than 4,500 "hits"—that is, records that did not match the database. These workers and their employers were notified of the discrepancy between their records and the government's. According to the INS, roughly 1,000 of these workers showed up for interviews, and only 34 lacked correct documentation (Bacon 1999). It is impossible to determine the fate of the rest, who left their jobs in fear of deportation or other entanglements with the INS. Although it is likely that many of the remaining 3,000 were undocumented, it cannot be assumed that all were. Legal residents have good reason to fear contact with the INS: Immigration laws give the INS broad powers to detain and deport them for minor offenses that may have been committed long ago, and there are occasional, well-documented examples of legal residents, even U.S. citizens, being deported improperly.

The impact of Operation Vanguard and other verification operations has been to destabilize entire communities, undermine immigrant families, and threaten their position in an industry that relies on their labor. It has also had a substantial impact on labor rights in meatpacking and similar industries in which working conditions are notoriously poor by eliminating those who organize their coworkers and increasing the fears of immigrant workers that participation in an organizing drive could lead to deportation.

Immigration Provisions of Other Laws: Welfare Reform

Although the debate that led to the enactment of welfare reforms in 1996 focused on the transition from welfare to work, the law itself was funded in part through an enormous cut in safety net services to immigrants who are legally in the United States. More than 40 percent of the cost savings of welfare reform resulted from removing immigrants from Medicaid, Supplemental Security Income, and the Food Stamp program. Some of these safety net services have been restored—but only for immigrants who are elderly, disabled, or children, and only for those living in the United States when welfare reform was enacted. Thus, many working adults who are legal U.S. residents lack access to federal programs that act as critical supplements to the wages of the low-wage workforce.

The Temporary Assistance for Needy Families (TANF) program, now the main welfare cash assistance program, is a state-level program, unlike its predecessor, Aid to Families with Dependent Children. Although most states have decided to preserve eligibility for pre-1996 immigrants, few give access to TANF for those who arrived since 1996. Similarly, the federal Food Stamp and Medicaid programs are unavailable to immigrants who have arrived since 1996—and to most immigrants who arrived before that date. While some states have created programs to provide nutrition or health care to immigrants who cannot access federal programs, even these efforts tend to be funded on a year-by-year basis, leaving their long-term stability in doubt (Community Catalyst 1999).

The application of such restrictions to legal immigrants—most of whom pay taxes that support these programs—and not to U.S. citizens reflects a new form of discrimination. Immigrant workers and their families have been severely affected by their inability to access these programs. Reports from both the health and nutrition advocates highlight these problems, which in some states are reaching crisis proportions (U.S. Department of Agriculture 2000). In California, for example, immigrants and members of immigrant families are far more likely than any other group to lack access to health care (Brown et al. forthcoming).

In addition to lacking simple eligibility for safety net services, legal immigrants and their families are less likely to use programs for which they remain eligible. The Urban Institute has documented that as many as 20 percent of American children live in "mixed" households—households with an immigrant parent and U.S. citizen children—and there is substantial evidence that the presence of immigrants in the family severely undermines access to the safety net for these children and other family members (Fix and Van Hook 2000). Immigrant workers are not alone in suffering the negative impact of these laws: Their family members, including children, spouses, and others living in the household, are also less likely to have access to health care, nutrition support, and other key services needed by low-income households.

Another recently documented issue for low-income immigrant women, in particular, involves the effectiveness of welfare-to-work programs designed to move welfare participants into the workforce. A recent study that included 75 Mexican women in California indicated that these women experienced problems accessing services (Equal Rights Advocates 1999). Many women reported that they had not received complete or accurate information about the job training or related services for which they were eligible, and several felt it was because they did not speak English. The majority, in fact, did not participate in either job training or English as a Second Language (ESL) classes—essential skill-building activities that they greatly need to improve their labor force opportunities. In addition, the study noted, some immigrant women who did not speak English were placed in training programs conducted in English. In other cases, women were steered toward job search activities, although they lacked skills needed to enter the labor force and had expressed a need for other services, like ESL.

Preliminary evidence shows that such policies, like the "work-first" approach, are deterring Latino participation in programs that might actually help to address their human capital barriers and position them for success in the labor market. In general, it appears that the same trends are true for these types of programs as for health and nutrition programs, and further tracking and documentation of such cases is needed to address the potential implications of these policies for Latino low-income workers.

This discussion strongly underscores the argument that access to the safety net for members of immigrant households is curtailed by policies that emerge from either immigration or welfare laws that aim to control who enters the United States. Often, the legislation is implemented aggressively by state or federal agencies that seek to deter immigrants and their families from using their services. For example, some local governments have placed signs at service agencies warning immigrants that undocumented family members will be turned over to the INS. This overly zealous interpretation of reporting provisions in both the immigration and welfare laws is a clear deterrent to immigrants, legal and undocumented, who fear entanglements with that agency (Schlosberg and Wiley 1998).

Similarly, federal agencies had until recently interpreted a very old feature of immigration law—that incoming immigrants must demonstrate that they are unlikely to become a "public charge"—to penalize immigrants whose family members had received health care services under Medicaid. Although these services were delivered properly to eligible recipients, the government used this fact to deny their immigrant family members the ability to adjust their status to reside permanently in the United States. This problem was resolved after nearly two years of deliberations by federal agencies, but the fear of safety net programs is still strong in immigrant communities. Indeed, enrollment in Medicaid, food stamps, and related programs has plummeted in the Latino community; these policies are largely to blame (Zimmerman and Fix 1998).

CONCLUSIONS AND RECOMMENDATIONS

In the context of both the nation's demographic transformation and the significant economic force that Latino immigrant and native workers represent, attention to the challenges these workers face is timely and relevant. Indeed, immigrants have been credited with immense contributions to economic growth through their high levels of work effort, productivity, entrepreneurship, tax inputs, revitalization of economically depressed neighborhoods, and consumption of goods and services (Greenspan 2000). Among Latinos, immigrants are more likely to own homes than native-born Latinos, an important factor in promoting neighborhood stability.[11]

Given Latino immigrants' vital contributions to the nation's economic growth, the labor market does not adequately reward their hard work. Insufficient education and skill levels and limited English language skills, coupled with low pay, lack of health and pension coverage, and insufficient occupational ladders to help immigrant workers improve their job status, all contribute to the disadvantaged economic position of Latino workers, despite their best efforts. Yet the economic prospects and outcomes of Latino immigrant workers are not solely "immigrant" issues. Indeed, how well Latino immigrants do economically will play a large role in America's prosperity and overall well-being.

The confluence of record levels of immigration and unprecedented economic growth with low unemployment and enormous federal surpluses creates an extraordinary opportunity to address the challenges facing low-wage workers, including immigrant workers. Moreover, if the productivity of our current economy is to be sustained, it would be wise to invest now in the very populations that will comprise the future workforce and who are already contributing so mightily, albeit without structures in place improving their economic status. In particular, policymakers must focus on low educational levels, the need for worker training, and lack of benefits. In addition, they must remove existing policy obstacles, such as those found in immigration and related laws, if not for the sake of the workers themselves, then for the sake of the nation's future prosperity.

A Rand Corporation study suggests some overall benefits of an "investment strategy" if the educational status of Latinos and immigrants were increased. According to the data, every Hispanic who now has a high school education would earn between $400,000 and $500,000 more over her/his lifetime if s/he had a bachelor's degree (as cited in Pérez and Kamasaki 2000). Even modest increases in educational attainment for Latinos would result in substantially higher wages for those workers and enormous corollary payoffs in terms of tax revenues and contributions to the nation's social insurance system, and to Social Security in particular.

A recent analysis of Latinos in California—where a significant portion of the state's Latinos are foreign-born—lends further support to these findings. López, Ramírez, and Rochín (1999) show that increasing the education levels and economic status of Latinos would provide "indirect benefits to the state in the form of higher expenditures on goods and services, increases in tax revenues, and a reduction in the need for public programs for the poor." Even if the nation were still living in an era of government deficits, the wisdom of investing in order to achieve these kinds of outcomes is clear; in the current environment, there is simply no rationale for neglecting these important investments.

It has also become evident that the immigrant workforce and the communities these workers represent are not isolated from the rest of the U.S. workforce or the U.S. community. The Urban Institute's revelation that fully 20 percent of American children live in immigrant families demonstrates the far-reaching nature of these issues. Improvements in the economic well-being of immigrant workers and their families will translate into gains for a large share of American families—and for the cities and states in which they live. The potential rewards for strengthening immigrants' position in the workforce are substantial, as are the risks for failing to do so.

In light of these considerations, a number of public policy changes must be carefully considered and implemented to ensure that immigrant workers and their counterparts in the low-wage workforce benefit as much from their labor as the larger society does from their presence in the workforce. These policies fall into five broad areas: investments, job quality, community-based responses, immigration and related policies, and civil rights.

Investments

There is a clear need to develop, enact, and implement strategies to address the human capital issues that deter immigrants from advancing in the workforce. These strategies would include comprehensive targeting of the educational system to better prepare young immigrants and children of immigrant families. Immigrants and their families are not well served by the educational system in general, and they are underserved by federal and other education programs that have demonstrated success. Indeed, increasing Hispanic education levels should be the top domestic priority for policymakers, with a particular focus on immigrant Latino children and on narrowing the gaps in high school and college attainment between Latinos and others.

In addition, an investment strategy should seek to improve dramatically both the number and quality of public and private workforce development programs and policies. These should incorporate elements that serve the particular needs demonstrated by immigrant workers, including English language instruction, development of literacy and numeracy skills, and targeted training for skilled positions in industries in which Latino workers are underrepresented.

Job Quality

Despite the strong economy, restructuring has reduced the quality of the low-wage and entry-level jobs available to low-skilled workers. Complementary to an investment strategy would be policies and initiatives to address the larger dynamics of the low-wage labor market, including inadequate pay, lack of benefits, limited training opportunities, and the absence of job ladders to promote economic mobility. Immigrant workers, in particular, appear to be in the greatest need of both income supports and access to health care.

A long-term, comprehensive approach would include shifting the nation's broad economic strategy to focus as much on job quality as on the number of jobs available, as well as on developing some form of universal health coverage that includes immigrant communities. In the short term, a number of effective approaches can make work more rewarding without demanding massive policy changes. These include improving immigrant participation in unions, expanding the earned income tax credit, increasing the minimum wage, and expanding eligibility for health programs like Medicaid and the Children's Health Insurance Program.

Another important aspect of job quality relates to job ladders: Immigrant workers who enter the labor market at the bottom of the economic scale should be able to acquire skills and move up to better-paying jobs, as previous cohorts of immigrant and

American workers have done. Employer-based training and lifelong learning programs would help address this gap. Overall, enhancing the quality of jobs in the low-wage labor market and creating economic ladders for upward mobility would benefit not only immigrants but all low-wage workers.

Community-Based Responses

The labor market challenges of the low-wage immigrant workforce can be addressed, in part, by the unique characteristics of Latino community-based organizations: They are often located within Latino communities, understand the barriers immigrants face, and have the trust of community residents. For decades, Latino and other community-based organizations around the country have helped address the needs of immigrant and low-income communities. They have filled the gaps in services when Latinos have been underserved by or underrepresented in federal social and economic programs.

Such organizations have responded with English language instruction and employment training programs to help Latino immigrants and other low-skilled workers. Funding should be expanded for community-based English language and civics programs, which are in high demand.

There are additional opportunities for community-based organizations to play a role in improving the labor market outcomes of Latino immigrants. First, to address the job search networks issues outlined earlier, Latino community-based organizations can be effective in serving as intermediaries between employers and prospective employees. This would supplement their already-effective workforce development programs for Latino immigrants by making connections to other high-paying employers or those in industries in which Latinos are underrepresented.

Moreover, in states with large concentrations of immigrant workers, Latino community-based organizations should be significantly represented in the governance structures and decisionmaking bodies established under the Workforce Investment Act of 1998 to ensure that their communities have a say in appropriately shaping training and funding opportunities for this population. Third, sectoral analysis offers some promise in helping community-based organizations influence job creation and labor market growth in local economies (Dowds and Hinojosa 1999). These efforts should be pursued to help improve access to well-paying jobs and entrepreneurial opportunities for Latino immigrants and low-wage workers.

Immigration and Related Policies

Immigrants face unique barriers that result directly from immigration laws and related policies that target them specifically. By creating a dynamic in which immigrants enjoy significantly fewer rights in the workplace, these laws have undermined the position of the entire low-wage workforce and made it more difficult to raise overall workplace standards, particularly in low-wage occupations. Ultimately, this situation cannot be remedied without reversing the laws that create these disparate standards, particularly the immigration and welfare reforms of 1996 and the employer sanctions policy, with its verification and enforcement schemes that make the workplace the focus of immigration control. Recent developments in immigration policy have only served to divert much-needed social and economic policy attention away from the needs of low-skilled, low-wage immigrant workers.

Civil Rights

Latino immigrant workers face "traditional" discrimination based on national origin, as well as discrimination on the basis of citizenship status. Their civil rights have further been eroded by the employer sanctions policy, which exacerbates employment discrimination and offers weak remedies once discrimination has occurred. A full commitment to the enforcement of equal protections in the workplace must be embraced as an essential element of an overall strategy to improve the status of low-wage immigrant workers. This means vigorous enforcement of national-origin claims, so that individuals denied jobs or equal wages because they are immigrants have some confidence their claims will be addressed. In addition, there is a need to create specific protections for vulnerable immigrants who run the risk of deportation if they report abusive employers, such as new visa categories that allow "whistleblower" immigrants to remain in the United States legally as their claims against abusive employers are addressed. Finally, public policies that put immigrant workers at specific risk of employment discrimination, such as employer sanctions, should be eliminated.

The broad framework of recommendations outlined above offers some strategies that will not only help to strengthen the path to upward mobility for Latino immigrants low-wage workers, but also benefit other workers trapped in the low-wage labor force.

NOTES

1. The terms "Latino" and "Hispanic" are used interchangeably by the U.S. Census Bureau to identify persons of Mexican, Puerto Rican, Cuban, Central and South American, Dominican, and Spanish descent; they may be of any race.

2. This does not include the 3.8 million residents of Puerto Rico who are U.S. citizens by birth.

3. See also a letter from the Essential Worker Immigration Coalition (which includes the American Health Care Association, American Hotel and Motel Association, American Meat Institute, National Restaurant Association, U.S. Chamber of Commerce) to the House of Representatives and Senate, February 14, 2000.

4. For a detailed examination of Hispanic educational issues, see Fisher et al. (1998).

5. Figures taken from the 1990 Census, as cited in Maceri (1999).

6. Current data show that 29 percent of Latinos who are U.S. citizens are uninsured, compared with 23 percent of blacks and 13 percent of whites.

7. For instance, when asked to select from a list of statements that describes them, foreign-born Latinos were more likely to agree it is pointless to save for retirement because it is too far away, it takes too much time and effort, saving for retirement is harder than saving for other things, and if they just save some money each month they will be fine. Retirement Confidence Survey, Washington, D.C.: Employee Benefits Research Institute, 2000.

8. For a recent discussion of the role of community-based training for Latinos, see Meléndez and Falcón (2000).

9. Information obtained from the Web site of the National Clearinghouse for Bilingual Education: http://www.ncbe.gwu.edu/askncbe/faqs/13adult.htm.

10. Information obtained from the Web site of the U.S. Immigration Naturalization Service: http://www.ins.usdoj.gov/graphics/aboutins/statistics/illegalalien/index.htm.

11. Census data show that more than half (57.1 percent) of Hispanic foreign-born householders were homeowners in 1996, whereas less than half (48.1 percent) of native-born Hispanics were homeowners that year.

REFERENCES

AFL-CIO. 2000. "Executive Council Statement." http://aflcio.org/publ/statements/feb2000/immigr.htm. February 16.

Bacon, David. 1999. "INS Declares War on Labor." *The Nation,* 25 October.

Bansak, Cynthia, and Steven Raphael. Forthcoming. "Immigration Reform and the Earnings of Latino Workers: Do Employer Sanctions Cause Discrimination?" *Industrial and Labor Relations Review.*

Brown, E. Richard et al. Forthcoming. *Racial and Ethnic Disparities in Access to Health Insurance and Health Care.* Los Angeles, Calif.: UCLA Center for Health Policy Research and Henry J. Kaiser Family Foundation.

Carliner, Geoffrey. 1996. "The Wages and Language Skills of U.S. Immigrants." Working Paper 5763. Cambridge, Mass.: National Bureau of Economic Research. September.

Chapa, Jorge, and Craig Wacker. 2000. "Latino Unemployment: Current Issues and Future Concerns." In *Moving Up the Economic Ladder: Latino Workers and the Nation's Future Prosperity,* edited by Sonia M. Pérez. Washington, D.C.: National Council of La Raza.

Chiswick, Barry R., and Michael E. Hurst. 2000. "Hispanics and the American Labor Market." In *Hispanics in the United States, An Agenda for the 21st Century,* edited by Pastora San Juan Cafferty and David W. Engstrom. New Brunswick, N.J.: Transaction Publishers.

Collins, Chuck, Betsy Leondar-Wright, and Holly Sklar, 1999. *Shifting Fortunes: The Perils of the Growing American Wealth Gap.* Boston, Mass.: United for a Fair Economy.

Community Catalyst. 1999. "Unfinished Business: The Restoration of Immigrant Health Access after Welfare Reform." *States of Health* 9 (2).

Del Pinal, Jorge, and Audrey Singer. 1997. "Generations of Diversity: Latinos in the U.S." *Population Bulletin* 52 (3).

Dowds, Curtis M., and Jorge Hinojosa. 1999. *The Subsector Approach to Community Economic Development.* Washington, D.C.: National Council of La Raza. July.

The Economist. 1997. "Immigrant Assistance." March 29.

Equal Rights Advocates. 1999. *From War on Poverty to War on Welfare: The Impact of Welfare Reform on the Lives of Immigrant Women.* April. http://www.equalrights.org/welfare/iwwp/finddisc.htm.

Fisher, Maria, Sonia M. Pérez, Bryant González, Jonathan Njus, and Charles Kamasaki. 1998. *Latino Education: Status and Prospects.* Washington, D.C.: National Council of La Raza.

Fix, Michael, and Jennifer Van Hook. 2000. "A Profile of Immigrant Children in U.S. Schools." In *Overlooked and Underserved: Immigrant Students in U.S. Secondary Schools,* edited by Jorge Ruiz-de-Velasco and Michael Fix, with Beatrice Chu Clewell. Washington, D.C.: Urban Institute Press.

Greenhouse, Steven. 2000. "Foreign Workers at Highest Level in Seven Decades." *New York Times,* 4 September.

Greenspan, Alan. 2000. Testimony before the U.S. House of Representatives Committee on Banking and Financial Services. February 17.

Grenier, Guillermo, and Peter Cattan. 2000. "Latino Immigrants in the Labor Force: Trends and Labor Market Issues." In *Moving Up the Economic Ladder: Latino Workers and the Nation's Future Prosperity,* edited by Sonia M. Pérez. Washington, D.C.: National Council of La Raza.

López, Elías, Enrique Ramírez, and Refugio Rochín. 1999. *Latinos and Economic Development in California.* Sacramento, Calif.: California Research Bureau. June.

Maceri, Domenico. 1999. "Spanish for All?" *Chicago Tribune,* 15 April.

Meléndez, Edwin, and Luis M. Falcón. 2000. "Closing the Social Mismatch: Lessons from the Latino Experience." In *Moving Up the Economic Ladder: Latino Workers and the Nation's Future Prosperity,* edited by Sonia M. Pérez. Washington, D.C.: National Council of La Raza.

Mishel, Lawrence, Jared Bernstein, and John Schmitt. 1999. *The State of Working America, 1998–99.* Ithaca, N.Y.: Cornell University Press.

Morales, Rebecca, and Paul M. Ong. 1993. "The Illusion of Progress: Latinos in Los Angeles." In *Latinos in a Changing U.S. Economy: Comparative Perspectives on Growing Inequality,* edited by Rebecca Morales and Frank Bonilla. Newbury Park, Calif.: Sage Publications.

Muñoz, Cecilia. 1990. *Unfinished Business: The Immigration Reform and Control Act of 1986.* Washington, D.C.: National Council of La Raza.

National Council of La Raza. 1997. "Hispanic Participation in Selected Federal Anti-Poverty Programs." Issue Brief. Washington, D.C.: National Council of La Raza. July.

Passell, Peter. 1998. "Benefits Dwindle Along with Wages for the Unskilled." *New York Times,* 14 June.

Pérez, Sonia M., ed. 2000. *Moving Up the Economic Ladder: Latino Workers and the Nation's Future Prosperity.* Washington, D.C.: National Council of La Raza.

Pérez, Sonia M., and Charles K. Kamasaki. 2000. "The Impact of Latino Workers on the U.S. Economy: Implications for Effective Employment Policy." In *Moving Up the Economic Ladder: Latino Workers and the Nation's Future Prosperity,* edited by Sonia M. Pérez. Washington, D.C.: National Council of La Raza.

Quinn, Kevin. 2000. *Working without Benefits: The Health Insurance Crisis Confronting Hispanic Americans.* New York: The Commonwealth Fund, Task Force on the Future of Health Insurance for Working Americans. March.

Santos, Richard, and Patricia Seitz. 2000. "Benefit Coverage for Latino and Latina Workers." In *Moving Up the Economic Ladder: Latino Workers and the Nation's Future Prosperity,* edited by Sonia M. Pérez. Washington, D.C.: National Council of La Raza.

Schlosberg, Claudia, and Dinah Wiley. 1998. "The Impact of INS Public Charge Determinations on Immigrant Access to Health Care." Los Angeles: National Health Law Program and National Immigration Law Center. May 22.

U.S. Bureau of Labor Statistics. Unpublished data tables.

U.S. Bureau of the Census. 1993. *We the American Foreign-Born.* Washington, D.C.: U.S. Bureau of the Census.

U.S. Department of Agriculture. 2000. *National Food Stamp Conversation 2000: Sharing a History of Accomplishment and Targeting Opportunities for Improvement.* Washington, D.C.: USDA.

U.S. General Accounting Office. 1990. *Immigration Reform: Employer Sanctions and the Question of Discrimination.* Washington, D.C.: GAO. March.

USA Today. 2000. "Immigrants Become Easy Targets for Abuse, Harassment on the Job." 27 July.

Vernez, Georges, Richard A. Krop, and C. Peter Rydell. 1999. *Closing the Education Gap: Benefits and Costs.* Santa Monica, Calif.: Rand.

Zimmerman, Wendy, and Michael Fix. 1998. "Declining Immigrant Application for Medi-Cal and Welfare Benefits in Los Angeles County." Washington, D.C.: Urban Institute.

13

Increasing Opportunities for Living Wage Employment

Targeted Industry Approaches for Less-Educated Males

John Foster-Bey, with Beata Bednarz

Since the early 1990s, "targeted industry strategies" have emerged as a framework for a number of workforce development and economic development efforts, including several major foundation-funded employment initiatives.[1] Industry targeting appears to offer the potential to improve both access to and the quality of employment. Two industry targeting strategies are particularly prominent: *sector employment initiatives* and *industry cluster development.*

Sectoral initiatives primarily seek directly to improve the access of low-income job seekers to employment opportunities in local and regional economies. The central goal is to restructure training, recruitment, and hiring patterns within selected industries to improve the access of low-income individuals to regional labor markets (Molina and Wiley 1995; National Economic Development and Law Center 1998).

Cluster strategies primarily seek to improve the competitiveness of businesses within a specified geographic area. They are based on the assumption that regional— and, indeed, state and national—economies have certain competitive advantages, leading businesses to cluster in geographic areas offering opportunities to take advantage of positive interdependencies. In the most common example, high-tech firms tend to locate near other high-tech firms. Clustering allows for the development of specialized labor, financial, technical, and organizational support for strong or promising local industries (Rosenfeld 1995).

Clustering also provides a framework to direct scarce resources according to a workforce development perspective, again suggesting that practitioners focus on identifying, supporting, and developing existing or emerging business clusters with the potential to achieve some level of competitiveness in national and global economies. The assumption is that these business or industry clusters will provide the greatest opportunities to support and develop high-quality employment. Unlike sectoral projects, clustering initiatives rarely focus on who gets the jobs (Porter 1990).

To a large extent, the judgment is still out on whether either sectoral or cluster approaches can achieve their expressed goals. A critical question is whether they improve not just access to employment but also the quality of employment available to low-skilled, low-income individuals. While these strategies share an interest in the quality of jobs available to residents in local and regional economies, they unfortunately operate from a relatively sparse empirical base.

This chapter explores how focusing on the quality of employment available to less-educated workers can inform the efforts of workforce development and economic development practitioners and policymakers interested in using targeted industry approaches. It addresses two empirical questions:

- *Which industries and occupations provide the best access to living wage employment for less-educated men?* Examining the experience of low-skilled workers in the labor market can improve how policymakers and practitioners identify, select, and target industries for economic and workforce development interventions. For example, certain industries have a stronger record of providing both access and quality employment to low-skilled workers. Moreover, the industries offering better opportunities may vary from area to area; targeted strategies would reflect local realities.
- *What differences in the industry and occupational employment concentration of African Americans, Hispanic Americans, and whites lead to racial and ethnic differences in living wage employment opportunities?* Understanding the causes of racial or gender inequity within an industry or a local economy may be critical to designing and implementing effective targeted industry development strategies. What are the connections between racial/ethnic patterns in occupations and access to living wage employment?

We examine these questions by analyzing full-time and living wage employment opportunities for a sample of noninstitutionalized adult males, 25 to 55 years old, with no more than a high school diploma (less-educated), stratified by race and ethnicity and drawn from the 1980 and 1990 Public Use Micro Data Sample. Welfare reform has focused public and policymaker attention on improving employment opportunities for nonworking female welfare recipients. However, several researchers and observers have asserted that declining opportunities for less-educated adult males have increased income inequality and contributed to the decline of many urban neighborhoods (Wilson 1987, 1996).

While it is also possible to examine industry and occupational opportunities for less-educated adult males using national aggregate data, most economic development and workforce development practitioners and policymakers operate at the local or state level. Therefore, we focus on metropolitan areas, specifically Chicago, Cleveland, Detroit, and Milwaukee. These four areas, situated in the nation's manufacturing heartland, have historically provided well-paying employment for less-educated men.

WHY EXPLORE RACIAL AND ETHNIC DIFFERENCES?

Since the 1980s, all low-skilled workers appear to have faced increasing challenges to finding decent, living wage employment, yet race and ethnicity appear also to play a persistent role in labor market outcomes. African Americans and Hispanic Americans consistently continue to experience higher poverty and lower income rates than whites. These higher rates among minorities seem to relate strongly to minorities' higher rates of unemployment and lower wages.

Against this backdrop, the issue of living wage employment seems particularly salient for low-skilled racial and ethnic minorities. To design effective employment strategies, practitioners and policymakers must understand whether racial and ethnic minorities have less access to living wage employment than white males.

Racial and ethnic differences in industry/occupation concentration might explain racial and ethnic labor market inequality. If so, then strategies focused on minorities' access to certain economic sectors might be critical to improving the labor market status of racial and ethnic minorities. On the other hand, if racial and ethnic minorities do less well within particular industries and occupations compared with non-Hispanic white males, a targeted industry approach must specifically address this imbalance, whether it results from overt discrimination or other causes.

CHANGES IN LABOR MARKET OPPORTUNITY FOR LESS-EDUCATED MEN

The unprecedented economic growth of the 1990s raised questions in many quarters about the distribution of benefits from economic growth (U.S. Department of Housing and Urban Development 1999). On the national level, an indicator of inequitable distribution is that jobs and productivity have grown much faster than wages, especially for individuals with little education.

> *The Chicago, Cleveland, Detroit, and Milwaukee metropolitan areas saw significant declines in their relative economic position between 1980 and 1990, and the declines were particularly severe for less-educated adult males.*

During this period, overall employment growth in all four areas was well below average for large metropolitan areas (table 13.1). More important, employment growth in manufacturing, a sector that historically provided significant levels of living wage jobs, was also well below average.[2] Over the decade, manufacturing's share of total employment declined in all four labor markets, although only Chicago and Cleveland lost manufacturing share faster than the national average.

Most of the relative economic stagnation in these four metropolitan areas resulted from the substantial economic declines for less-educated males. Not only did total employment decline, but manufacturing employment for less-educated workers also declined significantly except in Chicago. Even in Chicago, the increase, although substantial, was below average for similar groups in the 100 largest metro areas (table 13.2).

TABLE 13.1 Overall Employment Growth, 1980–1990

	Total Employment Growth (%)	Total Manufacturing Growth (%)	Change in Manufacturing Share of Total Employment (%)	Manufacturing Share of Total Employment, 1990 (%)
Chicago	34.2	−5.5	−29.6	20.0
Cleveland	13.9	−15.0	−25.4	22.9
Detroit	34.7	2.5	−23.9	25.4
Milwaukee	32.9	5.4	−20.7	26.0
100 Largest MSAs*	49.4	12.2	−24.9	16.7

*MSA = metropolitan statistical area

Moreover, as the access of less-educated adult males to manufacturing employment improved elsewhere, it fell significantly in Cleveland, Detroit, and Milwaukee. And while employment opportunities in general declined nationally for less-educated men, employment opportunities deteriorated faster in these four metro areas (table 13.2.)

While the situation improved during the 1990s, employment growth in all four metro areas was below both national and regional levels.

Cleveland experienced the greatest improvement in annualized ratio of metropolitan area growth to national growth between 1980 and 1998, followed by Milwaukee and Chicago (table 13.3). However, population growth was slow during the 1990s as well, so employment-to-population ratios rose noticeably. This suggests that despite relatively slow employment growth, labor markets became tighter, improving opportunities for employment for most job seekers (table 13.4).

Despite the deterioration in employment opportunities for less-educated adult males in Chicago, Cleveland, Detroit, and Milwaukee, three of the four metro

TABLE 13.2 Employment for Less-Educated Men, 1980–1990

	Total Employment Growth (%)	Total Manufacturing Growth (%)	Change in Manufacturing Share of Total Employment (%)	Manufacturing Share of Total Employment, 1990 (%)
Chicago	−16.4	4.6	25.1	51.2
Cleveland	−28.1	−29.8	−2.3	45.8
Detroit	−19.1	−30.0	−13.5	43.6
Milwaukee	−23.6	−35.1	−15.1	42.6
All 4 Metro Areas	−19.3	−14.6	−13.0	47.8
100 Largest MSAs	−5.0	59.1	67.4	51.8

TABLE 13.3 Ratio of Average Annual Metro to U.S. Employment Growth[3]

	1980–1989	1990–1998	1998
Chicago	.60	.75	.45
Cleveland	.20	.60	.45
Detroit	.50	.60	.36
Milwaukee	.50	.70	.45

areas had among the nation's highest living wage employment for this same group of workers.

These Midwestern metropolitan areas offered less-educated adult males with full-time employment a greater-than-average probability of holding living wage employment (table 13.5)[4] Except for Detroit, less-educated adult males in these metro areas were more likely to find and hold employment that earned above the level needed to keep a family of four out of poverty than elsewhere. This suggests that the economic sectors available to less-educated adult male workers in these four metro areas provided greater opportunities for quality employment than in other metro areas.

Racial and Ethnic Differences in Access to Living Wage Employment

Despite large declines in employment between 1980 and 1990, less-educated men in Chicago, Cleveland, Detroit, and Milwaukee still managed to maintain higher rates of living wage employment compared with similar workers in other metro areas. Nevertheless, there were noticeable racial and ethnic differences in labor market opportunities in all four metro areas.

Compared with both African-American and Hispanic-American males, white males had the greatest probability of holding full-time, living wage employment in all four metro areas (table 13.6). Moreover, these racial gaps were on average higher in these four metro areas than in others.

TABLE 13.4 Average Annual Employment-to-Population Ratios

	1980–1989	1990–1998	1998
Chicago	.54	.60	.62
Cleveland	.52	.58	.62
Detroit	.47	.53	.56
Milwaukee	.57	.64	.68

TABLE 13.5 Living Wage Employment Probability for Less-Educated Men, 1990

	Living Wage Employment to Total Population
Chicago	0.45
Cleveland	0.43
Detroit	0.38
Milwaukee	0.48
100 Largest MSAs	0.41

Even so, the picture varies from area to area. For example, Hispanics tended to have higher probabilities of being employed and holding full-time employment compared with African-American males. In Chicago and Milwaukee, Hispanics had a higher probability of holding living wage employment than African Americans.

INDUSTRY/OCCUPATION MIX AND EMPLOYMENT OPPORTUNITIES

What explains the racial and ethnic differences in employment, especially in living wage employment? We sought possible answers in connections between a region's industry mix and opportunities for living wage employment. For example, if less-educated African-American men, compared with similar white men, are concentrated in low-performing economic sectors, this might explain their relatively weak labor market performance. In this view, if minority males were clustered in retail trade and personal services, they might experience more volatility in employment, less full-time employment, and fewer opportunities to earn a living wage.

To determine which industries provided the greatest opportunities for living wage employment, this study asked:

TABLE 13.6 The White/Black and White/Hispanic Gap in the Probability of Holding Full-Time, Living Wage Employment for Less-Educated Men, 1990

	White	White vs. African American	White vs. Hispanic American
Chicago	0.50	1.43	1.19
Cleveland	0.46	1.31	1.39
Detroit	0.41	1.41	1.64
Milwaukee	0.52	2.17	1.33
All 100 MSAs	0.45	1.36	1.32

- Which economic sectors offer the highest probabilities for full-time, living wage employment for less-educated adult males?
- What if any racial differences exist for less-educated adult males in employment opportunities by economic sector?

Are the Jobs Full-Time?

For less-educated workers, part-time jobs seldom provide a living wage. If the goal of a practitioner or a policymaker is to improve not just job access but also job quality, then it is imperative to target industries with good opportunities for providing full-time employment. We measured the availability of full-time employment by examining the ratio of less-educated adult males holding full-time jobs to the total number of less-educated adult males by economic sector. The ratio indicates the probability that an individual can obtain full-time employment in a given industry.

On average across all four metro areas, less-educated men were more likely to work full-time in construction, manufacturing, transportation and communication, and retail trade than similar workers in other industries (table 13.7).[5]

While construction, manufacturing, and transportation fit most observers' expectations about where to find quality employment, retail trade is somewhat of a surprise. Indeed, retail trade provides as much opportunity for full-time work as construction, and more than nondurable manufacturing. There were also several other industries that offered reasonable opportunities for full-time work. For example, less-educated men also had a higher probability of working full-time in wholesale trade and business and repair than in areas such as finance, insurance, and real estate (FIRE), or health care.

TABLE 13.7 Probability of Full-Time Employment for Less-Educated Men, by Industry and Metro Area, 1990

	Chicago	Cleveland	Detroit	Milwaukee
Construction	0.09	0.07	0.06	0.08
Manufacture, nondurable	0.07	0.06	0.03	0.08
Manufacture, durable	0.16	0.21	0.25	0.23
Transportation and communication	0.10	0.09	0.06	0.08
Wholesale trade	0.05	0.05	0.03	0.03
Retail trade	0.09	0.07	0.08	0.08
FIRE*	0.02	0.02	0.01	0.01
Business and repair	0.04	0.04	0.04	0.04
Health	0.01	0.01	0.01	0.01
Profession services	0.02	0.02	0.02	0.02
Across all industries	0.70	0.68	0.64	0.73

*FIRE = finance, insurance, and real estate

Which Industries Provide the Highest Probability of Full-Time, Living Wage Employment?

While full-time employment may be considered a prerequisite for quality employment, full-time hours alone are not enough. Low-wage industries may provide full-time work at meager wages. Therefore, having identified the industries with better opportunities for full-time employment for less-educated men, the next question is which industries provide the best chance of living wage employment. These are the jobs with enough hours at high enough wages to keep a family of four out of poverty.

Because living wage employment is a function of both the wage rate and the number of hours available to work, it is useful to examine differences in average wages for less-educated males by economic sector. Table 13.8 looks at the average wages of less-educated men for full-time employment by economic sector.[6] For the most part, in all four metro areas, economic sectors with high concentrations of full-time employment also had above-average hourly wages. However, several sectors with relatively good opportunities for full-time employment, such as retail trade and nondurable manufacturing, also had below-average wages.

While average wages, along with full-time employment, provide a good measure of job quality, they can be slightly misleading. For example, average wages may be skewed by a relatively small number of workers with very high wages. As a result, an industry with high average wages may not have a high probability of providing living wage employment. Therefore, part of identifying the sectors with the best opportunities for less-educated men to gain living wage jobs is to reduce the possible distortions that might accompany average-wage measures. Table 13.9 presents the probability that a less-educated male is employed in a full-time job that earns enough to keep a family of four out of poverty. The probability of full-time living wage employment by industry is an indicator of the likelihood that a less-educated worker will hold a living wage job in a particular industry or economic sector. This probability (or ratio) is not influ-

TABLE 13.8.   Average Hourly Full-Time Wages, by Industry and Metro Area, 1990

	Chicago	Cleveland	Detroit	Milwaukee
Construction	$14.15	$13.20	$15.11	$13.31
Manufacture, nondurable	12.83	12.20	14.58	11.78
Manufacture, durable	13.47	13.18	15.85	13.83
Transportation and communication	14.94	14.09	15.00	14.76
Wholesale trade	13.25	13.87	14.29	13.46
Retail trade	10.90	11.29	10.64	10.18
FIRE	11.90	10.38	9.95	13.74
Business and repair	10.35	10.52	12.70	8.80
Health	9.95	10.30	9.20	9.43
Profession services	12.40	15.12	12.85	11.52
Across all industries	$12.96	$12.59	$14.08	$12.64

TABLE 13.9 Probability of Less-Educated Adult Males Holding Full-Time, Living Wage Employment, by Selected Industry, 1990

Economic Sectors	Chicago	Cleveland	Detroit	Milwaukee
Construction	0.06	0.05	0.04	0.05
Manufacture, nondurable	0.05	0.05	0.02	0.05
Manufacture, durable	0.11	0.13	0.16	0.17
Transportation and communication	0.07	0.06	0.04	0.06
Wholesale trade	0.03	0.03	0.02	0.02
Retail trade	0.04	0.04	0.04	0.04
FIRE	0.01	0.01	0.01	0.01
Business and repair	0.02	0.03	0.02	0.02
Health	0.01	0.01	0.01	0.01
Profession services	0.01	0.01	0.01	0.01
Across all industries[7]	0.45	0.44	0.38	0.48

enced by a skewed distribution (i.e., some workers with very high wages, others with very low wages). Rather, the probability indicates how many workers can meet a minimum standard of job quality. It reduces the impact of a few workers with very high or low wages.

> *In general, three sectors—construction, durable manufacturing, and transportation—offered the greatest opportunities for full-time, living wage employment and above-average hourly wages. In addition, nondurable manufacturing and retail trade offered a relatively high probability of living wage employment, although in both sectors wages were below average.*

Industries with high average wages did not always have high living wage employment opportunities. For example, wholesale trade offers above-average wages but a below-average probability of full-time employment or full-time, living wage employment. On the other hand, retail trade had below-average wages, yet this sector offered a relatively high opportunity for living wage employment. This suggests that there is more wage equality for less-educated workers in retail trade than in wholesale trade.

For practitioners and policymakers considering industry-targeting approaches to economic and workforce development, a key strategic question follows from this data. Should economic development and workforce development strategies target industries with high average wages? Or, should targeting efforts be directed toward industries and sectors with high probabilities of living wage employment for full-time work? In the best of all possible worlds there is no conflict. However, the data suggest that high average wages may not always be consistent with a high living wage employment probability. Such calculations could be critical to improving the decisions made by economic and workforce development practitioners and policymakers. In this case, for example, they might decide to target retail trade rather than wholesale trade.

Comparing the Probability of Employment by Economic Sector and Race

Having identified the economic sectors with higher opportunities to provide full-time, living wage employment for less-educated men, the issue remains of whether the opportunity to hold living wage employment varied by race/ethnicity.[8] To evaluate any possible racial disparity in the labor market, we calculated a racial disparity index for both full-time and living wage employment.[9] The index uses less-educated, non-Hispanic whites as the reference group. A value of 1 indicates that African Americans or Hispanics have the same probability of holding full-time or living wage employment as non-Hispanic whites. A value above 1 indicates that African Americans or Hispanics are lagging behind. A value below 1 suggests that minority males are doing better than non-Hispanic whites.

In general, the data suggest that white males had a higher probability of holding employment than African Americans or Hispanic Americans in economic sectors with high rates of full-time and living wage employment.

With only a few exceptions, non-Hispanic white men held a substantial advantage over African-American men in full-time employment in most sectors. However, the size of the racial disparity differed by metro area. In Milwaukee, for example, less-educated non-Hispanic white men were almost twice as likely to hold full-time employment as comparable African Americans. The greatest disparity was in the construction sector; the smallest in the transportation sector. On the other hand, Cleveland had the smallest (though still substantial) gap between non-Hispanic whites and African Americans (table 13.10).

There was also a measurable, but smaller, disparity in full-time employment between less-educated, non-Hispanic white and Hispanic-American males. For Hispanic Americans, the gap was highly dependent on metro area. For example, in Chicago and Cleveland, the racial disparity gap for Hispanics was relatively modest. At the same time, Detroit had a rather large racial disparity index. The racial disparity index also varied substantially for Hispanics by economic sector. For example, less-educated Hispanic males did relatively well in nondurable manufacturing in Chicago and Cleveland, but in Detroit and Milwaukee nondurable manufacturing offered below-average opportunities (table 13.10).

Given these findings, does the probability of living wage employment for full-time workers also differ by race and ethnicity?

To answer this question, we calculated the racial disparity index for full-time workers holding living wage employment. In general, less-educated, adult non-Hispanic white males had a greater probability of finding full-time, living wage employment than either African-American or Hispanic-American males. Just as with full-time employment, the racial disparity gap varied by sector and metro area. Less-educated African-American and Hispanic-American males tended to trail comparable non-Hispanic white males in construction across all four metro areas. For African

TABLE 13.10 Racial Disparity Index for Full-Time Employment, by Industry and Metro Area, 1990

	Chicago	Cleveland	Detroit	Milwaukee
White/black				
Construction	5.92	2.38	5.31	8.38
Manufacture, nondurable	1.26	0.99	1.35	1.50
Manufacture, durable	1.57	1.94	1.27	2.56
Transportation and communication	1.18	0.79	2.35	1.20
Retail trade	2.95	1.26	1.72	5.67
All industries	1.57	1.38	1.66	1.97
White/Hispanic				
Construction	2.74	4.72	1.58	n.a.*
Manufacture, nondurable	0.53	0.73	2.20	1.58
Manufacture, durable	0.75	1.12	1.32	0.63
Transportation and communication	2.43	0.92	1.71	n.a.
Retail trade	0.95	3.97	1.31	1.41
All industries	1.13	1.10	1.50	1.31

*n.a. = Not available

Americans, Milwaukee and Chicago offered the fewest opportunities for living wage employment. On the other hand, Hispanics found fewer opportunities in Cleveland and Detroit (table 13.11).

In general, minority males tended to have lower access to full-time, living wage employment than non-Hispanic white males in the high-quality economic sectors in all four metro areas. The analysis suggests that African Americans and Hispanics may not receive the same benefits from development strategies that target the high-quality economic sectors identified here. Minority males' lower probability of full-time employment in the high-quality economic sectors seems to have limited their capacity to hold full-time, living wage employment. African-American males seemed particularly disadvantaged.

What Explains Minority Males' Low Probability of Holding Full-Time, Living Wage Employment?

Despite some overlap, the three groups of males did not always find their best opportunities for living wage employment in the same economic sectors. This underscores the idea that targeted industry development strategies could have very different impacts for each of these three groups of less-educated men, depending upon which industry was targeted. However, it is important to determine if race itself is a factor in lower employment rates.

One reason African Americans and Hispanics may have had lower employment rates than less-educated, non-Hispanic white males may have been because they had much lower human capital factors (e.g., education, work experience). To test this

TABLE 13.11   Racial Disparity Index for Full-Time, Living Wage Employment, by Industry and Metro Area, 1990

	Chicago	Cleveland	Detroit	Milwaukee
White/black				
Construction	4.00	3.00	5.00	7.00
Manufacture, nondurable	1.25	0.80	1.00	3.00
Manufacture, durable	1.38	1.56	1.00	2.25
Transportation and communication	0.88	0.86	2.50	1.00
Retail trade	2.50	1.33	1.33	n.a.
All industries	1.39	1.24	1.32	2.21
White/Hispanic				
Construction	2.67	n.a.	2.50	n.a.
Manufacture, nondurable	0.63	0.67	n.a.	1.00
Manufacture, durable	0.73	1.75	1.33	0.64
Transportation and communication	2.33	1.20	2.50	n.a.
Retail trade	1.00	n.a.	2.00	n.a.
All industries	1.19	1.39	1.64	1.36

hypothesis, we calculated a linear probability model using full-time employment and living wage employment as dependent variables.

The results indicate that after controlling for education, work experience, net family and household income, and metropolitan areas, African Americans and Hispanic Americans had lower rates of both full-time and living wage employment (see chapter appendix 2). However, African-American males had substantially lower rates of both full-time and living wage employment than either Hispanics or white males.

The findings suggest that factors related to race may be responsible for the lower employment rates of less-educated, adult African-American males relative to less-educated non-Hispanic white and Hispanic-American men.

The low employment rates for African Americans could not be attributed to differences in education or work experience. Obviously, these findings might be evidence of labor market discrimination; however, there may be other reasonable explanations. First, this sample of white and Hispanic males might have had labor market skills not observed in the data set that gave them an advantage over African-American males with similar education and work experience in gaining employment.

A second explanation might be spatial mismatch: Less-educated, adult African-American males may disproportionately reside in locations isolated from employment opportunities in higher-quality economic sectors. For example, if minorities resided in racially segregated neighborhoods or central cities, they might lack information about available employment or access to suburban jobs (see, for example, Kain and Persky 1969). All four of these metro areas have high levels of residential separation by race and class. These areas also had significant job growth in the suburbs compared with the central cities. So the coefficients on the racial variables may actually be quantifying the cost of residential segregation and spatial mismatch on less-educated minority males.

A third explanation may be that minority males—especially African Americans—have withdrawn from the labor market. This might be the result of cultural factors often cited in the literature (see, for example, Meade 1986 and Wilson 1987). Assuming that African-American males are as economically rational as European-American and Hispanic-American males, they would only choose to stay out of the labor market if they had alternative sources of income. We attempted to control for this by adding variables for net family and household income. The results for these supply-side controls were either insignificant or had minimal impact. However, it is possible that African-American males had large sources of unreported income that allowed them to stay out of the labor market. It is also possible that African-American males placed a higher value on their leisure time than did either non-Hispanic white or Hispanic-American males.

One other explanation may be that African-American males had a higher reservation wage—that is, the minimum wage required to enter the labor market—than either white or Hispanic males. While there is no direct measure of differences in reservation wages among the three groups, it might be useful to examine whether there are statistically significant racial differences in actual wages. Such differences in wages might represent another barrier to address in designing an effective workforce development intervention using industry-targeting techniques.

To examine this issue, we analyzed racial differences in average hourly wages for full-time employment (tables 13.12 and 13.13).

The primary observation is that the average wages for white males were consistently $2.00 to $6.00 higher an hour than those of minority males in all four metro areas.

Except in Milwaukee, the largest wage gaps were between white and Hispanic males. Again, construction, manufacturing, transportation, and wholesale trade tended to be the highest wage sectors for all three groups in all four labor markets, despite clear racial and ethnic differences within economic sectors.

TABLE 13.12 Average Wages for Less-Educated White Males for Full-Time Employment, by Industry and Metro Area, 1990

	Chicago	Cleveland	Detroit	Milwaukee
Construction	$14.54	$13.03	$15.84	$13.21
Manufacture, nondurable	16.44	13.65	16.50	14.36
Manufacture, durable	16.73	15.34	17.35	15.09
Transportation and communication	16.60	16.20	16.41	14.50
Retail trade	13.70	13.07	11.99	12.19
Across all industries	$15.23	$14.09	$15.38	$13.57

TABLE 13.13 Racial Gap in Average Wages for Full-Time Employment, by Industry and Metro Area, 1990

	Chicago	Cleveland	Detroit	Milwaukee
White/black				
Manufacture, nondurable	1.33	1.08	1.60	1.45
Manufacture, durable	1.22	1.00	1.03	1.10
Transportation and communication	1.20	1.35	1.29	1.20
Retail trade	1.43	1.64	1.52	n.a.
All industries	1.28	1.13	1.14	1.31
White/Hispanic				
Construction	1.04	2.41	2.64	n.a.
Manufacture, nondurable	1.65	1.14	4.10	1.44
Manufacture, durable	1.50	1.90	0.96	1.19
Transportation and communication	1.18	2.49	1.09	n.a.
Retail trade	1.96	1.62	1.29	4.71
All industries	1.48	1.73	1.22	1.27

It appears that holding industry and occupation constant does not eliminate racial and ethnic differences in wages for less-educated men. At least for full-time work, on average non-Hispanic white males received higher wages than African-American and Hispanic-American males in most industries and occupations.

However, this analysis may not capture the impact of differences in actual work experience and years of education. For example, if white males were older and tended to have higher high school graduation rates than African Americans or Latinos, they probably had higher wages. Again, the regression analyses test whether differences in wages were the result of race or some other factor.

> In all four metro areas, less-educated, adult African-American and Hispanic-American males had statistically significant lower wages than white males, after controlling for education, work experience, industry, and occupation.

Moreover, Hispanics had the lowest wages in all four labor markets.[10] In Chicago, Cleveland, and Milwaukee, the differences between Hispanics and white males were relatively large, ranging from $3.00 to almost $5.00 an hour. African Americans' average wages were between $0.90 and $2.26 an hour lower than white males' wages. This suggests that minority males, especially Hispanics, were paid less than non-Hispanic white males working in the same industries and occupations and with the same level of education and experience.

Despite these troubling findings, it remains difficult to say whether this was actual evidence of labor market discrimination. Possibly white males had some unmeasured labor market skill that gave them a justifiable advantage. It is also possible that minority males were willing to work for less than white males in order to improve their employment status. Yet if this were so, minority males' employment rates should be equal to or better than whites. This does not appear to be the case. The results of the regression analysis do seem to provide some support for the reservation wage hypothesis as regards African Americans and Hispanic Americans. It appears that African Americans have higher wages than Hispanics, after controlling for human capital and industry and occupation. Latinos may have higher employment rates than African Americans because they are willing to accept lower wages.

OBSERVATIONS

Can the effectiveness of targeted industry strategies and their impact on low-income individuals be improved by examining the opportunities for living wage employment, specifically for less-educated workers and job seekers?

The findings here suggest that employment opportunities for less-educated men could be improved by specifically focusing on those economic sectors and occupations that provide the greatest opportunities for living wage employment. The analysis shows that it is possible to identify economic sectors by the level of living wage employment opportunities available to less-educated adult workers. Construction, manufacturing, transportation and communication, and retail trade all provided above-average opportunities for both full-time and living wage employment. Both the levels of employment concentration and the average hourly wages confirmed this finding.

Can the effectiveness of targeted industry strategies for less-educated workers and job seekers be improved if racial differences in living wage employment could be identified and explained by racial differences in the industry and occupational employment mix?

Opportunities for employment appear to be strongly related to race and ethnicity. An effective workforce development strategy would have to ask what can be done to improve the access of African-American and Hispanic males to employment opportunities in sectors of the regional economy that offer the greatest opportunities for living wage employment, such as construction, manufacturing, transportation, and wholesale and retail trade. While the lower probability of employment may not be entirely the result of racial or ethnic discrimination, directly addressing the barriers to employment for less-educated African-American and Hispanic males is critical to any successful targeted industry strategy.

There is also evidence that employed minority men are at a wage disadvantage as compared with white men. There is strong statistical evidence that both Hispanics and African Americans are paid less than whites, after controlling for education, work experience, and industry and occupation. This problem is particularly significant for Hispanic males. *This implies that a targeted industry strategy that hopes to improve the quality of labor market opportunities for low-skilled minority males must address what appears to be racial and ethnic wage inequality.*

Finally, an agenda for further research follows from a limitation of the data used for this paper: the 1980 and 1990 Public Use Micro Data Sample (PUMS). Although roughly 10 years old, this is the most recent data available for extensive analyses of labor market outcomes for individual adult males by individual metropolitan areas. Given the strength of the economy in the 1990s and what appear to be significant technological and structural changes in the U.S. economy, PUMS data may give only a modest insight into what is happening now in the labor market for less-educated workers.

However, the goal here has been to provide a starting point for empirically examining how living wages differ by race and ethnicity across metropolitan areas.[11] The hope is that the results will help provide insight to policymakers and practitioners, and help frame questions about the living wage issue for future research.

Moreover, similar methodology using other data sources could yield more current results for use in designing and implementing industry-targeting strategies. For example, table 13.14 presents employment growth by sector for selected counties in each of the four metro areas between 1993 and 1997. Assuming no significant change in the distribution of full-time living wage employment within industries from the 1990 patterns, the estimates, derived from the most recent County Business Patterns, paint a modestly encouraging picture of sectors with large and growing numbers of living wage employment opportunities.

While manufacturing in all four metro areas except Detroit experienced flat or negative growth, construction, transportation, and wholesale and retail trade experienced modest growth, indicating continued opportunities for living wage employment in these sectors for less-educated men. Table 13.14 also suggests that it might be useful to look again at living wage employment opportunities in the services sector. With few exceptions, these sectors experienced large annualized growth in all four metro areas.

The question that is more difficult to answer is whether the racial and ethnic inequality observed in the 1990 data continued through the 1990s. Given our findings, answering this question is critical to designing effective industry-targeting workforce and economic development strategies aimed at improving opportunities for low-skilled, low-income individuals.

TABLE 13.14 Annual Employment Growth in Selected Industries, by Metro Area Counties, 1993–1997

	Chicago (%)	Cleveland (%)	Detroit (%)	Milwaukee (%)
Total	1.29	1.58	2.26	0.63
Construction	2.19	−0.18	5.62	0.48
Manufacturing	−0.95	−0.25	1.46	0.26
Transportation and public utilities	1.56	1.34	2.45	−0.14
Wholesale trade	0.92	1.03	2.08	1.60
Retail trade	1.03	2.01	1.13	0.26
FIRE	0.84	4.44	1.36	−0.05
Services	2.67	2.29	3.26	1.17

APPENDIX 1: NOTES ON THE METHODOLOGY

This chapter focuses on three indicators:

- *Full-time employment for 1990 for less-educated men by race and ethnicity.* Full-time employment is defined as an individual employed 35 or more hours a week, 40 or more weeks a year. Full-time employment is used to calculate the rate of full-time employment, which is defined as full-time employment divided by total employment. We also calculated full-time employment as an individual employed 35 to 45 hours or more a week, 40 or more weeks a year. This more restrictive definition of full-time work assumes that a good full-time job requires no more than 45 hours a week.
- *Living wage employment for 1990,* or the number of the less-educated men holding employment and earning a living wage. Living wage employment is used to calculate the probability that a less-educated adult male can find and hold a job that earns a living wage. Living wage employment is defined as an individual employed 35 to 45 hours a week, 40 or more weeks a year, earning more than the poverty rate for a family of four.
- *Average hourly wages for full-time work by race and ethnicity.* The average hourly wage is calculated by dividing annual wages for full-time employees working 35 to 45 hours a week, 40 weeks a year, by 52 weeks and then by 40 hours.

All indicators were calculated for European-American (non-Hispanic white), African-American (non-Hispanic black), and Hispanic-American (Latino) males 25 to 55 years old with no more than a high school diploma. All indicators were analyzed by placing them into industry occupation tables that were then compared by race and across metro areas.

Key Assumptions and Definitions

To partially reduce the confounding effects of supply choices (e.g., family size and hours worked), our definition of living wage employment does two things. First, it defines a living wage as the annual earnings that would keep a family of four out of poverty, disentangling individual choices about family size from the quality of an individual job. Second, the definition is limited to 35 to 45 hours a week, separating decisions about how much an individual chooses to work from the quality of the available jobs. If an individual has to work 50 or more hours to earn income high enough to keep a family of four out of poverty, this is not considered a living wage job.

We use "less-educated" as a synonym for a high school diploma or less. The term is also used as a proxy for "low-skilled." The assumption is that a worker with no more than a high school diploma is at a competitive disadvantage in the current labor market. This is clearly an imperfect assumption: For example, a 55-year-old high school graduate may have many more job-related skills and much more experience than a 25-year-old college graduate. However, given the current premium on technical skill and knowledge, workers with a high school education or less tend to be at a disadvantage and are appropriately labeled low-skilled.

Another important assumption is that individuals with similar education and in the same age group have similar labor market skills and should, therefore, experience similar rewards in the labor market. This may not be the case. There is no guarantee that two individuals of the same age with high school diplomas have achieved equal competence or employability skills.[12] Given this, variations in the dependent variables may actually measure differences in the quality of individuals' labor market skills, not the quality of the jobs available in the labor market. Unfortunately, the data set does not allow us to directly observe differences in the quality of individuals' labor market skills. However, despite these potential limitations, the use of education and age as proxies for skill is generally well established in the literature.

Finally, we use the term "adult males" to refer to men 25 to 55 years old. The underlying assumption is that all men in this age group have roughly the same experience in the labor market. It is reasonable to assume that men age 25 have different labor market experiences than men 45 or 55 years old, but it also seems reasonable to expect that overall changes are likely to have similar effects on all less-educated adult males. For example, if we assume that younger adult males have lower rates of living wage employment than older adult males, it still seems reasonable to expect that the impact of economic changes would affect them in roughly the same manner.

APPENDIX 2: IDENTIFYING RACIAL AND ETHNIC DIFFERENCES IN EMPLOYMENT AND WAGES

This study used regression analysis to test several hypotheses concerning racial/ethnic differences in employment and average wages. The key assumption was that because each regression was done within a metro area, each racial/ethnic group would be subject to the same place-specific factors, such as unemployment or industry mix or the overall strength of the local economy.

Because the model was primarily descriptive rather than predictive, it did not attempt to include all factors that might influence employment. Given this assumption, only supply characteristics—education, work experience, race, and net household and family income—were used as control variables. Net family income and net household income were used as supply constraints because the expectation was that individuals would choose to work less if they had other sources of income. Therefore, the higher the net family and household income, the lower the employment.

Individual regression models were estimated using a pooled sample of white, black, and Hispanic males, 25 to 55 years old, with no more than a high school diploma, in each of the four metro areas. The null hypothesis for the pooled model was that racial differences in employment resulted from differences in education and work experience. The alternative was that observed differences in employment resulted from racial and ethnic factors.

Regression Analysis Variables

Variable	Description	Hypothesis
Average Hourly Wages	Calculated by taking the annual wages for all workers in the sample and dividing by 40 hours and then by 52 weeks	Dependent Variable
Total Employment	Number of individuals in sample who worked at least 1 hour the previous year	Dependent Variable
Full-Time Employment	Number of individuals in the sample who worked at least 35 hours a week for 40 or more weeks	Dependent Variable
Living Wage Employment	Number of individuals working 35–45 hours a week, 40 or more weeks, with earnings above the poverty level for a family of four	Dependent Variable
Education	A dummy variable equals 1 if high school graduate, and 0 if did not finish high school	Sign should be positive; theory suggests employment and wages rise with increases in education
Work Experience	A continuous variable equal to age minus years of education minus 6	Sign should be positive; theory suggests employment and wages rise with increases in work experience

(*continued*)

Variable	Description	Hypothesis
Industry	Dummy variables indicate which industry an individual is employed in; value is 1 if in the industry, 0 if not in the industry	Sign will vary; high-wage industries should be positive for wages
Occupation	Dummy variables indicate which occupation an individual is employed in; value is 1 if in the industry, 0 if not in the industry	Sign will vary; high-wage occupations should be positive for wages
Net Family Income	Supply side continuous variable indicating level of family income minus individual earnings	Expect sign to be negative for employment variables; the higher the net family income, the less the need is to work
Net Household Income	Supply side continuous variable indicating level of household income minus individual earnings	Expect sign to be negative for employment variables; the higher net family income, the less the need is to work
Metro Area	0-1 Dummy variables representing fixed effects for each metro area, such as differences in economic growth, or institutions	Sign depends on hypothesis being tested
Race	0-1 Dummy variables for African Americans and Hispanic Americans, with European Americans as the reference variable	Sign depends on hypothesis being tested

	Total Employment	Full-Time Employment	Living Wage Employment	Wages
Intercept	0.58*	0.43*	0.20*	7.31*
Chicago	0.006	−0.002	0.003	1.44*
Cleveland	−0.04*	−0.04*	−0.03	0.28
Detroit	−0.06*	−0.07*	−0.08*	1.91*
Education	0.11*	0.16*	0.12*	1.99*
Work Experience	0.001*	0.004*	0.003*	0.18*
African American	−0.18*	−0.20*	−0.07*	−1.74*
Hispanic American	−0.01	−0.03*	−0.03**	−3.05*
Net Family Income	−0.0000*	−0.0000*	−0.0000*	n.a.
Medium-Income Industries	0.18*	0.14*	0.02	−0.51
High-Income Industries	0.17*	0.17*	0.13*	2.32*
Service Occupations	0.16*	0.08*	0.03*	−3.02*
Skilled Occupations	0.12*	0.08*	0.09*	−0.18
Semiskilled Occupations	0.08*	0.03*	0.07*	−1.65*
Mean	0.80	0.68	0.43	13.50

*Indicates significance at 0.05 or less
**Indicates significance at 0.06–0.10

NOTES

1. The Annie E. Casey Foundation operates a multisite national jobs initiative that uses the targeted industry approach. The Ford Foundation has supported the National Economic Development and Law Center to manage a multisite, targeted industry employment project. Also the Charles Stewart Mott Foundation recently launched its own multisite, targeted industry employment initiative.

2. We define "living wage" as wages high enough to keep a family out of poverty. It refers here to annual wages for full-time work high enough to keep a family of four out of poverty.

3. Data for both tables 13.3 and 13.4 are derived from the Economic Information Systems' Economic Insight/State Edition (1999), http://www.econ-line.com.

4. Unfortunately, not enough detailed data are available at the metropolitan level to analyze employment outcomes from 1990 to 1998 in all four metropolitan areas for the target group.

5. The manufacturing sector includes durable and nondurable manufacturing. Transportation refers to the transportation, communication, and public utilities sector.

6. The definition of full-time employment was 35 to 45 hours a week, 40 or more weeks a year. This definition was used to make it consistent with the definition of living wage employment.

7. This is the cumulative probability across all industries.

8. From this point forward, the analysis focuses on the four sectors with the greatest opportunities for full-time, living wage employment.

9. The racial disparity index is calculated by dividing the full-time employment probability for whites by the full-time employment probability for African Americans or Hispanics. A similar index can be calculated for living wage employment.

10. However, using 90 percent confidence intervals, black and Hispanic wages do overlap, indicating some statistical probability that their wages are equal.

11. As part of a larger research project on living wages, the Urban Institute's Program on Regional Economic Opportunity is also using Current Population Survey data to provide descriptive and multivariate analysis at the national and regional level on variations in the living wage during the 1990s.

12. Harry Holzer and others call such employability skills "soft skills." Employers often see these so-called soft skills as a prerequisite for any employment.

REFERENCES

Kain, John F., and Joseph Persky. 1969. "Alternatives to the Gilded Ghetto." *Public Interest* 14 (Winter): 74–87.

Meade, Laurence. 1986. *Beyond Entitlement: The Social Obligations of Citizenship.* New York: Free Press.

Molina, Frieda, and Jean Wiley. 1995. "Sectoral Employment Intervention: A Strategy to Capture Jobs." *Economic Development & Law Center Report,* 1.

National Economic Development and Law Center. 1998. *Sectoral Employment Intervention: A Handbook.* Oakland, Calif.: National Economic Development and Law Center.

Porter, Michael. 1990. *The Competitive Advantage of Nations.* New York: Free Press.

Rosenfeld, Stuart. 1995. *Industrial-Strength Strategies: Regional Business Clusters and Public Policy.* Washington, D.C.: Aspen Institute.

U.S. Department of Housing and Urban Development. 1999. *Now Is the Time: Places Left Behind in the New Economy.* Washington, D.C.: GPO.

Wilson, William Julius. 1987. *The Truly Disadvantaged: Inner City, the Underclass, and Public Policy.* Chicago: University of Chicago Press.

———. 1996. *When Work Disappears: The World of the New Urban Poor.* New York: Vintage Books.

PART 4

Institutions That Can Improve Low-Wage Workers' Prospects

Community Colleges, Employers, and Labor Unions

14

Second Chances in Changing Times

The Roles of Community Colleges in Advancing Low-Skilled Workers

W. Norton Grubb

Now that the 21st century has arrived, we can see a little better what it looks like. Some aspects are not pretty. One characteristic of the new economy is its bifurcation and inequality: Many workers can find work but not enough of it, and not work of high enough productivity and skill to pay them much.[1] A second characteristic is its uncertainty and turnover. With the growth in contingent work of all kinds, many more workers have to create their own careers, moving among firms and occupations as the economy changes, as regions rise and fall, and as firms expand and contract in response to location decisions, foreign competition, and macroeconomic swings.

None of this is new, and we shouldn't find it particularly surprising. The turn of the last century was also a period of increasing inequality (Williamson and Lindert 1980), when skilled craft work was being displaced by semiskilled operatives on the one hand, and by people in newly skilled occupations (like machine repairers and electricians) and the professions (like engineers) on the other. Because of alarms about skill shortages, that period, too, was one of intense focus on the institutions preparing people for work, such as vocationalized high schools and universities, with professional schools emerging in engineering, business, law, and other occupations.

Fortunately, since then, the United States has developed an education system and a job training analogue that are better equipped for an economy marked by change and instability. In several ways, we have created a complex of second-chance institutions for individuals who find they have to restart their work lives—because of changes in the economy itself, because of geographic mobility, because individual preferences change, or simply because individuals figure out that their earlier choices about schooling and work were mistakes. These second-chance institutions include community colleges;

four-year colleges somewhat more open to older students; youth programs and dropout prevention programs; short-term job training programs, including special programs for dislocated workers; welfare-to-work programs; and proprietary schools open to all who will pay. Most are publicly funded and subsidized, and even private alternatives are publicly subsidized through federal grants, loans, and now the Hope and Lifelong Learning tax credits. If we live in an economy of change and instability, at least we have created the education and training institutions that can—potentially—respond to those conditions.

We should be proud of these second-chance institutions. At the individual level, they allow people to rejoin the economic mainstream, even if they face substantial challenges. One of the current rags-to-riches myths describes a welfare mother who enrolls in a short welfare-to-work program to become a hospital orderly. She returns while working to a community college to get a certificate and then an associate's degree in a health care occupation. Next, she transfers to a four-year college after working for a while, and finally enters medical school, the very pinnacle of the educational system!

From a collective perspective, second-chance institutions allow the economy to adjust to changes in the requirements of work and shortages and surpluses of labor. They may, therefore, be part of the complex of institutions that have made our economy more flexible and robust since the 1960s. These second-chance institutions also respond to another slogan of our times: the need for lifelong learning. As distinct from the pedagogical approach of preparing individuals to be independent learners, the institutional approach to lifelong learning is to make educational institutions more hospitable to older learners, providing them the supports necessary to gain additional competencies throughout their working lives.

But the existence of second-chance institutions doesn't mean that they work well in any absolute sense. The fable of the welfare mother who climbs through the second-chance system to become a doctor illustrates that paths of mobility exist, not that they are likely. The problem, now that we have a complex of second-chance institutions in place, is to examine them carefully and unsentimentally, and then to improve them so they work better for both individuals and the economy.

This chapter examines the challenges of reforming existing second-chance programs—specifically the community college, the most pervasive and promising of these institutions—so that they can respond more appropriately to the challenges of advancing low-skilled individuals. The first section clarifies that the individuals in need of such institutions include several different groups. They pose different challenges in the kinds of institutions they can use, in the services they need, and in appropriate pedagogical approaches. The second section examines the institutions and programs we have created and concludes that the comprehensive community college is the institution best able to address the challenges of advancing low-skilled workers.

But community colleges often don't work well, particularly for poorly informed individuals without much sense of their options. Therefore, the third section examines several discrete areas in which community colleges might be improved—in their approach to instruction, the support services they offer, their links to other programs, and their links to employment. This, in turn, creates a substantial reform agenda, and yet another problem: Because there are few reform pressures in community colleges, it is difficult to know how to make progress.

The next section briefly examines another part of the overall problem. If we as a nation ask educational institutions to provide more sophisticated competencies for low-wage workers, then a complementary policy—expanding the demand for skilled labor—is necessary in order to create the jobs for which they are being trained. In the long run, schools and colleges, by themselves, are inadequate to the task of reshaping the distribution of opportunities, and employment policies need to be created for the volatile economy that has emerged.

TARGET GROUPS: THE CHARACTERISTICS OF LOW-SKILLED WORKERS

The individuals who lack the skills for well-paid employment in our current economy comprise a heterogeneous group. When they show up in one institution—as they often do in comprehensive community colleges—they create special challenges for instructors who have to teach simultaneously to several distinct groups. It's useful to distinguish at least five, although they overlap:

1. *Recent high school graduates* face a bewildering variety of alternatives: employment, education in community colleges, education in four-year colleges of enormous variety, enrollment in a variety of short-term trade schools (e.g., in cosmetology or secretarial work), and the combination of further education and employment that has become so common. Some of these individuals, especially the well-educated offspring of middle-class parents, are well-informed about their alternatives and prepared for any college they might enter. Many others, however, are unprepared for the choices they must make: Their knowledge about employment options and what they require is weak, their ability to make rational decisions among alternatives is limited, and their command of basic academic competencies is also limited. These are students with "misaligned ambitions" (Schneider and Stevenson 1999)—many of them from low-income families, many of them black and Latino, many educated in low-quality urban schools—who enter community colleges and nonselective four-year colleges and drop out relatively quickly. They face uncertain prospects in a labor market where education beyond high school is increasingly necessary.
2. *Experimenters* come to community colleges seeking information about their options.[2] In a country with poor guidance and counseling at the high school level, there are few sources of information available to experimenters. Many are well aware that education beyond high school is necessary. As one said (Grubb 1996b, 68):

   When I first came here [to this community college], I had no idea what I wanted to study. . . . I didn't really have much idea of what I wanted to do. I knew I needed to go to school, though.

Experimenters are often frustrating to have in class because they are there to see *if* they want to learn a subject, not necessarily to learn it. As one community college instructor noted, "I have some people who want to take the class for information, and don't intend to do any of the work" (Grubb et al. 1999a, 5). Recent high school students and experienced workers may be experimenters, too, so this is a large and varied group—but all of them need special services in addition to employment-related competencies.

3. *Experienced workers seeking advancement* have found their promotion blocked without further formal education. Sometimes, these are individuals in licensed occupations—health care workers, for example—who need more formal schooling in order to pass subsequent licensing exams. More often, these are simply individuals who need additional competencies to advance. They are usually knowledgeable about their goals and intentions, unlike experimenters, and they often need one or two courses rather than an entire certificate or associate's program.

4. *Dislocated workers and others switching occupations* want to find another kind of work—either because they have become unemployed when jobs in their occupation or sector have dwindled (e.g., forestry workers in the Pacific Northwest) or because they want to switch into better-paying jobs. These individuals usually have substantial experience, but it may be unrelated to potential new jobs. Many of them may also need help in finding new occupations, and therefore behave like experimenters. As one such individual commented (Grubb 1996b, 69–70):

> *It'll be nine years this August that I've been licensed [as a manicurist], which is the longest I've ever done anything, and I really do enjoy it. But I feel like . . . you can only go so far, and I would just like to have an opportunity someday to do something else. I just don't happen to know what it is right now.*

5. *Populations with special needs* vary widely and are difficult to describe succinctly. Welfare recipients are one such group, and usually have multiple barriers to employment. The long-term unemployed, high school dropouts with young children, recent immigrants, former inmates, and the disabled (with access to vocational rehabilitation) are other such groups. In addition to occupational education of some sort, each of these groups needs specialized supportive services—sometimes child care and transportation services sometimes remedial or developmental education, sometimes bilingual education or English as a second language (ESL), sometimes mental health services or complex accommodations for specific disabilities. Short-term job training programs, formerly funded by the Job Training Partnership Act and now by the Workforce Investment Act, have served many of these groups, but largely in short-term programs of limited effectiveness and poor long-run prospects.[3]

So the different groups that need access to more extensive education and training vary. All of them need some supportive service in addition to occupational skills. And so when we consider how to construct effective programs, it's important to remember the variety of both needs and necessary services.

THE CASE FOR COMMUNITY COLLEGES

Over the past 40 years, a bewildering variety of institutions and programs has been developed to meet the needs for work-related education and training. Forty years ago, virtually the only work-related education and training took place in high school vocational programs and in the professional programs of four-year colleges and universities. Since then, short-term job training programs have proliferated—some targeted to specific populations, like programs for dislocated workers and welfare recipients. Area vocational schools have also developed programs for adults. Community colleges and public technical institutes have expanded, and public support for the training of incumbent workers has expanded through customized training and many economic development activities. Private trade schools have surely expanded, and employers have expanded training they provide their own workers.

In evaluating different education and training programs, I have developed a set of five heuristics or precepts for effective programs, drawn in part from evaluations of existing programs and in part from visits to exemplary ones, that seem useful in judging the *potential* effectiveness of various institutions and programs (Grubb 1999b). Briefly, they are the following:

1. Effective programs understand the local labor market and target those jobs with relatively high earnings, strong employment growth, and opportunities for individual advancement.
2. Effective programs contain an appropriate mix of academic (or remedial, or basic) education, occupational skills, and work-based learning, in the best cases integrated with one another. The intensity of both academic and vocational education is appropriate to the jobs being targeted. Finally, effective programs pay attention to the pedagogy of everything they teach, whether classroom based or work based.
3. Effective programs provide a variety of supportive services, as appropriate to the needs of their clients or students.
4. Effective programs provide their clients or students with pathways or "ladders" of further education opportunities, so they can continue their education and training when they are able to.
5. Effective programs collect appropriate information about their results and use it to improve their quality. Furthermore, ascertaining the *actual* effectiveness of these programs requires some kind of outcome evaluation, which has been common for job training programs but less common in education.

In light of these precepts, there have consistently been several problems with particularistic programs—those targeted on specific groups judged most in need.

First, particularistic programs have typically been of very short duration (violating precept #2): Job training programs have rarely exceeded 15 weeks, and some—for example, the job search assistance offered in welfare-to-work—last only three or four weeks. The scale of such programs has rarely been adequate to the task of preparing individuals for middle-skilled jobs.

A related problem is that particularistic programs are rarely connected to further education and training opportunities (violating precept #4). When an individual completes one program, there is no obvious next program to enter—a serious problem when programs themselves are short and specific.

A third problem is that the range of supportive services has always been limited (violating precept #3). While job training programs have offered some remedial education (or ESL), it has been (by definition) limited in amount, and is usually provided with the worst kind of pedagogy—routine "skills and drills" (violating precept #2). These programs, and some community-based organizations, have offered guidance and counseling on occasion, but the amount has always been much less than the need. Some programs have provided support services—for example, welfare-to-work programs have often provided child care and transportation—but others have not provided such services. Except in model or experimental programs, the range of supportive services—for example, mentorships or mental health services—has usually been quite limited. And so, particularly for low-wage workers, the programs cannot be very effective.

Some of the same problems apply to certain types of education programs open to all. For example, the offerings of area vocational schools for adults are usually quite limited in duration (again, about 15 weeks) and focused on specific entry-level jobs. These are neither long enough nor advanced enough to provide access to middle-level employment, and they are typically not connected to further educational opportunities. The system of adult education in this country provides some remedial education, as well as ESL for recent immigrants; however, most adult schools do not provide links to other programs, fail to offer much in the way of vocational skill training, and (except perhaps for recent immigrants wanting ESL) are supremely ineffective.[4]

This leaves the community college, which is the institution most likely to provide the array of services necessary for low-skilled workers and to meet the five precepts outlined above. There are several clear advantages to the community college.

First, most offer a wide array of programs, ranging from short-term programs for welfare recipients to two-year associate's degree programs. While the articulation among them is not always well established—for example, some short-term programs are offered on a noncredit basis, and therefore cannot be used as a bridge to longer, credit-based programs—at least these options are available within the same institution, and it is more likely that individuals enrolling in short-term programs can find their way to more intensive programs.[5] Furthermore, the credit courses and associate programs of community colleges are virtually always connected to further education opportunities: Certificate programs lead to associate programs, and associate programs lead to four-year colleges through articulation agreements. Therefore, community colleges can take individuals from short and limited programs to the mainstream of American education—as the rags-to-riches story of the welfare mother becoming a doctor illustrates. The community college is the only institution that can bridge the world of short-term training and mainstream education. (This "bridging" role will be discussed below.)

Second, community colleges offer a full range of coursework—academic, vocational, and remedial or developmental—rather than the restricted range typical of job training, area vocational schools, or adult education. This means that students need-ing remedial education before entering an occupational program can find it within the same institution. Occupational programs can offer balanced coursework, includ-ing supportive academic courses like math for engineering technicians or biology and chemistry for health care workers. A further possibility is that hybrid courses and learning communities integrating academic and vocational content can develop—something that is much more difficult in specialized institutions. Such approaches, promoted by federal legislation for vocational education during the 1990s as well as by the School to Work Opportunities Act of 1994, have the potential for providing stu-dents with a more powerful and contextualized approach to learning academic ma-terial at the same time as they provide the necessary academic underpinnings of occupational instruction.[6]

In most cases, community colleges have developed occupational offerings that mirror local labor markets. Often, they respond to local employers serving on advisory committees, or employers contacted through needs assessments; some provide cus-tomized programs for the employees of local firms, potentially providing another way of keeping in touch with local employment trends. Because their funding is enrollment driven, the demands of students for certain locally available occupations provide another mechanism keeping them in balance with local employment.

In contrast to short-term training programs, with their low employment benefits declining over time, community colleges can be highly effective. Individuals who com-plete associate's degrees, for example, increase their earnings by about 20 to 30 percent over the earnings of high school graduates; these advantages are even larger for certain occupations—business, health occupations for women, technical occupations for men—and for individuals who find employment related to their field of study. For those earning one-year certificates, the average gain is low for men but about 20 percent for women, again with substantial variation among fields of study. Community college education also reduces unemployment and increases access to professional and managerial positions with prospects for advancement, reducing the likelihood that individuals are in clerical, operative, and unskilled occupations.[7]

Fourth, community colleges are much more likely than four-year colleges to rec-ognize the special needs of adult students. They usually offer a range of courses in late afternoons and evenings; they often devise intensive programs for students who can-not afford to be out of work for long periods of time, including welfare recipients (Grubb et al. 1999a). They usually offer a range of supportive services, including guid-ance and counseling, child care, placement offices, and special education services. The nature and range of these services is sometimes a problem (see next section, "3. Guidance and Counseling"), but the rationale and structure are usually in place.

Finally, community colleges belong to the culture of *education* rather than *training*. Among the many strands to this division (Grubb 1996a, chapter 1), a crucial one is the connection to issues of teaching. Preparing individuals for employment is, inevitably, an instructional activity, and the quality and nature of teaching are central to its success. Community colleges pride themselves on being "teaching institutions," and, at least in theory, the improvement of teaching is a central goal. In contrast, most job training programs, adult schools, and area vocational schools are completely disconnected from discussions about the quality of teaching, instructor preparation, or methods of improving instruction—and inattention to instructional issues usually means that the worst approaches to pedagogy and the most mediocre teaching prevail. In addition, the connection of community colleges to the world of education means that the broadest conceptions of education can be found within these institutions—including a reverence for the political and moral dimensions of education, for liberal education connected to the great humanistic traditions—in addition to occupational education.

Comprehensive community colleges are part of a broader American tradition of comprehensive institutions, in preference to more specialized institutions. In the main, we have comprehensive high schools, rather than academic and vocational high schools; our public universities have developed from specialized institutions (like teacher colleges, religious colleges, and technical colleges) into comprehensive institutions, providing an array of academic and professional majors; and elite research universities are also comprehensive institutions—"multiversities," in Clark Kerr's (1963) phrase—rather than specialized research institutes or graduate programs. Comprehensive institutions have been promoted on the grounds of equity—because they do not create the separate tracks of specialized institutions—as well as choice: They allow individuals to choose among a range of options within the institution. In a period of uncertainty and turmoil, the argument about choice is particularly important, because specialized institutions may not provide appropriate options for individuals uncertain of their futures.

In conclusion, of the great variety of education and training institutions developed over the past 40 years, the community college has the greatest chance of providing the education necessary to advance low-skilled workers. However, it is appropriate to raise one last question: Whether this kind of "either-or" discussion, focusing on community colleges *rather than* community-based organizations, or education *rather than* short-term training, is the appropriate way to pose the issue. Is there some way that community colleges could work *in cooperation with* other programs providing job-related education and training, to the benefit of students?

One way of doing so has emerged in a few states and localities that have developed a division of labor, with different institutions specializing in different but complementary services. For example, the local Private Industry Council in Miami tried to put together recruitment, counseling, and placement services from community-based organizations (CBOs)—which they could better provide because of their close links to specific racial and ethnic communities—with academic and occupational instruction from local community colleges (Grubb and McDonnell 1991). A similar kind of collaboration exists between community colleges in San Antonio and Project QUEST, a local CBO: QUEST has recruited Latino students who would otherwise not enter the college, pressured the college to provide appropriate services (e.g., bilingual education, special counseling), and targeted a set of relatively well-paid jobs with prospects for advancement, while the colleges provide remedial and occupational education in two-year programs with credit-bearing courses.

In these cases, community-based advocacy organizations represent the special needs of their communities to community colleges, which in turn respond more effectively with the guidance and pressure of the CBOs.[8] However, this collaborative approach is probably limited because CBOs cannot easily represent certain populations—for example, experimenters or recent high school graduates with inadequate basic skills—and because dedicated CBOs like Project QUEST are not widespread (and certainly cannot be legislated into being). Under these conditions, this cooperative model will remain relatively rare.

One final alternative would be to upgrade the competencies of low-wage workers through choice mechanisms or voucher-like arrangements. Such market-like mechanisms have become popular in K–12 education, for example, and the Workforce Investment Act allocates funding for adults through Individual Training Accounts that have many of the characteristics of vouchers. Perhaps we should abandon the kinds of comparisons of different institutions emphasized in this section, let a thousand institutional flowers bloom, and allow the consumer to pick among them.

In my view, this approach is wholly inadequate for the populations under discussion: experimenters, those with low skill levels, and those with multiple barriers to employment. Market-like mechanisms work best when sophisticated, well-informed consumers face "strong" providers of education and training, who are stable, sure of their educational offerings and their instructional methods, and committed first and foremost to education rather than (for example) growth, profit, or higher status (Finkelstein and Grubb 2000). For example, the market in elite colleges is one with sophisticated consumers and strong providers. But most low-skilled workers are precisely the individuals who lack the information to choose wisely, and they sometimes lack the stable preferences by which they might judge their best interests—and many of the institutions they consider are "weak" according to this conception. Market mechanisms at this point would be counterproductive, as the British experience with Training Credits clarifies (Finkelstein and Grubb 2000; Hodkinson, Sparkes, and Hodkinson 1996; MacDonald and Coffield 1993). In the short run, then, we should avoid market-like mechanisms, while working over the longer run to create more sophisticated consumers and strong providers of education and training. These are precisely the goals of many reforms outlined in the next section.

THE EFFECTIVENESS OF COMMUNITY COLLEGES: SPECIFIC REFORMS

Community colleges are undoubtedly effective for certain kinds of students—particularly middle-class students with their parents behind them and some working-class students with clear ambitions but without the resources to leave home. For such students, community colleges live up to their promise of low-cost institutions responsive to student needs, providing access to students' academic and occupational goals.

But there are other indicators that community colleges are not as effective as they could be. One of the most straightforward—and contentious—is the completion rate: For example, of all students entering community colleges in 1989–90, 48.6 percent had not earned a degree and were not enrolled five years later (Berkner, Cuccaro-Alamin, and McCormick 1996, table 2.1b). Whether low completion rates indicate high rates of dropping out for financial or family reasons, high rates of students attaining their goals through limited amounts of coursework, or high proportions of students who never intended to earn a credential are issues that have never been empirically resolved.[9] However, it is clear that those with small amounts of coursework do not increase their earnings substantially on the average (Grubb 1999a, table 5), although it's quite likely that individuals in certain well-targeted programs do. Another indicator of shortcomings is the transfer rate, which can be calculated in many different ways with many different answers (Cohen 1990; Grubb 1992). Unfortunately, none of the conventional transfer rates is particularly high, and there is some evidence that transfer rates have been falling (Grubb 1991).

Furthermore, the problems of noncompletion are systematically higher for low-income students, minority students, and recent immigrants—precisely the groups for which community colleges exist as virtually the only point of access to postsecondary education. The problems become even worse when we consider the students who enroll in remedial or developmental programs, an increasing proportion of entering students: While there are no national figures, it's clear that completion rates in such programs are quite low. All in all, many community colleges have substantial difficulty in getting students to complete the coherent one-year and two-year programs that lead to the largest and most certain economic rewards.

Of course, many reasons for noncompletion have nothing to do with the quality of community colleges. Community college students, and most of the groups needing greater education and training, tend to have low incomes and face fiscal barriers to completing college. Many are first-generation college students, and they have neither financial nor experiential guidance from their parents. Many have family responsibilities that distract them from education.[10] Those who are unsure of their direction (the experimenters) are often ambivalent about completing coursework; others need a variety of support services, varying from group to group.

But the important question here is whether community colleges could improve the programs and services they provide, and in ways that would enhance learning and retention among the students most in need of greater competencies. Substantial improvements are possible in at least seven areas. The first two—institutional support for the college to enhance the quality of teaching, and remedial/developmental education—involve instructional issues, the heart of any educational institution. (See also precept #2 above.) The next three—guidance and counseling, financial aid, and other support services—address the specific ancillary services that low-skilled workers and experimenters need. (See also precept #3.) And the sixth and seventh involve the nature of connections to other programs and to employment. (See also precept #1.)

1. Improving the Quality of Teaching

The great variety of students in community colleges itself provides a challenge to instructors, and many students are woefully underprepared. In the face of various pedagogical challenges, community colleges pride themselves as being "teaching institutions," and try to distinguish themselves from research-oriented universities on this ground. In some ways, community colleges enjoy certain conditions conducive to good teaching: They tend to have relatively small classes, and most instructors are dedicated to teaching. But in most colleges there are virtually no institutional practices that enhance teaching, and so the quality of instruction is random. Some instructors are exemplary, usually having developed their own approaches to teaching by trial and error, but they are likely to be teaching alongside mediocre instructors.

In colleges that are truly teaching institutions, a variety of institutional mechanisms enhance the quality of teaching.[11] For example, they are likely to have hiring procedures in which the quality of teaching is carefully assessed; they support new instructors through mentorships, special seminars, and other forms of staff development; and their promotion and tenuring procedures evaluate teaching carefully. Their staff development usually emphasizes ongoing workshops in which groups of instructors work on particular teaching issues collectively, rather than the conventional, one-shot workshops. They take pains to include part-time instructors as well as full-timers and the full range of faculty, including occupational and remedial faculty. Many colleges have developed mechanisms by which instructors and administrators observe teaching, with the goal of improvement. Often, these colleges have teaching centers that coordinate this variety of activities and respond to other, individual demands for assistance, sometimes through mini-grants. And, invariably, colleges devoted to teaching have administrators who are knowledgeable and supportive of instruction, in contrast to the majority of colleges, which seem to have administrators whom faculty deride as "bean counters" . . . "so busy in the mechanics [of running a college] that the creative and the innovative is way, way in the back seat" (Grubb et al. 1999a, 303).

There are, then, many ways for colleges to improve the overall quality of instruction. Some require additional funding, but many simply require an institution to turn its full attention to developing a consensus about teaching and implementing some obvious reforms. Now, the extent to which such reforms would by themselves enhance completion remains unclear, given the complex reasons that cause students to leave. But it is relatively certain that enhancing the competencies of low-skilled workers, particularly for a world of shifting opportunities, cannot be accomplished without high-quality teaching.

2. Enhancing Remedial/Developmental Education

There's no dispute that the amount of remedial education in community colleges has increased. The issue is highly contentious: As recent debates at the City University of New York attest, the very presence of remediation in postsecondary institutions is objectionable to some, although to others such programs are testimony to a commitment to second-chance students. But in these debates about remediation, its quality and effectiveness are virtually unmentioned.

Most colleges offer two or three levels of remediation—in reading, writing, and math. In some cases, courses customized for certain occupations—biology for health occupations, business math—provide other forms of remedial content. In addition, there is a great deal of "hidden" remediation, which occurs when an English or math instructor in a college-level course discovers that the students cannot compute or write, and then converts the class into an impromptu remedial course. In most cases, the dominant approach to teaching is "skills and drills," in which complex competencies are decomposed into small skills—subject-verb agreement, sentence construction, long division—on which students drill. The more difficult tasks—writing persuasive papers, reading complex instruction manuals and rate books, reasoning through complex problems with multiple steps—that they will face on the job or in four-year colleges are typically ignored.[12] Completion rates for remedial courses are quite low. For example, figures from Miami-Dade Community College confirm that passing required remedial coursework does enhance completion somewhat, but only 63 percent of students needing one remedial course completed that coursework, as did 42 percent of those needing two remedial courses, and 24 percent needing remediation in three areas (Morris 1994). The prospects for students needing considerable remediation are often dismal.

Some colleges have developed alternatives to conventional remediation. In many institutions, individual instructors have shifted away from skills and drills. They have generally switched to more constructivist and student-centered teaching, with a greater variety of real activities, problems, and issues drawn from the lives of students and a greater variety of instructional methods. In other institutions, entire developmental education departments have taken this approach, codifying their practices in manuals and staff development for new instructors. These departmentwide approaches have the distinct advantage over individual and idiosyncratic efforts, ensuring that all developmental courses within a college are reformed, rather than just a few.

Finally, some institutions have shifted to learning communities, teaching remedial education in the context of other academic and occupational courses. For example, "Reading, Writing, and Wrenches" was devised to improve the reading and writing of automotive students; business courses have been joined with remedial math and English courses; and an innovative program for welfare mothers wanting to go into health sciences joined math, English, and introduction to biology in a learning community. These complexes of courses allow basic subjects to be taught in some meaningful context, and allow students to proceed with their "real education" while learning basic skills. There's some evidence that learning communities are more effective at retaining and promoting students,[13] and virtually all faculty and students participating in them are highly supportive.

There are, then, solutions to the inherently difficult problem of creating effective remedial programs. Unfortunately, relatively few colleges have self-consciously tried to examine and improve their remedial programs. Very few states have enunciated a coherent policy that might improve the quality of such programs or provide special funding for improvement.[14] The national organization, the American Association of Community Colleges, designated 1999–2000 as the "year of remediation," but did little to provide guidance or policies for those who might want to improve the quality of remediation.[15] For large numbers of students who enter higher education through community colleges, as well as for virtually all those whose low skills prevent them from entering the mainstream of the economy, greater attention to this issue is necessary.

3. Guidance and Counseling

The large numbers of experimenters coming to community colleges need more than appropriate coursework and excellent teaching. While they take courses to discover what they might want to do, these are sometimes random, flailing efforts, because courses are not designed to be mechanisms for helping students learn what they might want to do. Some students find their way on their own, but many more do not; as one student described the process (Grubb 1996b, 75):

> I know lots and lots of people out of high school who go to community college because they have nothing else to do, and have no idea what they want to do. And for some people that's fine—they go and they take their classes and eventually, a couple years down the road, they'll pick a major, and then they end up getting their bachelor's. But just as many don't. They just, you know . . . "What am I doing here? I have no idea why I'm taking these classes. I don't enjoy it." That's the situation that I found myself in and a lot of my friends.

In student use of counseling services, a kind of triage seems to emerge. Those students with the clearest career goals (including students trying to upgrade their skills for specific employers) do not go to counselors because they do not need to. But the students with the greatest trouble making decisions about their futures also report not going to counselors—partly because of limited resources and awkward schedules, and partly because they don't know what to ask. As one student admitted, in explaining why she had not been to see a counselor:

> I don't know, though—it's so hard to get appointments there for the counselors. There are only specific times, and each counselor, too, that you see—it seems like they tell you a different thing. . . . Well, it's sort of hard for someone to give you direction if you don't have one.

Another student noted the need for student initiative in conventional counseling situations: "In order for someone to help you out at the college, you have to look for help." So the best-informed students don't see counselors, and the worst-informed don't either, for quite different reasons.

Most community colleges provide an array of services, including counseling centers, transfer centers to help students understand the requirements of four-year colleges, and, sometimes, programs specifically for low-income or minority or disabled students. However, several problems emerge consistently. One is a general lack of counselors: The average student-counselor ratio is just under 1,000:1, and it appears to have increased over time. Counselors spend most of their time on academic counseling, helping students figure out coursework requirements, rather than career counseling. And many counselors seem to limit themselves to providing information rather than helping students explore their conceptions of employment options, their preferences, and their decisionmaking abilities.[16] As a result, the students most in need of direction are unlikely to find the appropriate help.

As in the case of remediation, some institutions have moved beyond conventional counseling to offer a broader array of activities and experiences. Some colleges offer semester-long or year-long courses in which students explore the local labor market and the nature of career options. Miami-Dade and some other community colleges have developed programs that track students' progress against their self-declared goals: When students' progress lags behinds their own goals, they are alerted to revisit a counselor (Roueche and Baker 1987, chapter 3). LaGuardia Community College has a program requiring students to take two internships (recently reduced from three for budgetary reasons); for liberal arts students, the college considers these internships forms of career exploration, allowing students to explore careers they might like. More generally, internships and cooperative education allow students some direct experience in the world of work, helping them decide on alternative directions.

But such experiments seem to be rare, and the need for community colleges to experiment with alternative approaches to career guidance is substantial. Furthermore, the guidance and counseling community in this country—and many policymakers— have developed a limited view of career decisionmaking. In most cases, the central assumption is that students need more information to make rational decisions. But— as British researchers have clarified, with their longer history of voucher and choice mechanisms—decisionmaking is not a simple "skill" that requires only information to exercise.[17] In addition, individuals must have well-formed preferences, which experimenters lack. They need to be able to weigh present and future possibilities and the trade-offs among them; they must understand probabilistic events, and alternatives with different probabilities of success. To make use of information, they need to be able to judge the information they receive, and to distinguish among well-intentioned but inaccurate information (from friends, for example), deliberately misleading information (from proprietary schools, for example), and accurate but unhelpful information (from statewide surveys of labor markets, for example). They need to be able to consider a wide range of alternatives, including some that are unknown to them and others (like formal schooling itself) and some that have been places of disappointment they may not be able to consider dispassionately.

And so decisionmaking proves to be a complex competence in its own right, one that is increasingly necessary in a complex economy of shifting occupations—but one that conventional guidance and counseling does not address. More substantial experiences—semester-long courses, internships or co-op placements, service and experiential learning—may be necessary.

4. Financial Support

Community college students have fewer financial resources than those in four-year colleges. If they are young, their parents have lower incomes; many older students are likely to be in low-wage jobs they are seeking to escape. Thus, financial barriers to attending and completing are serious, and colleges often find themselves helpless when faced with the financial catastrophes their students experience.

Now, providing financial aid is not (and should not be) the responsibility of individual colleges. Federal grants, loans, and tax credits (the Hope and Lifelong Learning tax credits) exist for low-income students, and welfare programs can also provide support for those eligible.[18] However, there is still a problem, because community college students appear to receive much less federal aid than their peers in four-year colleges or proprietary schools. For example, in 1986 only 28.4 percent of community college students received any federal aid, compared with 47 percent of students in public four-year col-leges, 65 percent of those in private four-year colleges, and a whopping 84 percent in proprietary schools. Even when these figures are corrected for the differences in char-acteristics of community college students versus their peers, substantial differences still remain (Grubb and Tuma 1991). Furthermore, there are good reasons to suspect that community college students will also underutilize the Hope and Lifelong Learning tax credits: In addition to considerable institutional confusion in the initial implementation of these credits, many community college students do not have incomes high enough to qualify for them (or to benefit from deductions).

Thus, what federal aid to low-income students does exist is not extensively used by those most in need. There appear to be at least three reasons. First, federal aid seems designed for conventional students in four-year colleges who are accepted the spring before they enroll and have substantial time to complete financial aid applications. Students who decide to enroll at the last minute or for only one or two courses, and are not eligible for certain grants, may miss their opportunity to apply. Second, many com-munity colleges seem to have poorly staffed financial aid offices, which cannot provide students enough information and help about the options available.[19] And, of course, tax credits are poor mechanisms for subsidizing low-income students who pay low or no taxes anyway, so the recent Hope and Lifelong Learning tax credits are of little addi-tional help. Thus, resolution to the problems of supporting low-income students in community colleges lies partly in the design of federal aid and partly in strengthening financial aid offices on local campuses.

5. Other Support Services

The issue of support services is a difficult one in virtually all educational institutions, and the solutions are varied, sometimes inventive, and almost always inadequate. Many community colleges provide child care; in the past, job training programs have pro-vided additional support (e.g., child care, transportation, materials) for eligible stu-dents, and welfare-to-work programs—now dwindling—have done the same for welfare recipients. But more extensive services for those in greatest need have always been difficult to find because they are rarely part of community college budgets.

The solution should be part of an overall approach to helping low-skilled individ-uals access and complete community college programs. One general approach is that of coordinating with other community agencies that are funded to provide such ser-vices. For example, urban K–12 schools sometimes gain access to various health and social services by creating ties to local community-based organizations or having such organizations locate on their campuses. A few such schools have hired school social workers to bridge the very different cultures of the school and the social service agen-cies, and to help integrate the provision of social services into the instructional pro-gram (e.g., by including health-related materials in social studies and life skills classes). A similar solution might be possible for community colleges. An alternative is for social services funding to "follow the student" wherever he or she enrolls. Whatever the potential solutions, the issue will continue to prevent special needs students from gain-ing access to additional competencies until it is resolved.

6. Enhancing the Bridging Role

Community colleges are virtually the only institution that can bridge the world of short-term job training/adult education programs and the conventional world of education programs. Colleges often provide some short-term training, on their own or under contracts with job training and welfare programs; in some regions, they provide all of adult education. And they all have articulation agreements with four-year colleges and aspire to greater transfer rates. They can therefore be the bridge among different programs, including the bridge necessary for welfare mothers to reach medical school! While a few colleges have thought of themselves in such ways—for example, by providing short-term programs through credit-bearing courses that can then be used to progress to certificate and associate's degrees—most have failed to consider such possibilities, even when they participate in job training or welfare programs. Constructing "ladders of opportunities" for low-wage workers requires articulating short-term training with longer-term education, and then providing students with the information necessary to climb these ladders.[20]

7. Connections to Labor Markets

The most effective education and training programs are in close touch with the nature of the local labor market; they identify, and often target, jobs with relatively high wages and substantial prospects for wage growth over time. (See precept #1 and King et al. 2000.) For community colleges, certain occupations yield much higher economic returns than others, and, at the very least, students need to be informed about these alternatives. Furthermore, the returns are much higher for students who find employment related to their fields of study. Because community colleges are often local institutions, with students searching for employment in local or regional labor markets, some contact with or information about local employment may be necessary for students to find related employment and thereby realize the benefits of their occupational programs.

Community colleges have a vast array of mechanisms for keeping on top of local employment, including advisory committees; formal studies of local demand conditions; placement offices; student tracking to determine which students find employment; contract education providing training for incumbent employees, a potential source of information about what employers find lacking in their employees; and co-op education or internships, which lead employers and educators to develop programs jointly. Some community colleges have distinct advantages in maintaining contacts with employers, particularly through customized training and through networks of former students. In other cases, however, the quality of these connections to employment vary widely (Grubb 1996b, chapter 6). Some advisory committees provide real information about the direction of employment and technology and provide help with materials, curricula, and placement, but others are merely symbolic. Some colleges have changed their offerings according to information about labor market trends and wage conditions, while others offer programs as long as students enroll, regardless of their prospects for the future. So, programs persist in such low-wage areas as child care, cosmetology, and clerical work.

Student tracking is improving, particularly as states develop data systems based on Unemployment Insurance wage record data. But in many states, these are unavailable, and colleges simply do not know where their students go—and anecdotal evidence tends to stress the positive. Contract or customized training has expanded in many colleges, but it is often organized in a separate unit that fails to provide information back to regular programs. And internships and co-op programs, as promising as they are for connecting employers and instructors, are still too uncommon to have much influence. As in other areas, like the improvement of teaching, the problem is not the lack of mechanisms to connect colleges to the local labor market but, rather, inattention to making each of these potential mechanisms as powerful as it could be.

THE NEED FOR DEMAND-SIDE POLICIES

Imagine now that the quality of community colleges has improved for the students described at the outset of this chapter. If the recent increases in earnings inequality are to be reversed, there still remains a further task: The employment opportunities for these better-educated workers must be enhanced. Otherwise, we might simply see the same individuals at the bottom of the occupational hierarchy, somewhat better educated than before but still in relatively poorly paid work. It is asking too much for educational institutions alone to shoulder the burden of decreasing inequality. What is needed, in addition, is an employment policy that might complement an education policy. Such a policy would be necessary even now, when unemployment is relatively low, because poverty and low-wage work persist. When economic conditions turn down, as they inevitably must, then the need for a demand-side policy will be even more critical.

A 10-point program will not be presented here because its details would be premature. But there are some broad directions to pursue. In recent simulations by Isabel Sawhill (1999), the large amount of part-time work and unemployment spells are to blame for a great deal of poverty and inequality: The overall poverty rate would fall from 12.2 percent to 3.6 percent if all family heads of household could work full-time. The growth of temporary, contract, or contingent work has exacerbated the amount of involuntary part-time work, the spells of employment between short-term bouts of employment, and the lack of access to benefits. National and state policies need to find some mechanisms of countering these trends, which appear to be getting worse despite relatively low unemployment. In Sawhill's simulations, other more familiar (and presumably federal) policies also help: Subsidizing child care costs would further reduce poverty by 1.3 percentage points, increasing the value of the earned income tax credit would reduce poverty a little more, and instituting universal health care coverage would presumably also help. But there's no substitute for providing sufficient employment.

Other initiatives have been proposed over the years. One would help those living in inner cities gain access to the booming job markets of suburban areas. Problems of racial discrimination in employment persist, especially for black men, and renewed efforts to identify and eliminate discrimination—a tactic that was beginning to succeed in the late 1970s until Reagan and his lieutenants undermined the enforcement of civil rights legislation—constitutes another promising avenue. A variety of programs for "making work pay" has been proposed, ranging from living wage ordinances to gender equity campaigns to union drives.[21]

States have started to devise their own demand-side policies, again under the theory that developing a more-educated labor force without increasing the demand for better-prepared workers is likely to be ineffective.[22] Many states have instituted small-business development centers, providing assistance that might reduce the turnover rates of small businesses. Oregon's efforts to diversify its economy require local Regional Strategies Boards to target three key industries, coordinating incentives to expand with education for their workforces. Virtually every state has a program to lure employers from other states; some are surely ineffective and others are zero-sum from a national viewpoint, but state experiences are often valuable as laboratories for experimenting with alternatives. A national program to encourage states to target policies for their depressed areas—many central cities, Appalachia, the Mexican border, certain regions of the South—might be able to eliminate pockets of poverty through carefully devised state policy, rather than a uniform and clumsy federal policy like tax incentives.

In a few cases, community colleges themselves have engaged in stimulating demand as well as preparing workers. Colleges with small-business development centers and incubator programs help small firms survive and expand by providing help with modern technology and business practices; at the same time, they create a pool of trained employees. So, they enhance both demand and supply. In other cases, community colleges have created career ladders and wage progression strategies, trying to convince employers to create more middle-skilled jobs, rather than relying on a low-skill, low-wage strategy (Fitzgerald and Carlson 2000). While the effectiveness of such efforts is unclear, they provide a vision of improving opportunities in the labor market directly.

There is no lack of alternatives to stimulate the demand for educated workers, even if there is little evidence and less consensus on what might be effective. But the issue is not whether there is a ready-made, demand-side policy to implement; of course there is not, because there has not been any real discussion of this approach since the late 1970s. The issue, instead, is whether as a country we can recognize that relying on educational reform is not enough to correct inequality—that our long history of efforts to resolve social problems through schools and colleges cannot work without complementary employment policies.

GETTING FROM HERE TO THERE: THE WILL TO REFORM

Among existing education and training programs, community colleges are the most appropriate for providing enhanced competencies of many kinds to low-skilled and low-wage workers. As comprehensive institutions, community colleges have precisely the structure necessary to respond to the varying needs of this large and heterogeneous group. That is the good news; the bad news is that community colleges need to improve a variety of their offerings if they are to be as effective as they could be.

The reforms outlined here should be addressed at a variety of levels. At the federal level, grants, loans, and tax credits need to be scrutinized to see why they are less available to community college students. Rather than continuing to provide post-secondary funding through demand-side policies, the federal government could fund more efforts for program improvement. For example, it could fund a series of instructional centers and student centers at relatively low cost, and these could help improve the quality of teaching and the availability of support services for a wide variety of students.[23]

In addition, given the dearth of research on community colleges, particularly describing and evaluating the variety of practices in more than 1,000 institutions, the federal government could play a much stronger role in research than it has so far. It is in a much better position than are state governments or local institutions to examine the variety of practices in remedial education, in guidance and counseling, in establishing connections with local labor markets, and in providing support services; the federal government could undertake research and technical assistance in these areas, with national rather than state or regional information.

At the state level, again there are policies that states could articulate. For example, they could provide networks of instructional centers to improve the quality of teaching on campuses. As Iowa has done with some success, they could require community college instructors to complete certain coursework related to community college teaching methods. They could convene colleges in collective efforts to examine the conditions of remediation, of guidance and counseling, and of other support services, and to clarify the alternatives available, including the development of more coherent state policies and funding. Even in states with weak state agencies, at the very least the convening power of the state—its potential role in identifying solutions, even if it does not require or fund them—would serve a valuable role. And in states with more centralized power, such efforts might suggest valuable directions for state policy.

Inevitably, many of these reforms need to take place at the local level, in specific colleges. Any federal and state policy needs at the very least to be appropriately implemented locally. There is no substitute for local competence. Those colleges that are truly teaching institutions provide examples: They identify potential areas of instructional improvement and use the institutional mechanisms at their disposal to make systematic advances. Their presidents and other administrators are knowledgeable about teaching, the core activity of the institution; they and their faculty work collegially on these issues, without the antagonism and infighting of other institutions that are too distracted to pay attention to teaching and learning. The changes necessary for converting "weak" institutions into "strong" colleges are multiple and complex to be sure, but they need to be implemented if community colleges are to be effective for low-wage workers.

But here we need to confront an unpleasant aspect of community colleges. There is very little reform energy in these institutions, or in the state and federal governments that fund them. Unlike K–12 education, which has been in a frenzy of reform at least since 1983, there are few widespread pressures from employers and policymakers to change. Unlike job training programs, which have been under federal pressure and performance standards for almost 20 years, there is no central funding agency responsible for improving the quality of results. A few states have initiated their own reform measures, particularly Florida, with its series of market-like reforms culminating in performance-based funding; North Carolina, with its performance measures and technical assistance to local colleges; and Oregon and Washington, with their efforts to have community colleges lead workforce development efforts. But state oversight of community colleges is weak in most states, and state agencies are often powerless against local control. At the local level, there are some colleges with reform-minded administration and faculty, but many others without either.

So the critical issue is one of political will. There is a long list of improvements possible in community colleges, improvements that would increase their ability to meet the needs of low-wage workers and respond to the demands for lifelong learning. Doing so will require state governments, in particular, and the federal government, in a more limited way, to concentrate on multiple dimensions of reform and improvement, rather than continuing to fund community colleges as if all is well. States (and the federal government, too) should consider a variety of mechanisms of institutional improvement, rather than relying solely on the accountability mechanisms that have become so popular; in particular, various forms of support and technical assistance are necessary to improve the weakest institutions. And both states and the federal government need to consider demand-side policies more carefully in order to match improvements in education with improvements in employment. Only then will it be possible for our second-chance institutions to realize their potential as mechanisms for improving the well-being of low-wage workers.

NOTES

1. According to the figures of Danziger and Reed (1999), inequality rose between 1973 and 1993, and since then has been relatively constant.

2. On experimenters, see Manski (1989), who clarifies that college going as a form of information gathering may be positive. See also Grubb (1996b, chapter 2), Grubb et al. (1999a, Introduction), Schneider and Stevenson (2000, chapter 9), and Gittell and Steffy (2000) on experimenters in a specific college.

3. There is substantial literature reviewing the studies on the effectiveness of job training programs. In addition to Grubb (1996a) and Grubb and Ryan (1999), see also LaLonde (1995), U.S. Department of Labor (1995), Fischer and Cordray (1996), O'Neill and O'Neill (1997), and Strawn (1998). It's too soon to tell how the Workforce Investment Act will operate, although the limited evidence available so far, based on pilot projects and local programs that have developed vouchers, suggests that spending limits on vouchers will perpetuate low resource levels in most job training even though a broader range of providers may emerge (Maguire 2000).

4. See Grubb and Kalman (1994). There is almost no evidence about the effectiveness of adult education programs; see, for example, the poor quality of the evidence in the National Evaluation of Adult Education Programs (Young, Fitzgerald, and Morgan 1994).

5. Having made this claim, I should admit that I have never found a community college that has calculated the proportion of students in short-term programs, or noncredit courses, who transfer to credit programs.

6. I have previously written about the integration of academic and occupational education in Grubb (1996b, chapter 5), Badway and Grubb (1997), and Grubb et al. (1999a, chapter 7).

7. See Grubb (1999a) for a review of the evidence on the employment effects of community colleges.

8. It is important not to understate the potential conflict between a college and a CBO. Initially, relationships in San Antonio were strained when Project QUEST challenged local colleges over their lack of success with Latino students. Conflict gave way to collaboration only after the CBO showed the colleges ways they, too, could benefit from the collaboration. On Project QUEST see Grubb (1999b) and Osterman and Lautsch (1996).

9. For a recent study for one college, see Gittell and Steffy (2000). They conclude that many students (perhaps 45 percent) had no intention of earning a credential. For those who did want to complete, the lack of financial resources and the strain of combining work, family life, and schooling were the most prominent reasons for dropping out.

10. In the recent work of Gittell and Steffy with two City University of New York colleges (1998, 2000), the primary reason for leaving involved the difficulty of combining college, work, and family.

11. This is a desperately brief statement of a book-length argument in Grubb et al. (1999a), one that is reasonably consistent with two other empirical works on community college teaching by Richardson, Fisk, and Okun (1983) and Seidman (1985).

12. On remedial education in community colleges, see Grubb and Kalman (1994), Grubb and Associates (1999, chapter 5), and Grubb (2001). See also Shaw (1997) on three types of community colleges and their responses to remedial education.

13. See Gudan et al. (1991), Tokino (1993), Tinto, Goodsell-Love, and Russo (1994), and MacGregor (1991). On learning communities in general, see Matthews (1994a, b).

14. North Carolina is an interesting exception: It has developed common competencies for remedial courses, imposed performance measures, and funded pilot projects around the state, generating six different approaches to developmental education that other colleges can adapt (Oral communication, Edith Lange, North Carolina Community College System). A few other states (e.g., Florida, Minnesota) are reputed to have state policies, but few states have done much (Oral communication, Hunter Boylan, National Center for Developmental Education).

15. The AACC has sponsored some research by Robert McCabe, but extensive empirical results are not available; for recommendations see McCabe (2000). For an earlier AACC document, stressing the importance of remediation but avoiding the institutional and pedagogical problems, see Day and McCabe (1997).

16. These empirical statements are based on Keim (1988), Coll and House (1989), and research in progress with the Community College Research Center, Columbia University.

17. See especially Hodkinson, Sparkes, and Hodkinson (1996), especially chapter 8 on technical versus pragmatic rationality, and Reay and Ball (1997) on class differences in conceptions of choice.

18. Access to allowable education and training opportunities has become much worse under Temporary Aid for Needy Families (TANF), despite a few efforts to examine education and training alternatives under TANF. See Equal Rights Advocates (2000), which reports the experiences of welfare recipients in California where caseworkers often fail to inform their clients of available services, and Grubb et al. (1999a), which clarifies how many states have eliminated education and training as options for welfare recipients. On the alternatives available, see Strawn and Martinson (2000) and other Manpower Development Research Corporation publications, and Ganzglass (forthcoming).

19. See especially the information on staffing in various California colleges, in Grubb and Tuma (1991).

20. Information about career ladders can be found in Grubb (1996a, b); see also Fitzgerald (2000).

21. See the June–July 2000 issue of *The American Prospect.*

22. These examples are all drawn from Grubb et al. (1999b).

23. I have estimated that the federal government could support Faculty Development Centers and Lifelong Learning Centers for students in every community college through matching grants for a total of $200 million; see Grubb (1998).

REFERENCES

Badway, Norena, and W. Norton Grubb. 1997. *A Sourcebook for Reshaping the Community College: Curriculum Integration and the Multiple Domains of Career Preparation,* vols. 1 and 2. Berkeley, Calif.: National Center for Research in Vocational Education.

Berkner, Lutz K., et al. 1996. *Descriptive Summary of 1989–90 Beginning Postsecondary Students: Five Years Later* (NCES 96-155). Washington, D.C.: U.S. Department of Education.

Cohen, Arthur. 1990. "Counting the Transfers: Pick a Number." *Community, Technical, and Junior College Times,* 24 April.

Coll, Kenneth, and Reese House. 1989. "Empirical Implications for the Training and Professional Development of Community College Counselors." *Community College Review* 19 (2): 43–52.

Danziger, Sheldon, and Deborah Reed. 1999. "Winners and Losers: The Era of Inequality Continues." *Brookings Review* 17 (4): 14–17.

Day, Philip, and Robert McCabe. 1997. "Remedial Education: A Social and Economic Imperative." Executive Issues Paper, American Association of Community Colleges. http://www.aacc.nche.edu/research/remediation.htm. October.

Equal Rights Advocates. 2000. *The Broken Promise: Welfare Reform Two Years Later.* San Francisco: ERA.

Finkelstein, Neal, and W. Norton Grubb. 2000. "Making Sense of Education and Training Markets: Lessons from England." *American Educational Research Journal* (3): 601–32.

Fischer, R., and David Cordray. 1996. *Job Training and Welfare Reform: A Policy-Driven Synthesis.* New York: Russell Sage Foundation.

Fitzgerald, Joan. 2000. *Community Colleges As Labor Market Intermediaries: Building Career Ladders for Low-Wage Workers.* Boston: Center for Urban and Regional Policy, Northeastern University.

Fitzgerald, Joan, and Virginia Carlson. 2000. "Ladders to a Better Life." *The American Prospect* 11 (15): 54–60.

Ganzglass, Evelyn. Forthcoming. *Strategies for Expanding Postsecondary Opportunities for TANF Recipients and Low-Income Workers.* Washington, D.C.: National Governors' Association.

Gittell, Marilyn, and Tracy Steffy. 1998. *The Benefits of College Attendance: A Case Study of BMCC.* New York: Howard Samuels State Management and Policy Center, City University of New York.

———. 2000. *Community Colleges Addressing Students' Needs: A Case Study of LaGuardia Community College.* New York: Howard Samuels State Management and Policy Center, City University of New York.

Grubb, W. Norton. 1991. "The Decline of Community College Transfer Rates: Evidence from National Longitudinal Surveys." *Journal of Higher Education* 62 (2): 194–222.

———. 1992. "Finding an Equilibrium: Enhancing Transfer Rates while Strengthening the Comprehensive Community College." Working Paper 3(6). Washington, D.C.: National Center for Academic Achievement and Transfer.

———. 1996a. *Learning to Work: The Case for Reintegrating Job Training and Education.* New York: Russell Sage Foundation.

———. 1996b. *Working in the Middle: Strengthening Education and Training for the Mid-Skilled Labor Force.* San Francisco: Jossey-Bass.

———. 1998. "Making Lifelong Learning a Reality: Capitalizing on America's Community Colleges." Unpublished note, School of Education, University of California, Berkeley.

———. 1999a. *Learning and Earning in the Middle: The Economic Benefits of Sub-Baccalaureate Education.* New York: Community College Research Center, Teachers College, Columbia University.

———. 1999b. "Lessons from Education and Training for Youth: Five Precepts." In *Preparing Youth for the 21st Century: The Transition from Education to the Labour Market. Proceedings of the Washington, D.C., Conference* (363–83). Paris: OECD Publications.

———. 2001. "From Black Box to Pandora's Box: Evaluating Remedial/Developmental Education." Occasional Paper. New York: Community College Research Center, Teachers College, Columbia University.

Grubb, W. Norton, et al. 1999a. *Honored but Invisible: An Inside Look at Teaching in Community Colleges.* New York and London: Routledge.

Grubb, W. Norton, et al. 1999b. *Order from Chaos: State Efforts to Reform Workforce Development "Systems."* Berkeley, Calif.: National Center for Research in Vocational Education.

Grubb, W. Norton, and Norena Badway. 1998. *Linking School-Based and Work-Based Learning: The Implications of LaGuardia's Co-op Seminars for School-to-Work Programs.* MDS 1046. Berkeley, Calif.: National Center for Research in Vocational Education.

Grubb, W. Norton, and Judy Kalman. 1994. "Relearning to Earn: The Role of Remediation in Vocational Education and Job Training." *American Journal of Education* 103 (1): 54–93.

Grubb, W. Norton, and Lorraine M. McDonnell. 1991. *Local Systems of Vocational Education and Job Training: Diversity, Interdependence, and Effectiveness.* MDS-259. Berkeley, Calif.: National Center for Research in Vocational Education.

Grubb, W. Norton, and Paul Ryan. 1999. *The Roles of Evaluation for Vocational Education and Training: Plain Talk on the Field of Dreams.* London: Kogan Paul, and Geneva: International Labour Office.

Grubb, W. Norton, and John Tuma. 1991. "Who Gets Student Aid? Variations in Access to Aid." *The Review of Higher Education* 14 (3): 359–82.

Grubb, W. Norton, Norena Badway, Denise Bell, and Marisa Castellano. 1999. "Community Colleges and Welfare Reform: Emerging Practices, Enduring Problems." *Community College Journal* 69 (6): 30–36.

Gudan, Sirkka, et al. 1991. *Paired Classes for Success.* Livonia, Mich.: Schoolcraft College.

Hodkinson, Phil, Andrew Sparkes, and Heather Hodkinson. 1996. *Triumphs and Tears: Young People, Markets, and the Transition from School to Work.* London: David Fulton Publishers.

Keim, Marybelle. 1988. "Two-Year College Counselors: Who Are They and What Do They Do?" *Community College Review* 16 (1): 39–46.

Kerr, Clark. 1963. *The Uses of the University.* Cambridge, Mass.: Harvard University Press.

King, Christopher, et al. 2000. "Training Success Stories for Adults and Out-of-School Youth: A Tale of Two States." In *Improving the Odds: Increasing the Effectiveness of Publicly Funded Training,* edited by Burt Barnow and Christopher King. Washington, D.C.: The Urban Institute.

LaLonde, Robert. 1995. "The Promise of Public Sector-Sponsored Training Programs." *Journal of Economic Perspectives* 9 (2): 149–68.

MacDonald, Robert, and Frank Coffield, F. 1993. "Young People and Training Credits: An Early Exploration." *British Journal of Education and Work* 6 (1): 5–22.

MacGregor, Jean 1991. "What Differences Do Learning Communities Make?" *Washington Center News* 6 (1): 4–9.

Maguire, Sheila. 2000. *Surviving, and Maybe Thriving, on Vouchers.* Philadelphia: Public/Private Ventures.

Manski, Charles. 1989. "Schooling as Experimentation: A Reappraisal of the College Dropout Phenomenon." *Economics of Education Review* 8 (4): 305–12.

Matthews, Roberta S. 1994a. *Notes from the Field: Reflections on Collaborative Learning at LaGuardia.* Long Island City, N.Y.: Office of the Associate Dean for Academic Affairs, LaGuardia Community College.

———. 1994b. "Enriching Teaching and Learning through Learning Communities." In *Teaching and Learning in the Community College,* edited by Terry O'Banion and associates. Washington, D.C.: American Association of Community Colleges.

McCabe, Robert. 2000. *No One to Waste: A Report to Public Decision-Makers and Community College Leaders.* Washington, D.C.: Community College Press.

Morris, Cathy. 1994. *Success of Students Who Needed and Completed College Preparatory Instruction.* Research Report No. 94-19R. Miami: Institutional Research, Miami-Dade Community College.

O'Neill, Dave, and June O'Neill. 1997. *Lessons for Welfare Reform: An Analysis of the AFDC Caseload and Past Welfare-to-Work Programs.* Kalamazoo, Mich.: W. E. Upjohn Institute for Employment Research.

Osterman, Paul, and Brenda Lautsch. 1996. *Project QUEST: A Report to the Ford Foundation.* Cambridge, Mass.: MIT Sloan School of Management.

Reay, Diane, and Stephen J. Ball. 1997. " 'Spoilt for Choice': The Working Classes and Educational Markets." *Oxford Review of Education* 23 (1): 89–101.

Richardson, Richard C., Jr., Elizabeth C. Fisk, and Morris A. Okun. 1983. *Literacy in the Open-Access College.* San Francisco: Jossey-Bass.

Roueche, John E., and George A. Baker III. 1987. *Access and Excellence: The Open Door College.* Washington, D.C.: Community College Press.

Sawhill, Isabel. 1999. "From Welfare to Work." *Brookings Review* 17 (4): 27–30.

Schneider, Barbara, and David Stevenson. 1999. *The Ambitious Generation: America's Teenagers—Motivated but Directionless.* New Haven: Yale University Press.

Seidman, Earl. 1985. *In the Words of the Faculty: Perspectives on Improving Teaching and Educational Quality in Community Colleges.* San Francisco: Jossey-Bass.

Shaw, Kathleen. 1997. "Remedial Education as Ideological Battleground: Emerging Remedial Education Policies in the Community College." *Educational Evaluation and Policy Analysis* 19 (3): 284–96.

Strawn, Julie. 1998. *Beyond Job Search or Basic Education: Rethinking the Role of Skills in Welfare Reform.* Washington, D.C.: Center for Law and Social Policy.

Strawn, Julie, and Karin Martinson. 2000. *Steady Work and Better Jobs: How to Help Low-Income Parents Sustain Employment and Advance in the Workplace.* New York: Manpower Development Research Corporation.

Tinto, Vincent, Anne Goodsell-Love, and Pat Russo. 1994. *Building Learning Communities for New College Students: A Summary of Research Findings of the Collaborative Learning Project.* Washington, D.C.: National Center on Postsecondary Teaching, Learning, and Assessment, Office of Educational Research and Improvement, U.S. Department of Education.

Tokino, Kenneth. 1993. "Long-Term and Recent Student Outcomes of Freshman Interest Groups." *Journal of the Freshman Year Experience* 5 (2): 7–28.

U.S. Department of Labor. 1995. *What's Working (and What's Not): A Summary of Research on the Economic Impacts of Employment and Training Programs.* Washington, D.C.: U.S. Department of Labor, Office of the Chief Economist.

Williamson, Jeffrey, and Peter Lindert. 1980. *American Inequality: A Macroeconomic History.* New York: Academic Press.

Young, Malcolm, et al. 1994. *National Evaluation of Adult Education Programs: Fourth Report Learner Outcomes and Program Results.* Contract No. LC90065001. Washington, D.C.: U.S. Department of Education.

15

Opening College Doors for Disadvantaged Hispanics

An Assessment of Effective Programs and Practices

Edwin Meléndez and Carlos Suárez

The 1996 enactment of welfare reform has had a tremendous impact on the field of employment training. Since then, welfare-to-work initiatives have emphasized short-term employability training that follows a "work-first" strategy, which assumes that work experience is the most important factor leading to stable, permanent employment. As a result, community-based organizations and numerous employer-based or industry-based initiatives have rushed to expand or create programs that assist in the transition to work—as have community colleges.

The question of how—and how well—community colleges can serve disadvantaged Hispanics gains further relevance in the context of the Workforce Investment Act (WIA) of 1998. After years of study and negotiation (Meléndez 1997), Congress enacted and President Clinton signed this workforce development legislation, which replaced the Job Training Partnership Act (JTPA) and also consolidated federal employment and training law under one act. Among other things, WIA emphasizes the role of community colleges and other educational institutions in the workforce development system. It also establishes clear performance criteria for training providers, and mandates that clients have ready access to program performance data.

Welfare reform and WIA are particularly relevant to Hispanics. Although JTPA evaluations found strong, positive employment impacts on disadvantaged populations as a whole (Orr et al. 1994), the historical results for Hispanics have been relatively poor (Meléndez 1989; Romero 1990). As a group, Hispanics who complete programs have a relatively low job placement rate and, subsequently, relatively low average wages compared with their peers who were placed in jobs. Other studies assessing the Job Opportunities and Basic Skills program, formerly offered by the Aid to Families with Dependent Children program, found similar inequities (Rodriguez and Martinez 1995).

This context helps explain the interest in the role that community colleges and universities can play in the emerging realignment of workforce development institutions. Community colleges have traditionally served as the educators of nontraditional and disadvantaged populations. To various degrees, they award technical certifications in response to local labor markets, while providing a foundation of core academic competencies for those who would like to pursue a college degree. In some urban areas, community colleges have become an effective coordinating mechanism for workforce development, with strong working relationships with both social service agencies and employers. These institutions have become integral to a comprehensive system of skills training that effectively provides social and academic support to those who need it most. And when trainees complete their training, these colleges have the necessary connections with industry to place people in entry-level jobs within a chosen career path.

However, very few community colleges serving the inner-city poor have fulfilled their potential as regional workforce development intermediaries. Often, community colleges are preparatory schools for universities, offering a traditional liberal arts curriculum to students who plan to transfer to four-year colleges. In many cases, industry plays a major role in designing, developing, or supporting only a few programs.

Given the changes in welfare and employment training policy, the appropriate role for community colleges in training the disadvantaged is receiving renewed attention.[1] This study seeks to understand how colleges and universities can enhance the employment opportunities of disadvantaged populations. It focuses on the role of community colleges and universities in serving Hispanics. According to the *1997 Index of Hispanic Economic Indicators,* only 53.4 percent of Hispanics had graduated from high school in 1995, compared with 83 percent of whites and 73.8 percent of African Americans; fewer than one in ten Hispanics (9.3 percent) had college degrees. The *Index* also indicates that "in terms of poverty levels, Hispanics are economically worse off that they were five years ago during the height of the recession"; one in three Hispanics was poor in 1995.

This study assessed four demonstration projects funded by the U.S. Department of Labor.[2] Developed by the department in collaboration with the Hispanic Association of Colleges and Universities, each demonstration aimed to create or promote innovative strategies and approaches for community colleges and universities to provide training and employment opportunities for economically disadvantaged Hispanics. All four programs targeted individuals of Hispanic origin eligible for programs authorized by the JTPA. JTPA served youth, adults, and dislocated workers who experienced barriers to training or stable, long-term employment. The demonstrations focused on barriers—in the workplace or in the educational system—reflective of the cultural, social, and economic environments. The Employment and Training Administration was the department's administrative agency for the grants.

In conducting this study, our main objective was to understand and document factors that contribute to the development of effective strategies for community college–based employment training and educational programs for disadvantaged Hispanics. It is generally accepted that students and job seekers need both job-specific skills and also connections to employers to get an entry-level job and advance to a better one. Successful job training programs provide job seekers with skills demanded by industry, and they institutionalize relations with employers to facilitate job placement and the transition to work: In short, they are successful "matchmakers" (Harrison and Weiss 1998; Meléndez and Harrison 1998). Moreover, recent research and various reports suggest that programs that emphasize connections to the job market have expanded in recent years (Dresser and Rogers 1998; Molina 1998; Seavey 1998; Siegel and Kwass 1995).

With that foundation, this study focused on four interrelated areas identified in the literature as contributing to the success of programs targeting disadvantaged populations: (1) case management, financial aid, and support services; (2) curriculum, instructional practices, and academic support; (3) program design and institutional environment; and (4) links to employers and local industry.[3]

From the perspective of a demonstration project, our research also sought to ascertain the programs' broader impact upon the larger institution. That is, did the college institute some of the demonstrated effective practices, either by continuing the program with other funding or by adopting similar initiatives in other parts of the college?

REINVENTING COMMUNITY COLLEGES

To answer these research questions, we adopted a comparative case study method.[4] This is the preferred research method for assessments of programs' effectiveness. It can be particularly useful when assessing the design of employment training programs and workforce development systems.

We combined and examined multiple sources of information, including site visits, interviews with students, instructors and other staff, program files and documents, and visits to employers and other collaborators.[5] Based on them, the study assesses program design and implementation during the period covered by the U.S. Department of Labor grant, and draws lessons for other programs serving disadvantaged Hispanics.

The research looked at the four demonstrations:

- The Hispanic Network for Education and Training, Albuquerque Technical Vocational Institute (ATVI), New Mexico;
- The Better Opportunities for Hispanics Program, Miami-Dade Community College (MDCC), Homestead Campus, Florida;
- The Direct Care Workers Program, Borough of Manhattan Community College (BMCC), New York; and
- The Accelerated Associate's Program for Licensed Nurses, Inter American University of Puerto Rico (IUPR).

Each program was unique in its design, in part reflecting the selection panel's desire for diversity in the demonstrations. Perhaps the greatest contrast arose in the relation of programs to host institutions. As a result, we compared programs that had a "dedicated" program design—IUPR and BMCC—with those having an "integration" program design—MDCC and ATVI (table 15.1).

TABLE 15.1 Program Structure at a Glance

	IUPR	BMCC	MDCC	ATVI
Financial aid	Based on need	Full assistance	Full assistance	Regular package and emergency financial aid
Academic support and instructional practices	Tutorial services and board exam review sessions	Tutorial services and classroom discussions	Tutorial services and workshops	Tutors and peer mentors
Case management and counseling	Responsibility of program coordinator	Integrated to program	By program director and school counselor	Primary service offered by program
Program design and specialized curriculum	Accelerated trimester system	Package of certifications	Life and job skills added to regular curriculum	Not part of program design
Administrative innovation	Problem solving by administration team	Self-contained structure	Program mediates relation to other programs within the college	Centralized support system
Links to jobs and employers	Present as in-hospital practices	Strong through internships and part of exit step	Not part of program design, but students had access to internships through college certificate programs	Not part of program design

The term *dedicated* denotes a self-contained program—that is, a curriculum designed to satisfy a particular certification or academic degree, and students who take classes as a group. Students receive other social and academic support as part of their affiliation with the program. In contrast, the term *integration* denotes a program that supports students who are in regular or existing programs in the college. They receive academic support as individuals, depending on the particular subjects in which they have enrolled. Counseling and other social support services are primarily offered through the college's student support system, and the main objective is to help students take advantage of existing services and succeed in regular college programs.

The Hispanic Network for Education and Training: Networking within Boundaries

The Hispanic Network for Education and Training (H-NET) at Albuquerque Technical Vocational Institute created a network of comprehensive services to support the efforts of Hispanic students to earn an associate's degree or complete a certificate program leading to employment. Services included orientation, counseling, peer mentoring, diagnostic testing, job and life skill courses, and emergency financial aid. The program was designed to ease the transition into college or the workplace. Through a variety of support service strategies, it provided assistance developing social, academic, and employment skills. The aim was to increase ATVI's retention rates for disadvantaged Hispanic students and, by extension, increase their employability.

The program provided services to students who were recruited during the fall, spring, and summer sessions of the 1996–1997 academic year. Out of a total of 112 students, 85 percent were female, 81 percent economically disadvantaged, and 70 percent educationally disadvantaged. Approximately 19 percent also participated in the Community Corrections program, and 3 percent had limited English proficiency. According to estimates by JTPA providers in the Albuquerque area, about 215 Hispanic participants attended ATVI; thus, H-NET served about half these students.

At the conclusion of the program, it was too early to quantify the effects of H-NET on the overall retention of Hispanic students at ATVI. Nevertheless, it is encouraging that the college's Counseling Center will maintain several program elements as permanent features, including emergency financial aid, as well as testing material, equipment, and orientation information. The key personnel will also continue working at the Counseling Center as director and counselors. Given ATVI's administrative and organizational structure then, it is expected that H-NET's culturally appropriate counseling services and referrals will continue. In fact, the ability to provide a cluster of services, including orientation, counseling, emergency financial assistance, referrals, Hispanic mentors, and culturally appropriate tutorial services, constituted the most significant feature of the H-NET program. In many ways, H-NET accomplished the core objective of the demonstration project: to promote institutional change to serve the needs of disadvantaged Hispanics.

Better Opportunities for Hispanics Program: A Focus on Students

Among the greatest challenges facing community colleges and other large educational institutions is how to create a welcoming atmosphere and a student-focused support system for disadvantaged students attending college for the first time—often when they are the first in their families to do so. Any student may find it difficult to negotiate financial aid, admissions and enrollment, deciding on courses, and other challenges of academic life; this is particularly difficult for disadvantaged students.

The Better Opportunities for Disadvantaged Hispanics program of the MDCC, Homestead campus, provided "client-driven" services in an effort to increase students' employability or their chances to complete an associate's degree. The program offered financial assistance, enrollment in certification courses, remedial and regular college classes, and supportive case management to 21 students. Students were unemployed, displaced agricultural workers, or individuals lacking English-language proficiency. The goals were to provide high school dropouts with an opportunity to pursue vocational training and develop job skills, as well as to facilitate their attainment of higher education.

The program was very successful in providing students with a safe "home" within the larger institution. The retention rate of 75 percent is slightly higher than for traditional students. Thirty-five percent of the students were placed in jobs, and the majority continued their education. Further, the program allowed students to pursue career paths in business management, elementary education, and airline ticketing through certifications and college credits. The program attributed its success to the individualized case management that was central to its "client-centered" approach, which also included ongoing support for students through counseling and nontraditional workshops in life skills and job skills.

The Direct Care Workers Program: Bilingual Vocational Training As a Pathway to Industry

The Direct Care Workers Program (DCWP) of the Borough of Manhattan Community College is a classic example of the role that community colleges can play in providing a pathway to industry for disadvantaged Hispanics. Nineteen students completed a six-month program of bilingual vocational training to become paraprofessionals in the field of mental retardation and developmental disabilities. Designed and taught by experienced instructors, the program provided training, financial and academic assistance, and an internship in a community residence or treatment agency. It also offered ongoing supervision to and advocacy services for participating students.

The DCWP was designed as an entry point for a career ladder in the health industry. It targeted bilingual students with poor academic experience living in New York City. As such, it facilitated access to college, while training participants with skills demanded by industry. The program offered English-language skill development in the context of learning job-related content and basic academic skills. To structure contextual and experiential learning, it combined classroom instruction with 126-hour workplace internships. By the end of the program, students were matched with employers and also earned three state certifications and three credits toward a college degree.

Conventional outcome measures indicate that the DCWP was highly successful: For example, 80 percent completed the program, and 63 percent were placed in jobs. Based on interviews with program staff, students, employers, and other sources familiar with the program, it appears that this success derived from a number of methods (by now well documented) associated with best practice training programs. These practices include a strict selection of students based on early orientation and counseling; the integration of basic education, language acquisition, vocational education and counseling; team teaching as support services; and the active participation of and connection to, employers and industry.

Accelerated Associate's Program for Licensed Nurses: Creating Career Ladders in University Systems

Thirty licensed practical nurses (LPNs) completed an innovative, accelerated program to earn an associate's degree in nursing from the Inter American University (Universidad Interamericana de Puerto Rico). The one-year program—three trimesters and two summer sessions—provided financial and academic assistance to disadvantaged students living in the San Juan metropolitan area. It allowed students to take advanced placement exams in areas they had covered as part of their practical nursing training, further reducing required classroom time. By training unemployed LPNs to pass the Registered Nursing (RN) Board exam, the program increased their chances for better employment, and increased the pool of registered nurses serving the health care needs of their communities.

The program was extraordinarily successful, as measured by several conventional indicators. The retention rate of 73 percent is about average for students enrolled in a regular two-year program leading to an associate's degree in nursing. The 95 percent who passed the Associate's Nursing Board exam is slightly higher than average. Several things make these outcomes remarkable: The students were economically and educationally disadvantaged, and they completed the program in less time than regular students.

Along with the students' level of commitment, perhaps the most important factor contributing to the program's success was that the university administration, in general, and the nursing school leadership, in particular, made a strong commitment to it. Although the program encountered a series of problems (as is common in the initial stages of any new initiative), the nursing school administration implemented numerous institutional changes to accommodate the learning needs of nontraditional students. They extended the accelerated program an extra trimester to accommodate students' academic requirements and personal circumstances, they granted accreditation based on practical experience through written exams and practice tests, and they waived math and English prerequisites for admission. These initiatives are even more significant in the context of a large university system, which rarely offers associate's degrees.

In addition to institutional changes, the nursing school administration also promoted the use of innovative teaching methods to facilitate student learning. Promoting new instructional practices is never without perils, yet the program negotiated every challenge.

The program also provided academic support services and case management to participants. It called upon the services of the financial aid staff to offer orientation workshops, and offered study habit tutorials as a way to supplement classroom instruction and help students overcome academic shortcomings. The program also appointed a full-time program coordinator, who provided overall orientation, information, and advocacy.

Inter American University's nursing school maintains a close professional relationship with a number of local hospitals as part of the in-hospital practices students must perform during their training. Through these connections, the program links students to prospective employers; remains abreast of current hospital practices and approaches; and can develop cooperative ventures involving professional development of hospital staff, instructors, and university students.

Ultimately, the program's success is reflected in the determination of the nursing school to continue it, supported with regular tuition fees. From the perspective of the U.S. Department of Labor, as sponsoring agency, the demonstration's most important outcome was program institutionalization. Thus, the Inter American University of Puerto Rico associate's degree nursing program exemplifies the potential role that university systems can play in creating career ladders for nontraditional students.

MODELS FOR SUPPORTING HISPANIC SUCCESS

Each of the programs and models in this study was designed to respond to the needs of the Hispanic community in a particular context. Each targeted a specific group of disadvantaged workers and, using different institutional arrangements, integrated them into other programs within the host college or university. Indeed, a common strength of the four case studies springs from the *sui generis* nature of each program, designed to address the specific needs of its targeted population.

At the same time, many elements the programs had in common also contributed to their effectiveness, and the research has sought to understand the contrasts and lessons learned. To facilitate the interpretation of research findings, the discussion is organized along the guidelines for successful programs serving the disadvantaged, particularly Hispanics.

Case Management

Prior research has shown that in effective programs, strong case management assists or links students with counseling, financial aid sources, and social services (Creason 1994; Kangas 1994).[6] When attending educational programs, disadvantaged Hispanics need to overcome multiple barriers, including low income and financial difficulties, parenting and other family responsibilities, emotional and substance abuse problems, and discrimination (Henriksen 1995).

Some of the case management questions that we explored include:

- Did the college establish a dedicated program to serve Hispanics, or did it serve them through existing, more general programs?
- Did it provide additional financial aid? Were counselors bilingual?
- Were services provided through the college, through community-based organizations, or through social service organizations? How were these links made?[7]

The most important commonality in this study is that every program had a strong case management component, even though each offered such services in its own way. The programs at Miami-Dade Community College and Albuquerque Technical Vocational Institute primarily supported students who were attending existing programs in the colleges. Nonetheless, Miami-Dade created a dedicated program, with its own counseling services and an emphasis on fostering group identity for program participants. In contrast, Albuquerque relied on staff from existing programs and focused on linking each student to a needed academic or social support service.

The Inter American University and Borough of Manhattan Community College programs were dedicated certification or degree programs targeting disadvantaged Hispanics. Case management, counseling services, financial aid, and other support services were integrated into the programs. Both targeted and developed strong links to the health care industry. However, the focus of New York's bilingual vocational training was to provide a pathway to the industry for a population disconnected from work. The Puerto Rico program for upgrading licensed practical nurses aimed to provide a career ladder for those already connected to the industry, but needing higher credentials to advance. In each program, support staff dealt simultaneously with academic issues and social problems.

Regardless of how a program structured case management, students benefited from having someone responsible for mediating their interactions with the institutions. This student-focused support system seems to have played a critical role in building student satisfaction and fostering success. Each program had a strong component of providing individual and academic counseling and coordinating other social and academic support services. In addition, each also offered a variety of life skills workshops, which offered a safe environment in which students could discuss problems, get information on resources within the college and the program network, and learn strategies for dealing with individual problems.

Another important finding was that programs that created student support groups and fostered a sense of group identity were more effective in helping students mediate multiple social and academic problems. Students used the support groups to solve day-to-day problems and learn from one another. Whether the programs were dedicated, self-contained, and relatively isolated from the rest of the college (as in the Manhattan and, to some extent, Puerto Rico cases) or depended more on regular class offerings and existing programs (as in Albuquerque and Miami-Dade), students' participation in regular group activities created a sense of belonging. In this context, common ethnicity played an important role in reinforcing group identity in relation to other students and the institutions.[8]

In a qualitative study, it is difficult to attribute exact causality to different outcomes, but there is no ambiguity in the four demonstrations regarding the positive role of strong case management in program success. Similarly, while it is hard to determine the relative impact of individual case management by dedicated staff versus group activities and group solidarity among students, both contributed significantly to program success and complemented one another.

Instructional Practices, Curriculum, and Academic Support

Student-focused instructional practices are essential for disadvantaged Hispanics to succeed in college. Given their educational background, many need noncredit, remedial courses in order to complete college-level math and English courses. Also, given nontraditional students' previous experiences with the educational system, integrated work and learning programs often provide an appropriate context for success (Camacho 1995; Jalomo 1995; Kangas 1994; Kraemer 1996). In this study, we posed such questions as:

- Did the program offer these and other successful strategies (e.g., combining English as a Second Language [ESL] courses with vocational training)?
- Did the program facilitate the creation of small, peer support groups and peer mentoring?
- Did the program implement faculty training to promote empathetic teaching and a positive classroom experience?

A common element among the demonstration projects was the provision of academic tutors and, in some cases, student (or peer) mentors. Academic support played a major role in students' success in approving finishing courses and programs. In fact, the typical student could not have succeeded in college-level courses without first taking noncredit remedial courses. Or, if they did take regular college-level courses, the students would have needed continuous academic support to succeed.

The demonstrations provided academic support in different ways. In addition to tutors or student mentors, the Puerto Rico and Manhattan programs also had faculty teach special sections or labs in which students discussed class materials in a less formal setting. Students considered these sections extremely useful, not only in helping them understand the material better, but also, in many instances, in creating a more positive learning environment. The students felt more confident about asking questions and developed personal relationships with the instructors more easily. Few of these sections were structured into the programs, however; often, instructors organized them informally on the basis of need or as requested by students.

Not all professors took similar initiative or demonstrated strong empathy toward the students. However, in Puerto Rico and Manhattan, the two programs structured as dedicated, self-contained units, most instructors offered labs or review sessions. They often provided handouts summarizing the most important points of a lecture and distributed other supplementary material to students. They also organized small group discussions during regular class times and practiced other student-focused techniques that facilitated learning. The most effective professors were attracted to these programs because of their own philosophical predisposition to and prior experience in teaching disadvantaged students. Very rarely did the other programs incorporate these student-focused instructional practices as part of their program design.

Another area in which the dedicated programs at IUPR and BMCC had an advantage was in curriculum design. Their courses and competencies related directly to industry expectations or state certification, and the nexus between employability and education was readily apparent. In the Manhattan program, the whole curriculum was designed to integrate vocational education with ESL and other scientific concepts necessary to work in the mental retardation field.

In sum, these demonstrations were more successful when they incorporated a strong academic support system for students, student-focused instructional practices, a curriculum developed in agreement with industry expectations, and faculty that played a proactive role in mentoring.

Program Design

Student-focused program design matters. For instance, school-based programs designed to integrate certificate-granting with degree-granting instruction provide an educational continuum that allows nontraditional students to complete a college degree while earning income. A student-focused program design might also accommodate working parents' schedules or offer distance learning opportunities. Another example of student focus is the development of life skills and employability workshops as integral curriculum components (Abbot 1978). In assessing program design, therefore, we asked the central question: Did it incorporate effective and successful student-focused strategies when serving the needs of disadvantaged Hispanics? As noted, the demonstrations used two main approaches: the dedicated-service approach and the integration, or mainstreaming, approach; each had its own advantages.

The nature of *dedicated* programs enhanced their influence over curriculum design and faculty participation. Beyond that, they were much better at fostering group identity and promoting solidarity among students. The more cohesive the group, the more support they could give one another. Students interviewed across all programs reported that peer support and encouragement were critical for success. Students in dedicated programs spent a significant amount of time in daily activities performed collectively. In contrast, the weekly or sporadic group activities in the integration programs were insufficient to facilitate academic and social connections, and the development of group identity and networking was relatively weak.

Dedicated programs developed closer links to industry and employers, and they had more clearly articulated career ladders within specific industries. IUPR, for example, made an accelerated associate's degree program accessible to displaced or underemployed practical nurses. This clearly represented an extraordinary effort from a large university system to open its doors to a nontraditional student population. The year-round/trimester format allowed students to finish a two-year degree in one year.[9] In conjunction with the block scheduling of classes in either the early morning or mid-afternoon to accommodate working students, this design facilitated the ability of employed nurses' aides, most of them with family responsibilities, to participate in and finish the program.

The Borough of Manhattan Community College created a career ladder by bringing a six-month training program to a typical two-year educational institution. As at IUPR, students could apply course work completed during the program toward a more advanced degree—a bachelor's degree in the case of the IUPR, and an associate's degree in human services in the case of the BMCC. Both programs also eased demarcations among vocational skills, training, and education—creating, in fact, a smoother continuum for professional development.

Dedicated programs were better at integrating various support services, providing academic support, and promoting a work-oriented education. In both the Puerto Rico and Manhattan programs, scheduling shared classes and workshops for all participants allowed for more interactions among counselors, instructors, and program staff. In the case of BMCC, the staff formed a program team that met regularly to discuss student progress, frequently solving problems before they became too difficult to resolve. For example, even when counseling and job placement responsibilities clearly belonged to specific team members, all shared responsibilities for advising students, establishing contacts with employers, and teaching the employability and life skills workshops.

On the other hand, programs promoting the *integration* of participating students into regular college courses could more easily open existing support services to students and offer a diverse set of educational options. Albuquerque Technical Vocational Institute, for instance, used existing counselors to staff the Hispanic Network program. The counselors coordinated social and academic support services for students.

Their location in the central facilities for student support services greatly facilitated the coordination of counseling, financial aid assistance, monitoring of student tutors, and other support services.

The Miami-Dade experience illustrates how an integration model could be more flexible in accommodating student schedules and career choices. Its Better Opportunities for Hispanics Program took advantage of the college program for providing industry certifications. About one-third of the participating students opted to take certification courses in airline ticketing, office administration, or child development. These 10- to 12-credit options had direct connections to industry in terms of financial assistance, internships, and job opportunities. The credits earned could be applied toward an associate's degree in business administration or education.

As an added advantage, Florida regulates the transfer of credits and program requirements, so students can easily transfer course credits from one college to another. This universalization of college credits greatly benefits those who face the greatest difficulties in finishing college, require flexible schedules, or who must move often— common issues of concern for disadvantaged Hispanics. The MDCC system offered this flexibility, and the South Dade Better Opportunities program took advantage of it as part of the program design.

Such access to diverse career programs discourages the tracking of disadvantaged Hispanic students into programs that could be in low demand by industry, and makes it easier to offer opportunities to enroll in "hot" programs.[10] Tracking occurs when a disproportionate number of students are clustered into particular programs. The greatest danger in dedicated programs is that they indirectly serve to track disadvantaged Hispanics into certain occupations.

The most evident weakness of the integration strategy was that both program design and instructional practices were of secondary importance. In this respect, the MDCC design offered an interesting model, maintaining the advantages of an integration strategy while steering students to the college's certification programs, which offered advantages similar to those of dedicated programs regarding connections to employers and industry. However, only a fraction of participating Hispanic students enrolled in the certification courses.

Finally, an important advantage of integration comes from the potential to institutionalize a program within the college's regular operations after grant funding has ended. In both institutions implementing this strategy, the college administration intended to continue the package of support services for Hispanic students. Regarding the dedicated programs, the continuation of BMCC's program was contingent upon additional funding. However, the IUPR program, which pursued a dedicated approach initially, is now part of the nursing school's regular programs.

From this perspective, the demonstrations were a complete success. Hispanic-serving universities and colleges are seeking ways to better serve the needs of a nontraditional, disadvantaged student population. Although each program featured a distinct design, all shared a focus on students' needs, and the end result benefited participating students and promoted their success.

The clear lesson is that a student focus is important. Designing accommodating schedules, encouraging staff to work as a team and be aware of barriers to student progress every step of the way, being flexible in accepting credit transfers—all are important program components that have a cumulative effect on student success.

Links to Industry and Employers

Links to employers and local industry are invaluable for defining skill competencies and curricula and providing students with internships and job placements. Programs that connect with the local labor market are better positioned to attract financial support, receive donations of equipment and other resources, and become part of regional business networks. Moreover, linkages to local industry and "networking" are more effective when colleges target a particular industrial sector (Fitzgerald 1997, 1998; Rosenfeld and Kingslow 1995). In this context, it was pertinent for this research to ask:

- Did the program promote active involvement from employers?
- What kind of support did it receive from local industry?
- How did learning and support services relate to workplace experiences and long-term employability?
- How did the program help students/participants get a job?

The range and depth of activities linking the four demonstrations to employers and industry varied greatly. They ranged from a concerted effort that constituted a central part of the program design to a minimum programmatic effort with a few workshops on employment topics. All programs included workshops on workplace norms and behavior and employability skills, such as how to search for jobs. The two dedicated programs, at IUPR and BMCC, had structured internships as part of the program requirements. Students at the former practiced at local hospitals, while the Manhattan program required the completion of a 126-hour worksite internship. In addition, the BMCC program provided ongoing career-support services for graduates.

Connections to employers helped these programs in other ways. BMCC program staff consulted on curriculum with staff at inpatient care facilities. This collaboration helped BMCC develop certified, industry-standard skill competencies. The IUPR instructors had extensive experience working in hospitals and supervising certified nurses, which proved extremely useful when placing students in permanent jobs. Some graduates from both programs found jobs at the institutions where they had interned; others benefited from job referrals from these contacts.

In contrast to these direct linkages with industry, the programs following an integration model relied on other college programs to establish links. This system functioned relatively well for students enrolled in programs with existing industry connections, such as MDCC's airline ticketing certificate program. For the most part, however, the MDCC and ATVI programs remained at a basic level of employment-focused activities. Job placement was not a major goal for either program.

In short, continuous and extensive relations with employers and industry provided significant benefits to students. Employers' participation in curriculum design helped align course content with industry standards and focus it on the competencies most in demand by the local job market. Students who participated in internships benefited from valuable learning experiences that could help relate classroom learning to the world of work. In the end, program efforts to build bridges to industry aided students' transitions to permanent employment.

REINVENTING COMMUNITY COLLEGES: RECOMMENDATIONS FOR POLICY AND PRACTICE

At the most general level, there is good reason to be encouraged by the overall response of these four demonstrations to the urgent need to provide disadvantaged Hispanic job seekers with quality educational opportunities. Dedicated staff and faculty responded quickly to the Department of Labor request for project proposals, and all programs started within a few weeks of award notification.

The results proved similar to findings from previous survey data studies (Creason 1994) and program-focused, case study research (Kangas 1994): The combination of counseling, tutoring, mentoring, and networking services was a major positive influence in helping Hispanic students succeed, measured primarily as program completion. The overall conclusion is that programs designed to support disadvantaged Hispanics should, at a minimum, offer a comprehensive package of support services, including proactive case management, counseling, and tutoring in basic academic subjects. Programs should also encourage and assist students to form support networks.

It is also apparent that both dedicated and integrated strategies have advantages and disadvantages. Understanding them is important for the design of effective programs to serve disadvantaged Hispanic students. In this context, other factors also must be considered. Instructional practices and connections to industry are important programmatic areas in designing community college programs that target the disadvantaged. As previously explained, some colleges in these demonstrations were careful to incorporate these two areas in their programs, but in general, the emphasis on new instructional practices or connections to industry was weaker than the emphasis on case management, counseling, and academic support. As Henriksen (1995) has pointed out, only a small fraction of Hispanics attending community colleges transfer to a four-year college (12 percent compared with 23 percent of white students). Hence, for disadvantaged Hispanics, the emphasis in a technical program must be on defining a career path and establishing connections to industry. In innovative programs, a six-month or one-year certification can provide the first steps toward an associate's or bachelor's degree.

More specifically, several sets of policy recommendations, derived from workforce development principles for effectively serving disadvantaged Hispanics, follow from the case studies:

- Offer comprehensive case management.
- Promote student-focused instructional practices.
- Design training to be student friendly.
- Keep your eye on the prize: Create links to industry and employers.

A successful program does not need to emphasize or allocate resources in all four areas. Indeed, it may focus on just one and excel in fulfilling its mission. That said, most successful programs have developed each of these programmatic areas to some degree, and assigned and prioritized resources in two or more, depending on existing resources and student support programs.

Offer Comprehensive Case Management

Colleges designing programs for disadvantaged Hispanics should include comprehensive case management. This would take into account the multiple barriers affecting the academic success of disadvantaged populations.

These strategies should also consider the strengths that Hispanics bring to their college experience, such as group identity and ethnic solidarity. Other students who have faced or are facing similar challenges often provide the best support system. They share experiences that illustrate how to solve specific problems and suggest resources to help solve the situation. Students can strategize about how to succeed in classes and form study groups. These groups and exchanges also give students a sense of belonging in the institution.

Promote Student-Focused Instructional Practices

Recent studies on Hispanics' college experience indicate that teaching methods and other instructional practices are critical factors leading to student success in college (Camacho 1995; Jalomo 1995; Kraemer 1996). However, most community college programs designed to assist the disadvantaged place greater emphasis on counseling and tutoring (what happens outside the classroom) than on instructional practices (what happens in the classroom). Thus, program designers assume that the success of Hispanic students depends primarily on the students' preparedness and responsibility, minimizing the importance of the institutional context and pedagogical practices along with the responsibility of faculty and other staff. Pedagogy is left to the instructors, and there seems to be limited scrutiny regarding instructors' effectiveness. The classroom becomes a "black box" into which administrators and planners alike are reluctant to look.

In contrast to this pattern, we found that good teaching matters. Students describing a significant positive influence in their college experience universally acknowledge good teachers and engaging learning experiences. In one of our cases, students found math and accounting to be "easy" and "fun." These so-called hard courses worked better for students when the subject matter was taught in a clearly applied context, often as part of a specific skill competency. Most students reported working hard for a course when they felt engaged. In a recent study, however, Perrin (1998) reports that faculty resistance is a major obstacle to the integration of academic and occupational education.

It is imperative to focus attention on improving instructional practices and promoting student-focused pedagogues. A well-trained instructor uses culturally and socially relevant methods. Students prefer active learning; good teachers have learned how to engage students in projects and workplace internships that promote active learning. While committed teachers are constantly searching for new methods and better approaches to engaging students, teachers often learn best from other teachers: Teacher collaboration and training in team building should be encouraged. Good teachers engage in active mentoring of students and look at the learning experience as a multi-dimensional process that is affected by social, nonacademic factors.

Teachers' associations can provide a measure of leadership by encouraging members to use demonstrated student-focused instructional practices. It is, however, the role of administrators to promote practices that enhance learning at their institutions. In addition to facilitating the systematizing of instructional best practices among faculty, administrators also can promote ongoing professional development, for example, by organizing faculty study groups and sponsoring expert seminars on student-focused instructional practices. Colleges can organize discussions, workshops, seminars, and ongoing professional development that focus on current pedagogical developments.

Design Training Programs to Be Student Friendly

Community colleges should design programs that accommodate the time constraints and learning styles of disadvantaged Hispanics. Dedicated programs seem to provide a more encouraging learning environment. They make disadvantaged Hispanics feel welcome at the institution, encourage the formation of peer support groups, and promote students' engagement in their studies. Dedicated programs also organize instruction to facilitate attendance and accommodate parental responsibilities. Class participation encourages active learning in what students perceive to be a safe environment.

Further, dedicated programs encourage faculty to be more involved in counseling, mentoring, and promoting relations with industry. As Moscovitch (1997) and Grubb (1996) have proposed, short-term student training should be a step toward a college degree. Whether competencies are achieved through approved courses or learned in a community college or community-based organization, all training should offer the opportunity to earn credits toward a certification, and all certifications should be articulated to a college degree.

In this conceptualization, the connection between learning and work is direct and clear. Programs concatenate and build upon one another to create an educational continuum. And for students with limited English-language proficiency, contextual and vocational ESL should be an integral program component.

Create Links to Industry and Employers

Community colleges with strong connections to employers enhance students' learning experiences and employment opportunities. In these colleges, curriculum and resources are more synchronized with technological change and the skills demanded by industry. Supporting the view of Fitzgerald and Jenkins (1997) and Rosenfeld and Kingslow (1995), this study found that community college–based technical training programs are more effective when they are closely linked to employers and industry.

NOTES

This chapter is based on *Opening Doors for Hispanics: An Assessment of the HACU* [*Hispanic Association of Colleges and Universities*] *Demonstration Project* (Boston: Mauricio Gaston Institute, 1998). The research has been supported by a grant from the U.S. Department of Labor, Employment and Training Administration, Office of Employment and Training Programs. The full report is available from the authors upon request. This research project could not have been completed without the support and encouragement from Josephine Nieves, Alicea Fernandez, and Gloria Salas from the department. Thanks are also due to the program directors and other staff who sponsored visits to the colleges, and to the support provided by the staff of the Mauricio Gaston Institute at University of Massachusetts, Boston.

1. See Brint and Karabel (1989) for a survey of the literature and analysis on the contending views on the appropriate role of community colleges in servicing the skill-training needs of local industry and in educating disadvantaged populations.

2. An assessment, in this context, consists of a review and interpretation of the evidence following a case study method. We used multiple data sources including interviews, group discussions, analysis of program documents, quantitative indicators, and others. An assessment is not a research strategy similar or comparable to formal program evaluations that follow the experimental designs of demonstration projects and carefully monitor the impact of programs on participants.

3. See, for example, Giloth (1998), Harrison and Weiss (1998), Joyner (1996), Grubb (1996), Moscovitch (1997), Meléndez (1996), Morales (1998), Orr et al. (1994), Stokes (1996), and U.S. Department of Labor (1995).

4. For an introduction to this method, see, for example, Yin (1984). For examples of applied research in this field, see Fitzgerald (1998), Fitzgerald and Jenkins (1997), Joyner (1996), Harrison and Weiss (1998), Meléndez(1996), Meléndez and Harrison (1998), Molina (1998), Seavey (1998), Rosenfeld and Kingslow (1995), Siegel and Kwass (1995), and Stokes (1996).

5. The data were collected between September 1997 and June 1998, and thus may not reflect more recent developments.

6. Case management is that part of program staff (counselors, coordinators, etc.) dedicated to monitor student progress, facilitate access to services, and provide assistance in problem solving so participants can complete a program successfully.

7. The research protocol for the case studies is included as an appendix to the report *Opening Doors for Hispanics.*

8. Group identity was also evident in the IUPR case in which ethnic identity played a lesser role, given Puerto Rico's more homogeneous cultural context, compared with ethnic diversity in the states. Group identity and solidarity were also important among students enrolled in TANF-sponsored welfare-to-work programs in community colleges. For a more detailed analysis of community colleges' involvement in welfare-to-work programs, see Meléndez (1999).

9. This design proved to be very ambitious, and eventually administrators extended courses for one more trimester; even so, this substantially reduced the time required to complete the program.

10. Generally, "hot" programs are defined as those in which graduates are employed in their chosen career track within 30 days of completing the program. Typically, these students are offered better salaries than in other occupations requiring similar training or education, and they find more internships and advancement opportunities.

REFERENCES

Abbot, William L. 1978. "Beating Unemployment through Education." *The Futurist* (August).

Brint, Steven, and Jerome Karabel. 1989. *The Diverted Dream: Community Colleges and the Promise of Educational Opportunity in America, 1900–1985.* New York: Oxford University Press.

Camacho, Julian. 1995. *The Latino Experience: New Implications for Compton Community College.* Compton, Calif.: Compton Community College.

Creason, Paul. 1994. *An Analysis of Success Indicators for Latino Students at Long Beach City College.* Long Beach, Calif.: Long Beach City College.

Dresser, Laura, and Joel Rogers. 1998. "Networks, Sectors and Workforce Learning." In *Jobs and Economic Development,* edited by Robert Giloth. Thousand Oaks, Calif.: Sage Publications.

Fitzgerald, Joan. 1997. *Making School-to-Work Happen in the Inner City Schools.* Chicago: Great Cities Institute, University of Illinois at Chicago.

———. 1998. "Is Networking Always the Answer? Networking among Community Colleges to Increase Their Capacity in Business Outreach." *Economic Development Quarterly* 12 (1): 30–40.

Fitzgerald, Joan, and Davis Jenkins. 1997. *Making Connections: Community Colleges' Best Practices in Connecting the Urban Poor to Education and Employment.* Chicago: Great Cities Institute, University of Illinois at Chicago.

Giloth, Robert, ed. 1998. *Jobs and Economic Development: Strategies and Practices.* Thousand Oaks, Calif.: Sage Publications.

Grubb, W. Norton. 1996. *Learning to Work: The Case for Reintegrating Job Training and Education.* New York: Russell Sage Foundation.

Harrison, Bennett, and Marcus Weiss. 1998. *Workforce Development Network: Community-Based Organizations and Regional Alliances.* Thousand Oaks, Calif.: Sage Publications.

Henriksen, Janel A. S. 1995. "The Influence of Race and Ethnicity on Access to Postsecondary Education and the College Experience." ERIC Document Reproduction Services No. ED386242. Office of Educational Research and Improvement, U.S. Department of Education. Los Angeles, Calif.: Clearinghouse for Community Colleges.

Jalomo, Romero, Jr. 1995. *First Year Student Experiences in Community Colleges: Crossing Borders, Making Connections and Developing Perceptions about Learning.* State College, Pa.: National Center on Postsecondary Education Teaching, Learning, and Assessment.

Joyner, Carlotta C. 1996. "Employment and Training: Successful Projects Share Common Strategy." Testimony before the Subcommittee on Human Resources and Intergovernmental Relations, Committee on Government Reform and Oversight, U.S. House of Representatives. Washington, D.C.: U.S. General Accounting Office.

Kangas, Jon. 1994. "ENLACE Success Rates Compared to Success Rates of Other Chicano/Latino Students in the Same Courses, Spring 1994." Research Report #861. San Jose, Calif.: Evergreen Community College.

Kraemer, Barbara. 1996. "Meeting the Needs of Nontraditional Students: Retention and Transfer Studies." Paper presented at the annual meeting of the North Central Association, Chicago, Il., March 23–26.

Meléndez, Edwin. 1989. "Towards a Good Job Strategy for Latino Workers." *Journal of Hispanic Policy* 4.

———. 1996. *Working on Jobs: The Center for Employment Training.* Boston: Mauricio Gastón Institute, University of Massachusetts.

———. 1997. "The Potential Impact of Workforce Development Legislation on Community-Based Organizations." *New England Journal of Public Policy* (Fall/Winter): 175–86.

———. 1999. *The Welfare-to-Work Policy Shock: How Community Colleges Are Addressing the Challenge.* Boston: Mauricio Gastón Institute, University of Massachusetts.

Meléndez, Edwin, and Bennett Harrison. 1998. "Matching the Disadvantaged to Job Opportunities: Structural Explanations for the Past Successes of the Center for Employment Training." *Economic Development Quarterly* 12 (1): 3–11.

Molina, Frieda. 1998. *Making Connections: A Study of Employment Linkage Programs.* Washington, D.C.: Center for Community Change.

Morales, Rebecca. 1998. *Project QUEST: An Embedded Network Employment and Training Organization.* In *Networking across Boundaries,* edited by Bennett Harrison and Marcus Weiss. Boston: Economic Development Associates Consortium.

Moscovitch, Edward. 1997. *Closing the Gap.* Boston: Mass Inc.

Orr, Larry, et al. 1994. *The National JTPA Study: Impacts, Benefits, and Costs of Title II-A.* Cambridge, Mass.: Abt Associates, Inc.

Perrin, Dolores. 1998. *Curriculum and Pedagogy to Integrate Occupational and Academic Instruction in the Community College: Implications for Faculty Development.* New York: Community College Research Center, Teachers College, Columbia University.

Rodriguez, Eric, and Deirdre Martinez. 1995. *Latinos and Jobs: A Review of Ten States and Puerto Rico.* Washington, D.C.: National Council of La Raza.

Romero, Carol. 1990. *Training Hispanics: Implications for the JTPA System.* Washington, D.C.: National Commission for Employment Policy.

Romero, Carol, and Frank Romero. 1997. *The Response of Federal Policy: Job Training Programs.* Washington, D.C.: National Council of La Raza.

Rosenfeld, Stuart, and Marcia Kingslow. 1995. *Advancing Opportunity in Advanced Manufacturing: The Potential of Predominantly Minority Two-Year Colleges.* Carrboro, N.C.: Technologies Strategies, Inc.

Seavey, Dorie. 1998. *New Avenues into Jobs: Early Lessons from Nonprofit Temp Agencies and Employment Brokers.* Washington, D.C.: Center for Community Change.

Siegel, Beth, and Peter Kwass. 1995. *Jobs and the Urban Poor: Publicly Initiated Sectoral Strategies.* Somerville, Mass.: Mt. Auburn Associates, Inc.

Stokes, Robert. 1996. *Model Welfare-to-Work Initiatives in the United States: Effective Strategies for Moving TANF Recipients from Public Assistance to Self-Sufficiency.* Report prepared for the Connecticut Business and Industry Association by RSS Associates, Hartford, Conn.

U.S. Department of Labor. 1995. *What's Working (and What's Not): A Summary of Research in the Economic Impacts of Employment Training Programs.* Washington, D.C.: U.S. Government Printing Office.

Yin, Robert. 1984. *Case Study Research.* Newbury Park, Calif.: Sage Publications.

16

Workplace Education Investments and Strategies for Lower-Wage Workers

Patterns and Practices in Employer-Provided Education

Amanda Ahlstrand, Max Armbruster, Laurie Bassi,
Dan McMurrer, and Mark Van Buren

Learning is the foundation for change, and, in an era of unusually rapid change, it takes on special significance. For workers with the capacity to learn and adapt, change can create opportunities for higher wages and better jobs. Without it, however, change is a threat. For workers, this threat can come in the form of reduced wages, job loss, or prolonged periods of unemployment.

After people leave the education system, they get much—possibly most—of their ongoing, formal education and training through their work. Consequently, workplace education is critical to workers' capacity to prosper in a rapidly changing economy.

There are two sides to this equation. First, workplace education must be available. That is, there must be an adequate supply from employers who believe it is in their self-interest to provide opportunities for ongoing education. Second, there must be demand: Workers must see it as in their interest to avail themselves of workplace education.

It is now well established that the probability that workers receive workplace education is directly proportional to their wage and education levels.[1] Workers with the highest wages and the most formal education receive the most workplace education; lower-wage workers and those with the least education receive the least. This is problematic from a public policy perspective, because the available evidence indicates that workplace education is typically more successful in raising earnings among lower-wage workers than government-provided training programs. In short, those who could arguably benefit the most from workplace education are the least likely to get it.

327

Less clearly understood is why. The supply side of the equation might be the cause, or it may be a dearth of demand. Alternatively, it could be that both the supply of and demand for workplace education for lower-wage workers lead to its disproportionate distribution.

In addressing that issue, we summarize what has been learned in a major, ongoing study of workplace education and training for lower-wage workers. To date, the study, funded by the W. E. Upjohn Institute and the Ford Foundation, has tackled the "supply" side of the equation—employers; that is the primary focus here. As the study unfolds, we will undertake a more detailed examination of the issue from the perspective of workers.[2]

METHODOLOGY AND SOURCES OF DATA

For the most part, this study defines a lower-wage worker as an individual who earns less than $10 an hour. At some points in the analysis, education (high school or less) is added as a second factor.[3]

The primary source of data has been generated by the ASTD Benchmarking Service, a major initiative launched by the American Society for Training and Development in 1997. This effort gathers data on employers' education and training investments and practices. Employers submit their data to ASTD, using common definitions and metrics; ASTD returns a customized benchmarking report that enables employers to compare their investments with those of other comparable employers. This generates a large database that ASTD can use for a variety of research.

In 1998, the initiative was expanded: (1) to collect "benchmarkable" data on the outcomes of employers' education and training practices; and (2) to provide additional data on education investments and outcomes for lower-wage workers. The data collection mechanism remained more or less unchanged in 1999 and 2000.[4] The database now contains information on education and training investments and practices for approximately 2,500 employers (about two-thirds are U.S.-based), as well as summary information on "learning outcomes" from more than 300,000 individual assessments from some 230 employers. This database serves as the primary source of quantitative information for this study.

The database includes U.S.-based responses to the *ASTD Measurement Kit*™ for 1998 and 1999. These responses are based on firms' 1997 and 1998 fiscal years, respectively.[5] Some information varies; data for 1997 reflect the responses of 754 organizations, and data for 1998 reflect the responses of 548 organizations.

A variety of other sources of data and qualitative information is also being gathered and analyzed, including a more qualitative perspective based on telephone interviews in February and March 2000 with 40 employers identified as having particularly interesting education programs for lower-wage workers. The next phase will involve more detailed case study analysis that will include a more direct focus on workers' decisionmaking with regard to education and training.

THE EMPLOYEE PERSPECTIVE

The population of lower-wage American workers is by no means homogenous. They range from upwardly mobile college students, who are working part-time, to former welfare recipients, who recently entered the workforce for the first time. The wages of the former are likely to improve as they become older, more experienced, acquire additional education, and move from part-time, temporary work to full-time, permanent jobs. For them, a dearth of workplace education opportunities may not represent a significant problem.

For other lower-wage workers, however, a lack of opportunities or incentives to learn new skills at work represents a significant problem. These are workers whose lower-wage status is unlikely to be ameliorated simply by the passage of time. This group consists disproportionately of women, immigrants, and those with little formal education.

Workers at the bottom of the earnings distribution are much less likely to receive education at work than those with higher earnings. For example, according to the National Household Education Survey, in 1995 only 22 percent of workers in the bottom quintile of the earnings distribution reported receiving employer-supported education during the previous year; 40 percent in the top quintile reported receiving such training (Bassi 2000). Similar findings emerge when the data are tabulated by education level. Moreover, opportunities for informal training are also unequally available for workers with the least formal education.

The best available evidence on the impact of workplace education and training indicates that workers receiving it earn significantly higher wages than comparable workers who do not. For example, the wage-rate benefit of 40 hours of workplace education is estimated to be 8 percent, which is as large as the return from an entire year of schooling (see, for example, Frazis and Loewenstein 1999).

Taken together, these findings point to a problematic distribution: Although workplace education is a potential tool for helping narrow the gap between the top and the bottom of the earnings distribution, it is, in fact, not serving that purpose. Instead, workplace education may well be contributing to the growth of the wage gap.

Workers consistently at the bottom of the wage distribution are likely to need a wide variety of educational remedies if they are to escape from their current status (Frazis and Loewenstein 1999). Among them can be:

- Basic skills, which are often a necessary prerequisite for pursuit of more advanced, job-specific training;
- English as a second language (ESL), for non–native English speakers;
- Computer skills, because computer usage is an increasingly important predictor of wage levels; and
- Problem-solving and interpersonal skills.

THE EMPLOYER PERSPECTIVE

Even if employer-provided training is important to employees' earning potential, why should employers provide it? In fact, economic theory predicts that employers typically will not find it in their economic interest to provide education and training, particularly for skills that have broad applicability: If an employer pays for education and training that makes an employee more productive, another employer will be able to offer the "trained" employee a higher wage. That is, employers who provide generalized education and training will experience higher turnover and be less profitable than employers that do not. This is a prediction that pertains to both high- and low-wage workers.

Of course, some very strong assumptions serve as the foundation for this prediction: Labor markets are perfectly competitive; employees work only for wages, and employers can, in fact, "buy" the skills they need. As tight labor markets drive up the price of "buying" skills, so, too, do the economic incentives to "make" skills by providing more and better training to workers earning lower wages. Nevertheless, the benefits to employers must exceed the costs. In addition, as the theory suggests, underlying forces can make it difficult for employers to recover their investments in training, particularly if their workforce is subject to rapid turnover, which is often the case with lower-wage workers.

ASTD's database makes it possible to provide a statistical overview of employers that provide unusual amounts of education and training to their lower-wage workers. In 1998, ASTD asked employers what percentage of their total training expenditures went toward training employees with less than 12 years of education. Of those that responded, 47 percent reported spending nothing; only 10 percent reported spending 15 percent or more.

Some caution in interpreting these data is warranted. Follow-up telephone surveys were made to verify responses of those who reported a percentage other than zero. This revealed that: (1) many respondents do not hire people with less than a high school education; (2) many cannot accurately distinguish this group from those who have a high school education but no more; and (3) some respondents, misinterpreting the question, responded in regard to employees with more than a high school education.

Fiscal year 1997 data were collected somewhat differently. The respondents were asked what percentage of their workforce earned less than $10 an hour, as well as what percentage had less than a high school education. Nearly 20 percent of respondents reported employing no one for less than $10 an hour; at least 10 percent of the employees of half the organizations earned less than that; and 15 percent of the organizations employed over half their workers at wages of $10 an hour or less. Fifty percent reported that 1 percent or less of their employees did not have high school diplomas. Only 2 percent reported that 50 percent or more of their workforce did not have high school diplomas.

Information was also collected on the percentage of each group receiving training. Half the organizations employing people for less than $10 an hour provide training to at least three-quarters of this group. Just over two-fifths of employers provide training to at least three-quarters of their employees who do not have high school diplomas.

With both the 1998 and 1999 *Measurement Kit*, identical questions were asked about employers' training expenditures on basic skills courses (one of 13 content categories covered by the survey). Only 25 percent of employers spent 1 percent or more on basic skills training; only 8 percent spent 5 percent or more of their training budgets on basic skills courses.

Identifying "Friendly Organizations" for Training Lower-Wage Workers

Combining variables, we identified employers that seemed to devote the most resources to training lower-wage workers, and flag them as "friendly."[6] These organizations constitute 15 percent of the sample, or 194 employers. Table 16.1 relates this subset of friendly organizations to the overall sample in terms of organizational statistics. Identifying the characteristics of friendly organizations provides a context for analyzing the barriers to and enablers for providing training for lower-wage employees. This, in turn, allows for better design of future public policy and employer practices to improve training opportunities for lower-wage employees.

As table 16.1 shows, mid-sized organizations are more likely than others to have training policies friendly to lower-wage workers. Higher concentrations of friendly organizations are found in trade and health care than in other industries. The highest representation of friendly organizations is found in the Midwest. Not surprisingly, publicly traded companies and for-profit employers are less likely to be deemed

TABLE 16.1 Percentage of Friendly Organizations and All Organizations Falling into Size Groups, Industry Groups, and U.S. Regions

	Friendly Organizations (%)	Overall Sample (%)
Size		
1–499 employees	34.9*	38.3*
500–1,999 employees	37.5*	31.1*
2,000+ employees	27.6	30.6
Industry		
Agriculture, mining, construction	0.5*	1.8*
Trade	7.2	5.9
Government	6.7	8.1
FIRE	8.8*	16.5*
Durables	10.8	10.0
Nondurables	10.3	9.0
Technology	11.9*	15.8*
Health care	20.1*	7.0*
Services	16.0	16.4
Transportation, public utilities	7.7	8.3
Region		
Northeast	17.0	17.8
South	28.9	30.7
Midwest	35.6*	30.9*
West	18.6	20.6
For-profit	58.6*	67.0*
Family owned	16.2*	12.2*
Publicly traded	30.9*	40.0*

* = Significant difference between means at .05 level.

friendly than nonprofits and government organizations, and friendly employers are disproportionately likely to be family owned.

Patterns in Key Training Measures

An examination of ASTD's key training ratios, which provide a variety of measures of training intensity, offers another avenue for understanding the differences between friendly organizations and others (table 16.2).

It is somewhat surprising that friendly organizations spend *less* per employee on training and *less* on training as a percentage of payroll compared with other organizations, although they devote more training hours per employee. A variety of factors likely explain these differences:

- Friendly organizations are typically smaller, both in terms of payroll and number of employees (table 16.3); smaller organizations typically spend less on training.
- Friendly organizations rely less on classroom delivery and more on other methods, including electronic learning, which is often less expensive.
- The training most commonly provided to lower-wage workers (e.g., orientation, safety) is likely to be less expensive than that provided to higher-wage workers (e.g., leadership and professional skills development).

Correlation analysis revealed positive relationships between friendly organizations and the following practices:[7]

- Percentage of employees that receive training;
- Percentage of training expenditures going toward new employee orientation;
- Use of job rotation/cross training;
- Use of mandatory annual training time;
- Use of skill certification;

TABLE 16.2 Key Ratio Means of Friendly versus Other Organizations

	Friendly Organizations	Other Organizations
Total training expenditures per employee	$557.09*	$762.81*
Total training expenditures as a percentage of payroll	1.61*	2.05*
Percentage of employees trained	88.67*	71.45*
Employee-to-trainer ratio	382 to 1	374 to 1
Percentage of training time via classroom instruction	74.33*	78.62*
Percentage of training time via learning technologies	9.21	8.98
Payments to outside companies as a percentage of expenditures	23.02	26.36
Total training hours per employee	34.10	27.16

* = Significant difference between means at .05 level.

- Use of documentation of individual competencies; and
- Self-rating the organization's ability to retain employees versus other organizations in the same field.

While it is not evident through correlation analysis whether being a friendly organization determines the existence of these practices or vice versa, it is interesting to note the types of training friendly organizations are likely to engage in. Conversely, training expenditures per employee, training expenditures as a percentage of payroll, percentage of training time via classroom instruction, and percentage of training expenditures on information technology skills are all negatively correlated with friendly organizations.

Although these correlations do not necessarily prove a causal relationship, they nonetheless suggest interesting possibilities.[8] For example, the positive relationship between friendly organizations and the percentage of employees receiving training suggests that these employers care more about training *all* their employees, and that their attention to lower-wage employees reflects their attention to their entire staff. Perhaps such organizations provide orientation to all new employees, regardless of job position or title.

Nor is it surprising that mandatory training correlates with training lower-wage employees. The telephone survey backed up these two correlations: Many respondents mentioned orientation and regulation-mandated courses as common training provided lower-wage employees. Moreover, the telephone surveys support the correlation between friendly organizations and their ability to retain employees. More than half the telephone survey respondents thought of their training for lower-wage workers as a recruitment and retention tool.

Table 16.3 provides additional insight into the traits and training practices differentiating friendly and other organizations.

THE IMPACT OF EMPLOYER-PROVIDED TRAINING

Part II of ASTD's *Measurement Kit™* is designed to provide "benchmarkable" measures of learning outcomes from training, so enterprises can assess whether their results fall within acceptable ranges. The *Measurement Kit™* enables enterprises to measure and benchmark learning outcomes at two different points in time: (1) an initial evaluation by learners at the conclusion of their learning event; and (2) a follow-up evaluation by learners and/or their supervisors from three to 12 months after a learning event.

Three measurements capture these outcomes. The "initial evaluation" is roughly akin to a Level 1 evaluation, in the terminology of Donald Kirkpatrick.[9] It measures learners' assessments of the potential *utility* of what they have learned, rather than a more traditional, "smile sheet," Level 1 assessment. The second and third measures are follow-up evaluations, similar to Kirkpatrick's Level 3 evaluation. One focuses on learners' assessments of the productivity effects of the learning, typically three to six months later; the other focuses on supervisors' assessments.

Respondents to Part II information of the *Measurement Kit* were asked the following background questions:

TABLE 16.3 Means of Various Organizational and Training Measures of Friendly and Other Organizations

Variable	Friendly	Other
Number of employees	3,590	6,392
Number of training-eligible employees	2,498	7,335
Payroll	$131,637,262	$236,454,376
Percentage of training expenditures on new employee orientation	9.8	7.1
Percentage of training expenditures on sales and dealer training	4.1	6.15
Percentage of training expenditures on information technology skills	10.0	12.5
Percentage of IT training expenditures toward administrative employees	25.5	16.0
Percentage of IT training expenditures toward sales employees	1.3	5.4
Percentage of employees who received training last year	84.7	65.4
Percentage of employees who will receive training next year	92.3	79.9
Use of four-year colleges/universities to deliver training (percent)	14.5	27.7
Use of product suppliers to deliver training (percent)	75.3	62.6
Use of federal, state or local government organizations to deliver training (percent)	31.2	22.5
Use of cable TV to distribute training (percent)	11.7	6.0
Use of intranet to distribute training (percent)	20.7	29.4
Use of local area network (LAN) to distribute training (percent)	28.3	35.9
Use of annual performance reviews (percent)	99.5	97.5
Use of skill certification (percent)	80.1	69.7
Use of teleconferencing to present training (percent)	41.7	30.0
Use of mandatory annual training time (percent)	68.6	49.6
Use of line on loan or rotational training staff (percent)	23.3	30.4
Use of job rotation or cross training (percent)	92.7	86.0
Use of total quality measurement (TQM) (percent)	78.6	72.1

Note: Differences are in means; all findings are statistically significant at the .05 level.

- "Do the majority of employees in these courses have fewer than 12 years of formal education?" (1998 and 1997 data); and
- "Do the majority of employees in these courses earn $10 an hour or less?" (1997 data only).

For purposes of analyzing the outcomes data, a "yes" to either question earned the course a friendly flag; using this criterion, nearly 10 percent of the 831 course types for which data were submitted were deemed friendly.

The average initial reaction of participants (i.e., their assessment of potential utility) taking friendly courses is lower than participants whose courses do not contain a majority of lower-wage coworkers (table 16.4).[10] However, in the follow-up evaluation (i.e., assessing the productivity effect of the course), on average, participants who took friendly courses were more favorable than those taking courses not deemed friendly.

TABLE 16.4 Comparison of Participants' Initial and Follow-up Evaluations of Friendly and Other Courses

	Initial Evaluation			Follow-up Evaluation		
	Friendly	**Other**			**Friendly**	**Other**
"My knowledge and/or skills increased as a result of this course."*	3.89**	4.28**	"As a result of this course, my performance on the course objectives has changed by __%."		34.50	21.16
"The knowledge and/or skills gained through this course are directly applicable to my job."*	3.97**	4.30**	"As a result of this course, my overall job performance has changed by __%."		30.42	20.14

* Initial evaluation questions are rated on a 5 point Likert Scale, with 1 = Strongly Disagree and 5 = Strongly Agree.
** = Significant at the .05 level.

Supervisors' assessments of the longer-term impacts of friendly courses are also better than for courses not provided to a majority of lower-wage/lower-education employees (table 16.5).

Since Level 1 evaluations are most common, especially in comparison with Level 3 evaluations, it is possible that some organizations have discovered less-than-desirable results through Level 1 evaluations and, therefore, directed more resources toward training other employees. Without waiting to gather follow-up information, the picture painted by initial participants is not necessarily good for justifying their training.

The Practice of Lower-Wage Employee Training

ASTD conducted 40 telephone surveys to collect information beyond that gathered by the *Measurement Kit*.[11] People from organizations in the database flagged as friendly,

TABLE 16.5 Comparison of Supervisors' Follow-up Evaluations of Employees' Performance after Receipt of Training

	Follow-up Evaluation	
	Friendly	**Other**
"As a result of this course, his/her performance on the course objectives has changed by __%."	24.35	20.07
"As a result of this course, his/her overall job performance has changed by __%."	30.83	19.14

as well as a few identified through published articles or by our advisory board, were contacted and asked for 20 to 30 minutes to participate in the survey. These surveys generated additional "qualitative" findings.

Organizational needs supersede those of individual employees in the initial phases of the training programs discussed in the surveys. That is, employers typically provide training for lower-wage employees because it is good for business, rather than simply to "do good." Nevertheless, some organizations have identified themselves as having *particularly* friendly cultures. These organizations tend to operate under a philosophy that providing training to all employees—especially voluntary training—benefits not only the organization (in terms of profits, productivity, and employee retention) but also the employees' skills, morale, work-life balance, and belief in their opportunities to advance within the organization.

The following summary of general findings from the telephone interviews helps frame the subsequent discussion:

- The mean reported percentage of an organization's workforce that is lower wage is 44.3 percent, with a range of 10 to 93 percent.
- Most lower-wage employees are concentrated in positions very much in line with the respondents' industry/business. For example, manufacturing organizations employ line workers, restaurants employ servers and cooks, and transportation companies employ bus drivers—all in lower-wage positions. In addition, lower-wage positions tend to fall into entry-level, seasonal, or part-time categories.
- Over the past few years, most organizations have experienced little change in the proportion of their employees who occupy lower-wage positions.
- Eighty-one percent of respondents use some type of technology to deliver training to lower-wage workers.
- More than 95 percent of surveyed organizations provide training for lower-wage workers on site.
- Most often, the organization's human resources department and departments with lower-wage employees shared responsibility for training lower-wage employees.

In terms of content, new-employee orientation is a major component of most organizations' training initiatives. Interestingly, some organizations mentioned that they have started to promote employees from within in order to keep orientation training costs lower.

In the service industry (tourism and restaurants, in particular), team building and customer service are key components of a successful training curriculum. Especially with respect to new hires, these types of training are of growing importance. Another major category is mandatory training, which includes such items as OSHA-required, sexual harassment, and diversity courses. Ironically, regulations seem to be both a key impetus for firms to provide training and a key factor in their lower-wage workers' lack of motivation and interest in completing it.

If the above are considered work-related programs, employers view courses on stress release, interpersonal relations (conflict resolution), English as a second language (ESL), and computer skills (when not directly job related) as personal-skills training.

Such training is often offered on a voluntary basis. Thus, not all employees are able, or encouraged, to take advantage of it.

While not all organizations offer voluntary training options, those that do tend to focus on basic skills acquisition (e.g., GED/ESL programs) and courses that may help qualify a person for a promotion or a new position. Tangible incentives to participate in voluntary training most often include pay raises and promotions; only 2 of the 40 organizations provide actual cash bonuses to employees who voluntarily take training to get certified with new skills.

Employers were also asked about feedback they receive from employees who participate in training. *The most common response was that employees are excited about the promotional opportunities and personal growth that go along with particular training programs.*

On the other hand, some respondents reported receiving less-than-enthusiastic feedback. For example, one employer said that training is always the first thing to be dropped when an employee has other things come up. Others mentioned that employees sometimes feel a lack of the managerial support that would encourage them to take advantage of a company education program. And one respondent mentioned that among employees who do not participate (a majority in this case), there is a general lack of desire to advance or improve their own skills. In this case, training and subsequent promotions do not result in significant pay increases. Thus, an employee's attitude that training not required for the current job is not worth the investment appears justified.

On the organizational side, *frequently mentioned benefits of training lower-wage employees include improvement in work quality, customer service, and employee recruitment and retention.* Other common organizational benefits are better safety and error records, increased employee satisfaction, and improved employee morale.

Tracking the training provided is increasing and becoming more consistent within the training departments surveyed. Using such measures as class hours, attendance, and expenditures, 62 percent of respondents track the amount of training they provide to lower-wage employees. Increases in employee turnover, as well as external factors (such as increased auditing), contribute to an increased focus on tracking training. One respondent reported, "Tracking helps predict future needs and is used in performance evaluations. It adds to the hiring process, helps determine the types of training that are necessary, is used in justifying training and development's existence, and is used in showing that training proactively enhances employees' job performance."

Within the sample of firms in the telephone survey, the amount of training provided to lower-wage workers is increasing. Many organizations report that their needs are evolving toward a more educated workforce. They also report they are seeking ways to compensate for a job market that does not seem to provide workers that are as skilled as they once were.

The reported lack of skilled employees does not *necessarily* translate into increased training, however. For example, one respondent remarked, "I'd rather have one employee off the floor [for lack of training] than two [because the trainer also has to leave his station to train that person]."

Only 47 percent of respondents formally assess the impact of training, using methods ranging from completely informal to formal Kirkpatrick models. With regard to the impact, respondents were also polled for their opinions on general characteristics of training that lead to better results. Keeping in mind that these answers are opinions, it is interesting to note that relatively "good" training was often related back to courses presented "closer to real life," those with energetic instructors, those in which participation was encouraged, and those with short classes. On the other hand, when asked about characteristics of courses that prove challenging, some respondents have found that classroom and lecture-delivered courses are not always well received, that soft skills are very difficult to teach, and that employees do not do well at retaining content presented in a passive manner.

Asked whether training varies in any way across employee groups, *content is the main difference between training for lower-wage employees and training for others.* Most often, the reported reason is that different groups of employees need different skills. However, several employers reported that while course content does not vary across employee groups, courses are sometimes customized to skill levels and language abilities. Most often, customized training courses are provided to lower-wage workers because they are more likely to require extra focus on basic skills, such as reading, and to require that courses be translated. One survey respondent noted that the "haves have it much better than the have-nots" as far as opportunities for training. Another respondent reported finding value in using different media (e.g., technology-delivered training) to deliver training to lower-wage employees, based on their need for slower-paced instruction. However, another respondent stated that technologically delivered training does not work for lower-wage employees, and is used only when training other categories of employees.

Respondents were also asked to discuss barriers they have encountered when training lower-wage employees. Time, language, literacy levels, managerial buy-in, shortage of staff, schedules, and attitudes were common barriers reported by many. Some organizations have overcome the more "fixable" barriers. Methods for dealing with them include translating training materials, using videos in place of workbooks, and making work schedules (of both trainers and employees) more flexible. Some organizations also have made communication with management a higher priority to promote the value of training and encourage managerial and participant buy-in.

Another survey question revealed that most of the respondents would like to provide more training to lower-wage workers. Keeping in mind that our respondents primarily were trainers, most said that, in an ideal world, the types of training they would add would include more of the training already offered: additional personal and basic skills training and refresher courses. On the other hand, some respondents reported that their organizations provide more than adequate levels of training; they were more concerned with getting people to take advantage of available opportunities.

To explore macroeconomic factors, respondents were asked about the affect of tight labor markets on training lower-wage workers. Interesting responses include:

- "The tight labor market has forced us to focus more on modifying/customizing training for lower levels of education and providing new basic skills training."
- "Turnover and the tight labor market have made it necessary to train people more quickly and thoroughly in order to get them onto the job ASAP. We cannot afford to

have people in training too long; but if the labor market loosens, we'd expect training to become a little longer again and more focused on developing skills once an employee is in the field."

- "Our practices haven't changed, but they should. We're getting a less-skilled class of employees in new hires today than five years ago, and the employees we're retaining do not often have the basic skills they need or that this group used to have."
- "There has been a dispute between HR staffing and training. HR is sending us the 'leftovers,' and training has needed to tighten up and become more of a weeding-out entity. This probably isn't too bad a situation, because it's in training that we can really tell who is going to work out and who is not. In essence, training has become the 'screen' for finding worthy employees, rather than their initial entrance test."

Respondents mention a number of other external forces also affecting training practices, such as cultural diversity, education gaps, use of technology, increased competition, the ability to use multimedia to deliver courses, and increased regulatory constraints. Also noted was training and development's shift in focus to performance consulting, which has helped bring education and training to lower-wage employees.

Tables 16.6 and 16.7 describe the organizations that participated in the survey and how they fit into the classification scheme devised to summarize findings. Table 16.6 depicts the key themes discovered through the telephone surveys; table 16.7 presents the demographics of survey participants according to these themes. The telephone survey organizations were classified into one of three groups: philosophy-driven, market-driven and nature-of-work-driven.

Philosophy-driven organizations: Training and development have historically been a part of the organizational culture and are believed to play strategic roles in increasing flexibility, employee retention, and the quality of services or products. The commitment to training stems from factors more cultural than economic. Philosophy-driven organizations represent a relatively small number of organizations surveyed.

Market-driven organizations: Training strategies are shaped primarily by economic factors, including the level of unemployment, the level of education of the workforce, the industry growth, and increases in customer service expectations. The key characteristics of training programs are strongly linked to external environmental factors, including industry standards, the level of unemployment, the level of education of the labor market, and the profitability of the sector.

Nature-of-work-driven organizations: Training strategies have evolved gradually, with the goal of better leveraging human resources in often highly specialized industries. As with market-driven organizations, the key characteristics of training programs are strongly linked to external environmental factors.

CONCLUSION AND IMPLICATIONS

Organizations that provide an above-average level of training for lower-wage employees are most likely to have between 500 and 2,000 employees. Health care and family-owned organizations also tend to provide more training to lower-wage

TABLE 16.6 Typical Actions with Respect to 10 Key Themes in Telephone Survey

Criteria	Group A: Philosophy-driven	Group B: Economic/market-driven	Group C: Economic/nature-of-work-driven
Retention	An explicit statement that the philosophy of the organization recognizes that training is an invaluable tool for recruitment and retention is made. Because of training, employees' perceptions of their workplace are improved and retention improves as a result.	Because retention is generally a problem, organizations are forced to train people because of high turnover or because they realize they must train their employees in order to help retain them.	Training is usually required by law or is so job specific that it is difficult to view training in terms of it being a retention tool.
Cross-functional training	Employees are trained to do other jobs within the organization, which helps them better understand the whole organization and how it operates.	Short on time and skills, flexibility is not pursued via training as much as hiring/letting go and/or outsourcing.	Cross-functional training is often required by the nature of the work—especially in manufacturing firms. Cross-functional on-the-job training (OJT) is implemented in order to reduce slips in the production cycle.
Employee motivation	Employees are highly motivated to participate in training because of the philosophy the organization holds toward training.	Employees are not that motivated on their own to take part in training, but when managers buy into training, they help boost employees' motivations toward training.	In an environment often highly regulated or unionized, some employees seem to have longer-term engagements with the organization. Employees' desires to stay with the organization over time have a positive impact on their motivations to participate in training.
Incentives	Tangible and intangible incentives exist for employees to take part in training. Paths toward promotions and/or pay increases are clear.	The better organizations provide a clear explanation of the payoffs and rewards to training.	Paths to promotion are often related to seniority, not performance, and there are very small, if any, financial incentives to participate in training.

(continued)

TABLE 16.6 Typical Actions with Respect to 10 Key Themes in Telephone Survey (*Continued*)

Criteria	Group A: Philosophy-driven	Group B: Economic/market-driven	Group C: Economic/nature-of-work-driven
Transferability	Education and training provide employees with new skills to move beyond their current level of employment. Employees are encouraged to take advantage of programs offering skills to move them out of the lower-wage category.	Some language or literacy skills are provided with the employers' needs in mind for maintaining their workforces, not with the improvement of the employees' marketability in mind.	The nature of the work is such that any time off the job for training strains the organization, so the provision of skills beyond those required for the job is not common.
Formalization of on-the-job training	Most training is provided in a formal fashion; thus, there is less focus on OJT training.	Because turnover is high and OJT training is relatively inexpensive, OJT training is formalized.	The nature of the work is such that formal OJT training is very common.
Managerial buy-in	Managers are key drivers behind the philosophy of the organization, so buy-in is not an obstacle to overcome.	Some managers realize that to successfully deal with fluctuations in the market, they need to support and encourage the training function.	Organizations struggle with managerial buy-in because managers do not necessarily see the need to pull an employee off the line or away from his/her daily tasks.
Differences	There are no fundamental differences between training provided to lower-wage and higher-wage workers.	Usually, the content of courses offered varies by occupation level. Lower-wage employees receive more specific job skill training and training required by outside regulatory entities.	Differences between higher and lower-wage employees are generally vast. "The 'haves' have got it, the 'have-nots' do not."
Innovative training	Training is not limited to the bare minimum—innovative programs have been put into place and are well received by employees. Receipt of awards and recognition from outside organizations is not uncommon.	Training departments spend almost all of their time designing, developing, and delivering training in order to react to the market, not in order to preempt the market.	Innovative training programs are very rare.
Technology	When appropriate, technology plays an important and useful role in the delivery of training.	It is not uncommon for organizations to not yet be ready to use technology to deliver training.	Training *on* technology is much more common than providing training *through* technology. However, when appropriate, CBT and other technologies are used to deliver training.

TABLE 16.7 Distribution of Philosophy-, Market-, and Nature-of-Work-Driven Organizations

	Group A Philosophy-Driven	Group B Market-Driven	Group C Nature-of-Work-Driven
Average number of employees	2,747	43,102	1,840
	Number of respondents	Number of respondents	Number of respondents
Size group			
1–499	3	4	6
500–1999	3	6	7
2000+	2	6	3
Industry			
Trade	1	4	0
Government	1	1	0
Finance, insurance, real estate	1	1	1
Durables	0	2	2
Nondurables	0	0	3
Technology	0	0	3
Health care	2	2	3
Services	3	3	3
Transportation/Public utilities	0	3	1

employees. However, these employers tend to spend less on training per employee and as a percentage of payroll, even though they generally train a higher percentage of their employees overall. They also tend to rely somewhat less on classroom training, dedicate slightly more resources to new-employee orientation, and are more likely to use governmental organizations to deliver training.

In terms of learning outcomes, courses that are delivered to a majority of lower-wage employees are not evaluated favorably by participants immediately following completion. However, after time has passed, participants and their supervisors assess the courses' productivity effects as being greater than those coming from courses provided to higher-wage employees. Further exploration of this finding is necessary to better understand its causes.

Telephone surveys made it apparent that there is a wide range of practices and policies with regard to training lower-wage employees. There are organizations that provide the bare minimum—lower-wage employees receive only training required by law. On the other hand, some organizations (few in number) have a deeply held belief that training is good. In these organizations, all employees, regardless of position, receive the same training and are actively encouraged to seek growth-oriented training opportunities on their own.

The tight labor market has most definitely affected training. Some organizations have viewed this market as an opportunity to use training to ensure current employees do not leave, while others have cut back training, fearing that production lines might shut down due to higher turnover. Some organizations report that electronic learning technologies are a highly effective method for delivering training; others report that they have been unsuccessful in using these methods.

A Note on Public Policy

Ultimately, the intent of this research is to help guide public policy aimed at increasing the quantity or quality of workplace education and training for lower-wage workers. At this point, only preliminary policy implications can be drawn; final conclusions must await completion of the case study phase.

Perhaps the most important insight is that no evidence has emerged that employer concerns about losing workers after (and perhaps because of) providing education and training are major impediments to its provision. In fact, most employers indicated just the opposite in the telephone surveys: They improve retention rates by providing education and training to lower-wage workers.

This does not rule out the possibility that the costs employers incur in providing education and training are a barrier to its provision. While virtually none of the employers in the telephone surveys mentioned the *direct cost* of providing training, some mentioned concern about the *opportunity cost* (lost productivity while workers are away from the job). This suggests that public policy interventions should take into account employer concerns that learning be delivered flexibly, with minimal lost production (e.g., where workers can access learning, particularly "developmental" learning, either before or after work).

The data also suggest that employers with training policies that are "friendly" to lower-wage workers tend to rely more on federal, state, and local government agencies for providing training than other organizations. Community colleges in many locations have become known for the flexibility and responsiveness with which they can deal with employers' requirements.

One of the most promising possibilities for reducing the costs of education and training (from both employer *and* employee perspectives) is the use of electronic learning technologies. While the fixed costs of developing high-quality content for electronic delivery can be quite high, the marginal delivery costs are very low. This appears to be a very important avenue for more in-depth inquiry in the case studies, in part given the mixed evidence from the telephone surveys on employer success using electronic learning technologies to deliver training to lower-wage workers. Some employers reported this was an important, highly effective component of their training; others indicated just the opposite. It may be that if the high fixed costs of developing quality learning content could be shared across employers with similar needs (through a learning consortium, for example), then electronic learning technologies might stimulate more provision of learning to lower-wage workers.

A related issue is a careful assessment of what works best, from the perspectives of both employers and employees. One barrier that must be overcome, mentioned by a number of those interviewed, is convincing senior management that delivering learning to lower-wage workers is worthwhile. Finding examples of what produces good outcomes may be a step toward overcoming this barrier. In the case study phase, we will focus on a small number of employers that have produced unusually good learning outcomes, based on data from the *ASTD Measurement Kit*.

Finally, public policy recommendations to stimulate workplace education for lower-wage workers must ultimately be based on the *needs* of both employers and employees. Understanding the latter will be an important component of the case study analysis that remains to be done.

NOTES

1. See, for example, Frazis et al. (1998).

2. Research for these grants was completed in late 2000, and a book examining our findings will be published by the W. E. Upjohn Institute.

3. Essentially, the individuals most of interest here are those "at risk" of harm from economic dislocation. Workers' skill level is the underlying concept of interest, but with no agreed-upon definitions or measurements of skill, the best available proxies are wage levels and, to a lesser extent, education levels.

4. The process was moved online in 2000.

5. Financial data for 1997 have been adjusted for inflation in order to be comparable with the 1998 data.

6. To identify organizations deemed "friendly" in terms of training practices for lower-wage workers, we used a combination of variables. First, we flagged all organizations reporting training expenditures of 15 percent or more going toward lower-wage workers as friendly in the 1998 data. For the 1997 data, the "percentage received" variables of both those employees earning less than $10 an hour and those with less than a high school education were ranked. After examining the rankings distribution, we flagged as friendly the top 25 percent of organizations training high percentages of lower-wage workers with less than a high school education. Next, using data pooled from 1997 and 1998, we flagged organizations where the expenditures on basic skills training fell into the top 10 percent of the distribution.

7. These correlations are statistically significant at the .05 level.

8. In addition to the descriptive statistics summarized in tables 16.1–16.3, numerous linear and logit regression models have been run. However, none shed light on the factors affecting the likelihood that an organization is friendly in its practice of training lower-wage employees.

9. In the 1950s, Donald Kirkpatrick proposed a four-level system for evaluating outcomes that result from education and training: Level 1, Student reaction; Level 2, Student learning; Level 3, Transfer of learning to the job; and Level 4, Business results. After Kirkpatrick's original work, a number of other authors also proposed Level 5, Return on investment.

10. This finding is statistically significant at the .05 confidence level. One possible explanation for these differences is that they result from a "composition effect" (i.e., if lower-wage workers are disproportionately likely to be taking courses that typically receive low initial evaluations but higher follow-up evaluations). However, regression results did not support this explanation. In fact, when we control for course type, a course's friendly designation has a statistically significant, negative effect on participants' initial evaluations. Regression results with respect to both participants' and supervisors' follow-up evaluations are inconclusive with respect to controlling for course type.

11. Organizations deemed friendly in terms of their practices of training lower-wage workers were targeted to participate in the telephone survey. All organizations reporting that their training expenditures going toward lower-wage workers were 15 percent or higher were flagged as friendly in the fiscal year 1998 data. Because the data collected as part of the *Measurement Kit*™ differed between 1998 and 1999, a different approach was used for FY 1997. Here, we used a combination of variables: (1) those ranking in the top 25 percent according to their provision of training to employees who earn less than $10 an hour and who have less than a high school education; and (2) firms ranking in the top 10 percent according to their

devotion of resources to basic skills training. We then used a list of 150 friendly firms to contact survey-eligible organizations via e-mail, fax, and phone calls. To date, we have found 40 firms willing to participate in the telephone survey.

REFERENCES

Bassi, Laurie J. 2000. "Workers at Risk." Unpublished paper prepared for the Russell Sage Foundation. February.

Frazis, Harley, et al. 1998. "Results from the 1995 Survey of Employer-Provided Training." *Monthly Labor Review* 121 (6): 3–13.

Frazis, Harley, and Mark A. Loewenstein. 1999. "Reexamining the Returns to Training: Functional Form, Magnitude, and Interpretation." Working Paper 325. Washington, D.C.: Bureau of Labor Statistics, U.S. Department of Labor.

17

Union Innovations

Moving Workers from Poverty into Family-Sustaining Jobs

Brian J. Turner

What is known about effective labor union strategies for helping low-income Americans advance into better jobs and out of poverty? What state and national policies would make it easier for unions and their partners to achieve this critical goal?

Recognizing that *the best answer to poverty is jobs* is an appropriate starting point. That means good jobs, not just any jobs—jobs with family-supporting wages, with such benefits as quality family health care and pension coverage, with support systems so workers can get to and stay in them, and with opportunities for advancing up skill progressions and career ladders. Unfortunately, these good jobs have become less and less the norm for working Americans over the past two decades, especially for people with limited education and skills.

Unions exist at the intersection of jobs, skills, and incomes. In recent decades—particularly the last 10 years—unions have created effective strategies for moving low-wage workers into good jobs. Often with new leadership and a renewed vision, labor organizations have undertaken a variety of strategies that aid low-wage workers. Their efforts include collective bargaining and public advocacy, as well as new kinds of training and job placement programs.

EDUCATION, TRAINING, AND UNION VALUES

Unions have a fundamental mission to create, sustain, and expand opportunities for good jobs, and to foster strong communities in which working families have an effective voice. Union-sponsored education and training programs fulfill this mission, because they promote the economic success of employers and their workforces. Yet, they also reflect a broader underlying commitment to improved workforce education and training.

While employers are more likely to promote workforce training in order to develop skills required in a worker's current job, unions see developing work-specific task skills as only part of their education and training mandate. Typically, union-sponsored programs seek to build the broad base of general knowledge and fundamental occupational and technical skills that can support a range of jobs. The result is not only higher levels of competence at work but also higher quality work, a better understanding of work and business practices, and wider opportunities for career advancement. Without a broad foundation of education and skill training, union leaders would likely say that, taken alone, "just-in-time training" is just too late (Sarmiento and Kay 1999).

The union commitment to workforce training rests on several building blocks. The foundation is the belief that access to education and training is a fundamental right for all—and that this access is basic to a healthy society and a strong democracy. Closely related is the union mission to create good jobs and strong communities for all working families.

While creating good jobs is fundamental to what unions do, good jobs are not very meaningful without strong communities, with an equitable distribution of income, rights, and opportunity for all—including those in poverty and suffering from discrimination. Thus, union-sponsored training and placement programs are best understood as part of two broad strategies that advance the interests of working families:

- Classically, unions raise labor and social standards through *collective bargaining,* directly raising standards for union members (including a growing number of workers in low-wage industries) and indirectly raising community or industry standards of what constitutes a good job.
- At the same time, *union advocacy* strengthens economic, labor, and social standards, policies, and services for all workers and their families, with those at the bottom generally receiving the greatest benefits.

Collective Bargaining: Union Jobs and Low-Income Workers

One basic purpose of unions is to transform bad jobs into good jobs—to sustain and expand those good jobs and to create new ones. The 16.2 million good union jobs in the U.S. economy are the product of organizing and collective bargaining campaigns. The better pay, higher benefits, and stronger worker voice that result have positive impacts for all workers, yet the impacts are greatest for those in low-wage industries and occupations and those who come from backgrounds of poverty. In fact, the most effective single step a low-wage worker can take to move out of poverty is to join a union (Freeman and Medoff 1984). Collective bargaining most directly benefits workers through improved wages, benefits, and working conditions for union members. The average weekly earnings of union workers are 33 percent higher than for nonunion workers: $615 versus $462 in 1999. For benefits, the average union advantage is more than 90 percent. Health care and pension coverage are the norm under union contracts, even as these benefits are becoming less prevalent in the overall economy. These advantages in wages and benefits often make the difference between the working poor and those with family-sustaining incomes.

Collective bargaining makes the biggest difference for workers who face the greatest barriers and the most discrimination: women and people of color (U.S. Bureau of Labor Statistics 2000b):

- For women, the union pay advantage is 38 percent.
- For African Americans, it is 42 percent.
- For Latinos, the union advantage is 52 percent.

Overall, a minority worker is more likely than the average U.S. worker to be a union member. In 1999, 17.2 percent of African-American workers were union members, while they made up only 13.9 percent of the workforce as a whole (U.S. Bureau of Labor Statistics 2000a). The percentage of Latino workers in unions is slightly lower than it is for white workers, but that gap has been closing in recent years.

The union focus on minority, female, and low-income workers has sharpened in recent decades as the weight of employment has shifted toward service industries with lower wages. Millions of union jobs have been lost in strongly organized manufacturing industries due to ballooning trade deficits and relatively rapid advances in manufacturing productivity. Even as overall union membership was stagnating from the early 1980s until the end of the 1990s, many unions in the service sector were growing significantly. This area of union growth has been a major factor in stopping the long-term decline in the union share of employment.

This new emphasis on organizing low-wage workers, along with strengthening union-community alliances (described below), is a hallmark of new leadership in the labor movement, especially but not only in service sector unions. In sectors from building services and health care to hotels and the public sector, as well as manufacturing and construction, these themes repeat. Broad recognition of the need for renewed union growth was a major factor in the 1995 election of John Sweeney as president of the AFL-CIO. In the previous 15 years, while Sweeney was president of the Service Employees International Union (SEIU), that union nearly doubled in size to more than 1 million members, with much of the increase among health care and building service workers. The new leadership of the AFL-CIO in Washington and around the country is helping generate a renewed commitment to organizing in general, and organizing low-wage workers in particular.

Recent organizing and bargaining victories have been prominent in low-wage sectors. For example:

- In Los Angeles in 1999, 8,500 janitors—mostly Latinos and other new immigrants—won a $1.90 an hour increase over three years; employers had proposed to freeze wages (at $6.00 an hour).
- SEIU has scored similar advances for low-paid building service workers through its Justice for Janitors campaign. In addition, in Los Angeles, 75,000 poorly paid home health care workers voted in 1999 to be represented by SEIU. This was the largest union organizing victory in decades.
- In the South, thousands of poorly paid textile workers—mostly African Americans and heavily female—have voted to be represented by the Union of Needletrades, Industrial and Textile Employees (UNITE).

- Twenty thousand laundry workers have joined in a national union campaign through UNITE for higher wages during the last year.
- At United Parcel Service, the major beneficiaries of the 1999 Teamsters contract agreement were part-time workers who had previously been restricted to less than full-time work and limited benefits.
- Low-income workers are organizing in health care and hospitality industries through a number of different unions. In April 2000, seven undocumented union hotel workers in Minnesota were allowed to remain in the United States after a court found that their employer had asked the INS to have them deported in retaliation for supporting an organizing drive of the Hotel Employees and Restaurant Employees Union.

Union Advocacy: Changing Public Policy

Beyond the confines of workplace and collective bargaining agreements, unions are active in campaigns and coalitions to raise labor and social standards for all workers, whether or not they are union members. Unions use their legislative advocacy in progressive coalitions focused on labor standards, education and training programs, economic development, civil rights, immigration rights, social rights, health care, and other benefits.

Raising the Minimum Wage: Unions have made the campaign to increase the minimum wage a high priority. This issue directly affects nearly 10 million workers and their families and indirectly raises wages and incomes for millions more (Bernstein and Schmitt 2000; Bernstein and Brocht 2000). By 1998, after 10 years of significant inflation and no congressional action, the value of the federal minimum wage had fallen to the lowest real level in more than four decades. Even today, after the 1998 increase, the federal minimum wage is worth 30 percent less than it was in 1968.

The AFL-CIO's call that "America needs a raise" applies most urgently to workers at the bottom of the economic ladder, those whose incomes have fallen most steeply since the 1970s. Raising the minimum wage has its major impact on low-income working families, with little direct benefit to union members. The same could be said for many other advances in labor standards, health care, and other public policies that unions actively support.

Achieving Living Wages: Living wage campaigns by local union-community alliances are an important new strategy, complementing efforts to raise the minimum wage for all workers. Between the mid-1990s and the middle of 2000, living wage coalitions raised the floor of wages and benefits for workers employed by suppliers and contractors to more than 45 city and county governments. The direct beneficiaries are tens of thousands of working families, and many others can benefit as well: The statutory living wage can become a moral minimum wage within communities. The enacted statutes have raised minimum wages for government contractors to as high as $11.42 an hour.[1] As of mid-year 2000, living wage campaigns were underway or in development in 87 additional cities and counties.[2]

Economic Development—New Policies for Good Jobs: Union-community alliances are also raising community labor standards through economic development programs that are broadly accountable to local stakeholders (Leroy et al. 1995, 1999). These coalitions ask why public economic development dollars should be invested to attract companies that depress community labor and environmental standards. Similarly, they ask, why should public policy help expand the pool of low-wage jobs that do not provide family-supporting wages or benefits?

As a result of these campaigns, the economic development programs of 26 cities, 16 states, and four counties now incorporate job quality, environmental, and other socially beneficial standards. These programs provide financial support only to employers who create jobs offering above-average wages and benefits. Low-income workers and their families again are the most immediate beneficiaries.

EDUCATION, TRAINING, AND PLACEMENT PROGRAMS

Just as unions have long advocated for expanded, high-quality public education for all, going back to the 19th century, they have also supported and sponsored high levels of worker education and training. This support has been consistent throughout the business cycle, not just when unemployment is low and unemployed skilled workers are scarce.[3] In other words, union support for education and training is not cyclical; nor is it limited to the largest firms. It recognizes that small and medium-sized firms currently provide very little training to their employees.[4]

The union rationale for skill development is both internal to the workplace and part of the broader commitment to improving communities.

The Internal Workplace Rationale for Skill Development: To advance the economic interests of present and future members and to secure jobs with good wages and benefits, unions typically recognize the need to increase the efficiency of organized employers. Through investments and workplace innovations that benefit both employers and workers, unions negotiate with employers to raise workers' skill levels through investments in training and workforce participation in workplace decisionmaking. Higher skill levels and greater autonomy at work confer an advantage in productivity that offsets higher wage and benefit costs. According to a recent comprehensive analysis, union-represented companies have an overall productivity advantage of 10 percent over nonunion companies that make similar investments in computer-based technology and participatory work practices (Black and Lynch 1997). A number of other studies, looking at different industries, have measured the productivity advantage of union workers at 11 to 51 percent (Brown and Medoff 1978; Allen 1984, 1986).

The Community Rationale for Raising Skill Levels and Living Standards: From their 19th century origins, American unions have recognized that they cannot achieve their goals if only some workers gain jobs with good conditions and wages. Good jobs in a few segments of the economy do not strengthen communities or support education systems and other public services that can broadly advance the condition of working families. That awareness has been sharpened during the last two decades, as social inequalities have widened dramatically and the economic viability of working families has eroded.

In many communities, regions, and industries, "high-road partnerships" are emerging that combine the goals of achieving higher skills, higher wages, and higher levels of worker voice at the workplace and in the community. These partnerships bring together unions, employers, community groups, educators, and local government to work together toward these goals. This high-road approach offers an attractive option for working families and their communities, compared with the discouragingly prevalent approach built on low skills and low wages.

High-road partnerships bring together people and organizations based on the understanding that the low road—with low skills and low pay and benefits—is insufficient for their communities or their industries. These coalitions are designed to actively shape a future built on good jobs and strong communities by retaining and expanding existing good jobs and creating new ones, and by building diversified, stable, regional economies that expand opportunity and provide for a broadly shared, equitable distribution of wealth (AFL-CIO Working for America Institute 2000).

While specific components may vary from community to community, the high road has several basic elements:

- Increased worker and community voice—through unions, community groups, and employers—to shape economic development within the region and its industries and to support the growth of jobs that have rising skill requirements and earnings potential;
- Good skills with continuing education and training opportunities tied to meaningful career ladders;
- Companies that compete in the marketplace by offering quality services and products incorporating technological innovations and unique qualities that customers value; and
- More equitable distribution of opportunities and incomes throughout the population.

As we have seen in recent decades, the "market" of business decisionmakers will not move the economy onto the high road on its own. Getting to the high road requires an active engagement by workers, their unions, and community allies. On this partnership basis, the high road is being consciously chosen in growing numbers of communities and industries by workers and their unions, by employers who recognize that their future success depends on a skilled workforce, and by community leaders who see that strong skills and good jobs in stable industries are the foundation of economic prosperity and social equity. Including low-income workers within union-sponsored education, training, and placement programs is a natural step within the framework of these emerging partnerships.[5]

This dual rationale—both internal to the workplace and community-oriented—is spurring several types of union-sponsored education, training, and placement services for low-wage, low-skill, and disadvantaged minority and new immigrant workers. Recent innovative approaches include the reorientation of long-standing programs as well as completely new kinds of initiatives. In general, these programs can be broken out into three different types:[6]

- Recruiting minorities and low-wage workers into unions and union jobs, with the provision of education and training to support initial placement and later career advancement;

- Raising standards for skills, wages, and benefits through training or through hiring hall placement in occupations or industries that lack union contracts; and
- Education, training, and job referral services for community and family members, with support for placement wherever jobs are available, whether in organized units or with unorganized employers.

Recruiting, Training, and Placing Low-Income Workers in Union Jobs

Many unions and union-sponsored programs reach out to new communities of workers, assisting in recruiting new hires through education and training. Operating through employers with union contracts and community-based organizations of all kinds—from congregations and interfaith groups to civil rights and neighborhood organizations—unions provide community members with access to existing skill enhancement and job placement programs. For example:

- *Through a variety of vehicles, unions are providing former welfare recipients, long-term unemployed and dislocated workers, and other low-income workers with access to quality job training programs linked to a concrete job with a union contract.* Specific examples include the Milwaukee Jobs Initiative; health care union programs; the training programs of the Hotel Employees and Restaurant Employees; and preapprenticeship, apprenticeship, and journeyperson training in a number of building trade unions. Most of these programs use negotiated private funding, while some also draw on public job training funds (i.e., Temporary Assistance for Needy Families [TANF] and Welfare-to-Work grants, Job Training Partnership Act [JTPA] funds, and funds from the U.S. Department of Housing and Urban Development).
- *UAW contracts with the "Big 3" auto makers have established an affirmative action, outreach, and training program to recruit minority workers for skilled-trades jobs in plants where minorities are underrepresented in these highly paid jobs.* The UAW won this program in its most recent contract negotiations, anticipating a major demographic turnover as tens of thousands of skilled workers reach retirement.
- *Union-negotiated career ladders and internal mobility policies require employers to provide new entry-level workers with opportunities to advance to secure, well-paying jobs.* These are part of negotiated training and upgrading programs in the health care, hospitality, construction, and other sectors.
- *Unions are providing ex-military personnel and ex-offenders with access to training, skill certifications, and job placement.* These efforts use funding from the U.S. Department of Labor, the Veterans Administration, and other sources.
- *A large number of unions and labor federations have built relationships with local school systems to provide at-risk students with productive work experiences and job placements upon graduation.* Leading examples include the Utility Workers in Southern California, the Hotel Employees and Restaurant Employees in Atlantic City, the Operating Engineers in Illinois, and the Electrical Workers (IBEW) in Seattle.[7]
- *Many unions are negotiating innovative, mandatory, apprenticeship slots for low-income and minority workers in socially oriented "project labor agreements"—PLAs—governing*

major construction projects. Social PLAs have been negotiated for major construction projects to reserve room for low-income and minority apprentices in Seattle, San Francisco, New Orleans, Boston, Washington, D.C., Los Angeles, and elsewhere. In these agreements, a percentage of apprentice slots are set aside explicitly for low-income residents, people of color, women, or economically disadvantaged populations to assure access to training and job opportunities in the construction trades. Sought by unions and community allies, these agreements focus on public construction projects, especially those that cut through low-income areas (e.g., the Alameda Corridor Project south of Los Angeles) or involve reconstruction of low-income housing. In these latter projects, low-income housing residents are specifically identified for training and employment in union-negotiated projects (e.g., in Philadelphia and New Orleans). Many unions have recently broadened the mission of their apprenticeship programs to support outreach to low-income workers and unorganized workers who lack the full set of journeyperson skills for construction crafts.

Raising Standards in the Absence of Unions

Unions are developing education, training, and skill certification programs in traditionally low-wage industries and creating hiring halls for traditionally low-wage workers—such as temporary office staff. These initiatives seek to raise wage levels and provide opportunities for upgrading skills and to provide access to support services for transportation and child care. In addition, unions are pursuing efforts to upgrade the legal employment status of the most highly exploited low-wage workers in a number of industries.

- *In Philadelphia, a program of the AFSCME Hospital and Health Care Workers 1199C is providing training and required certifications needed by child care workers.* This project enables participants, almost all of whom are minority women, to work in publicly funded child care facilities in the state (see below).
- *In Silicon Valley, Solutions@Work helps temporary office workers gain better wages, training opportunities, and support services, such as assistance with transportation and child care needs.* Started in early 1999, Solutions@Work is one of a number of union-based initiatives to provide better wages, benefits, and conditions for the 2.4 million workers now employed nationwide through temporary agencies. These workers typically receive far less than half the hourly fee paid to the agencies by the companies in which the temporary workers actually work. The Silicon Valley effort is a project of Working Partnerships USA, a labor-community nonprofit created by the South Bay Labor Council.
- *The Delmarva Poultry Justice Alliance is an example of union-community coalition programs to improve wages, benefits, and conditions for low-wage workers, many of them involuntarily caught up in contingent work arrangements.* In this alliance, a coalition of unions and civil rights, religious, and other community groups has joined with Baltimore's Public Justice Center to support a federal lawsuit on behalf of hundreds of poultry workers. Mostly minority workers, they lost low-paid jobs as Perdue

chicken catchers in 1992 when the company reclassified them as "independent con-tractors." The chicken catchers no longer receive the overtime pay, medical and pen-sion benefits, vacation, or profit-sharing options they had as Perdue employees. As former Perdue employee Clarence Heath told National Public Radio, "I'm told that I don't work for Perdue, but I climb into a truck that has his name on the side. I pick up chickens that belong to him. I put them in a pallet that belongs to him, which is moved by a forklift that's owned by him and put [it] on a truck, a trailer that's owned by Perdue" (AFL-CIO 1999).[8]

Education, Training, and Job Referral Services for Community Members

Many union-sponsored training programs provide free education and training for the families of their members, offering such classes as English as a second language (ESL), GED basic education, and introduction to computers and the Internet.

- *Philadelphia's Hospital and Health Care Workers Union, AFSCME 1199C, provides a job referral service for community residents—supported by collectively bargained funds—whether or not the residents are union members.*
- *Unions sponsor education programs for youth and community members in technical areas tied to their occupational skills.* Working Partnerships USA and the sign makers' local union in San Jose, California, provide training to low-income Latino high school students on computer graphics, using donated computers negotiated by WPUSA and located in the East San Jose High School. At night, the union uses the equipment for educating and training its membership.

PROGRAM PROFILES

Seeing how some leading programs have been established and grown gives a more con-crete sense of their operations and how the different parts of their work fit together. These thumbnail case studies from the health care, hospitality, and construction indus-tries suggest the range of union innovations in education and training initiatives that target low-wage and minority workers.

Hospital and Healthcare Workers Union

District 1199, the Hospital and Healthcare Workers Union, set up training and upgrade funds in its two largest areas of operations—New York (starting in 1969) and Philadelphia (in 1974). Both programs initially provided occupational skill training for new entrants and for career progression in a workforce that was (and is) largely minor-ity, and in occupations that were poorly paid before the unions were organized (e.g., food services, housekeeping, medical technician occupations). With the dramatic restructuring of health care delivery systems since the late 1980s, these programs have added dimensions of lateral job mobility and an even greater emphasis on job upgrades and job security.

In New York, where 1199A (now part of SEIU) represents 67,000 health care workers at facilities under the umbrella of the Hospital League of New York, the union negotiated an Employment Security Program in 1992 and an Industry Stabilization Program in 1994. In a period of major restructuring and turbulence, a joint Planning and Placement Fund makes it possible to track changing demand for workers in different occupations and to provide training for union members and others in occupations that will need workers. More than 150 employers have agreed to give hiring preference to laid-off 1199 members and to other workers referred through this program's new Employment Center.

With restructuring-connected layoffs rising from 1,150 workers in 1996 to 2,945 in 1997 and 2,291 in 1998, the active intervention of these programs reduced the percentage of workers who became unemployed from 53 percent in 1996 to 14 percent in 1997 and 7 percent in 1998. More than 98 percent of 1199 members participating in the Job-to-Job program complete the training they start, and more than 95 percent have been successfully placed in new positions. More than 7,000 workers had completed Job-to-Job training as of early 1999.

Beyond Job-to-Job, overall program activities reach an additional 17,000 workers annually. Negotiated employer contributions to the three core programs now total $21 to $23 million annually, and public funding provides an additional $10 million each year, with those amounts rising in recent years.

In Philadelphia, 1199C, now part of the American Federation of State County and Municipal Employees, likewise expanded its operations to train and retrain in order to prevent job loss for union members and to provide training for community members seeking employment in hospitals and health care. The program serves 17,000 union members in Philadelphia hospitals and health care, but approximately 40 percent of their training and counseling participants come from outside the union. A program that reaches beyond current union members is the training and certification described above, which enables participants to work in publicly funded child care centers.

One of the largest efforts of the AFSCME-1199C training and upgrade program is its extensive job referral and training service, which is not restricted to union members. The Community Job Referral Program annually serves some 18,000 low-income people who are not union members. Employers under contract with the union have agreed to consider applicants for job openings from a hiring hall that provides referrals and training to community members. About 10,000 calls a year come into the hiring hall program. This effort reflects the union's strategy to serve workers who are not currently union members in order to maintain and strengthen union-community links and to institutionalize an ongoing role for the union in the health care labor market. It is also providing training and required certifications for hundreds of child care workers who are not members of any organized bargaining unit but who are associate members of the union.

The program's collectively bargained budget comes to about $3 million annually. This is roughly matched by funding from public sources, including U.S. Department of Labor disadvantaged and dislocated workers grants; adult basic education, TANF, and Welfare-to-Work funds; and grants from the Philadelphia School District and the Philadelphia Health Department.

The Hospitality Industry: Hotel Employees and Restaurant Employees

In San Francisco and Las Vegas, locals of the Hotel Employees and Restaurant Employees (HERE) have used collectively bargained training programs to upgrade the skills of existing hotel staff and provide entry-level training for thousands of formerly low-income workers.

In San Francisco, the goal of HERE Local 2 in the early 1990s was to stabilize the union-represented share of the industry, which had experienced fractious labor-management relations and was failing to grow with the market. The union negotiated with a dozen major hotels to create the Hotels Partnership Project, which took effect in 1994, covering almost 5,000 workers. A preexisting, negotiated, joint labor-management training program was substantially enlarged to become the vehicle for strengthening basic skills, upgrading occupational skills, and improving the quality of hotel services with a highly diverse workforce.

The San Francisco program now features classes taught on a trilingual basis: Spanish, Chinese, and English. As the program became established, it added new dimensions, drawing on public funds from the California Employment Training Panel and other sources for a range of purposes, including recruitment, training, and referral of former welfare clients to jobs in the hospitality industry.

In Las Vegas, HERE Local 226 first negotiated the Culinary Union Training Center (CUTC) in 1989. Since opening its doors in 1992, CUTC has quickly grown to serve over 2,500 trainees each year. The center's dual purpose is to provide preemployment training for hourly workers entering the hotel industry and upgrade training for current union members. It offers occupational training to highly diverse groups of clients, including Bosnian refugees referred by the Las Vegas Interfaith Council for Worker Justice, workers coming off public assistance and referred by the Nevada Department of Human Services, and many other low-income people from the Las Vegas area or coming into Las Vegas seeking good jobs.

CUTC training courses cover a range of food service and housekeeping occupations in the hospitality industry. Instructors are union members with professional experience in those occupations. Being workers themselves, the instructors can more easily establish a worker-to-worker rapport with their students.

CUTC and the Department of Human Services report that the center has a very low dropout rate, even for "hard-to-employ" clients. More than 70 percent of program graduates are placed in union hotels; as of late 2000, the lowest wages were $10.70 an hour, with good health care benefits and opportunities for future promotions. According to the Department of Human Services, CUTC's average cost per trainee—$550—is the lowest among training providers for former welfare clients, while its graduation, placement, and retention rates are the highest, as are wage and benefit levels on placement. CUTC is also the largest training provider for Department of Human Services clients. Sixty-nine percent of CUTC graduates land jobs with HERE-represented employers, whereas an undetermined fraction of other graduates end up working elsewhere in the industry. Program graduates at represented hotels have half the turnover rate of new hires not trained at the center.

Beyond entry-level training, the CUTC provides extensive upgrade training. Union members who complete training for dozens of better-paying occupations have excellent chances of moving up with their present employers or other union-represented employ-ers in the rapidly expanding Las Vegas hospitality industry.

CUTC costs through 2000, totaling $1.5 million annually, have been borne 100 per-cent by collectively bargained employer contributions. Occupational training students are asked to pay a $22.50 enrollment fee, but the Department of Human Services pays it for their referrals. The center is exploring further expansion and considering apply-ing for public funds for its services to low-income and disadvantaged workers.

Building Trades Unions Outreach to Minorities and Women

A number of building and construction trades unions are opening their doors to work-ers who previously might not have had connections or opportunities to join previously.

Community project labor agreements create apprenticeship and preapprenticeship opportunities in many construction crafts for disadvantaged workers through contract requirements on publicly financed construction projects. Community PLAs combine two important features:

- A commitment from a broad group of building trades unions and contractors to bring specific numbers of low-income, minority, and women workers into craft apprenticeship training; and
- A preference or requirement in the contract bid specifications for having a signifi-cant percentage (e.g., 15 percent) of project construction workers enrolled in bona fide apprenticeship programs, with linked targets (e.g., 25 percent of all apprentices) for creating apprenticeship opportunities for low-income, minority, and women workers.

With these commitments in place from construction unions and these require-ments from those seeking bids for major construction projects, the result has been the creation of thousands of career opportunities in many construction crafts for under-represented groups with limited alternatives.

One of the first and most highly developed community PLAs began in the Seattle region in 1994. Seattle has an unusually rich and deep effort to bring minorities, women, and other disadvantaged workers into the trades, and serious efforts toward affirmative action in building trades apprenticeship have been underway for more than 20 years. The idea of a community PLA emerged there in the early 1990s and has grown consistently from that base, reaching significant scale. Many of the innovators seeking to create community PLAs in other regions look to Seattle as a point of reference.

Community-oriented project labor agreements in Seattle require that a certain percentage (typically 15 percent) of all labor hours on a covered construction project be apprentices in state-approved apprenticeship programs. Moreover, a minimum pro-portion (ranging from 20 to 35 percent) of these apprentices must be workers of color, women, or members of other disadvantaged groups. This policy was first adopted by the Port of Seattle and the King County Labor Council in late 1993. It has since been extended to other public entities, including King County, the city of Seattle, King County public housing, and work by Washington State that falls under the authority of the governor. A number of large private contractors have voluntarily adopted these "apprenticeship utilization requirements"—AURs—and applied them to private projects worth hundreds of millions of dollars.

In 1997, King County social PLA construction projects worth $1.113 billion created 890 union apprentice opportunities in jobs with starting wages ranging from $8 to $14 an hour (1997 dollars). The proportion of hours worked by minority apprentices on PLA projects had risen to 26.8 percent in 1997, up from 23.1 percent in the first few years of the program's operation (1994 to 1996). Women accounted for 21 percent of all PLA apprentices in 1997, up from under 15 percent in 1994 to 1996 (Office of Port Jobs 1999). As an indication of an accelerating acceptance of outreach to disadvantaged populations, minority workers made up 36.1 percent of the 983 King County construction apprentices who were newly enrolled in 1998 (Office of Port Jobs 2000).

Other construction union initiatives to recruit and train low-income minority and women also have begun reaching significant scale in recent years. In many cities, these efforts have been coordinated under the America Works Partnership, a national initiative launched in 1995 by the Carpenters and Painters Unions; the Sheet Metal Workers, Operating Engineers, Cement Masons, and Roofers Unions have all joined since then. The national program leverages Welfare-to-Work grants from the U.S. Departments of Labor and Health and Human Services to support the efforts of local union-community-employer partnerships to recruit low-income residents and welfare recipients, particularly from public housing, for preapprenticeship basic skills training and then entry into expanded apprenticeship programs.

As an important part of the America Works Partnership strategy, public construction contracts must include bona fide apprentices and apprenticeship programs, thus providing funding for apprentices directly within the public works contracting stream. In 13 cities, as well as rural Alaska, the Working Together for Jobs™ program and its local partnerships are moving workers from poverty into skilled trades with family-supporting wages and benefits. A survey of 143 graduates, conducted in Camden, Philadelphia, Dayton, and Miami between June 1999 and early 2000, found that 60 percent were women (in an industry that has a 2 percent female workforce) and 99.3 percent were people of color.

Individual construction unions are also taking major steps toward creating training and employment opportunities for workers of color. Many of these initiatives are built on education and training innovations that help bring new entrants into the union—often minorities, immigrants, and people who do not have the full skill set required of a craft journeyperson entering the unions.

The Southern Nevada Council of Carpenters exemplifies union expansion through inclusion. In 1996, new leadership began developing growth strategies for a union that had not grown in step with Las Vegas's construction boom of the 1980s and 1990s. In the past, the union had excluded potential members because they lacked all the skills of journeypersons who had completed the lengthy apprenticeship-training program provided by the negotiated Carpenters Union training program. That year, the union opened its doors to "anybody who uses a hammer at work," assessing their starting skill sets and filling the gaps of missing skills through a renamed Carpenters *Journeymen's and Apprentice* Training Center that increased the size of the training facility by tenfold.

In the first three months under its new leadership and with its new strategy, the Las Vegas Carpenters Union added 1,200 new members, a one-third increase. Most of the new members were Latino carpenters from the industry's essentially unorganized residential and light commercial segments. Within three years, the union had doubled in size and doubled the amount of work available—not only to union carpenters but to their union-organized employers, who now had the labor supply to increase their presence in the regional market. The local has also developed a bilingual staff, program, and culture.

Like the Las Vegas hotel workers union, the Carpenters Union has developed deep community ties, particularly through churches and the Interfaith Council for Worker Justice, women's groups (which have provided women carpenters for the trade), and social justice advocates. Both the carpenters and hotel workers union training programs provide ESL and other educational services to family members. These unions, with employer and community partners, now operate as an effective, high-road coalition that has a voice in shaping public policy and programs in the city and state.

CONCLUSION

The Working for America Institute, created by the AFL-CIO to support union strategies for building good jobs and strong communities, is continuing a research program designed to fill the knowledge gaps about union-sponsored education, training, and placement programs and how they benefit low-income workers. This is a subject of critical importance to communities, low-wage workers, and the union movement. The case studies and analysis of programs will be important to unions and union-sponsored education and training programs, which only rarely have had or exchanged information on these topics. Among other issues, differences of economic sector, region, types of union organizations, and skill level remain poorly understood.

With support from the Ford Foundation and other sources, the research will help develop a picture of the number of opportunities for training and jobs that are available for low-income workers and of the critical features that contribute to the success of these programs. It will be one among many efforts that seek to network the community of union-related education, training, and placement providers with one another; offer ideas about ways to add value to union members, employers, and communities; and educate the broader community about these resources with track records and connections to local jobs.

While this research effort will yield better quantitative estimates of the impact of union initiatives, it already seems evident that, across the country, some tens of thousands of low-income workers currently participate in union-sponsored education, training, and placement programs each year. Most of these low-skill, low-wage workers will probably gain access to higher-paying union jobs, particularly if the union movement continues expanding its presence in the service sector. Moreover, many other low-wage workers will have the benefit of improved education and training and even placement programs, even if they do not end up in a union-represented job.

Clearly, the participants who derive the greatest benefits from such programs are those who gain new skills, leading to a career setting that provides opportunities for further skill development, progression in job responsibilities, and advancement in income and benefits. Thus, it is significant that the retention rate in union-sponsored training programs is very high—even for those who wash out of other training programs because they are "hard to employ." Placement rates are very high because of the direct link between union training programs and union hiring halls. In addition, workers who participate in these programs increasingly have access to further training for career advancement.

IMPLICATIONS FOR PUBLIC POLICY

Innovative union-sponsored training and placement programs are developing skills and providing jobs that are helping move thousands of workers from poverty to family-sustaining jobs. These programs appear to be highly effective on such measures as graduation rates, initial placement, wages and benefits, retention, and opportunities for further skill development and career advancement. While they are meeting important goals of public policy, most programs receive little or no public financial support. With these public benefits, it appears that the public sector is underinvesting in union-sponsored education, training, and placement programs.

Given the contributions and growing potential of such union-sponsored programs, it is important to identify the public policy implications for bringing these strategies to scale within regional economies, industrial sectors, communities, the union movement, and ultimately the economy as a whole. A preliminary list of public policy steps in that direction would include:

- Increasing the number of union-sponsored, high-road partnerships by expanding funding and by encouraging the inclusion of union-sponsored programs in publicly funded skills alliances;
- Recognizing union programs as effective providers in TANF and welfare-to-work programs and by using union-sponsored training and placement programs as providers to a greater extent;
- More fundamentally, removing the accumulated barriers to the free exercise of workers rights to form unions; and
- Removing employer and employer enforcement sanctions for immigration violations, which are harshly and widely applied against low-wage workers.

NOTES

1. This is comparable to the national levels in many European countries. Decades ago, these countries made conscious choices not to endorse poverty wages in their economies.
2. The AFL-CIO Public Policy Department compiled these figures in April 2000.
3. By contrast, many companies that have advocated increased workforce training in the current relatively tight labor market had dismantled internal training systems in the weak labor market of the 1980s.
4. Despite the emergence of pervasive new technologies in the New Economy, an in-depth survey by the American Society for Training and Development, supplemented by BLS surveys, found that per-employee

investments in worker training by American business were lower in 1995 than they had been 10 years ear-lier. Investments in training for incumbent workers in the United States statistically fall considerably behind the comparable investments in other advanced industrial countries (Bassi and Van Buren 1998).

5. For more information on high-road efforts, see AFL-CIO Working for America Institute (2000).

6. Research is underway to develop a more comprehensive, more detailed picture of these union-sponsored programs and their benefits for low-income workers. The overview presented here is a preliminary report from this ongoing research.

7. Tabulation by Working for America Institute.

8. A union legislative priority is to end the abuse of providing lower wages and benefits for part-time, temporary, artificially defined "independent contractors" and other contingent workers. Many of these contingent workers, in all kinds of industries, including manufacturing and a variety of services, first became low-wage workers and members of the working poor when they were forced into part-time, tem-porary, and "independent contractor" work.

REFERENCES

AFL-CIO. 1999. "Winning Full-Time Rights for Part-Time Workers." *America@Work*. May.

AFL-CIO Working for America Institute. 2000. *High Road Partnerships Report.* Washington, D.C.: Working for America Institute.

Allen, Steven G. 1984. "Unionized Construction Workers Are More Productive." *Quarterly Journal of Economics* 99 (2): 251–74.

———. 1986. "The Effective of Unionism on Productivity in Privately and Publicly Owned Hospitals and Nursing Homes." *Journal of Labor Research* 7 (1): 59–68.

Bassi, Laurie, and Mark E. Van Buren. 1998. "1998 ASTD State of the Industry Report." *Training and Development* (January).

Bernstein, Jared, and Chauna Brocht. 2000. "The New Minimum Wage Proposals and the Old Opposition." Washington, D.C.: Economic Policy Institute.

Bernstein, Jared, and John Schmitt. 2000. "Making Work Pay: The Impact of the 1996–97 Minimum Wage Increase." Washington, D.C.: Economic Policy Institute.

Black, Sandra, and Lisa Lynch. 1997. "How to Compete: The Impact of Workplace Practices and Information Technology on Productivity." NBER Working Paper No. W6120. Cambridge, Mass.: National Bureau of Economic Research. August.

Brown, Charles, and James L. Medoff. 1978. "Trade Unions in the Production Process." *Quarterly Journal of Political Economy* 86 (3): 355–78.

Freeman Richard, and James L. Medoff. 1984. *What Do Unions Do?* New York: Basic Books.

LeRoy, Greg, R. Healey, D. Doherty, and R. Kerson. 1995. *No More Candy Store: States Move to End Corporate Welfare As We Know It.* Washington, D.C.: Institute on Taxation and Economic Policy.

LeRoy, Greg, Katie Tallman, Fiona Hsu, and Sara Hinkley. 1999. *The Policy Shift to Good Jobs: Cities, States and Counties Attaching Job Quality Standards to Development Subsidies.* Washington, D.C.: Good Jobs First.

Office of Port Jobs. 1999. *Apprenticeship Utilization Goals and Requirements: A Countywide Impact Study, 1997 Update.* Seattle: Office of Port Jobs.

———. 2000. *The Impact of AOP Referrals on Entrants into King County Apprenticeship Programs.* Seattle: Office of Port Jobs.

Sarmiento, Tony, and Ann Kay. 1999. *Worker-Centered Learning: A Union Guide to Basic Skills.* Washington, D.C.: Working for America Institute.

U.S. Bureau of Labor Statistics. 2000a. "Union Affiliation of Employed Wage and Salary Workers by Selected Characteristics." *Labor Force Statistics from the Current Population Survey.* Washington, D.C.: BLS. January 27.

———. 2000b. "Union Members in 1999." Press release, January 19.

About the Editors

Richard Kazis is senior vice president of Jobs for the Future, where he directs the organization's policy and research efforts. A former social studies teacher at an alternative high school for returning dropouts, he has also supervised a Neighborhood Youth Corps program, helped organize fast food workers, and written extensively on workforce, education, and economic development issues.

Marc S. Miller is director of publications at Jobs for the Future. Before joining Jobs for the Future, Dr. Miller directed publications and communications for Cultural Survival, an international human rights organization. He has also served as senior editor of *Technology Review*, MIT's policy magazine. As managing editor at the Institute for Southern Studies, he directed major publications projects on a variety of topics, including working women, electoral politics, and Southern history.

Jobs for the Future is a national, nonprofit organization that works to strengthen the foundation for economic opportunity and civic health in America by advancing the understanding of the skills and knowledge required for success in the new economy. Jobs for the Future works locally and nationally to develop innovative workforce development solutions that help people make effective, lifelong transitions between work and learning.

About the Contributors

Gregory Acs is a senior research associate at the Urban Institute's Income Benefits Policy Center. His research focuses on social insurance, social welfare, and the compensation of workers. In recent work, he has studied the employment patterns of young women and the impact of disabilities on the duration of welfare receipt and on welfare recipients' ability to work.

Amanda Ahlstrand is an associate in the research department at the American Society for Training and Development.

Max Armbruster is an MBA candidate at George Washington University and an intern in the research department of the American Society for Training and Development.

Laurie Bassi is the principal researcher on grants and the director of research for Saba Software. Before joining Saba, Dr. Bassi served as a vice president and general manager at the American Society for Training and Development (ASTD), where she was responsible for research and enterprise solutions. Her achievements at ASTD included creating internationally recognized standards for measuring and valuing firms' investments in education and training. Dr. Bassi is coeditor of *What Works: Training and Development Practices* (ASTD, 1997) and *Change at Work* (Oxford University Press, 1997).

Ray Boshara is program director at the Corporation for Enterprise Development (CFED) in Washington, D.C., where he leads the corporation's efforts on federal assets policy, including national policies for Individual Development Accounts (IDAs) and Children's Savings Accounts. He is the principal author of several CFED publications, including *Realizing the Promise of Microenterprise Development in State Welfare Reform* (1997), *20 Promising Ideas for Savings Facilitation and Mobilization in Low-Income Communities in the U.S.* (1997), and *Building Assets for Stronger Families, Better Neighborhoods, and Realizing the American Dream* (1998).

Anthony P. Carnevale is vice president for public leadership at the Educational Testing Service. He chaired the National Commission for Employment Policy during President Clinton's first term, while serving as vice president and director of human resource studies at the Committee for Economic Development. He has held senior staff positions in the U.S. Senate and House of Representatives and the U.S. Department of Health, Education, and Welfare. While serving as a research economist with the Syracuse University Research Corporation, he coauthored the principal affidavit in *Rodriguez v. San Antonio*, a U.S. Supreme Court action to remedy unequal tax burdens and educational benefits.

Carol Clymer is a senior program director at Public/Private Ventures. She directs several workforce development projects, provides technical assistance to labor market initiatives, and develops curriculum products for practitioners in the employment and training field. She has also worked with numerous public and private organizations in designing and implementing job training and adult literacy programs.

Colleen Dailey is a program manager at the Corporation for Enterprise Development. She oversees information management and programmatic issues related to Individual Development Accounts. Ms. Dailey is also a primary researcher on projects related to children's savings accounts and employer-based IDAs. She is coauthor of the fourth edition of the *Individual Development Account Program Design Handbook* (CFED, 1999).

John Foster-Bey is a senior associate and the director of the Program for Regional Economic Opportunity at the Urban Institute's Metropolitan Housing and Communities Center. The program focuses on research that examines the factors that improve the access of low-skilled, low-income individuals and communities to economic opportunity with local regional economies. Before coming to the Urban Institute, he spent 11 years in philanthropy and 10 years working in corporate finance, local government, and nonprofit youth programs.

W. Norton Grubb is the David Pierpont Gardner Professor in Higher Education at the University of California, Berkeley. His research includes the role of schooling in labor markets; the flow of students into and through postsecondary education; and the interactions among education and training programs, community colleges, the institutional effects on teaching, and social policy toward children and youth. His recent books include *Learning to Work: The Case for Reintegrating Education and Job Training* (Russell Sage Foundation, 1996) and *Working in the Middle: Strengthening Education and the Training for the Mid-Skilled Labor Force* (Jossey-Bass, 1996).

Heidi Hartmann is founder and director of the Institute for Women's Policy Research. Her work on issues such as welfare reform, pay equity, women's wages, and feminist theory has been widely published. In 1994, Dr. Hartmann received a MacArthur Foundation Fellowship in recognition of her pioneering work in the field of women and economics.

Harry J. Holzer, professor of public policy at Georgetown University and a visiting fellow at the Urban Institute, is a former chief economist of the U.S. Department of Labor. He is also a senior affiliate of the Joint Center for Poverty Research, research affiliate of the Institute for Research on Poverty, and a national fellow of the Program on Inequality and Social Policy. His books on the labor market problems of minorities and the urban poor include *What Employers Want: Job Prospects for Less-Educated Workers* (Russell Sage Foundation, 1996) and *Employers and Welfare Recipients: The Effects of Welfare Reform in the Workplace* (Public Policy Institute of California, 2000).

Vicky Lovell is a study director at the Institute for Women's Policy Research. She focuses on issues related to women's employment, including pay equity, discrimination, family and medical leave, and unemployment insurance.

Karin Martinson is a consultant for a number of policy research, advocacy, and public-sector organizations, including the Manpower Demonstration Research Corporation (MDRC), the Urban Institute, and the Center on Budget and Policy Priorities. She worked at the U.S. Department of Health and Human Services as policy analyst on a range of policy and research issues related to welfare reform and at MDRC as a senior researcher on several major welfare-to-work evaluations.

Daniel McKenzie was a research assistant at the Urban Institute's Income and Benefits Policy Center, where he focused on welfare reform, while this book was being written. He conducted data analysis using information from the National Survey of America's Families, and published several pieces for the Institute's *Assessing the New Federalism* project.

Dan McMurrer is a research manager at Saba Software.

Edwin Meléndez is a professor of management and urban policy and the director of the Community Development Research Center at the Robert J. Milano Graduate School of Management and Urban Policy at the New School University in New York City. Dr. Meléndez has conducted research in economic development, labor markets, workforce development, community strategies, and poverty, and coauthored *In the Shadow of the Sun: Caribbean Development Alternatives and U.S. Policy* (Westview Press, 1990) and *La Empresa Comunal: Lecciones de Casos Exitosos en Puerto Rico* (Puerto Rico Community Foundation, 1999).

Charles Michalopoulos, a senior research associate at Manpower Demonstration Research Corporation, is studying the effects of financial work incentives for welfare recipients in Canada, Connecticut, and Vermont. He has coauthored studies summarizing the effects of welfare-to-work programs studied by MDRC over the last 15 years, describing the effects of earnings supplements on employment and income, and studying what works best for whom in welfare-to-work programs. He has also published a number of articles on child care, welfare, and work policies.

Cecilia Muñoz is vice president for policy at the National Council of La Raza (NCLR). She is the editor of *Racing toward Big Brother: Computer Verification, National ID Cards, and Immigration Control* (NCLR, 1995) and other NCLR publications. Her opinion editorials on immigration policy have appeared in the *Washington Post* and the *Miami Herald*. In 2000, she was awarded a MacArthur Foundation Fellowship for her work on immigration and civil rights.

Paul Osterman is a professor at MIT's Sloan School and Department of Urban Planning. He is the author of *Securing Prosperity: The American Labor Market—How It Has Changed and What to Do about It* (Princeton University Press, 1999), *Employment Futures: Reorganization, Dislocation, and Public Policy* (Oxford University Press, 1988), and *Getting Started: The Youth Labor Market* (MIT Press, 1980). In addition, he has written numerous academic journal articles and policy issue papers on topics including labor market policy, job training programs, economic development, and antipoverty programs. He has worked as a senior administrator of job training programs for Massachusetts and as a consultant.

Sonia M. Pérez is deputy vice president for research at the National Council of La Raza. She is the editor of *Moving up the Economic Ladder: Latino Workers and the Nation's Future Prosperity* (2000), as well as other NCLR publications. She has studied and written extensively on the economic status of Latinos in the United States. Her articles have appeared in *Double Exposure: Poverty and Race in America, Crítica, The Journal of State Government, Trotter Review,* the *Journal of Hispanic Policy*, and other publications.

Katherin Ross Phillips is a research associate at the Urban Institute's Income and Benefits Policy Center. Her research focuses on low-income workers with children. She is currently studying the relationships between parental work and child well-being and the effects of family policy on parental work effort. She has published several reports for the Institute's *Assessing the New Federalism* project, including "Who Knows about the Earned Income Tax Credit?" (2001).

Anu Rangarajan is a senior economist and associate director at Mathematica Policy Research Corporation, specializing in welfare and nutrition. She has worked on several studies examining the employment behavior of welfare recipients, and directed the evaluation of the Postemployment Services Demonstration, a program aimed at providing case management–based job retention services to help newly employed welfare recipients keep their jobs. She is a principal investigator on the Work First New Jersey evaluation, a five-year study, and is responsible for the longitudinal client study that tracks current and former TANF recipients in New Jersey.

Brandon Roberts is a workforce and economic development consultant who works with public and nonprofit organizations across the country. He specializes in policy and program development matters, as well as program evaluation.

Stephen Rose is a senior economist at the Educational Testing Service. He has conducted research on labor market trends, using cross-sectional and longitudinal data to track individuals' career patterns. He has held policy positions at the U.S. Department of Labor, the National Commission for Employment Policy, and the Joint Economic Committee of the Congress. Earlier, in Seattle, he ran a consulting firm on public policy research and was a senior analyst with the Ways and Means Committee of the Washington State Senate. The fifth edition of his *Social Stratification in the United States,* originally published in 1978, was issued in January 2000.

Julie Strawn is a senior policy analyst at the Center for Law and Social Policy, where she studies workforce development and welfare reform, with emphasis on helping parents who receive welfare sustain employment and qualify for better jobs. From 1993 to 1996, Ms. Strawn was responsible for developing policy and legislative positions for the National Governors' Association in the areas of workforce development and welfare reform. She has also worked on welfare and workforce policy issues at the Welfare Information Network, the Center on Budget and Policy Priorities, the U.S. Department of Health and Human Services, and the U.S. House of Representatives.

Carlos Suárez is a researcher on educational programs for underserved populations. He has worked as a consultant for a substance abuse–prevention program, and writes regularly on Latin American politics. He is the program evaluator for the Hyde Square Task Force in Boston, Massachusetts.

Brian J. Turner is the director of the Transport Workers Union's transportation and technology and skills program and the Community Transportation Development Center, helping to develop opportunities for promotions and skill upgrades for transportation workers. He served as director of research and communications at the AFL-CIO Working for America Institute until 2001, focusing on developing union strategies to help workers move out of poverty. He was the founding president of the Work and Technology Institute (WTI), a union-sponsored research, development, and education organization supporting active union and worker roles in changing workplace technology, job design, and skills. Mr. Turner led the team producing *Making Change Happen: Six Cases of Unions and Companies Transforming Their Workplaces* (WTI, 1996).

Mark Van Buren is director of research at the American Society for Training and Development, where he has studied the effects of workforce development and creating information technology systems to more effectively support businesses.

Index